From Freedom Fighter to Statesman

MENAHEM BEGIN

by
Gertrude Hirschler
and
Lester S. Eckman

Introduction by
Howard L. Adelson

SHENGOLD PUBLISHERS, INC.
New York, N.Y.

ISBN 0-88400-051-6

Library of Congress Catalog Card Number: 78-54565

Copyright © 1979 by Gertrude Hirschler and Lester S. Eckman

Published by Shengold Publishers, Inc.
45 W. 45th St., New York, N.Y. 10036
In cooperation with Judaic Research Institute

Printed in the United States of America

Contents

Acknowledgments

The authors wish to express their deep appreciation to the following without whose constant counsel, assistance and encouragement this book could never have come into being.

To Prof. Tovia Preschel, of New York City, for permitting us to partake of his prodigious knowledge of Jewish and Zionist history and for his never-failing help and guidance;

To Alice Dukes Hirschler, of Baltimore, Maryland, for invaluable constructive criticism and advice and, above all, her devoted concern for and interest in every phase of the development of this work;

To Max G. Lowenherz, of New York City, for selfless friendship shown in innumerable ways;

To Dr. Howard L. Adelson, professor of history at the City University of New York, for reading this manuscript with painstaking care and pointing out inaccuracies that might have escaped the attention of a lesser scholar;

To Yitzhak ("Mike") Ben-Ami, of New York City, for his personal reminiscences about the tragedy of the S.S. *Altalena;*

To Dr. Judith A. Diesendruck, Jacob I. Dienstag, Moshe Giloni, and Alexander Schlesinger, all of New York City, for long talks which yielded important insights into the thinking of Menahem Begin and his followers;

To Chaim Lazar, of Tel Aviv, Israel, for most useful material;

To Sylvia Landress (director), Esther Togman (assistant director), Deborah Cassel, Gertrude Finkel, Rebecca Zapinsky Sherman and Judith Wallach, of the permanent staff of the Zionist Archives and Library, New York City, for help, support and personal friendship immeasurably beyond the bounds of ordinary professional courtesy.

Our thanks go also to the Memorial Foundation for Jewish Culture for their research grant.

Our sincere appreciation to Mr. and Mrs. Yitzhak Horn, Mr. and Mrs. Ben Milner of Montreal and to Mr. and Mrs. Joseph Tanenbaum of Toronto for their generous assistance in the publication of this work.

Introduction

HOWARD L. ADELSON

Professor, Department of History
The City University of New York

Adversity is a great fortifier of patience. Menahem Begin has known adversity and calumny to an unparalleled degree, and he has also learned the essential value of patience. His political struggle over the long years from the establishment of the State of Israel to his summons to serve as his country's prime minister was fueled by optimism and tempered by patience. Paradoxically, in recent months, he has seen his most inveterate political foes turn into his quasi-allies and some of his strongest supporters from the past become his sharpest opponents.

This shift in loyalties has had its effect on Begin's interpersonal relationships. From opponents of long standing he has never expected anything but opposition, and he is grateful if this opposition stops short of being vitriolic. The fact that his long-time political adversary David Ben-Gurion pointedly walked out of the Knesset chamber whenever he rose to speak did not deter Begin, on the eve of the Six-Day War of 1967, from urging that Ben-Gurion be returned to power. He recognized the value of Ben-Gurion as a symbol and leader for Israel in the hour of crisis. When, on assuming the premiership in May, 1977, Begin set forth the foreign policy of his new government, he gracefully accepted the attacks from the Labor Alignment as a fact of political life. But he was deeply stung by the criticism which has been leveled at him by some of his erstwhile supporters. When veterans of his "fighting family," the former underground members who constituted the backbone of his Herut (Freedom) party, turned on him for what they considered his abandonment of the principles taught by his mentor, Vladimir

Jabotinsky, the founder of the right-wing Revisionist movement in Zionism, Begin viewed this as disloyalty not only toward the party of which he is the leader but also toward his own person.

What has just been said is mirrored in Menahem Begin's concept of party discipline. In contrast to Israel's other political parties, in which a far greater degree of individual initiative is tolerated and even expected, party discipline has become a watchword in the Herut party and, by extension, in the Likud bloc, the right-wing coalition which now rules Israel under Begin's leadership. For this reason Herut — and Likud — has been identified with the person of Menahem Begin far more than any other party in Israel has been linked with the personality of any one political leader. The only other such instance of personal identification in Israel's political party spectrum was that of the short-lived Rafi, the splinter party which Ben-Gurion founded after his resignation as prime minister. Rafi and David Ben-Gurion, for all practical purposes, were one and the same thing. For a long time, Begin and Herut were similarly identified. Only in the most recent months has it been possible to pick out distinct factions within the Herut party, but even these factions have shown no sign of seeking to bolt from the party over questions of principle.

Over a period of almost three decades in the opposition, Begin experienced an ample measure of frustration. As leader of the opposition, he was unable to exercise that role in Israel's political life which he and his supporters felt would have best served the country. Because the Labor governments tended to downgrade the Knesset, Israel's parliament, he felt himself on the fringes of most of the crucial decisions in Israel's history. In many instances the leader of the opposition learned of important events either just before they occurred, or sometimes even after they had taken place. Some individuals in the Labor leadership might have been willing to discuss issues with him. But there were others who tried to govern the country as though Begin and his bloc were little more than a momentary inconvenience that could be largely ignored. It was under these conditions that Begin for nearly 30 years had to keep his party — and later his bloc — not only functioning as a unit but also to preserve the spark of hope that some day he and his supporters would be at the helm of Israel's goverment.

Begin's personal style is not typical of today's *sabra* society.

Ben-Gurion consciously tried to project the image not only of a philosopher and intellectual, but also that of *sabra*-type informality in dress, speech and behavior. Begin, by contrast, does not fit the stereotype which the Israelis have constructed of themselves. He has been eclectic in designing his personal pattern. His style is neither *sabra,* nor is it completely Western. He embraces friends and kisses the hands of ladies in the fashion of the middle and upper classes of Europe, but is given to a use of hyperbole in his speech that is not typically European. He is formal in a sense that is completely foreign to the *sabra,* but at the same time outspoken in a fashion that resembles the *sabra* more than it does the European style.

Begin is a complex individual. He can be firm and tough, but also pliant and conciliatory. In the *Altalena* affair, which could have thrown his country into civil war, and in his negotiations with the President of the United States, which could bring Israel into confrontation with her one ally, Begin has been both. Also, Begin has an intense awareness of his personal significance in the history of the Jewish people. He and his supporters have always viewed themselves as bearing the awesome responsibility for the evolution of a new type of Jew — one who lives in the context of modern Jewish statehood but at the same time considers himself part of a long chain of history and tradition shaped over two millennia of dispersion.

Whatever one might think of Begin's self-image, one must agree that since his assumption of the premiership, his role in the government of Israel has been a strong and decisive one. Israel's present foreign policy is not derived from a consensus among the members of Begin's government; it is Begin's voice that has consistently predominated. If the course which his government has adopted will prove successful, the credit will belong almost entirely to Begin. If it fails and leads to new bloodshed, it is Begin who will bear the blame. Begin is the leader of his party, but he is not a party man. He has chosen many of his advisers and assistants from other parties.

Gertrude Hirschler and Lester S. Eckman have tried to show the various facets of Menahem Begin's character and personality not merely by utilizing material descriptive of Begin's personal life but also by detailing the events in which Begin played a role, and by analyzing Begin's part in these events. They have, in a manner of speaking, written a history of Israel from the perspective — but not the bias — of those whom the Israeli establishment for years considered as dissidents. Much of the data in this book is derived from interviews and private papers. From these pages the reader will gain a conception of Begin as a man and leader which is neither so critical as to be distorted, nor so laudatory as to be gigantic. Each reader will see the composite picture from this new perspective and understand the persons involved in a critical yet sympathetic light.

New York
February, 1979

1. "The Courageous Will to Peace"

Oslo (AP) — President Anwar el-Sadat of Egypt and Prime Minister Menahem Begin of Israel, who buried 30 years of bitter enmity to sit down together as partners at the negotiating table, were awarded the 1978 Nobel Peace Prize yesterday for their historic efforts toward a settlement of the Arab-Israeli conflict . . .

The Nobel Committee . . . congratulated the two men for what it called their "courageous will to peace."

. . . Israel radio reported that Mr. Begin, observing the Jewish Sabbath at home, was "extremely excited" about the award but would not violate the Sabbath by commenting publicly on his prize.

— Associated Press Dispatch, October 28, 1978

After three stars had become visible on the evening sky, signifying the end of the Sabbath, Menahem Begin emerged from the seclusion of his official residence in Jerusalem. Television viewers the world over saw a dapper, smiling man of late middle age, followed by his trim, gray-haired wife and several of his eight young grandchildren, step up to a battery of microphones set up in the garden of the Prime Minister's residence. There was, he calmly told reporters, "no more important prize that man could aspire to," but "the real prize will be peace itself."

Since Anwar el-Sadat, as president of his country, outranked a prime minister, Menahem Begin had taken the initiative and had telephoned Sadat in Cairo, congratulating him on his selection as a co-recipient of the peace award.

During the 1940's Menahem Begin had founded the Irgun Z'vai Leumi and molded it into a highly-motivated, effective underground army which played a major role in ridding Palestine of a British regime that had become intolerable to the Jews. At the time, the British government had placed a £10,000 prize on his head. Not only the British, but also the official Zionist establishment consistently described Begin as a "terrorist." For years his most vehement political adversary, David Ben-Gurion, accused him of having sought to plunge the Jewish state into civil war in 1948. When he had first become prime minister, Israelis familiar with almost three decades of Begin's low-pitched ·but fiery oratory from the parliamentary opposition bench on questions of war and peace voiced apprehensions about life in Israel under the rule of an "extremist" who was likely to steer the country into another war and into a head-on political clash with its only ally, the United States.

Yet, on September 17, 1978 it was given Menahem Begin to achieve the goal which had eluded all the earlier prime ministers of his country: he became the first Israeli leader to sit at the same table with the leader of an Arab nation and, together with him, sign a comprehensive blueprint for peace in the Middle East.

Until quite recently few Israelis — including even Begin's followers — would have described Begin as a man of peace. Yet, through the five years he had served as commander of the Irgun Z'vai Leumi, his strategy for revolt against the British overlords was governed by one overriding consideration: that human life was precious and that he would not permit the men under his command to commit the indiscriminate killings usually associated with revolutionary armies. The Irgun Z'vai Leumi, popularly known simply as Irgun, was perhaps the only fighting force in the world to issue advance warnings, at the risk of losing the advantage of surprise, so that innocent civilians — British, Arab and Jewish — might have time to take cover and escape injury. Such a warning was given, among others, prior to the much-debated bombing of British headquarters at the King David Hotel in Jerusalem in 1946, and when British officials deliberately ignored the warning, so that over 100 civilians lost their lives, Begin was deeply shaken. The purpose of the Irgun raids on British installations was not to kill Englishmen, but to hamstring the British administrative machinery so completely that Britain would eventually realize it was not worth the price in frustration and loss of international prestige to remain in Palestine. Begin's horror at the thought of inflicting injury on civilians was manifest also after the raid on the Arab village of Deir Yassin in 1948. The Irgun had warned the population of the village to leave, but after the fighting had ended, Irgun men discovered the bodies of Arab civilians alongside fallen Palestinian and Iraqi soldiers. Begin was stunned and, almost a quarter-century after the incident, wrote to the London *Times* that it had been a "tragic and painful" thing.

Throughout its existence, the Irgun had been beyond the pale of the official Zionist establishment under the leadership of David Ben-Gurion, which had long believed that moderation would eventually persuade the British to open the gates of Palestine to survivors of the Nazi Holocaust. For a brief period Haganah, the semi-legitimate armed force maintained by the Zionist establishment, cooperated with the British authorities in bringing about the arrest and deportation of Irgun members. At that point, some members of the Irgun were ready to take up arms against Haganah. Begin recoiled at the possibility of civil war among Jews, and was able to keep his men from striking out against the "informers." It was to him unthinkable that Jews for any reason should shoot at one another. In the summer of 1948, due to a concatenation of tragic misunderstandings, the provisional government of the newly-created State of Israel became suspicious that the Irgun was about to start a civil war in order to topple David Ben-Gurion from power. The result was the shelling and sinking of the S.S. *Altalena,* which the Irgun had chartered to bring badly needed volunteers and weapons to the new Israeli army. There was shooting, and both Haganah and Irgun men were killed and wounded. Once again, there were Irgun men sufficiently enraged to demand a revolt against Ben-Gurion and his provisional government. But Begin went on the air to urge his men not to be carried away by their anger. "Raise not your hand against your brother. Not even today," he pleaded tearfully. And this time, too, the Irgun men obeyed their leader. Begin was probably the only underground commander in recorded history to liquidate his army voluntarily when it was no longer needed. He led his Irgun veterans into Israel's political arena where, as private citizens under the banner of the Herut (Freedom) party, they asserted their political views against those of the Labor government.

For almost 30 years, Begin led his party in Israel's parliament, the Knesset, always in the minority, but never hesitant to speak his mind. Though many Israelis detested his rightist political views and disagreed with his tough stand on Arab-Israeli relations, they came in time to understand that he was motivated not by personal lust for power but by love for his country, a land which he is convinced belongs to the Jewish people by the will of God, as expressed in the Bible. By the time he took over Israel's government, Begin, in the words of Harvard's Nadav Safran, "had long outgrown his reputation as a ruthless demagogue and was . . . highly respected, even by his opponents, as an honest, ascetic patriot and an able and dedicated leader."[1]

In an age of pragmatism, Begin has been a man of firm, deep and sincere convictions, of which he has never made a secret. For 20 years in the opposition, he acted as gadfly to an unbroken succession of Labor governments, but there were occasions when Begin the gadfly was more circumspect than some Israeli leaders generally respected for their statesmanship. Thus, Begin has harbored a violent dislike for Communism from childhood on, but he once kept Ben-Gurion from proposing to the Knesset that members who were Communists should be expelled from Israel's lawmaking body as "foreign agents." Ben-Gurion had come to Begin to seek the opposition leader's support for the move. Begin wanted no part of it. "These men were elected to the Knesset in free elections," he said to the Prime Minister. "If you can prove that they have endangered Israel's security, you can take action against them under our emergency laws, but as long as they were legally elected, you cannot expel them. You cannot do this to our parliament." Ben-Gurion never raised the question again.[2] A lawyer by talent and training, Begin is a firm believer in the due processes of law.

His law school education in Poland and his broad background in the humanities are both reflected in his skills as an orator. Though he hardly ever raises his voice nowadays, he keeps audiences spellbound, even when they do not agree with what he says. (In addition to Hebrew and his native Polish, Begin is fluent in Yiddish, English, Russian, German and French.) He can, and does, quote Shakespeare and Abraham Lincoln from memory as readily as he cites passages from the Bible or the Talmud. Yet his speeches are characterized by warmth, humor and at times a little sentimentality. Both on and off the platform, he seems at his best when he is confronted by a tough challenge. This did not change even after the near-fatal heart attack he suffered in the spring of 1977. It is said of him that he enjoys "psychosomatic good health."

Begin is the first of Israel's prime ministers to have left Europe during the Hitler era and to have lost members of his immediate family — his parents and only brother — in the Holocaust. This tragedy has had a profound effect on Begin's personal emotions, political attitudes and official policies. It has made him wary of pressures on his country to make concessions to hostile neighbors without tangible returns. It has also made him compassionate and very protective of those who cannot defend themselves. When he talks about Israel's determination to defend herself, he will speak in terms of Israelis defending their wives and children; the worst epithet he has in his vocabulary for the Palestine Liberation Organization (PLO) is that they are "killers of women and children."

He loves children, and they respond to him in kind. His conduct toward women is characterized by an old-fashioned courtliness that sometimes seems a little out of place in modern Israeli society. He endeared himself to Ben-Gurion's outspoken, no-nonsense wife Paula by kissing her hand whenever they met. He paid the same courtesy to Golda Meir when he tendered her his resignation from the Government of National Unity in 1970.

He demands absolute loyalty from his associates and subordinates, but is unfailingly considerate and solicitous of them. He makes a point of singling out his associates for credit; when he arrived at Camp David, he introduced his entire entourage to President and Mrs. Carter. At his office each morning Begin stops at the desks of his staff to inquire after their well-being. When he leaves the office on Friday afternoon, he gives each of his three office secretaries a fatherly "Good Sabbath" kiss on the cheek.

Begin's moral and humanitarian outlook is anchored in the religious tradition in which he was raised. He is said to be the first of Israel's prime ministers to hold the beliefs in God that are taught by Jewish tradition. He has never felt the need to seek a rationale for traditional religion in the context of modern Jewish statehood. To him, religious observance is part of Jewish national dignity. He is careful to maintain his personal standards of religious observance no matter where he goes. He will not travel on the Sabbath or on the major Jewish holidays, nor will he allow his ministers to do so when they are on official business. He keeps the Jewish dietary laws; unlike his predecessors, he has requested, and been served, kosher food, among other places, at the White House in Washington, at the official government guest house in Bucharest, Rumania, and at Birch Cottage in Camp David. Beginning with his Irgun days, his speeches and writings have included references to Divine aid, and when he uses, as he often does, expressions such as "please God" or "with the help of God" in his official statements today, it does not sound affected.

After Begin's first visit to the United States as Prime Minister in the summer of 1977, William Safire of *The New York Times* described him as an "authentic," a man with a powerful sense of who he is, what he stands for, and with the ability not only to survive in the jungle of domestic and international politics, but to prevail.[3]

To this day Begin insists that nothing he has accomplished in his life, including his assumption of the prime ministership, could stand comparison with the years during which he participated in the struggle for an independent Jewish state:

> In such a situation a man identifies with the basic idea of freedom. A man can have such an opportunity only once in a lifetime . . . No other task has ever been equal to it.[4]

This is how Menahem Begin sees his life's work, which began in a Zionist youth movement in Poland between the two world wars and which eventually brought him to the leadership of the country for whose freedom he fought.

2. The Boy

Menahem Begin was born in the city of Brest-Litovsk, then, as now, part of Russia, on August 16, 1913, a year before the outbreak of World War I. His father, Ze'ev Dov Begin, an Orthodox Jew and ardent Zionist, was the secretary of the city's Jewish community. His mother, Hasia Korsovsky, came from a rabbinical family. Menahem was the second son, the youngest of three children. He had an older brother, Herzl, and a sister, Rachel. His father also had a daughter from a previous marriage, but this much older half-sister was not part of Menahem's childhood world. She had left home at an early date, living first in Palestine and then in the United States.

Menahem in Hebrew means "one who brings comfort." The name had been chosen for the child because he had been born four days after the Fast of the Ninth of Av, the day of mourning which, in the Jewish calendar, commemorates the destruction of the Temple in Jerusalem. (His older brother had been named after Theodor Herzl, the founder of political Zionism).

Brest-Litovsk (in colloquial Yiddish, the name was corrupted to Brisk, or Brisk-de-Lita) on the eve of World War I was a thriving Lithuanian community on the shore of the River Bug, about four hours' railroad journey east from Warsaw. Located at a crossroads of commercial routes, it had long been a famed center of East European Jewish life and learning. The Jews had been farmers, traders and craftsmen, but Brest-Litovsk also produced an impressive number of Jewish scholars and was the home of a widely-known Talmudical academy. Over the centuries the relationship between the Jews of Brest-Litovsk and their Gentile neighbors had seesawed between toleration and pogroms.

During the first eight years of Menahem's life, Brest-Litovsk changed hands twice. During World War I, it was taken from Tsarist Russia by the German armies of Kaiser Wilhelm II. In 1921, it was incorporated into the newly-established republic of

Poland. In March, 1918, Brest-Litovsk enjoyed a brief moment of fame as the place where Russia, torn by revolution, signed a separate peace with the Central Powers. The chief negotiator from the Russian side was Leon Trotsky.

Menahem's childhood was marked by the dangers and hardships of war, followed by the intergroup hatreds fanned by an uneasy peace. During the war years, Brest-Litovsk was in the cross-fire of German and Russian artillery. Food was in short supply. The Polish, Russian, German and Ukrainian nationality groups were perpetually at loggerheads. Perhaps it was during the period of Russian occupation that the seeds were sown for Begin's lifelong hatred of Communism. A Red army unit was quartered not far from his parents' home. Among the soldiers was a female officer, apparently a Jewish girl, who boasted of the purges that had been taking place in Russia under the new regime and declared that she, for one, had no compunction whatsoever about shooting down opponents of the Revolution in cold blood. The sensitive child was horrified.

The Jews were caught in the middle of the political and ethnic tug-of-war. Especially after the Polish army, under the personal command of the Fascist-style dictator Joseph Pilsudski, occupied the city in 1921, Brest-Litovsk became a hotbed of anti-Semitism. Rocks were hurled through the windows of Jewish homes, Jewish cemeteries were desecrated, Jewish merchants were impoverished by confiscatory taxes, Jewish students came home from school with bloodied heads, and rowdies — in and out of uniform — cut off the beards of aged rabbis in the streets and at railroad stations. On one occasion the Polish officer whom Pilsudski had left in charge of Brest-Litovsk ordered the arrest of a number of prominent Jews, each of whom was sentenced to twenty-five lashes for alleged "sympathy with the Bolsheviks." The other Jews were herded into the city's principal park and compelled to look on while the prisoners were whipped. One of the victims died several weeks later. Begin, who was then only seven years old, had also been in the crowd watching the spectacle. He never forgot it.

For centuries, the typical Jewish response to oppression had been one of quiet resignation. But as other minority groups began to assert themselves, Jews, too, became active in their own defense. The task of defending Jewish rights in Brest-Litovsk had been quietly but effectively assumed by the secretary of the Jewish community, Ze'ev Dov Begin. His son often says that his own efforts on behalf of Jewish freedom were inspired in large measure by his father's example. "In all my life, I never met a more courageous man than him. It has been given me almost all my life to work with people of courage, but I will never forget the way in which my father fought for the defense of Jewish dignity."[1]

During the years immediately following the Polish takeover in Brest-Litovsk, Ze'ev Dov Begin was called upon again and again to intervene on behalf of Jews arrested by the Poles on charges of having passed vital information to the Communists. On at least one occasion the elder Begin's work brought him into personal contact with Pilsudski. The Polish dictator, a notorious anti-Semite, summoned the leaders of the city's Jewish community to his headquarters. He ordered them to "declare war" on the black market and to help eliminate profiteering, activities which were tagged as typically "Jewish" crimes.

"This is not our task," Ze'ev Dov Begin calmly replied. "We Jews are not informers and the Jewish community does not have a secret police. It's the government who has the secret police. Let them do the job." Those who were present at the encounter recalled that Pilsudski, though infuriated at this piece of Jewish impudence, seemed to be impressed by Begin's sheer pluck.

Another time — the boy Menahem was then about ten years old — Ze'ev Dov Begin and a rabbi were walking in the street when they were accosted by two Polish soldiers. One of them pulled out a knife and began to hack away at the rabbi's beard. Ze'ev Dov Begin thereupon struck the Pole on the shoulder with his cane. Both Begin and the rabbi were placed under arrest, ferried to the prison fortress on the other side of the River Bug, and horsewhipped. Then they were released. "When my father returned home," Menahem Begin recalled many years later, "he was in rather bad shape and we were worried about him. But his spirits were high. He was certain he had done the right thing, even though it could have cost him his life." The incident had an unusual sequel: Ze'ev Dov Begin received a formal letter of apology from Marshal Pilsudski himself.[2]

But there was one night when Ze'ev Dov Begin's luck almost deserted him. Menahem, then still a small boy, was already sound asleep at the time, and heard the story only afterwards. The Polish police had come to the Begin home with orders to arrest the secretary of the Jewish community. The two older children — the girl Rachel and the boy Herzl — wept and blocked the door in an attempt to keep the men out. But their father's self-control did not desert him. "Do you have a warrant for my arrest?" he demanded. The policemen, caught off guard, made a quick retreat.

In the view of Ze'ev Dov Begin, personal dignity included what he considered neat and appropriate attire. His son inherited this trait. In a country where open-collar, shirtsleeve informality has been the hallmark of Cabinet ministers and other high officials, Menahem Begin is hardly ever seen in public without a tie and jacket, no matter how hot the weather. His preferences tend to dark suits and conservative neckties.

Hasia Begin, the mother of the family, had to use all her housewifely skills and resourcefulness to stretch her husband's meager salary over the bare essentials of day-to-day living. She did not have much formal education but, according to her son, she possessed a good amount of native intelligence and was an avid reader. It was primarily due to her thrift and persistence that all her three children were able to attend university. Herzl Begin, who was to perish with his father during the Nazi Holocaust, became a mathematician. Rachel, who made her way to Israel during World War II, became a schoolteacher and married a lawyer.

All three children had to pitch in at an early age to help support the household; being good students, they earned money tutoring less gifted schoolmates. Life was hard for the Begins, but poverty was never permitted to damp the spirit of the Begin home. The family love and the gentle sense of humor which surrounded Menahem Begin during his childhood were to help sustain him through the trials and sufferings of later years.

Menahem received his early education at a Jewish elementary school. There, the teacher once asked the class to write an essay on "My Future Occupation." Menahem wrote that he wanted to become a lawyer so he could plead the cause of the downtrodden. Eventually he was to graduate from law school, but when he put his legal training to use, it was not before a judge and a jury.

His gift for public speaking was first revealed when, at the age of 12, he delivered his maiden oration standing on a table in a park before an audience of 5,000. The occasion was Lag B'Omer, the springtime holiday which Jewish tradition has dedicated to the school child. The young student was roundly applauded.

After completing elementary school, Menahem would have liked to enroll at one of the two Hebrew high schools in Brest-Litovsk, but the family was unable to raise the money for his tuition. He therefore entered a Polish gymnasium instead. There, he received a solid European-style general education; notably, he was introduced to a wide range of Polish and world literature. Begin and his classmates read the works of Tolstoy, Dostoyevsky, Proust,

Goethe, Schiller and Shakespeare, largely in Polish translation. During his free time, he read the writings of modern Hebrew authors such as Hayim Nahman Bialik, Ahad Ha'am and Joseph Hayim Brenner.

Photographs from Begin's gymnasium days show him as a youngster with dreamy eyes behind dark-rimmed glasses. He created the impression of a sensitive, well-disciplined boy, who spent most of his time with books rather than as a natural leader of teen-age activities. But concealed behind his delicate appearance were a liberal measure of tenacity and will-power and a strong sense of personal worth and awareness.

Gymnasium life brought Begin his first personal experiences with student anti-Semitism. There were fistfights with Gentile schoolmates in which the frail-looking Begin gave as well as he got. He often came home from school bruised and battered, but it was a matter of personal pride to him that he had been able to fight back. During that period, Begin's religious convictions were put to the test. Since non-Jewish schools in Poland were closed only on Sundays, he had to attend school on Saturdays, but was excused from classroom activities, such as writing, which violated the Sabbath. But the day came when a Latin examination was announced for a Saturday and Begin was given to understand that if he would not take the examination, he would receive a poor mark in Latin, a subject which he loved and in which he excelled. His Gentile fellow students hooted at his religious scruples. For a moment, he was tempted to strike a bargain with his conscience and to report for the examination. But in the end it was precisely the taunting from his classmates that kept him from doing so. The laughter of the Gentiles made Begin see his compliance with the Sabbath laws as something more than mere religious observance. Keeping the Sabbath would be his way of demonstrating that his pride in his national heritage as a Jew was as great as the devotion of the Polish Gentiles to their own cultural values. He refused to take the examination. He got his bad mark, but he felt in his heart that he had done the right thing.

Menahem Begin's initiation into organized Zionist life came when he was about nine years old and he joined a Zionist youth organization called HaShomer HaTzair. This organization — its name, literally translated, is "The Young Guard" — was eventually to turn to the far left, in opposition to almost all of Begin's own hopes and ideals. But during the period immediately following World War I it was only a scouting movement, inspired both by the spirit of independence that had taken hold of contemporaneous youth movements in Europe and the pioneering ideals of labor and self-defense that had spurred the early Jewish settlers in Palestine. Given Menahem's admiration for his father's fight for Jewish dignity in his own home town, it was no surprise that his imagination should have been captured by a movement that had taken the first part of its name from HaShomer, a self-appointed group of pioneers which stood on guard in far-off Palestine to ensure the survival of the Zionist dream. In their day-to-day lives, the men of HaShomer — many of them refugees from Russian pogroms — had taught themselves to wield the sword and the plowshare with equal skill, working the soil while defending Jewish settlements against almost constant raids from their Arab neighbors. With their fighting prowess and their impressive appearance — they wore the traditional Arab headdress to guard against the desert sun and rode on swift chargers in pursuit of the attackers — the pioneer-defenders were fast becoming legendary figures in Palestine, and had imbued the Arabs with new respect for the European immigrants whom they once had contemptuously dismissed as the "children of death." Aside for the desire to emulate the heroic image of HaShomer in Palestine, HaShomer HaTzair was committed to the teaching of Jewish culture in the spirit of Jewish national rebirth. The leaders of HaShomer HaTzair groups taught their young charges Jewish history and the Hebrew language not as relics from the past, nor even as strictly religious values, but as tools to be utilized in the development of Jewish national awareness and eventually in the creation of new Jewish art, music and literature. These were views to which any Zionist, regardless of the religious and social ideas he held concomitantly with his belief in the restoration of the Jewish homeland, could have subscribed. At the time, Menahem Begin considered HaShomer HaTzair a "magnificent Zionist movement."[3]

But by the time Menahem Begin was in high school, there had been a change in HaShomer HaTzair. The leadership of the organization (which by then had branches also in Western Europe and on the American continent) had passed into the hands of Marxists who preached the doctrine of revolution and class struggle with almost the same fervor as they promulgated the ideal of Jewish national renaissance. By the time Menahem Begin was thirteen years old — the age of *bar mitzvah* — HaShomer HaTzair had turned into an avowedly leftist movement which taught its followers to strive for a Jewish homeland founded on militant socialism and to view traditional religious values and observances as having out-lived their usefulness in the preservation of Jewish peoplehood. These ideas did violence to the convictions that had taken shape in Begin's mind — his intense dislike of left-wing radicalism (derived from the increasingly hostile attitude of Communism toward Jewish national and religious aspirations) and his own adherence to Jewish religious tradition as a basic ingredient of Jewish national pride. And so Menahem Begin, disillusioned, left HaShomer Ha-Tzair.

Those years — the late 1920's — were a period of keen disil-lusionment for Zionists the world over. The British conquest of Palestine in the closing phase of World War I had raised high hopes among Jews. The realization of a 2,000-year-old dream seemed im-minent, for had not Britain's Foreign Secretary, Arthur James Balfour, in his famous "Balfour Declaration" of November, 1917, officially stated his government's support of the "establishment in Palestine of a national home for the Jewish people"?

But reality did not match the hopes of the Zionists. Britain's offer of a national home for the Jews in Palestine had been her in-genious way of gaining control of the much-coveted crossroads link-ing three continents without appearing "annexationist" in the eyes of world opinion. By expressing support for the noble ideal of providing the much-persecuted Jews with a home in the Promised Land, Britain was able to obtain Palestine as a "mandate" with the blessings of the League of Nations. But what Britain really wanted in Palestine was a colony, where Jews might "also" live. As Menahem Begin was to point out years later, the British did not then seriously consider the possibility that, apart from a handful of idealists and paupers, Jews might want to move to Palestine in large numbers. Truth to tell, the British military men and civil ser-vants who performed the day-to-day tasks of government in Palestine had no great liking for the Jews, whom they considered too independent and self-assertive to make compliant "colonials." The Arabs, with their quaint, exotic ways, seemed to fit the traditional British notion of "natives" far better than did the Jewish pioneers with their modern ideas. And so the British administrators applied the old colonial policy of "divide and conquer" also to their regime in Palestine. The Jews would not be allowed to gain suf-ficient numerical or political strength for independence; they would be kept under firm British control as a perpetual minority. Thus, the British did not act when Arab nationalists from neighboring countries, notably French-dominated Syria, played upon the fears and prejudices of the Arabs in Palestine at the expense of the Jews. As long as Jew and Arab were at each other's throats in Palestine, the British felt they could count on remaining firmly entrenched as "arbitrators" between the two warring sides. In 1920, 1921, 1929 (and again to an infinitely more threatening degree in 1936), the Arabs organized mass anti-Jewish demonstrations that quickly turned into bloody pogroms. Typically, these outbreaks were preceded by inflammatory anti-Jewish tirades in the mosques and statements in the press, mostly to the effect that the Jews were murdering innocent Arabs and desecrating Moslem shrines. The aroused Arabs then attacked Jews in the streets, Arab gangs blocked highways and raided isolated Jewish settlements, and Arab mobs invaded Jewish neighborhoods in the cities to loot and slaughter. The Arabs disrupted Jewish worship at the Wailing Wall, the last remnant of the Temple, by pelting the pilgrims with stones and covering the ground in front of the wall with donkey droppings. In every attack on Jewish life and property, the Arab watchword was *"El daula ma'ana* (the Government is with us)," and so, indeed, it seemed, for the British forces of law and order were forbidden to open fire on the Arabs except when, in the course of their looting and murder, the raiders threatened damage to British interests as well.

The Jews of Palestine had formed their own self-defense force, Haganah, to fend off the Arab attackers but the British authorities regarded Haganah as illegal and, more often than not, Haganah men found themselves arrested on charges of possessing arms without permission and of having murdered Arabs.

The reaction of the British government in London to the Arab outbreaks was a slow but deliberate retreat from the promise made first in the Balfour Declaration and subsequently in the provisions under which Britain had been awarded the mandate over Palestine. In 1922 (Begin was then a child of nine) Britain had partitioned Palestine for the first time. On September 16 of that year, she notified the League of Nations in Geneva that the provisions of the Mandate for the "Jewish national home" were no longer applicable to Transjordan, the part of Palestine lying east of the Jordan River. Transjordan was turned over to the Emir Abdullah, an Arab chieftain, (he was a son of the Sherif Hussein of Mecca, and brother of Feisal I, later King of Iraq),[4] as compensation for his inability to gain a more satisfactory prize from the Great Power maneuvers in the Middle East following World War I. In effect, almost three-fourths of the territory originally intended for the "Jewish national home" was thus given away to the Arabs almost at the outset, reducing the Jewish homeland to 10,000 square miles — almost half of it wilderness. This happened 25 years before the adoption of the United Nations resolution of November, 1947, which again divided the already truncated Palestine into two sectors, one for a Jewish state, the other for a new state of Palestinian Arabs. (The Palestinian Arab state did not materialize, for the territory reserved for it was promptly incorporated by Abdullah into his kingdom of Transjordan, or, as it subsequently became known, the Hashemite Kingdom of Jordan).

In subsequent attempts to placate the Arabs, the British government enacted legislation designed to keep additional Jews from settling in Palestine and to curtail the rights of Jews to purchase land there.

The Zionist leadership protested, but did not attempt concerted pressure on Britain or on world public opinion to reverse British policy. That was to come only years later, after millions of Jews had died for lack of a haven from Hitler's "final solution." During the 1920's, the years when Menahem Begin went through childhood and adolescence, influential Zionists in both Palestine and the rest of the world still trusted the British sense of fair play and believed that there was little to be gained by irritating London with too frank reminders of the Jewish claim to Palestine. And so the Zionist leadership soft-pedaled the political goal which Theodor Herzl, the founder of classic political Zionism, had explicitly set for the modern Zionist movement: not merely the rebuilding of Palestine by the Jews but the establishment in Palestine of an independent Jewish state open to all Jews who wished to settle there. The Zionist leaders of the post-1918 era, under the presidency of the Russian-born British scientist Chaim Weizmann, concentrated on the social and economic aspects of Zionism. Their immediate objective was the formation of a Jewish pioneer elite which would establish an economic base in Palestine by steady, plodding effort — "acre by acre, cow by cow," as a then-popular saying had it — and would create in the Jewish homeland a model society patterned on the tenets of socialism. As a consequence, the leadership of the Zionist establishment before long became synonymous with that of the Labor Zionist parties.

But there was one lone man in the World Zionist Executive who opposed the gradualist policy pursued by the Zionist leadership. It was too passive, he asserted, for the rebuilding and, indeed, for the survival of the Jewish homeland. This man was

Vladimir (Ze'ev) Jabotinsky, who was to become the dominant influence in the life of Menahem Begin.

Like so many other Zionist leaders, Jabotinsky was a native of Russia. A brilliant journalist, author, poet, linguist, ex-soldier and orator, he enthralled his readers and swept his audiences off their feet. Such giants of Russian letters as Maxim Gorki had forecast a great future for him in the literary world, but Jabotinsky had chosen instead to devote his gifts of mind and spirit to the Zionist cause.

"I was won over by his ideas," said Begin, "and it was from him that I learned the doctrine of Zionism."[5]

3. Vladimir Jabotinsky: "Teacher and Master"

Long before he met Jabotinsky face to face, Menahem Begin had been mesmerized by his articles and essays. In 1930, Jabotinsky himself came to lecture in Brest-Litovsk and Begin, then in his last year of high school, went to hear him. Jabotinsky, Begin's senior by over 30 years, left an indelible impression on the seventeen-year-old student. This man had traveled through the world and had created the first Jewish army since Bar Kohkba's unsuccessful revolt against the Roman conquerors of Palestine 1,800 years before. Also, much like Begin's own father, Jabotinsky extolled as the ideal type of Jew one who combined culture, personal dignity and pride in his spiritual heritage with the resolute determination to fight for the rights of his people not only in Palestine but wherever Jews suffered from persecution or discrimination.

What impressed Begin most of all was Jabotinsky's philosophy of "monistic" Zionism — a single-minded striving for the attainment of Jewish statehood in Palestine, without what Jabotinsky viewed as diversionary excursions into social and economic theories. In his outspoken political demands, Jabotinsky was the direct ideological heir of Theodor Herzl, for whom Menahem Begin had early conceived an admiration bordering on hero-worship. To this day Begin frequently dips into Herzl's Zionist writings and says he is deeply moved whenever he does so. But Begin feels that Jabotinsky outstripped even Herzl both in intellectual attainments and in Zionist vision.

Like Herzl, Jabotinsky was best known to the non-Jewish world as a writer, but he surpassed Herzl in depth and versatility. Herzl, the Viennese socialite, had been primarily a man of light-hearted belles-lettres. Jabotinsky's publications, by contrast, ranged from novels to studies in comparative phonetics. Fluent in

Russian, German, Italian, French, Spanish, Polish, Yiddish and Hebrew, Jabotinsky had translated Dante and Edgar Allen Poe into Hebrew and modern Hebrew poetry into Russian.

Like Herzl, Jabotinsky was far from orthodox in his personal observance of Judaism. But in contrast to Herzl, who remained largely ignorant of traditional Jewish literature, Jabotinsky from early adulthood came to love the Bible and the Talmud, from which he said he derived some of his best philosophical and literary ideas and he never ceased to stress the role of religion in the survival of Jewish national individuality over 2,000 years of political helplessness.

"I do not need to explain that I [personally] am now, as ever, for the freedom of thought, and that I see no holiness in the [religious] ritual," Jabotinsky was to write to his son Eri in 1935. "The issue is much deeper . . . Everyone agrees that there are in the Torah[1] sacred principles and 'really sacred' ones. It is worthwhile implanting them . . . I go much further; *we need religious pathos as such*. I am not sure that we will succeed in reviving it in the souls (of our generation) — maybe nowadays it is but an innate quality given only to a few, like being musically gifted. But I would be happy if it were possible to create a generation of believers."[2]

Jabotinsky's disciple Menahem Begin shares this ideal. Himself (unlike Jabotinsky) an observant Jew, Begin does not seek to play "missionary" to individuals in their personal lives, but he makes no secret of the fact that he regards the fundamental tenets of Jewish religious tradition as basic to the idea of Jewish national identity. When Egypt's President Anwar el-Sadat announced his intention to arrive in Israel on Saturday, November 19, 1977, Prime Minister Begin made it known that he wished Sadat to land at a time when the state reception accorded him would not necessitate a desecration of the Sabbath. The Egyptian government respected the wishes of the Jewish leader: on November 17, U.S. ambassador Samuel W. Lewis transmitted to Begin a query from Egypt's Vice-President Husni Mobarek as to the time after sundown Saturday when Sadat might properly land at Lod Airport. (Begin replied that Sadat could come at any time after 7:30 or 8:00 P.M.; Sadat's plane touched down on Israeli soil at 8:03.)

Like Herzl before him, Jabotinsky stressed the need for political activism. "Buy acres, buy houses," Jabotinsky told audiences numbering into the thousands, "but never forget politics; ninety per cent of Zionism may consist of tangible colonization and only ten per cent of politics. But that ten per cent is the precondition of success and the ultimate guarantee of survival."[3] If the Jewish state in Palestine was to become a reality, he declared, world-wide pressures had to be exerted on Britain to abide by both the letter and the spirit of the Balfour Declaration. But in addition, the Jews must move full speed ahead in the physical rebuilding of the land. A mere trickle of immigrants over an indefinite span of years would not be enough; the largest possible number of Jews would have to be brought to Palestine as quickly as possible. Here was the ideological parting of the ways between Jabotinsky and Labor Zionism: It was fine to have kibbutzim, and pioneers to work the soil, but agricultural settlement alone was too slow a process of upbuilding. Industrial development would be faster, and this in turn required a shift in emphasis from labor pioneering to middle-class immigration and individual initiative. In the face of Arab enmity and British resistance, he said, quick action, both political and practical, might well tilt the balance toward the fulfillment of the Zionist dream — or its demise.

These ideas, which Jabotinsky disseminated on three continents in powerful orations and masterly essays, found followers throughout the Jewish world, but particularly in that part of Europe where Menahem Begin grew to manhood. In the new republics — Lithuania, Latvia and Poland — which had emerged in Eastern Europe in the wake of World War I, resurgent Gentile nationalisms had only served to sharpen deeply-ingrained anti-Jewish prejudices. Hampered by political, social and economic restrictions, thousands of Jews in these "succession states" reacted with a nationalism of their own; they looked to Palestine as the land where they would be free not only to live and work as they chose but also to cultivate the heritage of their own Jewish nationhood. The possibility that they might settle in Palestine only to find themselves a minority there also, ghetto dwellers in a British-ruled, Arab-dominated enclave,without foreseeable prospects of political independence, was totally unacceptable to them. In their view, the objective of Jewish sovereignty in Palestine had priority over social and economic experiments, no matter what their merits. In the mid-1920's Jews who shared these political ideas rallied around Jabotinsky and formed the nucleus of a new movement which he founded within the Zionist framework: the Revisionist party. This was the party whose youth movement Menahem Begin was to join as a high school student, and whose Jewish national values, as formulated by Jabotinsky, were to be reflected in Begin's own Herut party a quarter-century later.

One of Jabotinsky's basic theses was that, given the realities of modern power politics, Jews might be called upon to fight against hostile armies for the survival of the Jewish homeland. Therefore he preached that young Zionists had to acquire training in physical fitness, military discipline and the skills of modern warfare. This training was to become an important activity in the Revisionist youth movement of which Begin was to become first a member, and, before long, the leader.

Yet nothing would be wider of the mark than to dismiss Jabotinsky as a trigger-happy adventurer. He was by nature a man of peace, a member of that pre-1914 generation which had grown to manhood believing in the inevitability of human progress, and in the conscience of civilized man. Thus, even after Britain's repudiation of her Balfour Declaration, Jabotinsky believed that the British people would listen to reason — if only the Jews would not mince words but would state their case with the proper cogency and tenacity. "We can achieve a great deal if only we express our wishes with firmness," he stated on one occasion. The Englishman, he felt, was a gentleman. If he was presented with a note, he would pay it, sooner or later:

> Strength is essentially polite and soft-spoken. But it is infinitely stubborn, absolutely impervious to rebuffs, unshakable in its convictions, with its Decalogue reduced to one sentence: the last word will be MINE, provided, of course, the cause [which] that strength is fighting for is a good one . . . [The Englishman] has one virtue . . . in his own heart he has a Court of Appeal that is open to those who are not afraid to appeal; and he respects those who fight and never acknowledge defeat.[4]

Jabotinsky's disciple Menahem Begin early made this attitude his own. In and out of power, Begin has been known over the past three decades for the courteous, soft-spoken but firm and persevering approach favored by Jabotinsky, of whom Israel's Prime Minister still speaks piously as "our teacher and master", much as a devout *hassid* might refer to his saintly *rebbe*. Begin speaks calmly, but he insists upon his right — and the right of his people — to be heard. When he met with President Carter for the first time in the summer of 1977, Begin made it clear at once that to him, Israeli control of the West Bank (Judea and Samaria) was not a question merely of Jewish history or Biblical promise, but one of life and death for every man, woman and child in Israel. Begin unrolled a map of his country to illustrate how, if the West Bank were to revert to the control of hostile Arabs, Arab tanks could cut Israel in half within a matter of minutes. Having lost his own parents and brother in the Nazi Holocaust, Begin placed his presentation solidly in the context of the sufferings of the Jewish people over the centuries, and of Israel's vital need to be able to defend the lives of her citizens. Eyewitnesses reported that Carter and the others present at the meeting were impressed and moved. Begin's lecture at the White House might have been old-fashioned Zionism, but, as Walter Eytan, the veteran Israeli diplomat, wrote at the time, it reflected an approach that had not been used in years and needed to be revived.[5] Early in 1978, dismayed by what appeared to be a sharp American about-face in favor of Arab demands, Begin called upon American Jewry to appeal to the moral greatness of the American people in presenting Israel's case. Even as Jabotinsky viewed the Englishman as a gentleman, so Begin today regards the grass-roots American as basically fair-minded. Begin honestly believes that the American, once he knows all the facts, will be guided in his decision not by political expediency but by the dictates of the simple human virtues.

Among the old-fashioned decencies in which Menahem Begin has emulated his teacher is the gentlemanly conduct which stood high in Jabotinsky's scale of values. Personal courage, along with courtesy, modesty, and devotion to family and friends, were traits which Jabotinsky sought to instill in his younger followers. The concept of *hadar* — a Hebrew term literally translated as "inner glow" or "radiance" — which Jabotinsky taught to his disciples, is a combination of self-esteem, respect for others, chivalry and loyalty. Jabotinsky shunned political intrigue within his circles; so does Begin, who becomes thoroughly upset when an associate does not reciprocate the personal loyalty which he himself feels toward former comrades-in-arms and present-day colleagues. Unlike Herzl, whose marriage and family life were sacrificed to the Zionist cause, both Jabotinsky and Begin were fortunate in having loyal and understanding wives. Johanna Jabotinsky and Aliza Begin shared devotion to the purposes for which their husbands fought. And despite the extraordinary demands of their careers — Jabotinsky's perpetual lecture tours and Begin's years as leader of an underground movement — neither of the two men is known for extramarital adventures.

Unlike Herzl, Jabotinsky was not a strikingly handsome man. He was short, and during the final years of his life — he was not yet 60 when he died — he looked frail, as Begin does today. But until the end, Jabotinsky retained his personal charisma. He inspired his opponents (including David Ben-Gurion) with genuine respect, and his disciples with the feeling of near-adoration which was to move Menahem Begin to describe the day of Jabotinsky's reinterment in Israel in 1964 — almost a quarter-century after his death — as a "day of joy, anticipation, love and sacred awe."

Jabotinsky's life, which ended in 1940 in New York's Catskill Mountains, a year after the outbreak of World War II, began in Odessa, Russia, on October 18, 1880. Unlike Begin, he was raised in a moderately prosperous home. (His father was a merchant.) Also unlike Begin, who lived and breathed his Jewish heritage almost as soon as he became aware of the world around him, Jabotinsky, aside from some Hebrew lessons, had had, as he later admitted, no inner contact with Judaism during his early youth. At the age of 18, he went to Switzerland and then to Rome to study law, working at the same time as foreign correspondent for a leading Russian daily. (It is interesting to note that Herzl and Begin, too, studied law. Herzl, like Jabotinsky, was a foreign correspondent for a newspaper in his native country; Begin at one point ran a one-man newspaper but never worked as a newspaper reporter.) In Italy, Jabotinsky studied the *Risorgimento,* the 19th-century movement for the liberation, reform and unification of Italy. He conceived a special admiration for Giuseppe Garibaldi, the hero of the movement. Similar sentiments were stirred in Menahem Begin, to whom Garibaldi represents "the ultimate freedom fighter, a man who hated war but fought for freedom, not only for the freedom of his own people but for that of other nations too."[6] Begin has collected some original material on Garibaldi in the hope of writing a book about him someday, after he retires from politics.

Just as the Dreyfus affair brought Theodor Herzl to the idea of a Jewish state, so it was the pogroms of Odessa and Kishinev that turned Vladimir Jabotinsky into a conscious Jew, an active Zionist, and an advocate of Jewish rights. In Russia, he helped form the first Zionist self-defense unit which secured weapons and used them to fend off the attacking Russian mobs. While still in his thirties, he was already regarded as a major spokesman for the Russian Zionist movement at world Zionist conferences (and had met Theodor Herzl). At the same time he pursued the literary career which made Gorki lament Jabotinsky's devotion to Jewish and Zionist concerns as a loss to Russian literature. When Turkey entered World War I on the side of Germany in 1915, Jabotinsky, then a war correspondent in France, began an almost single-handed campaign for the formation of a Jewish Legion as part of the British army to help liberate Palestine from the Turks. This, he felt, would give the Jewish people the right to state its claim to its homeland after the Allied victory which he considered beyond doubt. In his efforts to organize the Legion, Jabotinsky initially had the support of a friend, Joseph Trumpeldor, whose memory was to serve as an inspiration to thousands of young Jews, including Menahem Begin. A man exactly Jabotinsky's age, Trumpeldor had lost an arm in the Russo-Japanese war and had become the first Jew to win an officer's commission in the armies of the Tsar. But like Jabotinsky, he had chosen to devote his life to Zionism.

Two years were to pass before the British government finally consented to the formation of three Jewish battalions in the British army. These units, which comprised the first Jewish fighting force avowedly representing the Jewish people since the year 135 of the Christian era, eventually got to fight against the Turks in Palestine. Jabotinsky enlisted as a private, soon rose to the rank of lieutenant, headed the first company to cross the Jordan River into Palestine, and received a decoration.

After the war, Jabotinsky remained in Palestine. Following the demobilization of the Jewish Legion, he organized the Jewish community's defenses against raids from hostile Arabs which began almost as soon as the British and French had finished dividing the Middle East between themselves. From among the veterans of his Legion, he formed a Jewish self-defense corps, which was to become the nucleus of Haganah, predecessor of the Israel Defense Forces. Jabotinsky personally led these units in Jerusalem during the Arab pogrom of Passover, 1920. For this, he was stripped of his commission in the British army and sentenced to 15 years at hard labor. However, in response to protests from Jews and non-Jews throughout the world, he was released a few weeks later.

In 1921 Jabotinsky was elected to the Executive of the World Zionist Organization. From this platform he spoke out for a strong Zionist stand in the face of Britain's increasingly anti-Zionist attitude. Two years later, dissatisfied with what he considered a lack of Zionist resistance to British policy, he resigned from the Zionist Executive and traveled through the world, including the United States, preaching his own ideas on how to go about translating the Zionist dream into reality. He incurred the anger of the Labor Zionist movement by stressing the need for encouraging large-scale middle-class immigration into Palestine, and by favoring a welfare state but opposing the creation in Palestine of a totally egalitarian society with no reward for individual initiative. As for Arab-Jewish relations, he had no patience with the temporizing attitude of the Zionist establishment. Unlike Chaim Weizmann, Jabotinsky publicly declared the immediate aim of Zionism to be the attainment of a Jewish majority in Palestine. He did not see why the Jewish majority and the Arab minority would not be able to live peacefully side by side within a Jewish state that should include Transjordan, the region which had been amputated from the Jewish homeland in order to appease the Emir Abdullah. (As late as 1950, the population of Transjordan was to be still only four persons per square kilometer.)[7] He did not see how one small Jewish state amidst a multitude of Arab states already existing and still to emerge in the Middle East would represent a hardship to the Arab world. He said all these things openly before the Peel Commission which had come to Palestine in 1937 from England to explore solutions for the "Palestine problem":

> There is no question of ousting the Arabs. On the contrary, the idea is that Palestine on both sides of the Jordan should hold the Arabs, their progeny, *and* many millions of Jews. What I do not deny is that in that process the Arabs of Palestine will necessarily become a minority in the country of Palestine. What I do deny is that *that* is a hardship. It is not a hardship on any race, any nation, possessing so many National States now and so many more National States in the future . . .[8]

By that time Hitler had come to power and had enacted the Nuremberg Laws. Long before most other Jewish leaders and thinkers, Jabotinsky foresaw catastrophe not only for German Jewry, but for the Jews of the entire European continent. He explained anti-Semitism as a form of xenophobia, which periodically assumed such gigantic dimensions that it could not be overcome by rational arguments. The Jewish people was now in need of a homeland for sheer physical survival. In his testimony before the Peel Commission, Jabotinsky frankly admitted:

> It is quite understandable that the Arabs of Palestine would also prefer Palestine to be the Arab State No. 4, No. 5 or No. 6 — that I quite understand, but when the Arab claim is confronted with our Jewish demand to be saved, it is like the claims of appetite versus the claims of starvation.[9]

During the years immediately preceding the outbreak of

World War II, Jabotinsky negotiated with various East European governments for an ambitious solution to the problem of their Jewish minorities. He believed that the leaders of these countries, embarrassed by the virulent anti-Semitism of their citizens, would be glad to rid themselves of their Jews. Accordingly, he proposed an internationally-sponsored ten-year plan under which 1.5 million East European Jews would be evacuated to Palestine. The British, however, remained obdurate in their refusal to lift their restrictions on Jewish immigration into the country. As the Nazi danger grew, Jabotinsky supported the promoters of "illegal" entry into Palestine. He himself had been banished from there by the British in 1930. He lived in Paris, then in London, and finally in New York City.

During the last year of his life, Jabotinsky, though himself not in Palestine, was the supreme political arbiter of the Irgun Z'vai Leumi, the underground fighting organization which by then had taken shape in Palestine and which, four years later, was to be revived and reorganized under the command of his disciple Menahem Begin.

Following the outbreak of World War II, Jabotinsky wanted to create a Jewish army along the lines of the Jewish Legion to fight with the Allies against Nazi Germany. In the fall of 1944, the British government, after long negotiations with the Zionist establishment, was to accede to the formation of a "Jewish Brigade" within the British Eighth Army. But by that time Jabotinsky had been dead four years.

In 1925 Jabotinsky organized the Revisionist party, of which he was president until his death. The party soon had branches thoughout the world. In 1935, a congress of Revisionists, meeting in Vienna and representing over 700,000 voters, seceded from the World Zionist Organization. Only after World War II did the Revisionists rejoin the organization as an opposition party. Following the establishment of the State of Israel, most of those Revisionists who lived in what once had been Palestine joined the Herut party under the leadership of Menahem Begin.

The sector of the Revisionist party which most strongly expressed the influence of Jabotinsky's ideals and personality, to which he felt the closest, and with which his life was almost mystically interwoven during the 1920's and 1930's was the party's youth movement, B'rith Trumpeldor. In fact, B'rith Trumpeldor — or Betar, as it soon became known — had been founded in 1923, two years before its parent organization. It was named after Joseph

Trumpeldor, Jabotinsky's close friend from the Jewish Legion days, who had settled in Palestine after World War I and had been killed in February, 1920, while defending the Jewish settlement of Tel Hai, in the upper Galilee, against an Arab onslaught. Trumpeldor had become a legendary hero to young Zionists. The grave in which he and his five comrades who died with him are buried has remained a pilgrimage site to this day.

Through B'rith Trumpeldor, Jabotinsky sought to imbue the lives of thousands of young Jews with a spirit of pride in the past and confidence in the future. Members of B'rith Trumpeldor were trained for total self-dedication to the creation of an independent Jewish state, and for the realization of Jabotinsky's *hadar* — the transformation of the timid, awkward children of the ghetto into young aristocrats, clean-cut, gentle, courteous and at the same time sure of themselves and of the inherent worth of Jewish nationhood.

When B'rith Trumpledor was first founded in Riga, in the winter of 1923, Menahem Begin was ten years old and still a member of HaShomer HaTzair. But when, six years later, in 1929, a branch of B'rith Trumpeldor was organized in his home town, Brest-Litovsk, Begin, then 16 years old, joined immediately. He had been fascinated by what he called the "total Zionism" of B'rith Trumpeldor. "All the ideas which, from reading and listening to others, I had come to accept for myself, found expression in Betar," Begin remembers, "and I had no doubt whatsoever that this was the movement in which I would want to serve the Jewish people all of my life."[10]

Indeed, much of the political development of Menahem Begin must be viewed in terms of Betar, which, second only to Vladimir Jabotinsky, was the outstanding influence in his formative years and young adulthood.

4. Betar

The handful of activist students who had met in Riga late in 1923 to hear a lecture by Jabotinsky and had named their group B'rith Trumpeldor (the full name was "Joseph Trumpeldor Federation of Activist Zionist Youth") had set themselves an ambitious task: they were out to revolutionize Jewish thinking. If the Jewish nation was to rise again in the modern world, dedicated toil and willingness to endure hardships were essential but no longer enough. If they were serious about political independence, the Jews would have to behave like a nation even before they had their state. For almost 2,000 years the Jews had become used to bending with the wind, absorbing blows without retaliating, relying only on inner spiritual strength for survival. So they had remained alive over the centuries, but it had been an uncertain, insecure existence at best — not sufficient to revitalize a nation in a setting of twentieth-century realities. Fulfillment of Theodor Herzl's Zionist vision demanded a shift from passivity to activism, and this in turn called for a basic change in the psychology of a people which had suffered persecution for two millennia without striking back at its foes. The Jews would have to be trained, deliberately and systematically, in the skills of physical self-defense.

These views were at one with the ideas of the student Menahem Begin, whose father had once struck a Polish soldier in order to protect his rabbi, and who himself had shown his anti-Semitic classmates at school that Jews could and would use their fists against enemies impervious to more "civilized" means of persuasion.

The original founders of B'rith Trumpeldor, or Betar, regarded themselves as the nucleus for the revival of the Jewish Legion in Palestine, which had been disbanded by the British almost immediately following World War I. They did not achieve this aim but eventually they were able to instill their ideals into tens of thousands of youngsters in at least two dozen countries. Over and over, Jabotinsky and his "Betarim" hammered home the idea that a nation about to be born might well be called upon to fight enemies not with appeals to righteous outsiders for protection but with its own strength. If the Jewish nation wanted peace, it would have to know how to use the tools of war.

In order to impress these ideas upon the young people whom they drew into their ranks, the leaders of Betar, taught by Jabotinsky, adopted some trappings of military discipline — training camps, patriotic songs, flags, uniforms and parades. In the summer of 1930 the Betar in Poland — by then a mass movement of almost 250 local branches with a total membership of nearly 10,000 — held a jamboree. "Some 2,000 Betarim camped near Warsaw. They all arrived on their own; some were able to buy railway tickets, some hitchhiked, others came on foot. The 2,000 participants marched through the streets of Warsaw, all in uniform, with flags and military music, and were greeted by the mayor of the capital as well as by the chairman of the Jewish community. It was the first time in the history of Polish Jewry that Jewish youths appeared in military formation. This gave the Jews a sense if not of security, then certainly of pride. The Poles accepted us as the *Zidowska Armia* (the Jewish army) . . ."[1] Thus ran an eyewitness account by Aaron Zvi Propess, first "commander" of Betar.

In left-wing Zionist circles this show of nationalist pride was criticized as an imitation of the Fascist youth groups which were then on the rise. But nothing was further from the minds of the Betarim than Fascism with its obsessive hatred of all things foreign, its racist mythologies and its paranoid fairy tales of international conspiracy. Betar's aim was not to train a corps of mindless party troopers, but to educate a generation of builders and defenders in the spirit of Joseph Trumpeldor and his comrades, who had gone to Palestine as pioneers but also had the strength of body and spirit to put up an effective resistance against enemies who sought to destroy what the Jews had labored to create. "Betar" had a twofold meaning: besides being the acronym of "B'rith Trumpeldor", it was the name of the fortress near Jerusalem where Bar Kokhba and his followers staged the final Jewish rebellion against Rome. Thus, Betar, by its very name, linked the memory of ancient Jewish courage with the modern-day struggle for Jewish rebirth and self-respect. Betar kept many young adolescents from joining Communist youth groups by making them aware of the Biblical teachings on social justice as the natural basis for the Jewish national entity.

Above all, Betar taught the ideal of *noblesse oblige,* which Betarim were called upon to reflect in their personal lives. This was to be expressed not only in terms of Jabotinsky's *hadar,* but also in *giyut,* voluntary service to the Jewish nation. *Hadar* meant to be long on deeds but short on words, to state one's convictions firmly but quietly, without a "straining of vocal cords." Neatness and order at home and school, in the street and at public assemblies, along with cleanliness of dress and person were to be cultivated as outer expressions of an inner harmony of heart and mind, of a healthy and purposeful will.[2] The year Menahem Begin left HaShomer Ha-Tzair, the first contingent of graduates from Betar training farms went on *giyut* to Palestine. On settling in Palestine, every Betar member was required to devote the first two years to "national service" without thought of personal gain. Betar "mobilization platoons" worked on farms, primarily in the Galilee, which were the most obvious targets of attacks from Arabs in neighboring Syria. Betarim helped revive tobacco farming in Palestine and at one time were the sole producers of olive oil in the country. In Jerusalem, Betar members organized themselves into the *"Plugat ha-Kotel"* (Battalion of the Wall) which protected Jews praying at the Wailing Wall from Arab molestation.

Those who knew Begin during his early days in Betar remember him as a quiet young man whose outer appearance was neat but left no particular impression. However, he early acquired a reputation among his peers and his group leaders for intellectual aptitude and extraordinary diligence.

In 1931, after graduating from high school, he left home. He enrolled at the University of Warsaw to realize his childhood ambition; he became a student at the school of law. There, he received a thorough grounding in the humanities and in jurisprudence. In addition, he attended seminars in the methodology of research and in the writing of clear, precise legal briefs. He may also have availed himself of the special courses in diction and rhetoric which were given at the university especially for law students. Begin was never to practice law, but the humanistic knowledge and forensic skills which he acquired and cultivated during his law school days — the ability to speak effectively in public without notes, to quote Abraham Lincoln and the Greek and Latin classics from memory as easily as he does the Bible and Talmud, and to draft legal documents — were to serve him well in putting his ideas across as an underground leader and later as a parliamentarian and prime minister.

In the Polish capital, Begin soon attracted the attention of the Jewish community. He organized his fellow students for self-defense against attacks — physical as well as verbal — from the Polish anti-Semites who were conspicuous at the university. His oratorical talents impressed the national leadership of Betar, which had its headquartes in Warsaw. In 1932, Aaron Zvi Propess, the Betar commander, appointed Begin, then not yet 20, as one of the nine district commissioners for Betar in Poland, and chairman of Betar's Organization Department. Begin proved to be not only a forceful speaker who drew large audiences, but also a capable, painstaking planner and administrator. He was not a "soldierly" type. His active interest at the time lay not so much in Betar's military training program as in the propagation of Jabotinsky's philosophy. He criss-crossed Poland, traveling from community to community, delivering speeches in Hebrew and Polish as the occasion demanded, sometimes accompanying Jabotinsky on the latter's lecture tours. Before long, ideological essays by Begin appeared regularly in the Hebrew periodicals published by Betar's parent body, the Revisionist party: *HaMedinah* (The State), *HaMadrikh* (The Guide) and *HaMetzudah* (The Fortress).

In 1935, Begin graduated from the University of Warsaw with the degree of *magister juris*. But his Betar activities left him little time to prepare for his bar examination. Early the following year, the Betar leadership sent him on his first mission abroad, to visit Betar branches in Czechoslovakia. He arrived there in February, 1936. The original intention, apparently, had been to have him stay in Czechoslovakia for a longer period, but he remained only a few months, during which he managed to tour the length and breadth of the country. His greatest successes in the recruitment of new Betarim were in Slovakia and Subcarpathian Ruthenia, the eastern sector, where Zionism and Jewish activism were far stronger than in the more assimilated western communities of Bohemia and Moravia. In Bratislava, the capital of Slovakia, Begin found himself promoting not only Betar's work for the Jewish homeland, but, once again, Jewish self-defense against the hatred of the local Gentile population. The showing of a Jewish motion picture, *The Golem*, the story of the legendary robot created by the great Rabbi Loew of Prague, had set off a wave of anti-Semitic demonstrations throughout the city. Begin goaded Betar groups and their friends into action to inspire the Slovak rowdies with respect for Jewish strength.[3]

Meanwhile, Hitler was rearming Germany and had declared

war on the Jews. Those German Jews who could do so emigrated. In 1935 alone, some 60,000 Jewish refugees entered Palestine. (But so did uncounted thousands of Arabs from neighboring countries who were drawn by the economic opportunities the Zionists had created there.) The year 1936 marked the beginning of three years of particularly savage Arab rioting. These new disturbances, unique in their extent and duration, were directed — for the first time — not only against the Jews in Palestine, but also against the British.

The Arab riots of 1936-39 brought to a head a development which had begun as early as 1931: the emergence of a new military force in Palestine's Jewish community. Spearheaded by disciples of Begin's mentor Jabotinsky who were already living in Palestine, this armed force was initiated by disenchanted members of Haganah, the self-defense organization whose nucleus originally had been brought together by Jabotinsky in 1920 but which had gradually come under the control of the official Zionist leadership. Since the policy of the Zionist establishment then was one of cooperation with the British, Haganah had evolved into a police force rather than a military organization. Its mode of dealing with Arab attacks was known as *havlaga,* literally, "self-restraint." Whenever a Jew was murdered, Haganah would try to apprehend the Arab culprits and turn them over to the British authorities for trial and (it was hoped) punishment under due process of law. It made no attempt to put an end to Arab adventurism by retaliating or pursuing the raiders to their bases of operations. At the time, the official Zionist leadership under Chaim Weizmann considered that such self-restraint even in the face of constant Arab provocations would eventually pay off in terms of British appreciation and good will toward Zionist endeavors. But this was not to be the case. As Weizmann himself was forced to admit in retrospect many years later,". . . violence paid political dividends to the Arabs, while Jewish *havlaga* was expected to be its own reward. But *havlaga* did not even win official recognition."[4] Whenever the Arabs rioted, the British reacted with studied "even-handedness" in an effort to calm down the Arabs. In 1939, this policy was to culminate in a "White Paper" which permitted the entry of only 75,000 Jews over a five-year period, after which all Jewish immigration into Palestine was effectively to stop.

The former Haganah members who had lost their faith in Haganah's effectiveness originally called their alternate defense force *Haganah Bet* — "Haganah No. 2." Supported by a wide spectrum of non-Socialist Zionist parties in Palestine, Haganah No.

2 considered itself an army in the literal sense of the word, dedicated to one purpose only: the attainment of maximum efficiency in stopping Arab looting and murder. It subjected its recruits, including large numbers of young Betarim, to intensive, systematic military training. In 1937, it officially declared its independence from the original Haganah and adopted the name Irgun Z'vai Leumi — the "National Military Organization" to distinguish it from the original Haganah, whose name was the Hebrew word for "defense."

Thus began the Jewish underground army of which Menahem Begin was to assume command a little over six years later, in the middle of World War II.

Begin's first personal contacts with the Irgun Z'vai Leumi took place in Poland, during the late 1930's. Representatives of the Irgun, as the new armed force in Palestine soon became known for brevity's sake, regularly visited Poland to recruit new members, to build up a network of supporters among the Polish Revisionists and Betar — and, most interesting of all, to obtain arms and training from the Polish government. Among the Irgun emissaries whom Begin met in his capacity of leadership in the Polish Betar was Yaakov Meridor, whom he was later to describe as "one of the ablest Jewish military commanders"[5] he had ever known. In Palestine, Meridor was to become Begin's immediate predecessor as commander of the Irgun.

When Begin first met him, Meridor was one of a group of 20 Irgun volunteers from Palestine who had been sent to Poland to take a special officers' training course in secret communications, sabotage and underground warfare. The Irgun men were placed into an army camp in southwestern Poland; their instructors were officers of the Polish army. This was part of an unofficial arrangement in which Vladimir Jabotinsky had been a key figure. Plagued with a vicious anti-Semitism which they feared might eventually jeopardize domestic peace and order, the Poles were eager to have as many Jews as possible leave the country. In return for a promise from Jabotinsky's Revisionist party to move large numbers of Jews out of Poland for service in the "Jewish Army" in Palestine, the Poles had agreed to train new Irgun recruits from Poland as well as Irgun "veterans" from Palestine, and to supply them with weapons. Before returning to Palestine, Meridor supervised the packing of rifles, machine guns, revolvers, explosives and hand grenades for illegal shipment from Poland to Palestine — enough to supply the 5,000 Betarim who were expected to join the Irgun. To elude detection by the British, the weapons were sent to Palestine concealed in washing machines, in lift vans containing personal belongings of immigrants, and in mislabeled crates.

In the meantime, Betar elsewhere in Europe was training young people as sailors for the future Jewish state. As early as 1934, when Begin was still at law school in Warsaw, Betar had set up the first Jewish naval training school in history — again, as in Poland, with the cooperation of an official military institution. At an Italian naval academy in Civitavecchia, about 100 Jewish cadets, under the supervision of Betar leaders, were taught by Italian naval officers how to man and operate seagoing vessels. The Betar cadets lived separately from the other students, spoke Hebrew, held Sabbath services and received kosher food. (In those days, the Italians permitted foreign students to enter their naval schools. Perhaps, too, the Mussolini government, then not yet committed to Hitler and his rabid Jew-hatred, secretly admired the spunk of the Jews in standing up to the Arabs in the face of British indifference.)

Another naval training school was opened in Riga, Latvia, the birthplace of Betar. Training ships were purchased or chartered to sail along the Mediterranean and Scandinavian coasts. Graduates of Betar's naval training program were eventually to find their way into the Irgun under Menahem Begin; later, they were to form the nucleus of Israel's fledgling navy, where many of them subsequently became high-ranking officers.

On the urging of Jabotinsky's son Eri, Betar even took to the air. During the years immediately preceding World War II, Betar aviation training centers were established in Paris, in New York, in Johannesburg, South Africa and at Lod, today the site of Israel's international airport. The first aircraft ever to be produced in Palestine — a glider — was built by Betar aviation cadets in the late 1930's.

As the influence of Nazism spread beyond Germany, England, still eager to mollify the Arabs, became increasingly miserly in doling out Palestine immigration certificates to Jewish refugees. As early as 1932 Vladimir Jabotinsky had published an article entitled *On Adventurism,* calling upon young Jews to thumb their noses at British restrictions and to make "illegal immigration" into Palestine a "national sport." By 1936, with the Hitler menace growing unchecked by the Western democracies, the Revisionists and Betar had made Jabotinsky's "national sport" a vital part of their program. While the official Zionist leadership still hung back, pondering the wisdom and safety of such action, the Revisionists and Betar, notably in Poland and Austria, led the way, negotiating the purchase of boats, devising the needed documents and assembling the refugees, hoping that the little tramp steamers, crammed with passengers from stem to stern, would not only make it to Palestine in one piece but would also escape discovery by British patrols. After Hitler had activated his "final solution" in the concentration camps and gas chambers, the Zionist movement as a whole, spearheaded by Haganah, was to do heroic work in organizing "illegal" immigration. During the three-year period between Germany's surrender and the birth of the State of Israel, Haganah was to help bring a quarter-million Holocaust survivors to Palestine. But it was largely due to the initiative of Betar that thousands of Jews were able to reach Palestine before the Nazi Holocaust unfolded in its full horror.

During the years immediately preceding World War II, Menahem Begin, as chairman of Betar's Organization Department, not only arranged "illegal" transports of refugees to Palestine but also worked to rally public opinion against Britain's refusal to open the gates of Palestine wide enough for the hundreds of thousands of Jews who had no other possibility of saving themselves. In 1937 Begin organized a mass Zionist demonstration across the street from the British embassy building in Warsaw and placed himself at the head of the marchers. He was promptly arrested by the Polish police, but was soon released.

Hitler's annexation of Austria in March, 1938, and the Munich Agreement six months later, set off a reaction of near-despair among Jabotinsky's younger followers, including Menahem Begin. The anger of these young people was now directed not so much against the Arab terror in Palestine as against the British, who they felt were inciting the Arabs against the Jews. Besides, Begin and his friends were becoming disillusioned not only with the democracies but also with their own elders who seemed to sit by helplessly while Hitler was preparing to conquer Europe and destroy European Jewry.

In the fall of 1938, Betar's third world-wide congress met in Warsaw. Begin, who had just turned 25, mounted the speaker's platform and called upon Betar in Palestine to start an open revolt against the British. He urged the Jews of Palestine to follow the example of the Irish, who had rebelled to cast off the British yoke. In this, Begin had the support of the younger delegates to the congress, including Betar representatives from Palestine.

Begin's impassioned plea promptly got him embroiled in an

argument with his revered teacher, Jabotinsky, who was then both supreme commander of Betar and head of the Revisionist movement. Jabotinsky had consistently reiterated the demand for an independent Jewish state and had urged defiance of the British in the form of overt political pressures and "illegal" immigration into Palestine. But Jabotinsky, now 58 years old and no longer in the best of health, regarded the younger Betarim as hotheads. He considered an all-out Jewish revolt in Palestine, as distinct from other manifestations of activism, to be neither feasible nor the proper way of reminding Britain of the obligation she had taken upon herself under the League of Nations mandate. Notwithstanding Britain's sellout of Czechoslovakia at Munich only weeks before, Jabotinsky insisted that "we are not living in a world of robbers, but in a world of law and justice, where human conscience still holds sway." The younger man disagreed. "After Munich," Begin shouted, "who can still have faith in the conscience of the world?" Jabotinsky, still true to his basic belief in human decency, became visibly upset. "If you, Mr. Begin, have stopped believing in the conscience of the world," he told his disciple, "my advice to you is to go and drown yourself in the Vistula River." Then, after a pause, he added, "Your other alternative would be to take up Communism."

Jabotinsky compared Begin's outcries of despair to the creaking of a door on its hinges, an irritating noise serving no useful purpose. "What kind of Irish-style rebellion would we be able to wage in Palestine?" he demanded.

At that point Israel Eldad (Scheib), a scholarly young writer, took the floor in Begin's defense. Even the creaking of a door in its hinges, he suggested, could perform an important service by awakening a man from his sleep in time to save his house from burglars. Begin's plea for revolt should be taken in the same spirit; it was meant to rouse the Jewish people in time to save their homeland from a pair of powerful enemies: opportunism and defeatism.[6]

It seems that Jabotinsky's impatience with Begin evaporated quickly, for early in 1939 he consented to Begin's appointment as overall commander of the Betar organization in Poland, which by that time had 70,000 members.

In the late spring of 1939, a happy change took place in Begin's personal life; he married. Two years before, in 1937, he had taken a short leave of absence from his duties in Betar to obtain his license to practice law. For this purpose, he had stayed briefly in the Galician town of Drohobycz. "There, I found two important things," he was to recall forty years later. "My wife, and someone who taught me English."[7] (It seems that the teacher taught Begin only the rudiments of English grammar, then left him on his own to study the language by himself.)

The young Zionist leader soon became acquainted with the Jewish communal life of Drohobycz. At the time of Begin's visit, over one-third of the town's 33,000 inhabitants were Jews. Thanks to the discovery of a petroleum well nearby, Drohobycz had been the center of the Hapsburg monarchy's petroleum trade. The Jews had assumed a prominent role in the industry and many of them had acquired considerable wealth as a result. The political upheavals following the end of World War I in 1918 and the absorption of the petroleum trade by large oil companies had put an end to the prosperity, but Drohobycz had remained a bustling, purposeful Jewish community. One day, after delivering a lecture, Begin was invited to the home of Dr. Arnold, the leader of the local Revisionist party branch. There, at the dinner table, he met his host's sisters. There were twins, seventeen years old. Both girls impressed the young guest as well-mannered; as he later recalled, they did not talk much during the meal.[8] But one of them, Aliza (or Ala, as she was known to her friends), caught his eye the moment they met. The next day, from a trip out of town, he wrote to her that although he had met her only once, he felt as if he had known her all his life. During the two-year courtship that followed, Begin warned her that life at his side would not be easy. "I told her we would never have any money, but trouble there would be plenty, and probably prison, too, because we would have to fight for Eretz Yisrael."[9] Aliza assured him that she was not afraid of trouble. She was to keep that resolve faithfully over the hardships of separation and underground life that marked the first nine years of their marriage. Aliza was a woman of quiet, steady courage. She was to give birth to her first two children, Benny and Hasia, during the years of World War II and the underground. (Her third and last, Leah, was born early in 1948, midway between the end of the underground period and the official emergence of the State of Israel.) During the years she lived in hiding, she grew thin, became stooped from endless reading and knitting (she wears thick glasses today), and suffered from asthma.[10] But Aliza Begin's unquenchable vitality and her subtle sense of humor never deserted her, not then, nor during the thirty years of her husband's tenacious political struggle as opposition leader in Israel's parliament, nor when his serious illness in 1977 almost cheated him of his ultimate political and personal triumph. Throughout, she was to maintain the serene, cheerful outlook which, in New York's Waldorf-Astoria Hotel, as the wife of Israel's Prime Minister, she was to sum up in three brief words: "I love life."[11]

But all this was still light-years away on the winter night when her young suitor, after completing a last-minute speaking engagement, met Aliza at the Drohobycz railroad station for a visit home to Brest-Litovsk to meet his parents. After the engagement was announced, Begin shared the news at once with Jabotinsky, who wrote to him:

> I wish you what I would wish my own son. There have been bad days in my life, but I have known many good days too. Now that I have grown old, I know that the best of the good days was the day I put a ring on a girl's finger, and recited a verse of nine words to her.[12]

Begin recited that same "verse of nine words" — the Hebrew marriage vow — to Aliza on a spring day in 1939. Much to Begin's joy, Jabotinsky was able to be present at the ceremony. There was no honeymoon. The day after the wedding, Begin had to leave for Warsaw to organize yet another transport of "illegal immigrants" to Palestine. The Nazis had occupied Czechoslovakia, and it was feared that Poland would be next. The days of world peace were numbered, and as many Jews as possible had to be spirited out of Europe while there was still time. Begin never had a chance to open a law practice.

Until two weeks before the outbreak of the war, he assembled and escorted transports of refugees bound for neighboring Rumania. There, it was hoped, they would be able to reach Black Sea ports from where "illegal" boats chartered by Betar would take them to Palestine. But the day came when he led a transport of 1,200 young refugees to Rumania and found the border closed. Almost 40 years later, on a state visit to Rumania, Prime Minister Begin was to reveal what had happened. Rumania had acted under pressure from the British ambassador in Bucharest, who in turn had been instructed by London to stop the "illegals" from using Rumania as a transit country on the way to Palestine. For most of the refugees in that group, the British ambassador's action meant the end of every hope for escape. Hardly any of them survived the war.

On September 1, 1939, time ran out for Polish Jewry. On that day, Hitler's troops crossed the Polish border from the west. Two weeks later, Soviet Russia entered from the east. The second world war within a span of twenty-five years had begun.

5. Flight, Arrest and Imprisonment: 1939-1942

While Poland was crushed between the German and Soviet war machines, Begin and his young wife remained in Warsaw. As German troops moved relentlessly toward the Polish capital, Begin's friends begged him to flee, but he refused; it would be an act of cowardice for him to leave when there were still Jews to be saved.

Only days before the Germans broke into Warsaw, Begin learned that two precious Palestine immigration certificates had become available and had been reserved by the Betar leadership for him and his wife. With these documents, he and Aliza could have crossed into Rumania unhindered and made the journey to Palestine not aboard a packed, battered "coffin ship" in danger of British interception but openly, as legally-certified immigrants, by the best transportation obtainable under wartime circumstances. But even then, Begin would not yield. Precisely because he was the commander of Betar, he felt that he and his wife had no right to "desert" and perhaps deprive two other Jews of the chance to reach Palestine in safety.

Only when the fall of Warsaw was imminent did the Begins leave the city, traveling southeast in the direction of Rumania. With them were four others; Israel Eldad (Scheib), who had spoken in Begin's support at the Betar congress the year before, Nathan Friedmann-Yellin (Yellin-Mor), a leader in the Polish Revisionist party and editor of various Irgun and party organs in Warsaw, and their wives. The three couples traveled on foot, each person carrying a knapsack, under a steady barrage of bombs.

They all managed to cross into the Russian-occupied zone of Poland, but at Lvov they were stopped by a Russian patrol and detained. They were soon released, but then more trouble came. Aliza was ill; her husband took her to the home of her parents in

Drohobycz forty miles away. Aliza, however, refused to be parted from her husband and insisted on continuing on the journey along with the others. Since it was too risky at the time to attempt a crossing into Rumania, Begin and his friends changed their plans and decided to head due north instead for Vilna, which had been transferred from Poland to Lithuanian rule and was therefore still neutral. This was a journey of several hundred miles, but the Begins, Eldads and Friedmann-Yellins completed it without running afoul of military patrols or border officials.

They found that Vilna had become an island of safety for Jewish refugees from Poland. Polish Betarim by the hundreds streamed into the city in search of possible roundabout routes to Palestine. Begin, as head of the Polish Betar, set about organizing the young people to give them a sense of stability while they waited to move on.

There were times during Begin's months in Vilna when his sense of responsibility toward his position of command in Betar assumed somewhat exaggerated dimensions. One day he called a meeting of the Betar leaders in the city and informed them that he had decided to return to Warsaw, which had fallen to the Germans on September 27. He explained he had received a letter from Palestine criticizing him for having fled from the Polish capital when other Jews were still stranded there. As captain of Betar, the letter stated, he should have been the last to abandon the sinking ship. Begin was torn by feelings of guilt; it took strenuous efforts on the part of his comrades to keep him from this impulsive act, which probably would have cost him his life.[1]

The months that followed saw the spread of war over ever wider parts of the world. The year 1939 ended with Russia's invasion of Finland. The spring of 1940 brought the German invasion of Norway, Holland, Belgium, and Luxembourg, and the fall of France.

In the end, Lithuania, too, lost her freedom. On July 26, 1940, several hundred Jewish students assembled in a hall at the University of Vilna to commemorate the anniversary of the death of Theodor Herzl and the Hebrew poet laureate, Hayim Nahman Bialik. The meeting was also intended to mark the fifteenth anniversary of the opening of the Hebrew University in Jerusalem. The principal address was delivered by Menahem Begin; it was the first time that an audience at the University of Vilna heard a speech given in the Hebrew language.

The proceedings were suddenly interrupted by a stir in the

audience. A note was passed to the speaker's platform: Soviet forces had entered the city of Vilna. There was a frantic scramble for the exits. In the midst of the confusion Begin remained, as ever, the stickler for discipline. He called for an orderly adjournment of the meeting with the singing of *Hatikvah,* the hymn of the Zionist movement, which eventually was to become the national anthem of the Jewish state. While Russian tanks rumbled through the streets outside, hundreds of young Jews inside the university auditorium stood at attention, singing the song of the Jewish people's age-old hope for a return to the land of Zion and Jerusalem.

Nine days later Begin and his friends found themselves wondering bitterly whether, indeed, there was any reason left to hope for a rebirth of the Jewish nation in their lifetime. Vladimir Jabotinsky was dead. The news had come to Begin by cable from London. Israel Eldad remembers first hearing it at the restaurant where the Jewish refugees in Vilna met to have their meals and to discuss the latest political developments. The young Betarim, bereft of their homes and far from their loved ones, were shattered by the loss of their leader. They had looked to his image as a symbol of ultimate Zionist fulfillment much as the Zionist youth of the previous generation had looked to Theodor Herzl. Now Jabotinsky was gone, dead of a heart attack in the United States, where he had been seeking support for a Jewish army, a reincarnation of his Jewish Legion, to fight alongside the Allied forces. Death had come to him on August 3, 1940 while visiting the summer camp run by Betar in Hunter, New York. Begin was desolate. "The whole world blackened for me and my family," Begin was to write years later. "Jabotinsky to us was more than a leader; he was the bearer of hope. We looked to him to bring us out of bondage. He would bring about the establishment of the State of Israel. Now that hope was lost."[2]

Begin traveled to Kovno, some 50 miles away in central Lithuania, where he eulogized Jabotinsky in the main synagogue. By that time Begin was aware that he, along with other known Zionists, was being shadowed by agents of the NKVD, the Soviet secret police, but in his state of depression he was beyond caring whether or not he would be arrested for his public tribute to his departed teacher. Indeed, he felt that if he had to go to prison, so much the better; if he could not fight for the Jewish state, at least he would go on record as having suffered for it.

Shortly after the Russian occupation of Vilna, the Begins and the Eldads moved to lodgings on the outskirts of the city, where they lived together with Aliza's brother, Dr. Arnold. (Friedmann-Yellin and his wife had gone underground; they were to reach Palestine before Begin.)

On September 1, 1940, Begin received an official message from the local authorities: "You are invited to call at the Municipality, Room 23, between the hours of 9 and 11 A.M. in connection with your application." Since he had never made any kind of application to the municipality, it was clear to Begin that the message was a trick designed to propel him into the hands of the NKVD. By that time, however, he had recovered somewhat from his sadness over Jabotinsky's death and was not ready to jump into the trap. If the Russians wanted to arrest him, they would have to come and get him themselves.

During the ten days that followed, he noticed that the house in which he lived was under constant surveillance. Once he caught sight of three spies — one of them a woman — shadowing him.

The denouement came ten days after the Russian "invitation," just as Aliza Begin and Batya Eldad were preparing the midday meal. Begin and Eldad were playing chess. The two men had just started a new game, when there was a knock at the door. Three NKVD men entered the room and asked Begin why he had not reported at the town hall as he had been ordered to do. Begin put on a show of innocence; he knew, he said, that there was no Room 23 in the Municipality Building and he had never made contact with the authorities. The NKVD men thereupon informed him that they had come to take him with them. Begin remembered how his father, in a similar situation, had sent the Polish police away in embarrassed confusion by requesting them to show him their warrant for his arrest. The son tried the same stalling device with the Russian NKVD; unfortunately, to no avail. But Begin kept his presence of mind and also his good manners. Aliza Begin, outwardly just as composed as her husband, invited the three Russians to have some tea before they left. Just as politely, the NKVD men refused; they had no time. Begin asked Aliza for some bread to take with him, then excused himself, explaining that he had to get ready. He polished his shoes and put on fresh clothing. There was no need to pack any belongings, the Russians assured him; if he cooperated with the authorities, he would be back home soon. He asked for permission to take some reading material with him; he chose one English book — André Maurois' biography of Benjamin Disraeli — and his Bible. At the door, Begin stopped, turned and insisted that the NKVD men precede him out of the room since, after all, they had been guests in his home. Eldad remembers that his own wife broke down in sobs but that Aliza Begin did not shed a tear.[3] In the street, Begin turned to Aliza. Let Eldad wait for him until he returned, he called to her. They had been interrupted in the middle of their game of chess just when it looked as if Eldad would win.

Actually, Begin had no illusions that he would be permitted to return home in short order. He wrily remembered how, before their marriage, he had warned Aliza that he might be imprisoned because they would have to fight for the land of Israel. But during those courtship days he had envisioned his arrest under very different circumstances. He had pictured himself in a British prison cell in Palestine, not in a Russian jail in Vilna.[4]

At Vilna police headquarters, Begin was told the charge that had been made against him: as a Zionist leader, he was an agent of imperialist Britain. Later, Begin was to describe it as the supreme irony of his career as a freedom fighter that the two periods of greatest personal danger in his life were, first, the time when he was accused of being a British agent, and then the years when he was hunted as an anti-British terrorist.[5]

Begin's first interview with the Soviet police was a friendly chat with an examiner who assured him that if only he would confess his guilt, he would be allowed to go home at once. But when Begin admitted that he had been a Zionist leader, his questioner called Begin an enemy of the Soviet power. When Begin insisted that he had never done anything to harm Russian interests, the investigator replied, "You are lying."

The battle to wrest a full confession from Begin continued. He was placed upon a chair with his knees as close as possible to the bare wall of the interrogation room. He was forced to sit in this position for 60 hours without food, water or sleep.

From police headquarters, he was transferred to Lukishki, the main NKVD prison in Vilna, where he was to spend the next eight months. On his arrival there, he was led into a room where he found himself facing an interrogator across a table. The interview resembled a polite discussion more than an interrogation. The interrogator was a tall, handsome young man. "I'm Jewish myself," he told Begin at once, "so you can tell me the truth." The conversation that ensued ranged over a wide selection of subjects — the Russian revolution, Zionism, Britain, Theodor Herzl, Jabotinsky, Mussolini, Marx, Engels, Stalin, the Spanish civil war, capitalism versus socialism and communism, idealism versus materialism, and theology versus science. Night after night, at the midnight hour,

Begin was dragged from his cell for another talk in the interrogation room. The interrogator was courteous, but he made it plain from the start that he considered Begin guilty as charged. The true purpose of Zionism, the Russian insisted, was to divert young Jewish people from the revolution in Europe and to place them into the service of British imperialism in the Middle East.

Worn out by the nightly debates, Begin drew upon his legal training for a new defense. He conceded that his Zionist activities might be crimes under Soviet law. But he pointed out that they had been entirely legal in Poland, where he had conducted them long before the Soviet invasion, and that Soviet law could not punish a Polish citizen for acts which had not been forbidden under Polish law at the time they had been committed. The interrogator thereupon acquainted Begin with Article 58 of a Soviet code which he said was applicable to everyone, regardless of citizenship or nationality, who came within physical reach of the Russian police: anyone violating Soviet law, no matter what the time or place, was liable to punishment by the Soviet authorities.

The Zionist movement, said the Soviet agent, had ordered Begin to remain in Vilna so that he might carry on anti-Soviet espionage and counter-revolutionary activities. Begin protested that he had been looking for a way to reach Palestine, and that, in fact, only his arrest had kept him from leaving Vilna. If that was so, the Russian replied, Begin was guilty of yet another crime — attempted flight from the Soviet Union. Begin concluded that by Soviet standards only an unborn being could ever be free of sin.

Soon after this debate with the Soviet agent, one of the guards overheard Begin telling a Yiddish joke with a pun about an idiot. The insult being the same in Russian, the guard thought that Begin was talking about him. As a result, Begin was placed in solitary confinement for seven days, on bread and water, in a triangular, fetid cell without windows and with only three and a half paces of space in which to move his body. For sleep, there was only the bare stone floor, and — since the latrine bucket was never removed from the cell — there were, as Begin sardonically recorded, plenty of rats for nightly entertainment. During those seven nights of total isolation Begin found himself dreaming not of freedom, of a nice home or of a warm bath, but of the barred prison cell he had left behind, where at least there had been a thin mattress on which to sleep and other prisoners to keep him company. When at last he returned to his former prison cell, he learned that one of his cellmates, who was serving time for theft, had already demanded a share of his belongings. The man had been certain that the slim, slight Begin would never survive his stay in "solitary."

In *White Nights,* his recollections of his period of imprisonment in Vilna and Russia, Begin gives character sketches of his cellmates which are of interest primarily for what they reveal of Begin's own thinking and personality. He describes his first cellmate as a highly educated bachelor of middle years. Begin says he enjoyed not only talking with him but also watching him eat his meals. It pleased him to see this man observe the rituals of good table manners even in their malodorous prison cell. It made him feel that he was still part of civilized humanity. Yet Begin never was a humorless pedant; he pokes fun at his neighbor's obsessive neatness which caused him to sulk for days because Begin had unintentionally placed his wooden spoon on that part of the table which the bachelor had marked off as his own "territory."

Begin's second cellmate, a young corporal in the Polish army and a tailor by trade, was not educated, but he was intelligent. Begin says he enjoyed playing teacher to this youth, giving him informal lessons in a number of subjects, especially the history of Poland. The corporal — Begin refers to him as "my pupil" — told him that he had been born a Catholic but was no longer religious. He considered most priests hypocrites and had come to regard himself as an atheist. But one morning Begin saw him in a corner of the cell, making the sign of the cross and dropping to his knees in silent prayer. Afterwards, the young Pole announced that in the future he would pray every morning because he had "begun to believe again." It seemed, Begin noted, that faith took better care of man when things went wrong than man did of his faith when things went well. Begin himself remained consistent in his religious beliefs even in Lukishki Prison. Despite the patronizing smile of the prison warden, he insisted on fasting on Yom Kippur, the Day of Atonement, giving his own share of the daily ration to his cellmates.

Begin worried about Aliza. During the endless interrogations, he had thought of sending her a conditional divorce, formally stating that if she had no news from or about him within a given number of years, she was to consider herself free to remarry. Under certain circumstances, such a document had validity under Jewish religious law. Aliza was only 20 years old; he did not want her to spend the rest of her days alone because she did not know whether or not her lawful husband was still alive somewhere. But he never sent the letter. One of the considerations that kept him from doing so was lack of decent paper and ink for writing out the document, supplies which prisoners could obtain only by official permission.

One day a food package from friends in Vilna arrived for Begin. Among its contents was a handkerchief. Begin shook out the square of linen. Embroidered in one corner were the letters O-L-A. But Aliza's pet name was Ala. Why the changed spelling? Begin wondered. He showed the handkerchief to a cellmate who happened to be Jewish, Edouard (Mordecai) Bernstein, who, like himself, had been arrested because of his prominence in Jewish affairs. (Unlike Begin, however, Bernstein was not a Zionist but a member of the anti-Zionist, Socialist and Yiddishist *Bund*.) Bernstein solved the riddle. The letters on the handkerchief, O-L-A, were not "Ala" misspelled but the Hebrew word for "She is going up." "Going up" was the term used by Zionists to signify emigration to Palestine. So, Bernstein reasoned, the embroidered letters must be a secret code, informing Begin that his wife had left Vilna and was on her way to Palestine! Begin's relief at the news helped make the months that followed easier for him to bear.

On April 1, 1941, Begin and hundreds of other prisoners were herded into a large lobby where each prisoner was given an official document to sign, stating his offense and the final sentence meted out to him. The document handed to Begin for his signature certified that a special committee of the People's Commissariat for Internal Affairs had found "Menahem Wolfowitch Begin" (the "Wolfovitch" stood for his father's name, Ze'ev, meaning Wolf) to be a dangerous element in society and had therefore sentenced him to internment in a "correctional labor camp" for a term of eight years.

In May, Begin was notified that, before leaving Lukishki Prison for the labor camp, which was in Siberia, he would be permitted to receive one close relative as a last visitor. Bernstein's surmise about the letters on the handkerchief had been correct. The visitor who came to bid Begin farewell was not Aliza, but a young Betar girl from Vilna named Paula Daiches. The visit took place under the surveillance of a Russian guard. Paula handed Begin a package containing some clothing, food and two bars of laundry soap. In accordance with prison regulations, the two carried on their conversation in Polish, a language the guards would be able to understand.

Paula wanted to be certain that Begin knew of Aliza's escape — just in case he had not received the handkerchief, or had not understood the code. "Aunty Ala is with Uncle Shimshon," she told him. "Uncle Shimshon" was Shimshon Yunitchman, the leader of

Betar in Palestine. "Also, regards from Aunt Iggeret Be-Savon," the girl continued. *Iggeret Be-Savon* was Hebrew; it meant, "letter inside the soap."

The guard examined the contents of the package and cut each of the two bars of soap in half to make sure nothing was concealed inside. Luckily, he did not uncover the letter. Back in his cell, Begin, with the help of a friendly fellow inmate, a Polish sergeant, dissected the pieces of soap (carefully, in order not to waste the precious soap), and, pressed deep inside one of the halves, found the letter Paula had told him about. It was from another close Betar friend, Joseph Glazman, telling Begin that people in Palestine and America were hard at work to obtain his release and that Aliza and several other friends had left for Palestine.

Neither Paula Daiches nor Joseph Glazman was to share the good fortune of Aliza Begin. Like many other Betarim, they were unable to leave Poland. Glazman was to become a leader of the Jewish partisans — many of them Betar members — who revolted against the Nazis in the Vilna ghetto after the city had been occupied by the Germans. Both Glazman and Paula were to lose their lives, Paula in the ghetto and Glazman in the woods with his partisan unit.

Early in June, 1941, Begin and several hundred other prisoners boarded a freight train bound for the depths of Arctic Russia. The passengers in this transport were all political prisoners. Among them were physicians, lawyers, engineers, teachers, professional soldiers, and even a former assistant editor of *Pravda,* the official Communist party organ. This man was a Jew, known in the party by the name of Garin. He had fallen from grace in the Kremlin and had been arrested on charges of "Trotskyism."

About midway in their journey, the prisoners learned that Hitler had attacked the Soviet Union. For the Poles in the transport; this was to be an unhoped-for stroke of good fortune, but no one aboard the prison train could have known it at the time.

After a journey of several weeks, the transport arrived at its destination. When the prisoners filed out of the freight cars, it was two o'clock in the morning, but it was still broad daylight. These were the famous "white nights" of the brief Arctic summer.

From the train, the prisoners were transferred to a boat which took them to their first place of work, a slave labor camp on the banks of the Piechora River, close to the Arctic zone.

Life at the camp was intended to turn the inmates into nonpersons, without a will or spirit of their own. Everyone, sick or well, worked fourteen hours each day on highway and railroad construction projects in the tundra, and individual bread rations depended on whether the prisoner had fulfilled his "normal" production quota for that day.

Inmates were frequently transferred from one work site to another. Those "etapes," made by train and boat, held special terrors for the prisoners, because most of the year in Arctic Russia is winter, with temperatures at times plummeting to 60 and 70 degrees below zero Centigrade. As for the labor camps through which the prisoners passed in the process, Begin refers to them a "NKVD health institutes." The barracks were filthy huts, teeming with fleas and lice, but at least they provided a shelter of sorts from the incredible cold.

Some time during the winter of 1941-42, Begin, too, was assigned to an "etape." Eight hundred labor camp inmates, political prisoners and ordinary civilians, were packed into one small freighter for the northward journey down the Piechora River to a new construction project. The prisoners were quartered below deck, with no room to sit, much less to move; they could only lie on their bunks, which had been arranged in tiers along the damp walls of the ship's hold. During the weeks aboard this floating dungeon, Begin and his fellow passengers drank the icy water from the river. Most of the prisoners came down with diarrhea. The toilet facilities were on deck; two boards placed at an angle in the boat's stern served 800 people. On the deck stood a Russian sentry, his rifle at the ready to prevent the luckless passengers from attempting to jump overboard.

But nowadays, when the talk turns to those weeks aboard the Russian prison boat, Begin's recollections do not center on physical hardships. He prefers to relate an incident involving Garin, the former *Pravda* editor. At first, Garin had refused to talk about his Jewishness and had spoken to Begin only in Russian. A devout Communist despite his arrest, Garin had engaged Begin in endless arguments about Zionism, which Garin insisted was a product of bourgeois nationalism and irreconcilable with human progress. Then, one day at the labor camp, while unloading heavy rails from one of the river barges, Garin had gotten into a fight with one of the "Urki," not a political prisoner but one of the ordinary criminals who were serving terms at hard labor. In the heat of the quarrel, the Russian had called Garin a dirty Jew. From that time on, Garin was a broken man, terrified that one of the criminals would eventually kill him.

One night aboard the prison boat, Garin was convinced that his end was near. Until then, he had mostly kept aloof from the other Jewish prisoners, but now he approached Begin. He had one last request to make. Speaking to him in Yiddish for the first time, he asked Begin whether he remembered the song the Zionists had sung at their gatherings when he, Garin, had still been a boy in Odessa. It had been a Hebrew song and he wanted to hear it once more before he died. He remembered only one word from it — *La-Shuv* — but he was sure that Begin would know the song he meant.

Garin's pronunciation of the Hebrew word was odd, so it took Begin a few moments to understand. The song was, of course, *Hatikvah:* its closing lines began with *La-Shuv,* "to return to the land of our fathers." Over a year before, Begin had sung it in the hall of the University of Vilna along with hundreds of other young Jews while Soviet tanks had roared into the city. Now, with Garin sitting close beside him on a berth in a Russian prison ship, Begin sang it again. Three other Jewish prisoners lying near them joined in. The Urki in the hold heard it and started a discussion among themselves: What were the Jews singing? It was a prayer, one of the Urki volunteered. The Jews were praying to their God to help them. The rest of the Urki laughed aloud. But their comrade had been right. To this day, Begin regards *Hatikvah* not just as a national anthem, but as a prayer, a solemn affirmation of the Jewish spirit. As he went on singing, and Garin listened in silence, Menahem Begin felt as if he were reciting a confession with a Jew who had gone astray but who, after many tribulations and on the point of death, had found his way back to his people and his faith.

Some days later, the prison ship stopped at a port and rode at anchor while workmen were preparing her for the continuation of the voyage. One day, Begin heard the Russian sentry on deck shout his name, along with other names, in alphabetical order. All those prisoners whose names had been called, the sentry announced, were to collect their belongings and go ashore. Poland and the Soviet Union were now allies in the war against Hitler. Therefore, under an agreement between Marshal Stalin and the Polish government-in-exile, all Polish citizens were to be released from Soviet labor camps to help fight the Nazi enemy, and all the Poles aboard the prison ship were now free men.

Begin found it difficult to grasp what he had just heard. Months before, at the labor camp, there had been vague rumors that all Polish citizens were about to be set free, but he had been as-signed to the "etape" on the prison ship without a chance to investigate the report further. Now that freedom had come, it was totally unexpected and he felt both light-hearted and confused.

Moments later, after a hurried farewell to Garin (who somehow still clung to life), Begin found himself shoved from the large boat onto a smaller craft. They were being taken ashore to a transit camp, the other Poles aboard the pilot ship told him. From there they would travel south to make contact with a Polish liberation army that had formed in Russia under the command of a Polish general.

For the next few months Begin, along with a group of other Poles, traveled through Russia, crossing the vast distance from the Barents Sea, an arm of the Arctic Ocean, north of Norway, to the shores of the Caspian, which lay inland between Russia and Iran. Begin and the other ex-prisoners had no money for train tickets. They covered hundreds of miles standing on the steps of railroad cars and clinging to the door handles. Many times they were pushed off moving trains by angry conductors. They slept in railroad stations, parks and vacant lots, often going without food for days.

As he made his way south into the center of Asia, Begin was looking not only for the newly-formed Polish army of liberation but also for his sister Rachel, who had married a lawyer named Halperin and had been deported into Russia even before Begin's arrest in Vilna. The Poles who were traveling with Begin considered his search somewhat unrealistic. How would he go about finding two people among the millions of war refugees and released internees who were roaming the huge Asian continent? The Poles assured Begin that it was impossible.

But, as was to happen quite often in Begin's life, the impossible came true. Overhearing a chance conversation at a railroad station in Central Asia, he learned that his sister and brother-in-law were not only alive and well but were, in fact, living not too far away from where he himself now was. They had settled in a little town in the Soviet Republic of Uzbekistan, somewhere between the famous ancient cities of Samarkand and Tashkent.

He found the Halperins staying with a friend from Poland in a miserable mud hut. Once settled with his relatives, Begin sent a cable to his Betar friends in Palestine. Before long, he received a reply from Jerusalem. Among those who signed the reply was Aliza.

After several weeks of rest, Begin felt that it would be best for him to move on. Too many people in the town knew of his "past" as a Zionist leader. He feared that as long as he remained adrift in

Russia there always was a chance that, despite his Polish citizenship, he might be arrested again as a counter-revolutionary.

Early in 1942 he learned that a division of the Polish liberation army was stationed in the city of Margelan, a journey of about 400 miles from his sister's home. He traveled to Margelan and reported at once to the Polish headquarters. There, he found one of his old friends from his Betar days; he asked him what he should do next, join the liberation army or find a way of getting to Palestine. The friend told Begin that his prospects of obtaining a Soviet exit permit to go to Palestine on his own were as good as non-existent. He strongly advised him to join the liberation army, which was under the command of General Wladyslaw Anders. There was a good chance that the division from Margelan would be sent to the Middle East.

After cutting through a tangle of red tape — it seemed that the top brass in the Anders liberation army were not eager to have too many Jews — Begin was accepted and took the oath of allegiance to the Polish army. Weeks later, his hopes came true; his unit was ordered to Palestine. In May, 1942, after a long journey through Iran, Iraq and Transjordan, Begin crossed the Jordan River in a Polish army truck. He remembers stopping for a brief respite, taking his first steps on the soil of the Jewish homeland, and one of the Polish soldiers, not a Jew, saying to him, "Good to be home, eh?"

Begin's first stop was in Haifa, where he was to be stationed temporarily. And then there was the reunion with Aliza, whom he had not seen since his arrest almost two years before. (His sister Rachel and her husband, too, were eventually to arrive in Palestine.) He found Aliza in good spirits; after her arrival in Palestine in 1941, she had taken a furnished room in Jerusalem and had enrolled at the Hebrew University to continue her education. The courses she took were not of practical value for her future life, but they helped her through the long months of loneliness by absorbing her active mind; her field of study was archaeology. Thirty-five years later she was asked whether, if she had to do it all over again, she would have sought an independent professional career. "No, thank you," she firmly replied. "Thank God, I was able to fulfill my role as a wife and mother."[6]

6. "The Fighting Family"

For the next year and a half, Begin served in General Anders' Polish liberation army, first in Haifa and then in Jerusalem, where he was attached to the Polish commander as a translator from Polish into English, which he had learned so painstakingly in Poland. This was the only period in his life that Begin wore a uniform and held a military rank, though not an exalted one.

"I ran into Begin shortly after his arrival in Palestine," a friend from the days of the 1938 Betar congress in Warsaw recently told an Israeli journalist. "He and I were both in uniform. Begin's was that of a lowly Polish private. Mine was that of a corporal in the British army. No sooner did we come face to face than Begin gave me a snappy salute. At first, I thought he was teasing me. But no, he was in dead earnest. He was saluting me because, as a corporal, I outranked him."[1]

But on at least one occasion Begin attempted to bypass army discipline. He was sent on an errand to British headquarters in the south wing of Jerusalem's imposing King David Hotel. Regulations for those on official business in the south wing were strict: Only officers were permitted on the main indoor stairway; enlisted men were expected to use an uncovered fire escape that ran along the outside wall of the building. This was no great hardship when the weather was good, but it was not pleasant in the wintertime.

"One day in January, 1943," Begin remembers, "I had to go up to the top floor. It was a bitter cold day and I wasn't keen on climbing seven flights on an uncovered fire escape. So I went inside. Of course I wasn't foolhardy enough to walk into the elevator, but I started up the main stairway. I hadn't proceeded very far when a British soldier stopped me. He wore the insignia of a staff officer. 'Don't you know enlisted men aren't permitted on the indoor stairway? Outside, man, outside!' I had no choice but to go out again and climb the seven flights outdoors in the cold. I was cursing to myself in Russian all the way up."[2]

Most of the other Jewish refugees from Poland who had come to Palestine with the Anders army shed their uniforms almost immediately after their arrival without the formality of an official discharge. But Begin was not among those refugees who deserted from the Polish army. Like many of the others, he had joined the Anders army primarily as a means of reaching Palestine, but unlike most of them, he insisted that he had no right to ignore his oath of allegiance to the Polish armed forces. He could not permit himself to be branded as a deserter from an army which had been formed to fight Nazi Germany. He persisted in this attitude even when he found himself caught in a conflict between his duties in the Polish army and his almost desperate eagerness to resume full-time service to the Zionist cause.

Almost from the day of his arrival in Palestine, he had been in close touch with friends from the Polish Betar who had saved themselves from the European Holocaust. The mood in Palestine's Jewish community was grim. By April, 1942, the month before Begin's arrival in Haifa, the first reports of Hitler's "final solution" for European Jewry had reached the country. Mass deportations of Jews to the extermination camps had begun, and reports from Nazi-held Europe indicated that no more than 25 per cent of Europe's Jews would be left alive when — and if — the war ended in an Allied victory.[2a] Throughout these tragic events, Britain remained obdurate in her determination to keep Jews from entering Palestine. In the spring of 1939 she had issued the White Paper under which, in effect, Palestine would be closed entirely to Jewish immigration after 1944, with those Jews already in the country condemned to remain a permanent minority within a British-dominated Arab state. In February, 1940, legislation was passed placing additional limitations on the right of Jews to purchase land in Palestine.

Since immigration certificates were almost impossible to obtain, Jews by the tens of thousands attempted to reach Palestine by "illegal" routes. Britain's reaction was to blockade Palestine to boats carrying Jewish refugees. Governments of neutral countries through whose territory or waterways the refugees had to pass were subjected to British diplomatic pressures to stop the Jews and to keep shipowners from providing transportation for the "illegals." As a result, thousands of Jewish refugees found themselves abandoned by the captains who had taken them aboard ancient hulks at exorbitant fares, or turned back from ports where their boats, almost at the point of disintegration, had stopped for makeshift repairs.

The most horrifying example of British indifference to the fate of Jews who looked to Palestine as their only hope of survival was the *Struma* incident, which aroused a storm of protest from Jewish communities still free to speak their minds. Late in 1941 a member of the Revisionist party had chartered the S.S. *Struma,* an old Bulgarian coal barge flying the flag of neutral Panama, to transport 600 refugees from Rumania to Palestine. The boat was totally unseaworthy, but, fearful that their Rumanian transit visas might expire before they had another opportunity to leave, 769 Jewish refugees were aboard the ship when she left port. On December 14, 1941, the *Struma* put in at Istanbul because she was in no condition to go on. The Turkish authorities, however, would not permit her to land because the British refused to accept the passengers in Palestine. The Jewish Agency, the body of Zionist leadership originally created to help Britain establish the Jewish national home, protested, but to no avail. In February, 1942, after the *Struma* had been drifting for three months within sight of Istanbul harbor, the Turkish port authorities had her towed out into the Black Sea. There, the boat suddenly exploded, killing all but one of the refugees aboard.

This tragedy brought a change in relations between Britain and the Zionist establishment. In May, 1942, three months after the loss of the *Struma,* Zionist leaders from the United States and 17 other countries met in New York's Biltmore Hotel and ratified a declaration drafted on the initiative of David Ben-Gurion, leader of the Socialist Zionist Mapai (*Mifleget Po'ale Eretz Yisrael*) party, who was chairman of the Jewish Agency Executive. Rejecting the British White Paper of 1939, the declaration asserted that the ideals of peace, justice and equality could never become realities in the postwar world unless there were a permanent solution for the problem of Jewish homelessness. To this end, the declaration, which was to go down in Zionist history as the "Biltmore Program," called for the establishment of Palestine as a "Jewish Commonwealth" after the war. This was the first time that the official Zionist leadership openly acknowledged that which Jabotinsky, the Revisionists, Betar and Menahem Begin had never hesitated to proclaim all along: that the ultimate aim of Zionism in Palestine was not the development of a vaguely-defined "Jewish national home" but the creation of an independent Jewish state.

On his arrival in Palestine, then, Begin found the aim of Jewish statehood supported no less by Haganah, which was under the orders of the Jewish Agency (to all practical purposes, the Labor Zionist movement led by Ben-Gurion), than by the Irgun Z'vai Leumi, the military force which enjoyed the support of the Revisionists, Betar and other non-Labor elements in the Zionist ranks.

But during the early part of World War II, both Haganah and Irgun had temporarily set aside their opposition to British anti-Zionist policy and concentrated their energies on aiding the British war effort against the enemy whose defeat was vital for both Britain and the Jewish people. During that period, there was hardly any trouble from the Arabs in Palestine. Impressed by Jewish resistance during the bloody riots of 1936-39 and — for the first time — held in check by the British authorities who could not afford civil disorder in wartime, they had become relatively quiescent. A much more immediate threat to the Jews in Palestine came from General Rommel and his *Afrika Korps,* which seemed about to overrun Egypt and stood at the very gates of the Jewish homeland.

In the case of Haganah, which by then had been tacitly accepted by the British administration as a semi-legal organization, there was never a doubt that it would devote itself completely to the pursuit of the war. Thousands of Haganah members joined units of the British army fighting on every battlefront. Haganah fighters aided the British intelligence service and spearheaded the British invasion of Syria, the action in which Moshe Dayan lost his left eye. Palmach, Haganah's commando division, was trained by the British in guerilla warfare to harass the Germans in case Rommel's armies got through to Palestine. Haganah and the Jewish Agency (the latter representing the Zionist establishment vis-a-vis the British authorities) were motivated by the belief that in return for its contribution to the Allied war effort in the Middle East and elsewhere, the Jewish community in Palestine would be entitled to assert its claim to independence when the war was over.

The Irgun Z'vai Leumi, which had begun active warfare against the British shortly before the outbreak of World War II, followed the example of Haganah. Although the Irgun's leadership did not share Haganah's gradualist approach to the struggle for Jewish statehood, it announced the cessation of all anti-British action "for the duration" and offered to cooperate with Britain in the struggle against Nazi Germany. At one point early in the war, the Irgun even sought a reunion with Haganah, but apparently Ben-

Gurion was unwilling to consider the proposal. The commander of the Irgun at the time was David Raziel, a former rabbinical student in his early thirties who had excelled in mathematics and philosophy at the Hebrew University but had switched to an intensive study of military history and sciences which he felt he would need for his work with Irgun. Menahem Begin in later years was to describe this devoutly religious, calm, thoughtful man as "the great leader of the people of Israel in this generation." In 1941, during a pro-Hitler revolt in Iraq, Raziel and a small group of his followers volunteered to go to Baghdad on an important British sabotage and intelligence mission. A German plane machine-gunned the car in which Raziel was traveling, and he was killed instantly. Today, his remains rest on Mount Herzl in Jerusalem, alongside the leaders and heroes of the Jewish state.

When Raziel announced the Irgun's intention to defer the showdown with Great Britain until after the war, he provoked a sharp split within his organization. Avraham (Yair) Stern, an intense, handsome and highly gifted man three years Raziel's senior, considered the British no less an enemy of the Jewish people than Adolf Hitler. In June, 1940, Stern led a group of like-minded individuals away from the Irgun to form his own underground fighting force, which continued the struggle against England. He named it *Lohame Herut Yisrael* (Fighters for the Freedom of Israel) or, for short, LEHI. Soon, it was popularly referred to as the "Stern Group." It is true that in some cases members of Irgun and LEHI were linked by ties of personal friendship from earlier days. (Begin's friends Israel Eldad and Nathan Friedmann-Yellin, who had fled Warsaw together with him and had reached Palestine before him, were to join the "Sternist" high command.) It is true also that at various times during the final phase of British rule in Palestine, LEHI and Irgun engaged in joint operations. But it is not correct to lump the two groups together as one "band of terrorists." The Sternists, who were known to their opponents as the "Stern Gang," regarded the Irgun as far too moderate. When the Irgun, under Begin's command, eventually resumed the fight against the British, it sought to attain its objectives by destroying government property and disrupting communication lines rather than inflicting human casualties. Also, it took great care not to harm civilians. LEHI, by contrast, believed that war against England would be effective only if it was fought on a highly personal level. In Stern Group tactics, individual assassinations played a prominent role, with little concern whether the victim was a soldier or a noncombatant. Members of LEHI, not Irgunists, killed Lord Moyne, the British Resident Minister in the Middle East.In February, 1942, Stern himself was shot and killed by the British police.

Because of its notoriety for violence, LEHI had few sympathizers outside its immediate ranks. The Irgun, on the other hand, though considered a "dissident" movement in Zionism, enjoyed the respect and sympathy of many Jews, including rank-and-file members of the more moderate Haganah.

Still, in the middle of 1942, when Begin came to Palestine, the Irgun had reached a low ebb. Over 1,000 of its members had left to join the British army. Only about 600 Irgunists were in Palestine and within reach of Yaakov Meridor, who had taken over as commander after the death of Raziel. Haganah received funds through the Zionist establishment, but the Irgun during the early years of World War II was largely dependent on contributions obtained in the United States through emissaries and propagandists such as Hillel Kook and Arye Ben Eliezer. Kook operated under the alias of Peter Bergson to conceal his family relationship with Abraham Isaac Kook, late chief rabbi of Palestine and one of the most loved and venerated personalities in Palestine's Jewish community. Arye Ben Eliezer was to become Begin's firm advocate and subsequent collaborator in planning the Irgun's eventual revolt against British rule in Palestine.[3]

But in the year 1942, Begin's first in Palestine, the Irgun revolt against Britain was still in the future. The threat from the *Afrika Korps* in neighboring Egypt was still acute. As for Begin himself, he was still a soldier in the Anders army. He was, in fact, already leading two lives, for in the fall of 1942, he had been elected commander of the Betar organization of Palestine. At first it appeared that his work in Betar would not clash with his duties in the army, because it did not take too much of his time. Primarily, he wrote ideological articles for the bulletin put out by the Betar command under the editorship of a young schoolteacher, Israel Epstein. Written under the pen-name "Ben Ze'ev" (alluding to Begin's own father as well as to Vladimir Ze'ev Jabotinsky), these articles attracted favorable attention in Betar as well as in the Irgun circles with which Begin also maintained contact. But before long, Begin had reason to suspect that the British military intelligence service was watching him and reporting his "extracurricular" doings to Polish army headquarters. His superiors had begun to restrict his movements.[4] Begin therefore resigned from his official position in

Betar, hoping that, eventually, some way might be found for him to receive a legal discharge from the Anders army.

As the year 1942 drew to a close, the fortunes of the Allies took a turn for the better. General Montgomery's decisive victory over Rommel's armies at El Alamein, followed by the landing of American forces in Algeria, eliminated the immediate threat of a German invasion of Palestine. The following year saw the Allied invasion of Sicily and the Italian mainland, and Italy's surrender. With Britain no longer threatened by defeat in the war, but the Jews of Europe still faced with annihilation, the Irgun leadership increasingly felt that the time had come to resume the struggle against the British colonial administration in Palestine and to force open the doors of the country so that Jews could enter. During the summer of 1943 Arye Ben Eliezer, after four years of Irgun propaganda and fund-raising work in the United States, returned to Palestine and explored possibilities for the revival of the Irgun as an effective underground organization. He proposed a three-point strategy for the Irgun: to harass the British administration in Palestine, to establish an independent Jewish government, and to present the Irgun's ideology effectively to public opinion in Palestine as well as in the English-speaking world. Yaakov Meridor, commander of the Irgun, was a fine organizer who had shown expertise in training recruits and acquiring weapons from the most unlikely places, but he lacked experience in the art of propaganda, which at this juncture was considered all-important. It was therefore agreed that the command should be turned over to an individual who had demonstrated skills in formulating and publicizing the political ideals which the Irgun had meant to pursue. The choice fell on Menahem Begin. Ben Eliezer and the others who favored Begin pointed out that his "skills in analysis and style, and his leadership talents stemming from profound moral and spiritual strength, courage and his spirit of sacrifice"[5] more than offset the fact that, as a newcomer from Poland, he had not passed through the Irgun's ranks in Palestine and had never participated in the planning or execution of underground military operations. As for Begin himself, he was not at all certain that he was either willing or qualified to assume the commandership of the Irgun. But as a refugee from Nazi Europe and aware of what was happening to European Jewry, he no longer considered it morally defensible to hold the revolt against Britain in abeyance until after the war. He was determined to devote all his energies to the struggle which lay ahead once he found a way to separate himself decently from the

Early 1930's: Begin as a student in the uniform of Betar, the Revisionist youth organization.

Middle 1940's: Menahem Begin in the underground as "Rabbi Israel Sassover."

1942: Menahem Begin, in soldier's uniform and cap, shortly after his arrival in Palestine. At his right is his wife Aliza. On the far right (in light civilian suit) is Begin's close friend Israel Epstein.

September 17, 1978: The signing of the Camp David Agreements in the East Room of the White House. President Jimmy Carter is flanked by Prime Minister Begin on his left and by President Sadat on his right. Standing on the far right is U.S. Secretary of State Cyrus Vance.
Courtesy Israel Government Press Office.

September 22, 1978: Begin and his wife receive Jerusalem's official welcome on their return to the city following the Camp David Conference. Begin is standing at the speaker's lectern in front of the National Convention Hall. At Begin's left (in open-necked shirt) is Mayor Teddy Kollek.
Courtesy Israel Government Press Office.

Anders army. He saw the revolt as something more than a bid for the social and political rebirth of the Jewish people. He conceived of it not only as a fight for Jewish freedom in the land deeded to the Jews by a document thousands of years older than the Balfour Declaration — his belief in the Biblical promise to the Children of Israel is literal and absolute — but, in fact, as a last-ditch battle for the survival of the Jewish people no matter where they lived. Two thousand years in a role of passive homelessness had disarmed too many Jews not only physically but also psychologically, leaving them timid prey over the centuries to constant humiliation and persecution which had now culminated in the Nazi Holocaust. To Begin, revolt in Palestine would be rebellion "against the yoke of oppression and against the wanton shedding of Jewish blood" all over the world. He and those whom he was to lead were convinced "that our people truly had nothing to lose except the prospect of extermination."[6]

The full extent to which the Jewish people had been intimidated, Begin says, was brought home to him on Yom Kippur in 1943 when he and a group of friends went to pray at the Wailing Wall, to which Jews were to have access until Jordanian troops occupied the Old City of Jerusalem in 1948.[7] Following the Arab riots of 1929, the British authorities, citing consideration for Arab sensibilities, had forbidden the sounding of the *shofar* at the conclusion of Yom Kippur services at the Wall. Although the sounding of the ram's horn at the close of the Day of Atonement is an integral part of the traditional Yom Kippur liturgy, neither the Jewish Agency nor the religious leadership of Jerusalem's Jewish community had ever lodged an official protest with the authorities against this prohibition. But each year, inevitably, a young Betar man would materialize at the Wall and sound the *shofar* in defiance of the British order. Now, too, in 1943, despite the presence of British police who, armed with rifles and truncheons, mingled with the worshippers, a Betar man came forward to blow the *shofar*. To Begin's horror, the police set upon the Jews and struck them indiscriminately with their batons and rifle butts. Many were injured. Someone in the crowd began to sing *Hatikvah;* others joined in. Finally, the police withdrew.

Begin was shocked by the conduct of the British police, but he was even more heartsick over the failure of the Jewish leadership to uphold the religious rights of Jews in their own homeland. "A people that does not defend its holy places — that does not even try to defend them — is not free, however much it may babble about freedom," he wrote many years later. "People that permit the holiest spot in their country and their most sacred feelings to be trampled underfoot are slaves in spirit."[8] This spiritual servility would have to be eradicated, and he resolved to do something about it.

In the meantime, Arye Ben Eliezer and another friend, Meir Kahan, an older man who had practiced law in Warsaw, used their contacts with Polish army brass in the Middle East and leaders of the Polish government-in-exile to obtain Begin's discharge from the Anders army. They suggested that five Jewish soldiers from the Anders army in Palestine be released from regular service and sent to the United States to help inform the American public about Nazi atrocities in Poland. At the same time, they would work to muster American support on behalf of thousands of Polish Jews who, less fortunate than Begin, were still stranded in Russian slave labor camps. With these propaganda activities, the Irgun leaders pointed out, the five Jewish emissaries would indirectly help rally American public opinion in favor of Polish independence after the war. The Poles, who, it appears, had received various favors from Arye Ben Eliezer's Irgun "mission" in the United States,[9] agreed to the proposal, and the Irgunists from Palestine saw to it that the list of the five soldiers to be released from active duty included the name of Menahem Begin. Due to wartime conditions, the five were unable to make the trip to the United States, but their "leave of absence" from the Anders army for "welfare work" was understood by both sides to be indefinite, and in December, 1943, Menahem Begin found himself officially a civilian.

On the day of his discharge, Begin, at the request of Meridor, reported to a meeting of the Irgun command, which consisted of less than half a dozen men. According to one Irgun veteran, Begin told the group, "I am reporting to you in the uniform of an Irgun man — civilian dress."[10] His close associate Eliahu Lankin remembers that at the time of his discharge from the Polish army Begin in fact owned no civilian clothing whatsoever, and that the Irgun leadership had pooled its meager funds to buy him a winter coat and one gray suit. According to Lankin, Begin wore that one suit every day for many months.[11]

By that time Begin, now 30 years old, had become a father. Aliza had given birth to their first child, a son, whom they named Binyamin Ze'ev (Benny), perpetuating the memory of the two Zionist leaders of whom Begin considered himself a spiritual heir. Binyamin Ze'ev had been the Hebrew name of Theodor Herzl and

Ze'ev, that of Vladimir Jabotinsky. When the child was born, the fate of Begin's own father, Ze'ev Dov Begin, was not yet known.

Begin's first act as leader of the Irgun was to appoint a new command staff consisting of Arye Ben Eliezer, Eliahu Lankin and Shelomo Levi. Meridor, Begin's immediate predecessor as Irgun commander, went on temporary leave but soon returned to duty and was named Begin's deputy. Meridor, Ben Eliezer and Lankin were about Begin's age and, like him, had been born outside of Palestine, of East European parents — Meridor and Ben Eliezer in Poland, and Lankin in Harbin, Manchuria. Shelomo Levi was altogether different. Known as "Danny," he was a *sabra,* born of Sephardic parents in Petah Tikvah. In addition, he was the youngest of the group; he was only 19 when Begin picked him as his "chief of staff." A later addition was Yeruham ("Eitan") Livni, whose title was "chief of operations."

Eventually, all the members of the original Irgun command — except for Begin himself — were arrested and deported by the British authorities, but while they were out of action, their places were taken by others equally single-minded in their dedication to the cause. Begin called these men his "fighting family," a term which eventually came to include every member of the Irgun.

One of the first proposals which Begin put before his new staff at the beginning of 1944 was a "proclamation of revolt" announcing that, in view of Britain's conduct in Palestine, the Irgun considered its truce with Britain to be at an end. Jews in Europe were being killed by the hundreds of thousands but Britain still kept the gates of Palestine shut. Some of Begin's intimates, including Eliahu Lankin, an idealist pure and simple, had no patience for lengthy proclamations; they wanted the revolt to begin with a sensational act rather than with yet another ideological manifesto. Begin, however, was concerned about the long-range effects of the Irgun's activities not only on world public opinion but also on the daily lives of the Jews in Palestine:

> There would be suffering and we would be hounded incessantly. Consequently, it was our duty to elucidate the principles of the struggle and its aims . . . The people should know why they must be prepared, through our operations, to endure recurring troubles. The youth must know why they are risking their lives. We knew, too, that our fight would not be only military . . . Consequently, political explanation, clear and persistent, would have to accompany the military operations.[12]

The proclamation was, in fact, already prepared, for it had been drafted, largely by Begin, early in 1943 when he was still officially a member of the Polish army. Now, all that remained was to have the proclamation printed for public distribution. The printing was done by a Sephardi, whose shop had been turning out Irgun literature for some time. In the morning of February 1, 1944, citizens throughout Palestine on their way to work found walls and kiosks plastered with posters addressed "To the Hebrew People in Zion." Begin during that period frequently used the term "Hebrew" rather than "Jewish," which many Jews in Palestine found too reminiscent of exile and persecution.

The proclamation consisted of twelve points setting forth, in meticulous detail, the facts behind the Irgun's decision to terminate its "armistice" with Great Britain. Begin told how at the start of the war, the Jewish community in Palestine had immediately offered its full support to the Allied nations in their fight against Hitler, for the Fuehrer had made it plain that he considered the Jews as Germany's Enemy Number One. As a "mandate," Palestine was not a British colony whose inhabitants would have been subject to a draft. Nonetheless, over 25,000 young Palestinian Jews had enlisted in the British army. The Arabs of Iraq, Syria and Egypt had been siding with the Germans, and the Mufti of Jerusalem had fled to Berlin, from where he commanded his followers in Palestine to fight against the English. But the Jews of Palestine had remained steadfastly loyal to Great Britain even during the most difficult days of the war, contributing not only their skills and industries, but also, in many cases, the lives of their sons and daughters, to the war effort. In the meantime, the Nazis were systematically exterminating millions of Jews in Europe. These Jews might have found a haven in Palestine, the homeland of the Jewish people, had Britain not shut them out from there. It was clear, too, that even after the defeat of Hitlerism, the Jews would not be able to rebuild their lives in Europe; the lands overrun by the Nazis were too badly infested with anti-Semitism for that to be possible. These facts were well known; still, Britain had not abrogated the White Paper of 1939, which doomed the Jews to a ghetto existence in their own homeland and the surviving Jews of Europe to annihilation.

By ignoring the promises implicit in the Palestine Mandate and remaining unmoved while European Jewry was being slaughtered, the British had betrayed the Jewish people and there was no longer any moral basis for a British presence in Palestine.

We shall draw our conclusions without fear. There is no longer any armistice between the Jewish people and the British administration in the Land of Israel, which is literally handing over our brethren to Hitler. Our people are at war with this regime — a war to the end.

Begin then spelled out the Irgun's demand of the British overlords. It was all simple and straightforward: administrative authority in Palestine was to be transferred at once from the British administration to a "Hebrew Provisional Government." This government would establish a "Hebrew People's Army" and contract alliances with the Allied powers against Germany, their common enemy. Begin also proposed a mutual aid pact, "on the basis of the Atlantic Charter and the recognition of mutual interests," with Great Britain, the United States, a postwar democratic France, "and any other free nation that will recognize the sovereignty and the international rights of the Hebrew State." As for the adjoining Arab nations, the Hebrew government would offer them a "peace of honor and good neighborliness."

As soon as possible, the autonomous Jewish government would negotiate with other governments for the organized evacuation of Jewish refugees to Palestine, and it would create the proper conditions for the integration of the "returning sons" in the Jewish homeland. Among the governments with whom the negotiations were to be taken up, Begin specifically named the Soviet Union.

Within the Jewish state to be created, the government would undertake to ensure employment and "social justice" for every citizen of the state, and full equal rights for the Arab population. The Holy Places of the Christian and Moslem faiths would be guaranteed extraterritorial status.

Begin also set forth his view of the place of religion in the projected Jewish state. The government, he specified, would "implant the sanctities of the Torah into the life of the people liberated in their homeland." And he closed that part of the proclamation with an expression of confidence in Divine aid. "The God of Israel, the Lord of Hosts, will help us. There will be no retreat. Freedom — or death."

By way of a postscript, the proclamation urged all Jews in Palestine to help the Irgun in the struggle by acts of civil disobedience — refusing to pay taxes and organizing strikes and demonstrations.

It is significant that Begin did not specify how, or by whom, the "provisional government" was to be set up. Time and again, his associates were to urge him to appoint an underground government. This, they told him, would give the Irgun international status in competition with the Jewish Agency, which in the world's eyes was already functioning as the "shadow government" of the Palestine Jewish community. but Begin turned down the advice of his friends. The Irgun's concern, he insisted, was to fight for the freedom of the Jewish people, not to seize political power for itself.

In order to translate the demand for Jewish independence into reality, Begin proposed a strategy which he had evolved with Arye Ben Eliezer in long nightly walks through the dark streets of Tel Aviv, in clandestine talks at the home of Ben Eliezer's sister and in Room 17 of the Savoy Hotel, near Tel Aviv's seashore, where Begin had taken up residence with Aliza and their infant son under the alias of "Ben Ze'ev." Begin's plan was based on three considerations: his knowledge of the repressive methods used by colonial administrations to keep their "natives" in line, his assessment of the international situation, and his mental picture of Britain's position in the postwar world. His revolt called for a succession of underground operations calculated primarily not to kill or injure Englishmen but to destroy the prestige and credibility of the British authorities by making it impossible for them to govern Palestine. If everything proceeded according to Begin's plans, the British administration eventually would be confronted with the unpalatable choice of either crushing Jewish resistance by brute force or else quitting Palestine. Begin did not think that Britain could afford to retaliate with a full-blown war against Palestine's Jewish community. In addition to incurring her the hatred also of the more "moderate" Jewish elements in Palestine and elsewhere, such action would alienate her major allies, the Soviet Union and the United States, both of which sought to cast themselves in the role of anti-imperialists. Also, Begin pointed out, America after the war would have the largest and most influential Jewish community in the world. If Jews and others in the United States were sufficiently provoked by British outrages against Jews in Palestine, Britain might jeopardize the American economic assistance she would need for her postwar recovery. Finally, the public in England itself, dismayed at the prospect of British boys being killed or wounded fighting against the Jews after the Nazi Holocaust, would soon question the practical and moral justification of continuing the British presence in Palestine. Thus, in Begin's view, the revolt to be waged by the Irgun could have only one logical ending: the departure of the British, followed by the emergence of an independent Jewish state.

Since the war against Germany and Japan was not yet over, Begin, in addition to the avoidance of bloodshed, placed another temporary restraint on Irgun operations: the Irgun was not to raid British army bases or other installations vital to the war effort. Until Hitler would be defeated, the Irgun was to confine its works of harassment to non-military targets: telephone and telegraph lines (to disrupt communications), immigration and internal revenue offices (to destroy records of "illegal" Jewish immigration and hamper the collection of taxes), warehouses and police stations (excellent sources of materiel including small weapons for the Irgun stockpile). When bombs or explosives were employed to damage or destroy government property, every precaution was taken to avoid injury to personnel. Irgun men were under strict orders to refrain from killing except in order to save their own lives. Whenever possible, the Irgun gave advance warnings of its operations. Handbills were scattered or "practice explosions" set off to permit civilians enough time to leave the scene before the attack. Occasionally, the Irgun's concern for the personal safety of Englishmen left the British authorities dumbfounded. Several months after Germany had surrendered and the Irgun no longer considered British military installations "off limits," Irgun raiders attacked a British army payroll train, from which they "confiscated" banknotes in the value of £38,000. The quantity of explosives used to halt the train somewhere near the city of Hadera had been carefully measured out: enough to force the train to a sudden stop, but not enough to destroy the train or harm the personnel aboard. As it happened, a few of the British guards who traveled with the money were cut by flying glass; to their surprise their wounds were promptly treated and bandaged by members of Irgun's "first aid department" who had been kept in readiness for that purpose. (Meanwhile, other Irgun men spirited away the banknotes; the British authorities never did find out what had become of the money.)

The Irgun's organizational structure was not complicated. Operations and policies were planned by a small command headed by Begin. The rank and file, for practical purposes, was divided into two sections: the Assault Force, which carried out the operations, and the Revolutionary Propaganda Force, which produced and distributed public information material. Irgun operations proved so effective that at one point British officials thought the underground organization must have at least 1,000 full-time professional soldiers.

Actually, the Irgun never had more than a few dozen members on full-time service; sometimes less than 20, but never more than 30 or 40. The other hundreds (and eventually thousands) of men and women who belonged to the Irgun had ordinary jobs and lived openly with their families under their own names. But they were expected to be on constant call for furtive meetings in shuttered rooms and for operations large and small — from bearing messages and pasting propaganda posters to making underground broadcasts and blowing up bridges and railroad beds. They lived under the perpetual strain of having to conceal their secret lives from friends and relatives who disapproved of the Irgun or who could not be trusted to keep confidences. Then, too, there was the ever-present fear of being discovered by the authorities, of being arrested, or perhaps shot, by the British police.

Those men who spent full time on Irgun service were paid not according to their rank — a military ranking order of sorts, ranging from lance corporal to captain, had been introduced by David Raziel — but according to their personal circumstances. Drivers with families received higher salaries than some members of the command who had no dependents. But salaries barely sufficed even for basic subsistence. Money was scarce. The funds raised by contributions from Jews in Palestine and abroad, or obtained by occasional thefts of cash from British banks and goods from British warehouses, had to be conserved for other important expenses including illicit arms purchases from British soldiers willing to cooperate.

Irgun discipline was strict. Prospective Irgun members were screened by a three-man selection committee to eliminate adventurers and unstable characters. Candidates who passed that hurdle were put through four months of indoctrination seminars in groups of five to ten. During that period, too, many "washed out." Then came military training — night courses in tactics and in the handling of weapons, nighttime firing drills in the desert or on the seashore, and weekends of instruction at remote camps. The most rigorous training of all was reserved for those who had direct contact with the explosives stolen from British depots or manufactured at makeshift Irgun plants; that course extended over one full year.

Begin took pride in the fact that the Irgun was, as he put it, a melting pot of the Jewish nation in miniature. The Irgun included natives not only of Eastern and Western Europe, South Africa, the Americas, and Palestine itself, but also of the Oriental countries — Bokhara, Iran, Iraq, Syria, Tunisia and Yemen. "Our comrades from the Oriental communities," he writes in *The Revolt,* "felt happy and at home in the Irgun. Nobody ever displayed any stupid airs of superiority toward them, and they were thus helped to free themselves of any unjustified sense of inferiority they may have harbored."[13] Begin's freedom from prejudice against the "Orientals" was to be a prominent factor in the steady growth of his Herut party and his own electoral victory over the Labor bloc in 1977.

Though none of the Irgun's military operations could be planned or executed without Begin's approval, the Irgun activities that engaged his keenest interest were those of public information: the maintenance of the underground radio station and the Irgun newspaper, *Herut.*

The Irgun's first clandestine transmitter, which was kept in a suitcase at the home of David Raziel's sister, Esther Raziel-Naor, fared badly. It was captured by the British, who also arrested Esther and her husband. However, another transmitter was soon found and the broadcasts were resumed. At first, broadcasts lasted no longer than six minutes at a time, leaving the announcer and operator exactly one minute to escape with the radio. This scheduling was based on the assumption that British tracking devices would take eight minutes to home in on underground transmitters. Eventually the Irgun, weary of these "hit-and-run" maneuvers, published a warning to the effect that its radio station was under heavy armed guard. The British made no further attempts to capture Irgun broadcasting apparatus, evidently believing that a transmitter which could easily be replaced was not worth the risk of casualties in a possible shootout with the Irgun. Thereafter, the Irgun operators considered it safe to remain on the air for ten, fifteen and even twenty minutes at a time. When the British attempted to jam the Irgun broadcasts, the operator would skip from one wave length to another in order to elude the jammers. The British authorities never succeeded in silencing the Irgun radio, whose broadcasts, starting in 1944, were translated into foreign languages and distributed among foreign news correspondents and diplomatic representatives. (Sporadically, LEHI, the "Stern Group," also operated an underground radio. Haganah's radio station Kol Israel, no less "illegal" than the stations of the other two organizations, was the last to enter the field; it began broadcasting only after the war, in October, 1945.)

Herut was the personal, one-man bulletin through which Begin, whose face and whereabouts were known only to a few intimates, issued ideological statements, public appeals and official communiques reporting the latest Irgun operations. It appeared every two or three days, and sometimes even daily or nightly. At first, it was printed by the same Sephardi who had run off the "proclamation of revolt" but when he understandably grew nervous about keeping underground material in his shop, the Irgun set up its own printing plant in Tel Aviv, which also took in commercial orders to give it a mantle of legitimacy and to help raise much-needed funds for the Irgun treasury. Begin described *Herut* as a "wall newspaper" because it was posted on walls through the length and breadth of the country by members of the Revolutionary Propaganda Force, working at night to avoid being caught in the act.

Begin's news reporting was truthful to a fault. He accepted bluffing as a legitimate strategic device — as in the non-existent armed guard at the Irgun radio station — but he refused to inflate the results of actual Irgun operations. When a major raid on a British police station for arms yielded only 14 rifles (the police had intercepted the raiders, forcing them to retreat before they could complete their mission) Begin insisted on saying so although he could have avoided mentioning details and simply announced that the Irgun had succeeded in capturing "a quantity of arms." His staff argued that there would be no harm in stretching a point if it helped lift public morale, but Begin stood his ground. "We did not soil our mouths or our pens with falsehood," he wrote. "We told the truth. Good or bad . . . it was always the truth."[14] In an underground army surrounded by enemies and detractors, long-range public credibility was more important than temporary psychological boosts.

Later, the Irgun added to its publications a mimeographed bulletin meant for foreign observers. The editor of that newsletter was Shmuel Katz, a veteran Revisionist from South Africa who became head of the Irgun's "English department," worked as Irgun emissary in Europe, and was to serve briefly as Prime Minister Begin's public information advisor in 1977.

Thousands of Irgun leaflets were distributed in Arab towns and villages either by Irgun members who looked like Arabs or by friendly Arabs who had no love for the English and who relished Irgun's successes in upsetting the British authorities. Printed in Arabic, the handbills explained to the Arabs that the Irgun had no desire to fight or harm them, that it was only the British who sought to foment war between the Arabs and the Jews, and that the Irgun, along with all the Jews in Palestine, was eager to see the Arabs as peaceful citizens in the future Jewish state.

The command meetings to plan the Irgun's military and propaganda operations were brief and to the point. They were held at various hideouts, including the apartments where Begin lived with his wife and children under assumed identities. Eliahu Lankin notes that even at these "kitchen cabinet" meetings, under the pressures of time and secrecy, Begin insisted on strict parliamentary etiquette.

"As a rule," Lankin remembers, "we would rise when Begin entered the room. He would step up briskly to each one of us in turn, shake hands and then ask us to be seated." (Unlike the members of his command, Begin took no military rank because he had never gone through the Irgun course of basic training; he was known simply as "the commander".) He devoted hours of painstaking thought to the preparation of the agenda, carefully formulating each question to be discussed. At the meetings, those present were free to propose additions or changes, but Begin was very much the man in charge, opening each session with a detailed analysis of the latest developments, then presenting the agenda, point by point, giving the floor to each participant in turn, mildly reprimanding one or the other man who, in the excitement of the discussion, interrupted a colleague's presentation. As a rule, Begin showed little emotion while transacting Irgun business. "In the underground there was little time or opportunity for baring one's personal feelings," Lankin comments.

Begin never talked about his personal problems. "Nature did not bless Begin with robust health or a strong body. He was always thin, but his stamina was remarkable. He seemed to have no difficulty going without food or sleep or staying in his room for days on end without seeing sunlight or breathing fresh air.

"His one problem was money. We made it a rule to offer him cash loans every so often. When he answered, 'Oh, all right, let me have a couple of pounds,' we would know that his wife didn't have a penny left to spend, for as long as they had a couple of pounds, he would insist he didn't need any help."[15]

Though he rarely expressed them during the years of struggle, Begin's feelings for his men ran deep. Later, in his memoirs of that period, he was to use extravagant terms of praise and affection in describing his close associates. "We were all like brothers," he was to write. "And the mutual deep affection . . . was the source of our happiness, perhaps the only happiness in the darkness of the underground ... It was not by mere chance that one of the pseudonyms we used for the Irgun was 'the fighting family.' We *were* a family."[16]

7. "The Very Heart of Logic"

When his somewhat ambitious-sounding "proclamation of revolt" first turned up on walls and kiosks throughout the country, Begin was in his thirty-first year. When he emerged from the underground for the first time with a radio broadcast on May 15, 1948 — the day after the signing of Israel's proclamation of independence — he was exactly three months short of his thirty-fifth birthday.

As commander of his "fighting family," Begin was able to show a record of three achievements which had a basic impact on the history of the State of Israel.

First: He succeeded in rallying the shrunken, floundering Irgun and in reshaping it into a hard-hitting underground fighting force which fully accomplished its purpose: to hamstring the British administrative machinery so completely that Britain eventually realized it was no longer worth what it cost her in materiel, frustration and loss of international prestige to remain in Palestine.

Second: He attained this end without the unrestrained brutality and indiscriminate killings usually associated with revolutionary armies. The Irgun was perhaps the only fighting force to give advance warnings of its raids, foregoing the advantage of surprise in order to permit the escape of non-combatants in the area under attack. Begin's men came from many different backgrounds of culture, temperament and life experience, but with few exceptions he was able to keep them within the limits of moderation he had set for them.

Third, and perhaps most important: It was largely thanks to Begin's levelheadedness and strength of purpose that Palestine Jewry was not split by civil strife during the last years of British rule. During the final months of World War II, the Jewish Agency and Haganah, hard-pressed by the British administration, declared an "open season" on the Irgun, arresting or kidnapping hundreds of Irgunists and turning many of them over to the British authorities for imprisonment and deportation. Over the centuries, "informing" on a fellow Jew to the government had been regarded as the most despicable act a Jew could commit. Accordingly, many Irgun members — and not only hotheads — clamored for revenge against the "collaborators." But Begin, the commander, categorically rejected such advice. He was certain that in time the Jewish Agency and Haganah would realize the futility of temporizing and would join Irgun in an all-out fight for independence. Until then, Begin said, rather endure indignities and worse at the hands of fellow Jews than open an irreparable gap between brothers who eventually would become comrades-in-arms against the common enemy. Begin himself spent the years from 1944 to 1948 in double hiding — from the British, who offered a reward of £10,000 for his capture, and from the official Jewish leadership, which had informed him of its intention to "step in and finish" the Irgun. Only through his own ingenuity — and that of his closest associates — did Begin himself escape being arrested by the British, moving from apartment to apartment and changing his identity and outer appearance as the need arose.

The Irgun's operations against the British began in mid-February, 1944, with bombings of British immigration and internal revenue offices and police stations. In each instance, the raid was carried out after office hours, to avoid injury to employees.

The first three targets — all hit during the same night — were the government immigration offices in Tel Aviv, Jerusalem and Haifa, where records of "illegal immigrants" and expulsion orders were kept. In Tel Aviv, four Irgunists spirited the explosives into the building through the roof, which they had reached via an adjacent house opened by a friendly locksmith. In Jerusalem, the raiders staged a street brawl to keep the police busy while the explosives were planted. In Haifa, two Irgunists — a boy and a girl — acted out a torrid love scene across the street to divert the attention of the lone Arab policeman who guarded the building at night.

Two weeks later, the internal revenue offices in the same three cities fell victim to a similar attack.

In each of the six operations, the objective was accomplished: the files needed by the British authorities for the persecution of "illegal" Jewish immigrants and for the collection of income taxes were no more. Not one human being suffered so much as a scratch.

The next month, the Irgun bombed CID stations (the CID is the British counterpart of the American FBI) in Jerusalem, Jaffa and Haifa. This time, despite careful planning, there were casualties, both British and Jewish. In Jerusalem and Jaffa, unforeseen complications resulted in shootouts. In Haifa, a telephoned warning from the Irgun prior to the bombing had cleared the station, but four of the constables on duty had insisted on remaining. When the entire left side of the building crumbled (a land mine had been placed against that side), all four were crushed beneath the rubble. Three of them eventually died of their injuries.

The British response came only three days later, but it was no feeble gesture. A curfew was slapped on the three major cities, Jerusalem, Haifa and Tel Aviv, buildings were searched, suspects arrested and paraded in endless police lineups, and an old law imposing the death penalty for possessing arms and placing explosives was resurrected.

Begin was then staying in Tel Aviv at the Savoy Hotel, sharing his room, No. 17, near the end of the second-floor corridor, with Aliza and their young son. Only a few days before, he had had them brought to him from their apartment in Jerusalem on the advice of his associates; the police had already visited the apartment many times and there was reason to fear that, sooner or later, Aliza and the baby might be taken as hostages to flush out Begin. Begin had chosen the Savoy because, for some reason, he had not thought the British would look for him there. But one night during the curfew, a party of military police and plainclothesmen entered the hotel, which was close to the seashore, and searched it from top to bottom. Aliza and little Binyamin Ze'ev seemed to be asleep, but Begin was wide awake. As he heard the footsteps of the police approaching, he berated himself for not having left his wife and child in Jerusalem. What would happen to the child if he and Aliza were both arrested? As the heavy footsteps came nearer, he looked through his pockets, and was relieved not to find any of his documents there. At least he would have no incriminating evidence on his person when the police came to take him.

Then, suddenly, the voices and footsteps outside the room began to fade away. For another half hour, Begin was able to hear movements — then nothing more. The next morning, the owner of the hotel casually asked him whether he had heard anything unusual during the night. Begin, with an equally nonchalant air, asked what had happened. The hotel owner, a Mr. Ben Zvi (no relation to Israel's future President by the same name), told him that the police had been there looking for suspects in the bombings and had taken in some of the guests whose papers seemed suspicious. He, Ben Zvi, had guided the police from room to room, but had kept them away from No. 17, which was close to the balcony. He had seen no point in troubling the little family "with all this business," he explained. At any rate, the police had accepted his assurance that there were no more rooms on that floor, and had moved on.

Recalling that first narrow escape from the British police, Begin was to say that, aside from his concern about the fate of his wife and child, the prospect of his being arrested did not particularly frighten him. His only sadness was at the thought that he might be put out of action before the struggle for independence had made real headway. But then he told himself to be grateful for having been able to reach Palestine in time to help start the revolt. As for Aliza, it seems that, far from being asleep, she, too, had heard the footsteps outside the hotel room and realized what was going on. Thirty-three years later, when she was asked in New York how she had felt that night, she answered, "I wasn't frightened. I couldn't afford to be."[1]

Not long after the incident at the Savoy Hotel, the Begin family checked out and left Tel Aviv for Petah Tikvah, a city about ten miles to the northeast, which was famous for its citrus groves and, at the time, also as a center of Irgun activity.

The Begins' first home in Petah Tikvah was a small, old isolated house in Mahne Yehuda on the edge of the city's "Yemenite quarter."

The house had neither electricity nor central heating, and the broken shutters gave no protection from the wind and the chilly nights. His only luxury during the months he spent there, Begin ruefully recalls, was the bedding. Toward the end of his stay in the house, he was permitted to sleep on the fine linen sheets which had been prepared for no less a personage than Sir Harold Mac-Michael, the British High Commissioner in Palestine. MacMichael had angered all of Palestine Jewry with his anti-Zionist development program and, along with Lord Moyne, the British Resident Minister in the Middle East, had been blamed for the fate of the 769 Jewish refugees aboard the S.S. *Struma*. LEHI, the "Stern Group," once made an unsuccessful attempt on his life. The Irgun from time to time had contemplated plans for kidnapping Sir Harold, taking him prisoner, and declaring the end of British rule in Palestine. Determined to treat Sir Harold in a manner befitting so distinguished a captive, the Irgun had gone so far as to stock its warehouse in Petah Tikvah with articles intended for his comfort. But the Irgun command, evidently realizing that the idea was too fantastic and risky to execute, had shelved "Operation Mac-

Michael" indefinitely. As a result, the Begin family fell heir to the sheets originally intended for Sir Harold, who happily left Palestine in the late summer of 1944.

In the meantime, the Irgun continued its operations. In May, 1944, an Irgun raiding party marked the fifth anniversary of the enactment of the 1939 White Paper by seizing the central British broadcasting station in Ramallah, an Arab enclave near Jerusalem. Armed for the first time with Irgun-made mortars, the men arrived at night in trucks and, without firing a shot, occupied the building under the very noses of the British police who, at first, remained ensconced inside their "Tegart fortress."[2] Pointing his gun at the bewildered British and Arab officials inside the building, an Irgun officer told them that they would not be hurt provided they would help the Irgun make a broadcast from the station. As it happened, this was not one of the Irgun's great successes. According to Begin's recollections, it turned out that the actual broadcasting studios were not in Ramallah, but in Jerusalem.[3] Another source explains that the broadcasting equipment was indeed at Ramallah, but that the Irgun radio man was unable to work it. While he was tinkering with it, the Irgun team had to bring their homemade mortars into play in order to fend off the British police, which in the meantime had appeared on the scene.[4]

On July 14, 1944, Irgun men gutted the Land Registry Office in Jerusalem; in that raid, two Arab policemen were killed. The next day, Irgun men seized a truck filled with explosives. In one of his final reports from Palestine, High Commissioner MacMichael informed London that the security situation in Palestine appeared to be deteriorating, and that the outlook was "not encouraging."[5] The Irgun's campaign of harassment was clearly beginning to take its psychological toll.

On August 23, Irgun teams raided CID barracks in Jaffa, Abu-Kabir and N've Sha'anan for weapons. It was in one of these operations that the Irgun obtained its modest loot of 14 rifles which Begin had reported with such candor.

Throughout that spring and summer, the Jewish Agency under David Ben-Gurion became increasingly worried about what it called "terrorist" activity in Palestine. At the time, the Agency was negotiating with the British government for the establishment of a Jewish Brigade, an all-Jewish army group which would fight alongside the Allies against the Nazis even as Jabotinsky's Jewish Legion had fought the Turks during World War I. Now, just as a quarter-century before, the British government found it difficult to accept the idea of an all-Jewish army, and the Jewish Agency was concerned lest Britain's anger at the Irgun's activities in Palestine put an end to the whole project.[6] Worse, the official Zionist leadership feared that if the Irgun were to drive the British authorities beyond the limit of their patience, the result might be an actual British attack on Palestine's Jewish community, with an enormous loss of life and the destruction of everything the pioneers had built up over the years. Begin was convinced that this would not happen, but the leaders of the Jewish Agency took a more pessimistic view.

As early as April, 1944, the Jewish Agency had adopted an official program of counter-measures to increase what it called "anti-terrorist" propaganda and to isolate the "terrorists." Ben-Gurion, for the first time, recommended that Haganah be permitted to use force against the Irgun, but the rest of the Jewish Agency Executive was not yet willing to go so far; particularly the religious, along with other non-Labor members, refused to associate themselves with such a move.

During the summer of 1944 representatives both of the Jewish Agency and the Irgun felt out one another about the possibilities of arranging a meeting between Ben-Gurion and Begin. Begin was prepared to make Ben-Gurion an offer which he did not think the latter was in a position to refuse. After all, Ben-Gurion himself, in New York two years before, had proudly proclaimed the Zionist aim to be the establishment of an independent Jewish state in Palestine, thus in effect taking up the struggle where Vladimir Jabotinsky had left off. In Begin's view, therefore, the immediate objectives of the Jewish Agency and of the Irgun now officially coincided. Begin's proposal was simple and to the point. If Ben-Gurion would be ready to lead the Jewish community of Palestine in the struggle against British rule and for Jewish independence, the Irgun would be willing to place itself under Ben-Gurion's command. If Ben-Gurion had indeed been serious in his proclamation at the Biltmore Hotel, here was his opportunity to prove it.

The meeting between the two leaders was set for the night of August 10, 1944. Begin, accompanied by Eliahu Lankin, appeared at the designated place as scheduled. However, somewhat to their astonishment, the two men found themselves face to face not with Ben-Gurion, but with Moshe Sneh, a member of the Haganah high command, who explained that he had come as Ben-Gurion's personal representative. The political peregrinations of Sneh, then a man in his mid-thirties, would make an interesting study. Born in

Poland, he had graduated medical school and had started out not in the Labor Zionist movement but in the General Zionist party, which included political moderates as well as liberals. Arriving in Palestine two years before Begin, Sneh soon became a member of the Haganah staff. In 1945, he was to join the Jewish Agency Executive and play an important role in bringing survivors of the Nazi Holocaust to Palestine. After the establishment of the State of Israel he was to resign from the Agency, moving steadily leftward in the political spectrum until he ended in the Communist party, which he represented in Israel's Knesset from the mid-1950's on. In the mid-1960's, however, Moshe Sneh was to become increasingly critical of Soviet policy and led the mainstream of Israel's Communist party in adopting a program independent of the Moscow line. He was to die in 1974, leaving instructions in his will that he be given a traditional Jewish burial.

After the first few minutes of conversation between Sneh and Begin, it turned out that the two men were talking at cross-purposes. While Begin was offering to cooperate with Ben-Gurion in a country-wide uprising against the British overlords, Sneh had been sent to persuade the Irgun to give up its activities in order not to antagonize the British. He, Sneh, said he had it on good authority that Prime Minister Churchill was a friend of Zionism despite opposition within his own party, and that, after the war, Churchill would unveil "a new plan" for Palestine in which the Jews would "get the biggest plum in the pudding."

When Begin pressed Sneh for details about the "plum," Sneh intimated that Churchill was planning to propose a partition of Palestine such as already had been recommended by the Peel Commission in 1937 in order to permit the establishment of an independent Jewish state. If the partition arrangement would make a viable Jewish state impossible, said Sneh, Ben-Gurion would refuse it, and if it were imposed upon the Jews, he would be ready to revolt. But until the question became acute, it would be best for Haganah and the Irgun both to lie low until the war was over and do nothing to spoil the chances of a favorable settlement.

Begin replied that, aside from his own opposition to any further partition of Palestine, he did not share Sneh's trust in second-hand reports of British promises. He, Begin, had been following the British press, according to which British policy in Palestine was still firmly based on the 1939 White Paper. Churchill might drop hints about his postwar plans, but what if Churchill were no longer in power when the war was over? Besides, in view of what was happening to the Jews in Europe, did the Zionist leadership have a right to do nothing except wait passively to see whether or not the British would eventually permit the surviving remnants of European Jewry to rebuild their lives in their rightful homeland? The work of Zionist leadership should be the active struggle for Jewish sovereignty, not speculation about whether or not the Irgun represented a challenge to the authority of the Jewish Agency. The only chance the Jews would have of gaining anything from England would be if they were to "lift the Palestine problem into the orbit of public attention," and this could be done only by putting up an effective fight, not by talks about hopes and future negotiations. As for the Jewish Agency and Haganah, Begin said, they were free to continue on their temporizing path and dissociate themselves from the Irgun's activities, but they had no right to stop the Irgun from what it was trying to accomplish for the Jewish people.

Sneh had no real answer for these arguments except to say that internal discipline was a very serious matter and that in the Zionist leadership there was room for only one army and one policy.

The conversation did not come to an end until three o'clock the next morning. Begin immediately reported the outcome of the talks to Lankin, who had been waiting outside. Then, both men went off to sleep for what remained of the night.

Early in September, 1944, the British authorities mounted a huge "cordon and sweep" operation to flush out the Irgunists in Petah Tikvah, and Begin had his second hair's-breadth escape from arrest. The three Begins had left Mahne Yehuda and moved into a small house in the Hasidoff Quarter, a workers' suburb on the southeastern border of Petah Tikvah. This neighborhood consisted of a row of low houses on a highway, opposite an Arab village. Most of the dwellings had no electricity and frequently also no water, but the Begins found their new home much more pleasant than the old one because the environment was healthier; the area was then a "garden belt" of sorts, with lush fields, plenty of trees and fragrant orange groves. The Begins had chosen this particular place in accordance with the Irgun "open underground" tactics; it was assumed that the authorities would not expect to find an Irgun leader in a neighborhood where everyone knew everyone else. Some of Begin's nearest neighbors were members of HaShomer HaTzair (the affiliation of Begin's own preadolescent years), but they, too, did not then suspect that they were harboring the commander of the "reactionary terrorist" Irgun in their midst. The only one who "knew" was Begin's landlord, and he could be trusted to keep quiet.

During the months (according to Begin's recollection, it was almost a year) that he lived in the Hasidoff Quarter, Begin ceased to be "Ben Ze'ev" and assumed the identity of Israel Halperin, a refugee from Poland who had moved into the neighborhood because he had been unable to find suitable, inexpensive living quarters for himself and his family in the city proper. To forestall questions why he, a healthy-looking young man with a wife and baby to support, did not leave for work each morning, Begin volunteered the story that he was being supported by a refugee aid organization while studying for his law examination. To lend credibility to his explanation, he filled his living room with law books. No one suspected that the "friends" who periodically came to sit with Begin in the tiny kitchen of his apartment, lit only by a candle or an oil lamp, were members of the Irgun command. On Sabbath afternoons or on pleasant evenings, the men would move their command meetings outdoors, discussing policies and operations while strolling casually through the fields and citrus groves. Sometimes, the neighbors would ask the men to help make up a *minyan* — the quorum of ten required for Jewish public worship — at the synagogue nearby. Begin himself faithfully attended the synagogue, where he was called up to the reading of the Law by the name of "Israel son of Ze'ev Dov." He used Israel as his first name because of his close friendship with Israel Epstein, the schoolteacher who had edited the Betar bulletin when Begin first arrived in Palestine.

At dawn on September 5, 1944, the British police, assisted by army personnel, began their search of Petah Tikvah. The city was surrounded, a curfew was declared and soldiers rode on trucks through the streets of the city with loudspeakers, warning that anyone violating the curfew did so at the risk of his life. Over 40 Irgunists were arrested. At sunrise, a neighbor who knew Begin's true identity warned him that the British were coming and advised him to make a getaway through the orange groves. Oddly enough, the orchards until then had never been subjected to searches, although they were freely used by Irgun fighters for secret meetings and as hiding places for weapons. Begin, however, did not do as his neighber advised him. He was afraid that, in attempting to escape, he might attract the attention of a neighbor and risk being reported to the authorities.

Fortunately, the British search stopped short of the Hasidoff

Quarter, and the curfew was lifted at noon that day. Once more, Begin, his wife and the baby were safe, but the search of Petah Tikvah was probably the cause of a tragedy in Begin's family. Aliza's brother, Dr. Arnold, at whose home in Drohobycz she and Begin had first met, died in Tel Aviv on the day of the search. He had known where his sister and her family had been staying, and had been worried about their safety. Except for Aliza, Arnold had been the only one of his immediate family to escape the Nazi Holocaust. His small son had been torn from his mother's arms and flung into a gas chamber; the grief-crazed mother took her own life. The rest of the family, too, had been murdered by the Nazis and he had never recovered from the shock. Now Begin was distressed at the thought that his brother-in-law's anxiety over what was happening in Petah Tikvah might have been too much for his weakened heart. Because it would not have been safe for them to appear in public in Tel Aviv, neither Begin nor Aliza attended the funeral. Later, Begin was told that British spies had mingled in the crowd at the cemetery, hoping to corner him there.

Three weeks later, on Yom Kippur, the Irgun won a significant psychological victory. Begin had not forgotten how, the year before, he had seen British policemen strike Jews for sounding the *shofar* at the Wailing Wall at the end of the fast. Begin knew that he himself would be unable to worship at the Wall that year, but he was determined that the British should not be permitted to repeat their outrage with impunity. During the week preceding the Day of Atonement, members of the Irgun's Revolutionary Propaganda Force went out night after night to plaster Jerusalem's walls with posters in Hebrew and English, warning the British authorities against interfering with the Yom Kippur service at the Wailing Wall. The final warning to be posted invoked the memory of the victims of the Nazi Holocaust who might have been saved if the British White Paper policy had not kept them out of Palestine:

> 1. On the Day of Atonement, at the Western Wall, large numbers of people will unite with the spirit of the martyrs of Israel who fell victim to German cruelty and British treachery.
>
> 2. The principles of civilized humanity dictate that the sacred prayer should not be disturbed, nor the Holy Place violated.
>
> 3. The British Government — ruling temporarily against the will of the Jewish people in its Homeland — is required not to infringe upon these principles.
>
> 4. Any British policeman who on the Day of Atonment dares to

burst into the area of the Wailing Wall and to disturb the traditional service will be regarded as a criminal and will be punished accordingly.

As the warnings multiplied and Yom Kippur drew closer, Jews throughout Palestine grew increasingly apprehensive. Many feared that the Wailing Wall area might become the scene of a bloody battle between the British police and the Irgun. The official Chief Rabbinate of Palestine, dismayed at this possibility, issued a declaration bidding Jews to follow the orders of the authorities and refrain from sounding the *shofar* at the Wall.

Begin did not think that the British would defy the Irgun's threats. They had no way of knowing what the Irgun might do in retaliation and Begin was confident that the British authorities would not want to ruin their image as civilized gentlemen by provoking a shootout at a Holy Place. As for Begin, he, too, had no intention of staging such a battle on the spot; aside from the infringement on the sanctity of the Wall, his prime consideration was the safety of the elderly and of the women and children who would worship there on Yom Kippur. For this reason the Irgun command planned simultaneous attacks on the Tegart police fortresses in Haifa, Bet Dagan, Kalkilya and Katra to be carried out on the night after the fast. If, contrary to Begin's expectations, the British would provoke trouble at the Wall, the Irgun would announce that the raids on the police stations on the night after Yom Kippur had been a punishment for British disregard of Jewish religious sensibilities.

Begin's hunch about the British response to the Irgun's warnings proved correct. On that Yom Kippur, for the first time in fourteen years, the British police did not come near the Wailing Wall, not even when the perennial Betar member put the *shofar* to his lips and sounded it with all his might. The *shofar* was sounded at the Wall again every Yom Kippur during the three years that followed, without interference from the British authorities, until the Arabs annexed the Old City of Jerusalem in 1948 and barred the Wall to Jews.

For the first time, that fall day in 1944, Jewish freedom fighters had been able to intimidate the British police into retreat. And though the planned raids on the four Tegart fortresses took place as scheduled, the British did not retaliate then.

As an additional tweak of the British lion's tail, Irgun men broke into a government textile warehouse in downtown Tel Aviv eight days later, removing large quantities of cloth. Some of the textiles were sold and the money used to buy weapons. Others were distributed, Robin Hood-style, to needy families.

During the months that followed, a never-ending chain of communiques and propaganda pamphlets streamed from Begin's kitchen in the Hasidoff Quarter. The Irgun won many new members, and also regained some former ones who had drifted away.

The Irgun was one of the few underground organizations which permitted its members the option to drop out at any time. Yet, outright defections and betrayals by ex-Irgunists were extremely rare. Begin himself never believed in witch-hunting. In one instance, Begin's reluctance to accept the possibility of treason within his entourage enabled a known traitor to elude punishment. During the early part of 1944, a list of Irgun members from which the British had been making a conspicuous number of arrests throughout Palestine was traced back to a man named Chilewich, a product of the Lithuanian Betar who had come to Palestine in the 1930's. In Palestine, Chilewich had joined the editorial staff of the Revisionist party organ and had helped raise funds for the Irgun, but he had never actually joined the underground, preferring to remain on the periphery of the action. An unstable character, he was addicted to gambling and to expensive clothes. Still, his fund-raising activities brought him into the homes of many Irgun members, including the Jerusalem apartment in which the Begins lived before moving to the Savoy Hotel in Tel Aviv. One day, he visited the Begins. Finding only Aliza at home with Benny, he left a gift for the baby and went away. The next day, the apartment was searched by British police. Luckily, Begin himself was not in the apartment; he was already in Tel Aviv. But for weeks thereafter, the police kept turning up at the Begin apartment to inquire after Begin's whereabouts. This was the reason why Begin eventually moved Aliza and Benny from Jerusalem to Tel Aviv and into the Savoy Hotel. At the time, for some reason, no one connected the police search of the Begin apartment with Chilewich's visit there the day before. But after the large-scale British roundup of Irgunists several months later, the Irgun's "information officers" discovered that Chilewich, apparently in need of money, had supplied the British intelligence service with an Irgun list in return for a cash reward. It was he, too, who had reported the underground radio transmitter at the home of Esther Raziel-Naor, so that both she and her husband were arrested. Meanwhile, Chilewich had left Palestine and gone to Cairo.

The first reaction of the Irgun leadership was to want Chilewich liquidated. There were any number of Irgun volunteers ready to proceed to Cairo and put an end to Chilewich on the spot. But Begin would not hear of it. He had long arguments with his associates; he could not believe, he insisted, that a Jew could really sink so low. There was always a chance, no matter how slight, that an error had been made. To prevent a miscarriage of justice, Begin said, Chilewich should be brought back to Palestine and given an opportunity to defend himself before an Irgun court of honor. Finally, two Irgun sympathizers who happened to be stationed with the British army in Egypt were asked to find Chilewich and make arrangements for his return to Palestine. But by that time, Chilewich had vanished without a trace. Much later it was learned that he had gone to the United States, where he changed his name and went into business.

Begin himself tells part of the Chilewich story in *The Revolt,* his memoirs of the underground period. Apparently reluctant to call Chilewich by name in a book first published only a few years after the event, Begin refers to him simply as "Mr. Tsorros."[7] Tsorros, or *tzores,* happens to be the Hebrew-Yiddish word for "troubles."

Meanwhile, the British administration had intensified its pressures on the Jewish Agency to put an end to "terrorism" in Palestine. As far as the British were concerned, there was no difference between the irritating harassments devised by the Irgun and the deliberate killings done by members of the Stern Group. The Jewish Agency was given to understand that unless it took drastic action, it, too, would be regarded as disloyal and guilty by association.

In mid-October, 1944, the Haganah, on orders from the Agency, opened a special training course for 170 volunteers to wage an all-out campaign against the Irgun and the Stern Group. Borrowing a term from hunting parlance, the Jewish Agency declared an "open season" particularly on the Irgun which, unlike the Stern Group, was well organized and had a strong leadership.

Almost simultaneously, the British authorities went into action with a move that outraged Palestine's Jewish community: they began to deport Irgunists and Stern Group members who had been arrested for "terrorist activities." At four o'clock in the morning of October 21, 1944, the detention camp in Latrun, on the Tel Aviv-Jerusalem highway, was surrounded by British troops. Security forces dragged 237 internees from their beds half-naked, put them aboard a fleet of cargo planes and flew them to Eritrea, a part of Ethiopia from which the British had expelled Mussolini's armies three years before. These deportees were joined by 14 others who had been kept at the prison fortress in Acre.

The Jewish Agency gave public expression to its dismay that any Jew, no matter what he had done, should be punished by deportation from the Jewish homeland. But the protests were not backed by action and therefore futile.

At the end of October, 1944, Begin and Lankin had a second meeting with emissaries of the Jewish Agency. This time the spokesman for the Agency was Eliahu Golomb, a founder of Haganah and the Agency's unofficial "Minister of Security." He was accompanied by Moshe Sneh. A man in his early fifties, Golomb had first come to Palestine as a high school student and had later served with Jabotinsky's Jewish Legion. Prominent in Labor Zionist ranks, he was a brother-in-law of Moshe Shertok (Sharett), who at the time was head of the Agency's political department and later became the first foreign minister of the State of Israel. The meeting took place at night, on Allenby Street, Tel Aviv's busiest thoroughfare. Golomb and Sneh opened the discussion with an ultimatum: in the name of Palestine's Jewish community, they demanded that the Irgun should cease its anti-British activities at once and should make a public announcement to that effect. Golomb admitted that the Irgun's operations might have had some political significance: they had proved that when Jews began to fight for their homeland they were prepared to fight and even to die for their cause. However, he asserted that the Irgun had done quite enough and, as Begin was to recall, he characterized its military operations as "the consequence of a semi-childish pursuit of heroics."[8]

To this last argument, Begin replied that neither he nor the Irgun had any desire for heroics and adventures. What impelled them was a sense of mission, the conviction that if they laid down their arms now, the result would be the moral and psychological enslavement of the entire Jewish people. Begin, the refugee from Hitler's "final solution" and Stalin's war on "counter-revolutionaries," insisted that freedom could be obtained only through struggle. The leaders of Palestinian Jewry — the majority of whom had come to Palestine before the Nazi onslaught on European Jewry — mostly feared for the immediate present, for the tangible manifestations of Jewish pioneering. They were haunted primarily by the grim image of fields and orchards laid waste, of towns and kibbutzim destroyed by British soldiers because a handful of impatient Jewish dissidents would not wait for Britain to fulfill her promise. Begin and the Irgun, on the other hand, thought in terms of the long-range future, of meaningful Jewish survival not only in Palestine but in all the other lands where Jews would still be alive after the war. The survivors of the ghettoes and the concentration camps would view the open capitulation of Palestine Jewry to the threat of British force as the end of their last remaining hope. No country in the world relished the prospect of being burdened with Jewish refugees. Where, then, were the remnants of Auschwitz, Dachau, Buchenwald and Bergen-Belsen to go? As Begin saw it, the Jews of Palestine already living in in the Jewish homeland had an obligation to their brethren who had seen sufferings such as no human being should ever have been called upon to endure. Was history to record that the Jewish community of Palestine had been tested but had failed the test because of fear for its own safety?

The four men continued their debate long after the busy street had emptied for the night. Golomb and Sneh kept harping on the threat facing the survival of Palestinian Jewry if the Irgun continued its activities. Begin and Lankin pointed to the likelihood that there would be no Jewish survival anywhere in the world if the Irgun ceased to fight.

Apparently in order to lighten the grim mood of the meeting, Golomb attempted to inject a note of optimism. Unlike Sneh, he seemed to have little confidence in Winston Churchill's friendship for Zionism. However, he was certain that after the war, Churchill would be replaced by the Labor party. Citing speeches delivered by British Labor leaders at various political gatherings, the "Minister of Security" tried to convince Begin and Lankin to be patient just a little longer: the Labor victory would bring about a decisive change in Britain's attitude toward Zionism. In view of its promises over the years, the Labor party, once in power, could be counted upon to open Palestine to all Jews who would want to come there. Begin considered Golomb's hopes incredibly naive, but he was not able to shake his beliefs.

The meeting broke up long after midnight. As the men bade each other "Shalom" — Begin remembers that they even shook hands — Begin once again voiced his hopes that, before long, the Jewish Agency and Haganah would come around to the Irgun point of view and that they all would present one united front in the struggle against England. Golomb's parting words were anything but conciliatory. "We shall step in and finish you," he said. Begin never saw Golomb again. The following year Golomb was to die of heart disease at the age of 52.

Less than a week later, on the evening of November 6, 1944, Begin and his deputy Yaakov Meridor were sitting in one of the Irgun meeting places, waiting for two Sternist leaders, Itzhak Ysernitzky[9] and Nathan Friedmann-Yellin. They were going to discuss possibilities of a joint Irgun-Sternist operation. Though the Irgun disagreed with Sternist tactics, the leaders of the two "dissident" organizations kept in touch and from time to time explored areas where they might collaborate against the British.

While Begin and Meridor were waiting for their visitors, Meridor casually turned on the radio in the room. Begin throughout his years in the underground was an avid listener of the BBC broadcasts from London, to which he has given credit for helping him perfect his English. Meridor, however, happened to get Radio Cairo, just in time to hear a news bulletin. Lord Moyne, the British Resident Minister in the Middle East, had been assassinated in Cairo. Neither Begin nor Meridor was sorry that Moyne was dead. In his last post in Cairo and, before that, as Secretary of State for the Colonies, Moyne had been responsible for the enforcement of British colonial policy in Palestine and had never made a secret of his bitter opposition to Zionism. Two years before, he had delivered one of his most violently anti-Zionist and anti-Jewish speeches on the floor of the House of Lords, in a debate with Lord Wedgwood, a Christian friend of Zionism. Wedgwood, a long-time critic of Britain's policy toward Palestine, had been drawn to the militant Zionist spirit of Jabotinsky. He had advocated the establishment of a fighting force composed of Jewish refugees from Germany and proposed a motion that the Jews in Palestine should be allowed to organize an armed all-Jewish home guard. Moyne's response to Wedgwood's recommendations had shocked even those in Britain who did not favor Zionist aspirations in Palestine. He accused the Zionists of racism, suggested that there were grounds for comparing the Zionists with the Nazis and explained that Jewish refugees could always be settled in Syria, Lebanon and Transjordan, countries which, he said, would have no cause to fear Jewish domination in the Middle East.

When they heard the news of Moyne's assassination, Begin and Meridor did not doubt for a moment that LEHI had been responsible. The Irgun itself, in line with its policy not to engage in individual killings, had not contemplated murdering Moyne. In his recollections, Begin does not reveal his personal feelings about the wisdom of the action, but he says that at the time he had been "very angry" with the Stern Group for not having given the Irgun so much as a hint of its planned operation in Cairo. The assassins had been two young Sternists, a 22-year-land surveyor, Eliahu Bet Zouri, and a 17-year-old student, Eliahu Ben Hakim. Both were subsequently hanged in Cairo.[10]

The assassination set off a spate of condemnation in England as well as in Palestine. In a highly emotional speech in the British House of Commons, Churchill, a close personal friend of Moyne's, declared that if such acts were to become typical of Zionism, he and many others like himself would be forced to reconsider their attitude toward it. (His own position on Zionism, he claimed, had been one of good will throughout the years.)

The official Zionist leaders in Palestine expressed shock at what they called a "revolting crime." There were rumors that Britain was planning a pogrom in Palestine to avenge Moyne's death. The Jewish Agency and Haganah, dreading a violent British reaction to the assassination, now officially inaugurated their "open season" on the dissidents.

The Stern Group, led, among others, by Friedmann-Yellin, a much more astute politician than its founder, Avraham Stern, decided to lie low and did not engage in any operations during the six months that followed. With a membership of only 200 armed men[11] and another 200 supporters in all of Palestine, LEHI wanted to avoid becoming a target of the Jewish Agency. As a result, it was the Irgun which bore the full brunt of the concerted attack.

The Jewish Agency's official "declaration of war" on the Irgun took the form of an appeal drafted by Ben-Gurion and approved by the membership of Histadrut, the labor federation of Palestine Jewry, on November 20, 1944. As chairman of the Jewish Agency Executive, Ben-Gurion called for the expulsion of all "terrorists" from schools and places of employment. He urged the Jews of Palestine to give neither aid nor shelter to the dissidents, not to be cowed by any threats of civil war which the "terrorists" might make, and to cooperate with the British in the eradication of "terrorism." Not all the leaders in the Jewish Agency agreed with Ben-Gurion. Rabbi Judah L. Fishman (Maimon), veteran leader of the Orthodox Mizrachi party, and Itzhak Gruenbaum, a secularist author and historian (both men were to join the first cabinet of the State of Israel), temporarily resigned from the Executive in protest against Ben-Gurion's order. At the other extreme, there were Haganah people who not only accepted Ben-Gurion's "season" as a regrettable though necessary evil to pacify the British, but actually welcomed it because it dovetailed with their own ideological and social prejudices. These individuals were dogmatic leftists who felt real hatred for the Irgun as the offspring of Jabotinsky's Revisionist movement, which they had long reviled as reactionary. Considering themselves members of the pioneering elite — many of them were members of kibbutzim — they had only contempt for the Irgunists, whom they regarded as an inferior breed, a mixed bag of recent immigrants, Orientals and wild city youngsters who had to be taught a lesson once and for all.

The main work of the "open season" was performed by the Haganah unit of volunteers which had been trained especially for that purpose in the fall of 1944. Irgun men were shadowed, kidnapped and placed into improvised prisons at leftist kibbutzim. Most of them were eventually released because there simply was not enough room in the kibbutzim to hold them all, but in some instances, leading Irgun members were handed over to the British authorities. Worse, the British themselves were able to arrest hundreds of Irgunists with the help of lists turned over to them by Haganah.

Among those arrested and deported to East Africa were four of the members of the original Irgun command. Yaakov Meridor, the deputy commander, made four unsuccessful attempts to escape from an internment camp in Kenya. The fifth try worked, and he reached Paris in April, 1948. He returned to Israel on May 15, the day after the Jewish state had been proclaimed. Arye Ben Eliezer also arrived in Paris in 1948, after having escaped first from Eritrea and then from a prison in French Somaliland, where he almost had been extradited to the British authorities. He came back to Israel a month after Meridor. Eliahu Lankin, too, managed to escape from a prison camp in Eritrea. Like Meridor and Ben Eliezer, he returned to Israel via Europe. Shelomo Levi, the chief of staff, also attempted to escape from an Eritrean prison camp but he was less fortunate than his three colleagues. He was recaptured and was released only after the establishment of the State of Israel.

The arrested members of the Irgun command were quickly replaced by others. Bezalel Amitzur, short, heavy-set and Russian-born, was placed in charge of basic training. A distinguished-looking young man known only as Reuven directed the underground radio service and the medical department, and super-

1948: Begin at Herut party headquarters shortly after his emergence from the underground.

Safed, 1948: Begin (center, wearing hat) and his comrades pay tribute at the graves of Irgun fighters hanged by the British.

"To the Hebrew People in Palestine." The Irgun's Proclamation of Revolt against British rule issued in February, 1944. "There is no longer any armistice between the Jewish People and the British administration in the Land of Israel, which is literally handing over our brethren to Hitler. Our people are at war with this regime — a war to the end."

vised not only the production of weapons but also the Irgun's arms storage system. Yoel, a former British soldier (his full name was Yoel Bela Eilberg), a cool and collected type who looked and acted like an Englishman, became the head of intelligence. An older man, Yitzhak, dealt with financial and organizational problems.

When Yeruham ("Eitan") Livni was arrested in 1946 his job was taken over by Gideon ("Giddy") Paglin, a former Haganah man who was then in his early twenties. A skillful technician, Paglin invented such weapons as a contact mine for railroad sabotage, and the heavy electrically-operated mortar which later evolved into the Israeli army's famous "Davidka." It was "Giddy" who planned some of the Irgun's most daring operations after World War II, including the bombing of British headquarters at the King David Hotel, the attack on the prison fortress of Acre, and the conquest of Jaffa. In the fall of 1977, Paglin was to become Prime Minister Begin's advisor on combating Arab terrorism. Early in 1978 he was injured in an automobile crash. Three weeks later he was dead, only 55 years old.

Shelomo Levi was succeeded as chief of staff by Hayim Landau, who was known variously as "Avraham" and "Hayim Grossman." An architect by profession, Landau devoted eighteen hours a day to his duties with the Irgun, which required him to live alone in Tel Aviv. His wife and young son stayed at their home in Haifa and were able to see him only twice or three times a year. Among Landau's more interesting tasks was the coding and decoding of Irgun correspondence. He wrote his diary on long strips of paper, which he kept inside the long socks he always wore with his khaki shorts.

A later addition to the Irgun command was Shmuel Katz from South Africa, whose task was to produce English-language information material and to translate Irgun broadcasts into English.

The only member of the command who was never arrested, not even during the "open season," was Begin himself. As the "season" gathered momentum, he found that the Hasidoff Quarter on the outskirts of Petah Tikvah was no longer safe for him and his family. Some of his neighbors, members of HaShomer HaTzair, frankly favored cooperating with the British authorities in flushing out "terrorists." What if, by some chance, they were to discover the true identity of the man whom they still knew only as a mild-mannered, late-blooming law student named Israel Halperin?

The Begins moved back to Tel Aviv and took up residence on Joshua Bin-Nun Street, a small side street near the Yarkon River, which then formed the northern edge of the city. There Begin's friend Meir Kahan, who had helped secure his release from the Anders army, had bought a small detached house under an assumed name and leased it to Begin for a period of two years. The house had a seedy-looking garden in front and a rotting orange orchard in the back. The street was dusty in the summer and muddy during the rainy winter season. Among the Begins' closest neighbors were the municipal abattoir and the city dog pound. This was to be the Begins' home for the next two years.

As an added safeguard, Begin grew a beard and once again changed his name and life style. In order to complete the transformation before moving to Tel Aviv, Begin started raising his beard a month before leaving Petah Tikvah, explaining to his neighbors that a close relative had died and that he was observing the traditional mourning custom of not shaving for a period of thirty days. When he arrived in Tel Aviv, Begin was no longer Israel Halperin, the student of law, but Rabbi Israel Sassover, who spent his days poring over the Talmud and profound Rabbinical commentaries. Some of his new neighbors took him for a functionary in a political party organized by religious Jews. Others dismissed him as a type not uncommon among Orthodox Jews — a young man spending the early years of his marriage at Talmudic studies thanks to the generosity of an affluent father-in-law who wanted a learned husband for his daughter. He was asked to join the neighborhood synagogue, a small congregation whose members were simple folk — craftsmen, factory workers and small storekeepers. Since the congregation had no rabbi of its own, the members, who were extremely devout, took to consulting "Rabbi Sassover" on day-to-day religious problems. On one occasion Reb Simcha, the beadle, asked him for a favor: would he accompany him to the offices of the Chief Rabbinate downtown and testify that the neighborhood butcher was an honest, God-fearing man and that the meat he sold was kosher beyond a shadow of a doubt? Begin was convinced of the butcher's religious credibility, but he did not dare to risk exposure by walking with the beadle in broad daylight through the streets of downtown Tel Aviv and then undergoing a cross-examination by the rabbinical judges. He had a difficult time inventing excuses for not complying with the beadle's request. Sometimes the congregants would stop the "rabbi" after services and ask his opinion on the latest political developments. But "Sassover" merely shrugged his shoulders and said he never mixed in politics. This reply came as no great surprise to the questioners: one look at "Sas-

sover's" pale, bearded face was enough to see that he was a very unworldly man.

Meanwhile, Haganah's "open season" on the Irgun continued
unabated. Quite aside from the kidnappings, arrests and, most dis-
tasteful of all, the acts of outright "informing," Haganah's methods
in dealing with the Irgunists included cruelties for which neither
the Jewish Agency's fear of the British nor personal prejudice could
be accepted as rational explanations. In their interrogations,
Haganah men frequently resorted to third-degree tactics: there
were threats, burns and beatings.[12]

It would have come as no surprise to anyone in Palestine if the
Irgun would have answered these provocations with threats or outright acts of warfare against Haganah. When the civil war against
which Ben-Gurion had warned the community did not materialize
and the Irgun did not even escalate its anti-British operations, the
Jewish Agency leadership was persuaded that the "open season"
had succeeded in clipping the Irgun's wings.

But this was not true. When the "open season" had first
begun, Irgunists had been filled with rage, and not a few of them
had been eager to retaliate against the Haganah "collaborators."
But being members of a disciplined fighting force, they looked to
the Irgun command, and the commander himself, for their orders.
At ten o'clock on a bleak, rainy morning in mid-December, 1944,
Begin called a meeting of the command in Tel Aviv to decide what
the Irgun's answer to the Jewish Agency and Haganah should be.
There were three possible responses: unconditional surrender to
the Jewish Agency's orders; surrender, but with "mental reservations;" or retaliation.

Begin was opposed to unconditional surrender, but it was not
because anyone, including Begin himself, would have found it in his
heart to accuse the Irgunists of cowardice if they had given in to the
Agency's demands. After all, the Agency and Haganah did have the
edge on the Irgun in resources and in official Jewish backing. The
Irgun could take pride in the fact that it had been the first to raise
the banner of revolt, to strike out at the foreign oppressors, not
counting the cost in private happiness, personal liberty and, in
many cases, life itself. No one would deny that the Irgun had
already done its best for the Jewish people in Palestine.
Nevertheless, Begin, supported by the Irgun command, rejected the
Agency's ultimatum. Begin's main argument for doing so was still
the same as that which he had put to Golomb and Sneh at their
meeting on Allenby Street. In Begin's view, surrender at this point,

even in the face of extreme provocation from Haganah, would have implied tacit resignation to the physical destruction of European Jewry and acceptance of moral enslavement in Palestine for generations to come. Jews privileged to live in the Homeland had no right to kill the last hope of their brethren who had survived the Holocaust in Europe.

Also, Begin pointed out, there was the ideal of *hadar* that Jabotinsky had taught. *Hadar* meant adherence to the principles of common decency, and this included loyalty to one's comrades in arms. Neither Begin nor the Irgun command condoned the radical methods of the Stern Group. Yet, Begin regarded the Sternists as "comrades in revolt and partners in danger" because, like the Irgun, LEHI, too, was a "dissident" organization in Palestine Jewry. If the Irgun were to surrender to the Jewish Agency, Begin explained, LEHI would be left to fight its battles alone. One did not abandon one's fellow fighters in the hour of common peril. Only much later, when his hope for a change in the Agency's policy came true, at least for a short time, and Haganah joined forces with Irgun and LEHI, did Begin learn that there would have been no need for him to worry about the Sternists. They had promised Golomb on their own that they would stop their operations against the British.

As for the second choice, surrender "with mental reservations," Begin had eliminated *that* in his mind almost instantly. To agree to surrender, with the intention of breaking that agreement at the first opportunity, might have been acceptable in other underground movements, but Begin considered this, too, incompatible with his concept of *hadar* as self-respect and moral courage. Begin's closest associates apparently shared his outlook, for during the discussion none of those present even suggested surrender "with mental reservations."

As for the third option, retaliation against Haganah, not only Begin but also the rest of the Irgun leaders knew that this would plunge Palestine's Jewish community into civil war. In that case the only victors would be the British. "We did not want to give them this satisfaction," Eliahu Lankin, who attended the meeting, recalled. "Whatever went on within the Yishuv [i.e., the Jewish community of Palestine] was a family matter. But we would not permit our British adversaries to have their day of rejoicing."[13]

By noon the Irgun command meeting was ready to adjourn. The policy which the command had hammered out under Begin's prodding was the Irgun's own version of self-restraint. On the one hand, the Irgun was not going to accede to the Jewish Agency's demands; it would neither stop its active struggle against the British nor would it promise to do so while reserving the right to renege on its pledge later on. On the other hand, the Irgun would not allow itself to be provoked into retaliating for the arrests, kidnappings and other maltreatments to which Haganah had been subjecting Irgunists, nor would it take revenge for Haganah's unbrotherly conduct in handing over fellow Jews to the British authorities. There would be no surrender, but there would also be no civil war.

Begin admitted that, from the viewpoint of pure reason, such a policy did not sound very logical. But he explained that, in making this decision, he and his supporters were guided not by logic, but by faith and a deep sense of duty to the Jewish people. Begin still believed in the basic good will of the Zionist leadership. He was convinced that Haganah would eventually join the Irgun in the battle for freedom. Nineteen centuries before, the Jewish people had lost its independence because political factions within the walls of besieged Jerusalem had battled each other in bloody civil strife instead of fighting shoulder to shoulder against the Romans at the city's gates. Begin would not permit that to happen again. Not logic, but instinct, derived from centuries of a sorrow-laden Jewish past and from faith in the fundamental sanity of the Jewish spirit, dictated Begin's resolve that, no matter what the cost to the Irgun, there must not be a civil war in the Jewish homeland. "And who knows?" he mused. "Perhaps instinct is the very heart of logic."[14]

The self-discipline which rallied the entire Irgun to the command's decision against a retaliatory strike at Haganah earned the Irgun, and Begin, the respect even of their opponents. Moshe Dayan, who had returned to farming after the loss of his eye but still played an important role in Haganah, sought a meeting with Begin, and the two men got together for a candid exchange of views. Begin listened with frank admiration as Dayan, who was considered one of the "activists" in Haganah, gave him a detailed but completely dispassionate description of his own sabotage activities in Syria against the pro-German government of Vichy France. When Dayan was finished, Begin launched into an equally detailed account of the Irgun's activities and their political significance. Dayan refused to be drawn into a debate on the political value of the Irgun's methods; he said that there could always be two opinions on that subject. But he admitted that the Irgun's daring and its ingenious snipes at the British authorities, along with its idealistic refusal to break the peace within the Jewish community, had begun to capture not only the imagination but also the hearts of many rank-and-file Labor Zionists who did not care for the Irgun's ideology but enjoyed watching the Irgun boys make the British squirm. Whatever the future held, Dayan told Begin, "you have already performed a historic act; you have proved that it was possible to attack the British."

By that time most of the Jews in Palestine, mourning the loss of friends and loved ones in Europe, agreed that the only hope for the Jews who had survived the war was the establishment of a Jewish state in Palestine as soon as possible. Even those who did not consider the Irgun's methods the right way to the realization of this aim began to suspect that many Labor Zionists were overly zealous in abetting the Jewish Agency's "open season" on the dissidents, that the "hunters" might be motivated at least a little by partisan considerations; more specifically, to keep non-Laborites from gaining influence in the future Jewish state.

The Chief Rabbinate, which at first had expressed its disapproval of Irgun operations for fear of British retaliation, now was equally sharp in its condemnation of Haganah's kidnappings and other anti-Irgun excesses.

As the winter of 1944 progressed and gradually yielded to the spring of 1945 the Jewish Agency itself began to feel increasingly uncomfortable in its role as collaborator with the British authorities. Clearly, the "open season" was not fulfilling its purpose. The Irgun was still very much alive, and even more popular than before. All that the Jewish Agency's tactics seemed to have accomplished was to earn growing sympathy for the Irgun while casting a shadow of suspicion on the Agency's motives. In March, 1945, a meeting of "season" leaders held at Kibbutz Yagur, near Haifa, heard Eliahu Golomb and Moshe Sneh announce that activities against the "dissidents" were about to cease. By May, 1945, the month the war ended in Europe, the "open season," too, for all practical purposes, had come to a close.

8. Turning Points: 1945-46

Hitler was dead and his armies had surrendered, but for the Jewish people that was a hollow victory. Over one-third of the world's Jews had been destroyed. Those pitiful survivors who returned to their home towns from the death camps were often greeted by former neighbors with surprise and open hostility: "So you're still alive? We thought Hitler had taken care of you in the gas chambers!" Those who poured into the displaced persons' camps of Germany and Austria refused to be "repatriated" to the countries from which they had been deported in the Nazi "final solution." To the vast majority, Europe after Hitler could no longer be home.

"We know of no country," the Anglo-American Committee of Inquiry on Palestine conceded a year after the end of the war in Europe, "to which the great majority of Europe's surviving Jews can go in the immediate future other than Palestine. Furthermore, that is where almost all of them want to go. There they are sure that they will receive a welcome denied them elsewhere. There they hope to enjoy and rebuild their lives."[1]

Their fellow Jews in Palestine were indeed waiting to welcome them, but this did not help the survivors of Hitler's ghettoes and concentration camps because Britain, under the terms of the White Paper of 1939. had closed Palestine to all Jewish immigration as of 1944. The only way for Jews to enter was by braving inhuman hardships and perils to smuggle themselves into Palestine.

Menahem Begin saw the end of World War II as a turning point in the confrontation between Palestine Jewry and Great Britain. The Irgun no longer felt bound by the restraints it had imposed upon itself during the war in order not to hurt the British war effort. Also, Begin predicted — and correctly so, as it turned out — that following the Nazi Holocaust, Palestine would become a glass house for observers throughout the world. Their attention no longer claimed by developments on battlefronts in Europe and Asia, newspapermen and other molders of public opinion would focus their sights on Palestine, the final hope of the Jewish people, who had been Hitler's first victims. This was the time for an all-out revolt to force Britain out of Palestine. Then, at least the remnants of European Jewry would be able to enter Palestine not as fugitives at the risk of their lives but as free men ready to begin a new existence in the historic homeland of their people.

Begin was motivated not only by the sufferings of the Jewish people as a whole, but also by his own personal loss. He and his sister Rachel had learned that their father and mother, along with their brother Herzl, had perished in Brest-Litovsk. Until the very end, Ze'ev Dov Begin, secretary of the Jewish community, had comported himself in accordance with his concept of Jewish dignity. Brest-Litovsk had first been occupied by the Germans during Hitler's lightning thrust into Poland in the fall of 1939. Shortly thereafter, the city had been turned over to the Soviet Union, but not before the Nazi governor had taken several hundreds of Jews as hostages, demanding an astronomic ransom for their release. Ze'ev Dov Begin called on the governor and showed him the interpreter's identity pass that had been issued to him by another German occupation army a generation earlier, during World War I. As an official of the Jewish community of Brest-Litovsk, he now demanded the immediate release of the Jewish hostages. The governor did not free the prisoners, but he permitted Begin to visit them and to take messages back to their families in Brest-Litovsk.

The Russian occupation of Brest-Litovsk provided a short reprieve for the Jews. But after the outbreak of hostilities between the Soviet Union and Germany in 1941 the city was recaptured by German forces. The Nazis arrested 500 Jews, including Ze'ev Dov Begin and his son Herzl, and led them to the banks of the River Bug. One of the Jews who miraculously escaped that death march told Menahem Begin that Ze'ev Dov Begin had placed himself at the head of the procession and, under the guns of the SS escorts, had led the others in a chant reaffirming Jewish belief in Divine Providence even in the face of martyrdom:

> I believe, I believe
> With perfect faith,
> That Messiah will come;
> And although he may tarry,
> I daily await his coming.

Everyone joined in, and then, as they neared the river, all the

500 prisoners burst into *Hatikvah,* the anthem of unbounded hope for the restoration of Zion. On the bank of the river, the prisoners were met by a hail of Nazi machine-gun bullets. Hasia Begin was not with her husband and son because she had been ill in the hospital when the men were arrested. But the Germans eventually caught up with her also. They dragged her from her hospital bed and killed her.

When Menahem Begin, in Tel Aviv, was told what had happened to his parents and his brother, it was, as he later recalled, "the most terrible moment in my life."[2]

Begin's second child, a daughter, was born the year after the war. She was named Hasia, in memory of her grandmother. When Hasia was born, it was not safe for Begin to leave his house on Joshua Bin-Nun Street to visit his wife in the hospital. His friend Israel Epstein stood in as father of the baby, lending his own last name to Aliza Begin for registration purposes. When Epstein arrived at the hospital there was a slight misunderstanding. Another woman who was in fact named Epstein had given birth to a son, and the floor nurse took Israel Epstein to be the woman's husband. Told that he had just become the father of a son, Epstein raced to Joshua Bin-Nun Street to tell Begin that Aliza had had a boy. When the error was straightened out and he learned that the child was a girl, Begin could not help feeling relieved; a circumcision ceremony would have been inconvenient, to say the least, because he could not afford to attract public attention by becoming the center of a celebration, even if it was just in his own little neighborhood synagogue.

The underground, Begin recalled in his memoirs,[3] was a hard master. It did not permit mourning over parents killed in the Nazi Holocaust, nor rejoicing on the birth of a new-born baby. It also did not permit surrender to illness, but the time came when Menahem Begin's iron willpower was no longer sufficient to keep him going. The years of stress and anxiety, of life as a fugitive from the British and very often also from the official Zionist leadership, coupled with lack of fresh air — Begin's only outdoor exercise while he lived as "Rabbi Sassover" in Joshua Bin-Nun Street consisted of brief walks in the immediate neighborhood near the Yarkon River — had taken their toll. His body rebelled and literally went on a hunger strike. For weeks he was unable to keep down food, not even tea, which he usually relished. Despite Begin's protests that it was against the rules of the underground to call in outside medical help, Hayim Landau, the Irgun's chief of staff, insisted on sending for Dr.

Hermann Zondek, a well-known internist who had arrived in Palestine during the mid-1930's after fleeing Hitler's Germany. The kindly doctor examined the patient, then handed him a prescription and said, "Herr Sassover, you're still a young man. Why do you sit indoors studying all day long? If you want to stay well, you simply must get out more, have some exercise and fresh air."

Begin had the prescription filled, but he was in no position to heed Zondek's well-meant advice about the benefits of a daily airing. Still, he eventually recovered and, despite his frail appearance, remained in good health until his heart attack over 30 years later.

Begin had no time to attend to the needs of his body; the struggle against Britain preempted all his energies. He laid new ground rules for the Irgun's future operations against the British authorities. Now, with Britain's forces no longer engaged in a war of survival against Nazism, the Irgun was free to attack British military installations, to "confiscate" weapons and destroy army property. One rule, however, still remained unchanged: in its operations the Irgun, unlike the Stern Group, would continue to avoid taking lives, except in self-defense. The objective Begin had set for the Irgun was still the same as it had been when he had first assumed command: not to kill Englishmen (who, after all, were only carrying out the orders of their government) but to make the British in Palestine look so ridiculous in the eyes of world public opinion that sooner or later Britain would see no other alternative but to make as graceful an exit as possible and leave the Jewish homeland to the Jewish people.

Haganah had abandoned its "open season" on the Irgun; yet, it persisted in viewing Irgunists as dangerous dissidents. Begin openly urged that, instead of dissipating its energies on devising ways of neutralizing the Irgun, Haganah should apply its military skills and resources to the revolt against Britain. During the war it could have been argued that, despite her obnoxious policies in Palestine, Britain had been an ally of the Jews in the war against Adolf Hitler. But since she continued to keep Palestine closed to the survivors of Hitler's terror, she had ceased to be an ally and had in fact become an enemy of the Jewish people. It was high time for Haganah and Irgun to unite in the struggle against that enemy.

A month after the end of the war in Europe, Begin announced a plan in which he felt Haganah and Irgun could cooperate. He sent it, in the form of a memorandum, to 250 leading personalities — political and non-political — of Palestine's Jewish community. Basically, it was an elaboration of proposals which Begin had already set forth in his "proclamation of revolt" in February, 1944: the establishment of a Jewish provisional government in Palestine. In 1944, Begin had been somewhat vague, but now he was quite specific about the structure he wished the provisional government to assume. All those individuals — heads of official institutions, economists, scientists, and other prominent personages inside the Jewish Agency or outside it — who considered themselves the political, spiritual or intellectual leaders of Palestine Jewry were invited to meet for the purpose of declaring an independent Jewish state and forming a provisional government. The government was to consist of two branches: a cabinet, and a supreme national council. The council, to which the cabinet would be responsible, would be chosen from among all the Jewish political parties in Palestine, from extreme right to extreme left, with the exception of the Communists. The parties to be represented in the national council would maintain their independent policies but would unite on a common basic political, social and economic program: the establishment of a state which, while Jewish in every respect, would ensure equal rights for all its inhabitants regardless of religion or ethnic background, the mass ingathering of Jews from the diaspora, the right of workers to improved standards of living, social insurance, agrarian reform, and the national ownership of utilities and public services.

The first task of this government would be to lead the organized revolt of Palestine Jewry against British rule. Begin was aware that the revolt would exact a heavy price in human life and liberty. In his memorandum, he did not minimize the risks. If the members of the original cabinet did not go underground, they would be arrested almost immediately by the British. Such arrests would have a powerful impact on world public opinion. The plan, therefore, was precisely that these leaders should deliberately maintain a high visibility and expose themselves to arrest. "They should gladly accept this risk . . ." Begin noted, "bearing in mind what millions of ordinary Jews and thousands of their spiritual and religious leaders have given for the Jewish people. They should also bear in mind the political significance of this act, both externally, and more particularly, internally, in rallying the masses to their fighting leadership."[4] In order that the government should not remain leaderless following the anticipated arrests, Begin proposed that the national council should elect second and third "back-up" cabinets. As opposed to the original cabinet, the identities of these alternates would not be revealed. If the original members were arrested or killed, the alternates would carry on their work underground.

After sending out his memorandum, Begin waited for replies. When none came, he sent his associates to call personally on the recipients of the memorandum. The reaction was disappointing, but it came as no surprise to Begin. Most of the leaders of Palestine Jewry were afraid to put their lives and liberty on the line without support from their colleagues. Rabbi Meir Berlin (Bar-Ilan), a Mizrahi leader, said he would accept the invitation issued in the memorandum, provided that 50 of the other addressees would do likewise. Since not even five of the recipients responded, the memorandum yielded no practical results, However, Berlin, a longtime sympathizer with the Irgun, offered Begin a hiding-place in his own home if ever Begin should find his quarters on Joshua Bin-Nun Street no longer safe from British searches. Begin declined the offer; he felt he had no right to endanger Rabbi Berlin's safety.

Actually, Begin during that period felt reasonably secure in his home, although he and his family had been adopted by a stray female dog who perversely seemed to bark only when she scented British soldiers or police nearby. One night, an entire unit of the British army set up camp near the house and Roxy — the Begins' name for their inconvenient pet — went wild. Luckily, Roxy's yelps were drowned out by the loud voices of the soldiers who, fortunately, left the next morning without ever realizing that they had spent the night almost at the doorstep of the leader of the "Jewish terrorists."

The summer of 1945 was a period of suspense for the Jews of Palestine. Britain held her first postwar general election. For the Jews in Palestine, and in the DP camps of Europe, the mere possibility that the Labor party might win held hopes for a complete turnabout in Britain's Palestine policy. For years, the leaders of the Labor party had opposed the government's Middle Eastern politics, and throughout the election campaign they had put out statements even more Zionistic, if that was possible, than any public declarations ever issued either by the Jewish Agency under Weizmann and Ben-Gurion or by the Irgun under Menahem Begin. In one campaign statement shortly before the election, the annual conference of the Labor party called for unlimited Jewish immigration into Palestine. There was, the Labor leaders declared,

> neither hope nor meaning in a "Jewish National Home" unless
> we are prepared to let Jews, if they wish, enter this tiny land in

such numbers as to become a majority. There was a strong case for this before the war. There is an irresistible case now . . . The Arabs have many wide territories of their own; they must not claim to exclude the Jews from this small area of Palestine . . .

This statement went so far as to contemplate "the possibility of extending the present Palestinian boundaries."[5]

Neither the Jewish Agency nor Begin had ever expressed a desire to displace Palestine's Arab population in favor of Jewish immigrants. But in the spring of 1944, a Labor party conference had urged precisely such a policy as a solution of the "Palestine problem":

> Let the Arabs be encouraged to move out as the Jews move in. Let them be compensated handsomely for the land and let their settlement elsewhere be carefully organized and generously financed . . .[6]

In the election, the Labor party won a decisive victory and formally assumed office on July 27, 1945, with Clement Attlee as prime minister and Ernest Bevin as foreign secretary. Zionists of all persuasions were delighted. The Jewish Agency pressed the new British government to act on a series of requests made of Churchill late in May, calling for the immediate establishment of a Jewish state, authorization of the Agency to arrange for Jewish immigration, international assistance for the resettlement of a million Jews in Palestine, and reparations from Germany. Even the Irgun which, in the light of past experience, took a somewhat skeptical view of promises made in the heat of election campaigns, announced that it would hold off its operations for several weeks to allow Attlee and Bevin time to implement their party's pledges with regard to Palestine:

> In view of the fact that all the members of the British Government, as members of the Labour Party, subscribed to the programme of mass repatriation to Zion and the establishment of the Jewish state, we consider it our duty, out of a sense of responsibility and of our own free will, to give them an opportunity of proving whether they mean to go the way of all their predecessors, the way of denial and betrayal, or whether they mean to fulfill their solemn public undertakings without delay . . .[7]

As the summer of 1945 wore on, the way Attlee and Bevin meant to go became distressingly clear. Instead of firm promises,

Zionist leaders conferring with British government officials in London received only vague hints of possible future decisions. In August, Chaim Weizmann, president of the World Zionist Organization, learned from the British Colonial Office that the Attlee government had no plans for liberalizing its Palestine immigration policy. Foreign Secretary Bevin denied that his party had ever made promises to endorse Jewish independence in Palestine. "There is not one resolution carried by the Labor party that I know of that promised a Jewish state," he insisted. "If ever it was done, it was done in the enthusiasm of a Labor party conference."[8]

The official Zionist leadership, which had hailed the victory of the Labor party with so much enthusiasm, felt stunned and betrayed. In August, 1945, Ben-Gurion told a world Zionist conference in London what the Zionist movement would do if the Labor party were to go back on its election promises. "We will not shrink before the might of Britain; we will go to war against her," he said.[9] Until that summer, the Revisionists and the Irgun, particularly Menahem Begin, had been ridiculed by Ben-Gurion and his colleagues as Fascists and militarists who were out of touch with reality, unable to make compromises, to wait and to distinguish between what was possible and what was not. Now it seemed that Begin had been right in his pessimistic predictions. The British had no intention of rewarding Zionist moderation by giving the Jews their state in Palestine. The Jewish state was not going to be created by the founding of kibbutzim after all. The only way for the Jews to obtain their state would be by force.

Haganah and the Jewish Agency Executive announced that they had "gone to war with the 'White Paper government'," as Begin put it in his memoirs.[10] On October 9, 1945, Haganah opened an underground radio station, Kol Israel, and broadcast its own proclamation of revolt. "What Hitler did in his murderous *blitz* against the Jewish people is now being repeated in the form of slow-grinding political policy of the democracies . . . As we rose against the brutalities of the Nazi butchers in the ghetto, so shall we rise against the foul designs of the democracies."[11]

In the late fall of 1945, Haganah and the Jewish Agency Executive did exactly what Begin had foretold; they called upon the "dissidents" — the Irgun and the Stern Group — to join with them in forming a "united Jewish resistance movement." Begin and the leader of the Stern Group, Nathan Friedmann-Yellin, were contacted by Moshe Sneh, now commander of Haganah and a member of the Jewish Agency Executive, and Sneh's deputy, Israel Galili, a labor leader and kibbutz intellectual who had come to Palestine from Russia as a small child. What Sneh and Galili wanted was, in effect, that Begin and Friedmann-Yellin should merge the Irgun and the Stern Group with Haganah and place them under the control of the Jewish Agency. Begin, who the year before had offered to submit to Ben-Gurion's orders if Ben-Gurion would agree to lead Palestinian Jewry in the struggle for independence, consented to an alliance with Haganah but did not want the Irgun to lose its identity as an independent organization. He had no faith in the staying power of Haganah, which was under the command of the Jewish Agency. There was always the possibility that, out of political considerations, the Agency might do an about-face from one day to the next. "Yesterday," Begin told Sneh and Galili, "the Agency told you to fight us. Who can tell what orders they will give you tomorrow? The decision is not in your hands. Others decide for you."[12] Once it was absorbed into Haganah, the Irgun would be in no position to reconstitute itself as an independent fighting organization and to resume the revolt on its own if the Jewish Agency and Haganah lost their nerve or reversed their strategy. Begin therefore suggested instead the formation of a united resistance organization to consist of three equal, independent partners, Haganah, Irgun, and the Stern Group, operating under one united command, with all operations, except arms raids, subject to the approval of all three organizations.

The result of these negotiations was a united resistance movement known as Tenuat Hameri, commanded by a triumvirate consisting of Itzhak Sadeh, operations officer of Haganah, Yeruham ("Eitan") Livni, Irgun's chief of operations (after Livni's arrest, his place was taken by Gideon "Giddy" Paglin), and Yaakov Banai, who represented the Stern Group, which, along with the Irgun, had accepted the discipline of the united command.

Tenuat Hameri existed for nine months — from November 1, 1945 until August 23, 1946 — before it broke up again into its original components. During its lifetime, it carried out an impressive round of attacks on British railroads, bridges, police barracks and military objectives, beginning with the "night of the railroads" during the night from October 31 to November 1, 1945 (when railroad lines and bridges were blown up simultaneously in 153 places throughout Palestine) and culminating in the bombing of British government headquarters at the King David Hotel in Jerusalem on July 22, 1946.

On November 13, 1945, Foreign Secretary Bevin formally announced in the House of Commons that an Anglo-American Committee of Inquiry would be appointed to study the "Palestine problem." At the same time, he declared that for the time being there would be no change in the existing restrictions on Jewish immigration and land purchase in Palestine. Rather insensitively, he advised the survivors of the Nazi Holocaust in the DP camps not to emigrate but to stay where they were and help rebuild Europe.

Britain's response to the newly-launched revolt in Palestine was to send the Sixth Airborne Division of the British army to quell "Jewish terrorism." Begin was horrified to note what deep roots anti-Semitism had struck in many of the soldiers. Once, he found a threat scrawled on a copy of the Irgun newspaper *Herut:* "Oh Gee, oh Gee, Hitler killed 6,000,000 Jews. The Sixth Airborne will kill 60,000,000 if you don't bloody well behave yourselves." Still, Begin did not expect massive British reprisals. He remained convinced that the British did not want to see their soldiers killed, or to alienate world public opinion, in a war against the Jews in Palestine.

Irgun and its two partners, Haganah and the Stern Group, continued their endeavors to make life as miserable as possible for the 100,000 British soldiers who were now stationed in Palestine. And they kept on making use of British materiel for their operations.

For explosives, the Irgun made a purchase of Chilean nitrate from a British chemical firm in Haifa, without having to pay a penny for the merchandise. It presented the British company with forged documents purporting to be requisitions from the British authorities in Hebron. The order was duly processed, and a Jewish "friend," driving an official truck from the Hebron municipality, picked up nearly five tons of nitrate packed in 100-pound sacks. The nitrate was promptly put to use at Irgun's explosive manufacturing plants, while the British chemical firm was left, as British parlance has it, to whistle for its money.

Late in November, 1945, Irgun men stole two truckloads of arms from a Royal Air Force camp. Two days later, Haganah raided the police station at Givat Olga, riddling the station house with bullets from automatic weapons. Two days after Christmas, 1945 — which was marked by another "confiscation" of weapons from a British army camp — the Irgun, accompanied by Stern Group men, made a return visit to British CID headquarters in Jerusalem and Jaffa, blowing up the heavily fortified buildings and destroying many secret British intelligence files. "I saw the police buildings laid flat on the ground," an awestruck member of the British parliament who happened to be nearby at the time later reported in the House of Commons.

During the early part of February, 1946, Haganah attacked a series of mobile police units, while the Irgun and Stern Group devoted their attentions to three British air bases. Begin gleefully reports how Irgun men stormed two of the bases, climbed into the Halifax bombers they found there and packed the planes with explosives. Gideon "Giddy" Paglin, who had personally led the operation, reported how difficult it had been for him to persuade his men to stop gaping at the fireworks that followed and to run for their lives. The entire raid had been carried out without casualties on either side, but in London a member of the House of Commons angrily demanded an investigation of the conditions that had made it possible for "terrorists" to enter the closely-guarded air bases and to destroy so many precious British bombers.

Early in March, 1946, the Anglo-American Committee of Inquiry arrived in Palestine to hold hearings. On the same day, fourteen Irgun men, disguised as British Airborne soldiers, raided the central British army camp at Sarafand and drove off with a truckload of weapons. This time there was an encounter with British troops, but again, not one British soldier was killed. Nevertheless, the raid on Sarafand signaled a turning point in British methods of coping with the Jewish revolt. In his memoirs, Begin entitles this new, desperate era as "the ordeal of the gallows."

Two of the Irgun raiders had been wounded and taken captive by the British. On June 13, 1946, three months after their capture, they were tried by a military court and summarily sentenced to "hang by the neck until they are dead." When they heard the sentence, the two prisoners stood at attention and sang *Hatikvah*.

After considerable deliberation, the Irgun command decided on a new strategy to save the two men from the gallows. At first, the Irgun demanded that the condemned men should be treated not as criminals under British emergency laws but as prisoners of war. When the British rejected this appeal, the Irgun command warned the British that, if necessary, the Irgun could, and would, do more than destroy property. The killing of Jews would not go unavenged. If the British carried out the death sentence, the Irgun would "answer gallows with gallows."

Several days later, an Irgun unit surrounded a British officers' club in Tel Aviv. A small party went in, briefly occupied the building, picked out the five officers who seemed to be the highest-ranking in the house, took them prisoner and were gone with the captives before police and military units were able to arrive on the scene. The five officers were kept in Tel Aviv, three in one place and two in another. The British imposed a curfew on the city and conducted house to house searches, but were unable to locate the prisoners. After it had kidnapped the five British army officers from their club, the Irgun made no more public threats of "gallows for gallows." but newspapers and radio commentators proclaimed day after day that the Irgun would hang the five Englishmen if the British authorities hanged the Jews. On July 3, 1946, High Commissioner Sir Alan Cunningham commuted the death sentences of the Sarafand raiders. The Irgun thereupon released the British officers, each with a one-pound note as compensation for the wear and tear they had suffered.

While the Sarafand raiders' lives still hung in the balance, the Irgun continued its operations against British railroads, destroying three trains in the Lydda area, dynamiting a Jaffa-bound train between Tel Aviv and Sarafand, and damaging a Jerusalem-bound train just outside Tel Aviv. A week later the Irgun, aided by Stern Group men, destroyed eleven highway and railroad bridges within a period of 21 hours.

On April 23, 1946, an Irgun unit attempted another arms raid, this time on the fortified police station in Ramat Gan, on the outskirts of Tel Aviv. Some of the raiders were disguised as British soldiers, another dozen as Arabs. Pulling up at the station in an army truck, the Irgun men put on a carefully rehearsed act of British soldiers bringing in Arabs caught in the act of robbing the army camp at Tel Litvinsky. Once inside the police station, both "soldiers" and "Arabs" pulled their guns at the officers in charge and made for the munitions room. Since the bewildered British policemen were unable to locate the keys, the Irgun men had to use explosives to blow in the heavy iron door. They swiftly gathered up as many machine guns, rifles and ammunition boxes as their arms could hold and loaded them onto their truck. Unfortunately British reinforcements from two other police stations arrived and a battle ensued, in which three of the Irgunists were killed and others were wounded. The most seriously wounded among the Irgun fighters was Dov (Bela) Gruner, a 20-year-old immigrant from Hungary who had served with distinction in the British army during World War II and had lost his entire family in the Nazi Holocaust. His fellow fighters thought he had been killed, but in fact he had been taken captive by the British, more dead than alive. Half of Gruner's face had been blown away and he underwent fourteen operations before the British finally placed him on trial before a military court nine months later, in January, 1947.

As the Jewish revolt heated up, the British authorities were determined to break Jewish resistance once and for all, because the uprising now included not only groups they had previously dismissed as "terrorists" but also the Haganah, a body which they had grudgingly tolerated as the order-keeping arm of the Jewish Agency. For some months, the British had been retaliating in a particularly odious fashion. Wherever "illegal" immigrants had secretly landed, the Tenuat Hameri had crowds of *bona fide* civilians gather in order to detract attention from the new arrivals, enabling the refugees to get lost in the shuffle before the British could spot them. It was on these crowds that the British now turned, shooting indiscriminately into them and killing not only unarmed men but also women and children.

Saturday, June 29, 1946, has gone down in the history of the Jewish state as the "Black Sabbath." On that day the British authorities in Palestine launched an all-out attack to put an end to the Jewish revolt. At dawn, tens of thousands of British soldiers fanned out over the entire country. A curfew was imposed on all Jewish cities, towns and settlements. Thousands of Jews were arrested. Among the first to be taken were leaders of the Va'ad Leumi, the executive body formed under the British Mandate to administer the day-to-day internal affairs of Palestine's Jewish community. Also arrested were four members of the Jewish Agency Executive, including Moshe Shertok (later Moshe Sharett, Israel's first foreign minister), who was anything but an extremist, and Ben-Gurion's long-time friend, the religious Zionist leader Rabbi Judah L. Fishman (Maimon), who was to become the first Israeli minister for religious affairs. Fishman, who had never traveled on the Sabbath before, was forced at gunpoint to climb into the car which took him to the detention camp set up in Latrun for political prisoners. Ben-Gurion, the chairman of the Executive, escaped arrest only because he happened to be abroad on official Agency business. At the time, the noted Labor Zionist author and publicist Marie Syrkin wrote that "the members of the Jewish Agency were imprisoned not because of any suspected complicity in 'terrorism' but because they were the accredited leaders of a body whose function it was to secure the fulfillment of the Balfour Declaration. They were the leaders of the Jewish Homeland and, as such, were seized by the British as the natural adversaries of a policy intended to crush the idea as well as the physical being of a Jewish National Home."[13]

On that Sabbath, the British soldiers in Palestine behaved more like pogromists than like preservers of law and order. Arrests of Jews continued all day long. Raids were made on kibbutzim which had never had any ties with the Irgun or the Stern Group. The inhabitants of Kibbutz En Harod were herded into an area fenced in by barbed wire. When they asked what they had done, the reply was, "It's orders." By July 1, 1946, thousands of Jews had been arrested, interrogated and held for periods of days, weeks or months. Except for Fishman, who was released two weeks later due to ill health, the leaders of the Jewish Agency had to spend several months in Latrun before being freed.

During the day, British soldiers broke into the headquarters of WIZO, the Women's International Zionist Organization, which had always confined its activities strictly to social welfare work. The raiders destroyed not only WIZO's files and safes but also integral portions of the building. At the same time, British soldiers and policemen entered the headquarters of the Jewish Agency in Jerusalem, carrying off truckloads of documents.

This time the British authorities found they could not intimidate the Haganah into delivering Irgunists and Sternists into their hands. Speaking to newspaper reporters in Paris, Ben-Gurion said, "[Britain] will not find anyone, either of the left or of the right, who will agree to play the part of a Quisling or of a Pétain"[14]

In London, the feeling in much of public opinion was that the authorities had gone too far in Palestine. On July 2, 1946, Michael Foot, a Labor member of Parliament, defended the Jewish resistance. "In spite of all the acts of violence, I maintain that the Jews in Palestine have been only too patient. They have been only too patient for twenty years," he said in the House of Commons.[15]

The statements issued by Haganah began to resemble those made by the Irgun in earlier years. Throughout the "Black Sabbath," the Haganah broadcasting station called upon the Jewish people to fight and to drive the "unclean sons of Titus" from the Holy Land.

The Irgun proclaimed a "Freedom Charter" which, for the third time in a little over two years, urged the establishment of an independent Jewish state and a Jewish provisional government. This charter received prominent billing in the world press. But the Irgun would not confine its activities to calls for independence.

As early as the spring of 1946, Begin had proposed to the Haganah-Irgun-LEHI command of Tenuat Hameri an ambitious operation: a sabotage attack on the southern wing of the King David Hotel in Jerusalem which housed the central military and civilian agencies of the British mandatory government. The attack would be carried out jointly by Haganah, Irgun and the Stern Group. Begin recommended the use of a new explosive invented by "Giddy" Paglin — a homemade time bomb device which could be adjusted not to go off until half an hour or even one hour after it was planted. This delayed-action arrangement, Begin pointed out to Haganah representatives Moshe Sneh and Israel Galili, would permit ample time for the Irgun to warn the people inside the hotel and for the British authorities to evacuate the entire building before the explosion. Begin's prime concern still was to avoid loss of life; the Irgun was still interested only in disrupting the machinery of British government, not in killing or injuring British bureaucrats, much less guests and employees in other parts of the hotel.

Initially, Haganah had vetoed the operation as too ambitious and the Irgun, faithful to the discipline of the united resistance movement, had held off. But on July 1, 1946, two days after the "Black Sabbath," the Irgun received a letter from the Haganah command, authorizing the execution of "Operation Chick" at the earliest possible moment. ("Chick" was the code word for "malonchick", a Hebrew-Yiddish diminutive meaning "little hotel," a misnomer if ever there was one, since the King David at the time was, in fact, one of the largest and most elegant buildings of its kind in the entire region.)

Later, "Operation Chick" would be represented to world public opinion as an act of terrorism carried out by extremists and roundly condemned by the responsible Zionist leadership. However, Haganah's letter to Begin not only approved the operation but made it plain that the Haganah command, in fact, wanted it carried out at the earliest possible moment.

In Begin's opinion, Haganah's hasty turnabout was motivated by two considerations. The first was that an attack on British headquarters was only proper retaliation for the British invasion of the Jewish Agency building, which enjoyed semi-official status as "Jewish headquarters." The second consideration was even more important. The documents carried off by the British soldiers in their raid on the Agency building included highly sensitive material, which the Agency and Haganah could ill afford to leave in British hands. Among the papers was a typescript of a report made by Moshe Shertok (Sharett) to a closed Zionist meeting. In this report Shertok, whom a later generation would have described as "dovish" in his attitude toward the British administration, expressed praise for the propaganda and psychological significance of the joint 21-hour Irgun-Stern Group attack on the highway and railroad bridges. The Shertok report was only one of the many pieces of clear evidence that the Jewish Agency had given its sanction to the sabotage operation conducted by Haganah in concert with Irgun and the Stern Group. Three decades later, Irgun's "Giddy" Paglin was to tell a newpaper reporter that the documents could have led to the trial and hanging of the top Zionist leadership in Palestine.[15a]

How eager Haganah was to see these documents destroyed became apparent at the meeting between Itzhak Sadeh, the Haganah operations officer, and "Giddy" Paglin, at which plans for "Operation Chick" were discussed. Sadeh asked Paglin how much time would be allowed between the planting of the bombs in the hotel and the actual explosion. "Forty-five minutes," said Paglin. "With our advance warnings, this ought to give the British plenty of time to evacuate all their people before the bombs go off."

"That's too long, I think," Sadeh replied. "If we leave them three-quarters of an hour, it'll give them time not only to evacuate their people but also to take our documents with them. I think fifteen minutes should be ample."

"Fifteen minutes may not give them a safe margin for evacuating the hotel," Paglin insisted. "You don't have to worry about the documents. Look, I've had quite a bit of experience in this sort of thing. When the British authorities get a warning that one of their offices is going to be blown up, their first thought is to *get out*. They don't waste time on rescuing documents."

In the end, the two men compromised: The time to be allowed between the planting of the explosives and the detonation would be half an hour. The explosives were to be brought into the building in heavy milk cans by Irgun men disguised as Arab milkmen. They would be placed in the basement of the southern wing, where there was a kitchen and a café. It was calculated that this was precisely the proper location to produce an explosion that would destroy the entire government wing, from the basement to the roof, without seriously damaging the rest of the hotel. Paglin decided that the explosives would be planted in the basement at eleven o'clock in the morning, so that they would go off before lunch-hour customers would come to the café. Everything was planned in careful detail to produce maximum damage to British property without loss of British, Arab or Jewish lives.

Unfortunately, the operation was doomed to disaster from the very outset. There were upsets in the scheduling, last-minute mishaps and an unforeseen shootout. Worst of all, the British failed to evacuate the government wing before the explosives went off.

Perhaps the first untoward omen was the circumstance that the attack was not carried out until three weeks after Haganah had given its authorization. First, it was the Stern Group that asked for more time; they were not yet ready to perform their part of the task, they explained. Then, Haganah requested postponements — two or three times, as Begin remembers. Haganah's final request for deferment came in the form of a note from Moshe Sneh, which Begin received on July 19, urging him to put off the operation for a few more days. Finally, Haganah and Irgun agreed on a date — Monday, July 22, 1946.

Then, at the last moment, there were complications, with the result that the milk cans were brought into the café one hour later than the scheduled time — at twelve noon instead of at eleven. The Irgun men, in their Arab disguise, succeeded in depositing the milk cans at the right place, but as they were about to leave, two British soldiers turned up. Something about the "milkmen" had aroused their suspicion and there was shooting, in which one of the Irgunists was killed. However, the explosives remained in place.

At ten minutes past twelve — twenty minutes instead of one hour before the explosives were meant to go off — an Irgun girl made three telephone calls. First, she telephoned the King David Hotel, informing the switchboard operator that explosives had been planted in the basement of the hotel and would go off shortly. "Evacuate the entire building!" she shouted, then hung up. The next call went to the offices of the *Palestine Post* — today the *Jerusalem Post*, then as now Israel's major English-language newspaper — informing the staff that bombs had been placed under the King David Hotel and that the people in the hotel had been advised to get out. The final call was to the French consulate, which was in the immediate neighborhood of the hotel. The girl urged the consulate officials to open their windows wide in order to minimize the effects of the explosion. Because the employees at the French consulate heeded the Irgun girl's advice, their building remained intact.

As an added precaution against loss of life, firecrackers were set off opposite the hotel to scare off innocent passers-by.

The explosion came at 12:37 P.M., seven minutes after the half-hour time limit. The blast shook the whole city. The walls of the southwest corner of the hotel bulged outward, and the entire southwest wing crumbled. As a British news report put it, the entire government wing of the King David Hotel was sheared off from the rest of the building as with a sharp knife.

Tragically, the government wing was not empty at the time of the explosion. The top British officials who were in charge of the wing had ignored the Irgun's warnings. Perhaps they thought that the Irgunists would never succeed in getting past the heavy barbed-wire barricades and the intricate alarm system with which the British security forces had fortified the area around the hotel. The next day Begin was to hear from Israel Galili a report of a conversation overheard between a police officer and one of the high British officials at the hotel. According to Haganah's information service, the official had said to the policeman: "We are not here to take orders from the Jews. We *give* them the orders."

Due to the British bureaucrats' refusal to heed the warnings of the Jews, well over 100 employees at British headquarters, not only Englishmen, but also Arabs and Jews, men and women, were killed or injured.

Begin was shocked and angry at the cavalier attitude that had been responsible for the unnecessary deaths and injuries. When he learned that an American newspaperman, Richard Mowrer, had been among the injured, he wrote him a letter to the hospital where he was recuperating, expressing regrets on behalf of the Irgun and explaining that the Irgun had not wanted to hurt him, or anyone else for that matter. Mowrer had not been in agreement with all the Irgun's policies, but he had consistently sympathized with the Irgunists, arguing that they were not terrorists but freedom fighters who were waging their struggle "with their eyes open."

Begin was no less stunned and bewildered by the behavior of his comrades in arms, the leaders of Haganah. The night after the explosion he received a note from Israel Galili, asking him to publish a statement that the Irgun bore sole responsibility for the attack on the hotel.

The next day Kol Israel, Haganah's underground radio station, broadcast a denunciation of the heavy loss of life caused at the King David Hotel by the operations of "the dissidents." The newspapers carried screaming headlines attacking the Irgun. That same day, too, Galili sent Begin a note deploring the "grave consequences of your action in Jerusalem" which was "liable to cause tragic and grave complications in the continuance of the struggle"[16] for Jewish independence, and asking Begin to meet with him at nine o'clock that evening. Clearly, Haganah wanted its endorsement of "Operation Chick" quietly buried. The official Zionist leadership, horrified by the heavy casualties and, as so often before, fearful of British reprisals, was determined to dissociate itself completely from the Irgun and its activities.

At the meeting with Begin that night, Galili produced, among other arguments, a note from Itzhak Sadeh explaining that he, Sadeh, had been misled by "Giddy" Paglin as to the timing of the operation. Paglin, Sadeh asserted, had told him that the operation would take place between two and three o'clock in the afternoon, when most of the government employees in the hotel would be out of the building for their lunch period. Sadeh wrote nothing about the Irgun's warnings to make the British evacuate the government wing. At a subsequent meeting, with both Paglin and Sadeh in attendance, Begin insisted that there had been a misunderstanding, that Sadeh and Paglin had discussed all the details of the operation except, oddly, the hour at which it was to take place, and that the Irgun had done nothing contrary to what had been agreed upon in advance with Haganah. Begin offered to refer the dispute between the Irgun and Haganah to a formal arbitration panel. To assure the panel's impartiality, Begin went so far as to suggest that its chairman should be chosen from among three prominent public figures known for their open and consistent opposition to the political aims of the Irgun: Itzhak Gruenbaum, of the Jewish Agency Executive, or Itzhak Tabenkin, a member of Galili's own faction within Labor Zionism, or Dr. Judah L. Magnes, president of the Hebrew University, an American-born self-declared pacifist who had gone so far as to renounce the concept of Jewish statehood in favor of a "binational" Arab-Jewish state in Palestine although he could not produce so much as one Arab to endorse his idea.

A court of arbitration that included any one of those three individuals would hardly have been considered weighted in favor of the Irgun; yet, the Haganah representatives did not accept Begin's suggestion, nor did they act to stop the public denunciations of the Irgun as the sole party responsible for "Operation Chick." Finally, on July 29, 1946, the Irgun issued a communiqué defending itself and blaming the British for the deaths in the explosion, but the only response from Haganah was a public statement to the effect that the British had indeed been given ample warning to evacuate the hotel. The Irgun made no further effort to detail Haganah's complicity in the operation, for fear of causing harm to the Jewish Agency leaders then still in British custody in Latrun.

The results of the King David Hotel bombing were to be only the first in a series of tragedies born of misunderstandings which were to tarnish the public image of the Irgun and of its leader Menahem Begin for a long time to come. It took years to obliterate the discord and mistrust which, during the two years that followed, were sown between Jews who should have worked hand in hand for the objective they both sought to attain: the creation and furtherance of an independent Jewish state in Palestine.

The British response to the attack on the King David Hotel was swift. Tel Aviv, the all-Jewish city, was occupied by two British infantry divisions beefed up by swarms of police and intelligence agents. A day and night curfew was declared; anyone seen in the streets was to be shot on sight. Screening cages were set up, and the army conducted house to house searches. In the process, many of the British soldiers gave free rein to anti-Jewish feelings. Herbert Howarth, a British official who witnessed the events, later reported that some of the soldiers made obscene anti-Semitic remarks, and that one patrol opened fire on a child who happened to appear on the balcony of a house.[17] General Sir Evelyn Hugh Barker, commander in chief of the British armed forces in Palestine, issued an order declaring all Jewish stores, amusement places, restaurants, cafés and private homes off-limits to British soldiers. "I understand that these measures will create difficulties for the troops," he concluded, "but I am certain that if my reasons are explained to them, they will understand their duty and will punish the Jews in the manner this race dislikes the most: by hitting them in the pocket, which will demonstrate our disgust for them."

The curfew and searches continued until August 7, but they netted the British little beyond a bad press from a world after Auschwitz, shocked by the blatantly anti-Jewish overtones of the operation. The whole process yielded only two arrests of consequence: one active member of the Irgun, plus Itzhak Ysernitzky, then the leader of the Stern Group.

The British authorities put Begin's house through two thorough searches and several less formal inspections but though Begin was at home all the time, they never found him. He escaped arrest by hiding out for four days without food or water in a tiny cubbyhole which Yaakov Meridor had built into the house for just this sort of emergency, long before he himself had been arrested during the "open season."

Instructing Aliza to tell their son Benny, and British search patrols, that he had gone to Jerusalem, Begin climbed into the cubbyhole. Aliza turned up the volume of the family radio so that her husband would be able to keep track of the British troop movements through the city.

Before long, British troops had set up camp in the Begins' own garden, entered the house and come within a few feet of the cubbyhole where Begin crouched, unable to stretch his limbs, not daring to move. When asked where her husband was, Aliza Begin, whose English by that time was quite fluent, coolly answered that she could speak no English. Her husband, she explained in Hebrew, was in Jerusalem. She and the two children, Benny and Hasia, were taken outside for questioning to a screening desk that had been set up in the street less than a mile from the house. The British policeman on duty took one look at the young woman with her two small children and sent her home. Back inside, Aliza began to talk loudly to the children so that her husband would know all was well again, at least for the time being.

But the British returned to the Begin house for yet another search. This time they actually knocked at the wall of the cubbyhole in which Begin was locked. Once again, luck was with him; the British did not probe any further, but he did not dare emerge from his hiding place as long as the radio reported the searches still in progress. While the British were camped almost at the doorstep of the house, Aliza did not dare open the cubbyhole even long enough to give her husband a piece of bread or a cup of water.

By the third day Begin was dizzy and felt his body drying up. In retrospect, he was to say that if he were given a choice between hunger and thirst, he would prefer hunger. Going without water, he found, was sheer torture, made no easier to bear by the British soldiers whom he could hear strolling in and out of the house, casually asking his wife for such favors as matches, but most often for a cool drink.

Finally, on the fourth day, he heard a commotion outside, followed by the roar of truck motors, loud at first, then fading away. Then, complete quiet. Aliza banged the cubbyhole with her broom, the all-clear signal. Begin stumbled out of his hiding place and plunged his head into a basin of cold water, so parched that at first he could not even drink.

The first of his friends to come to house on Joshua Bin-Nun Street after the lifting of the curfew was "Giddy" Paglin, who shook his head in amazement when he was shown the cubbyhole.

"How on earth is it you didn't suffocate there?" he asked.

Begin did not know how to answer that question. Somehow, he had never worried about the air in the cubbyhole. All he had thought about for four days was water.

Later, Begin learned that during the curfew days Jews had risked their lives to leave their homes and to go to synagogues to pray for his survival and safety.

Meanwhile, the Jewish Agency, alarmed by the most recent developments, reviewed the whole question of united resistance. Moshe Sneh rushed to Ben-Gurion in Paris to urge that Tenuat Hameri continue its joint operations, but Ben-Gurion, who the year earlier had urged war on the British and only a few weeks earlier had called for Jewish solidarity in the face of the British mass arrests, backed down. Continued open resistance, he now said, would result not in a British withdrawal from Palestine, but only in the physical destruction of everything Zionist pioneers had built up over many decades. On August 23, 1946, to the relief of Israel Galili and other "doves" in the official Zionist establishment, Haganah, at the behest of the Jewish Agency, withdrew from the united command and Tenuat Hameri came to an end.

From that time on until the establishment of the State of Israel, Haganah concentrated its energies on a more subtle form of resistance, the "illegal" mass movement of refugees from the ruins and the DP camps of war-wrecked Europe to the shores of Palestine. As early as October 10, 1945, three weeks before the creation of Tenuat Hameri, a Haganah unit had attacked a British army camp in Atlit, south of the seaport of Haifa, overpowered the guards and released over 200 "illegal" immigrants who had been detained there. For the two and a half years that followed, Haganah representatives, along with members of Betar and Irgun, played a vital role in the "underground railroad" operation known as *B'riha* (the Hebrew word for "flight"). B'riha, which included many Haganah men in its top organizational echelons, smuggled endless transports of Jewish refugees from Communist countries in the east and DP camps in the west across closely-patrolled European borders to seaports from which ancient hulks chartered and officered by Haganah took them to the shores of Palestine.

But for the immediate future, the armed struggle against the British authorities and military forces in Palestine was left to the Irgun and the Stern Group.

9. The Final Round:
September, 1946 — November, 1947

S tarting with the fall of 1946, Irgun operations went into high gear. Almost every day brought a new Irgun raid on some British government or military installation. The Irgun even set up branches outside Palestine. In France, an Irgun representative, Dr. Shmuel Ariel, a highly educated man, thoroughly at home in French literature and politics, worked behind the scenes to win the French government for the Irgun's political objectives, and before long a "diaspora Irgun command" in Paris was recruiting volunteers for military training. Ely (Fershtei) Tavin, one-time contact man between the Irgun and the representatives of Haganah, became a member of the Irgun command in charge of diaspora operations. He was dispatched to Rome, where he helped speed former partisans and ghetto fighters to Palestine and train them in the fighting skills they would need once they got there. Among the other Irgun officers active in Italy was Begin's old friend, Israel Epstein. A few days after Epstein's arrival in Rome, in the early fall of 1946, an Irgun unit blew up the British Embassy building there. Again, no lives were lost because the bombs had been timed to go off when there would be the least chance of casualties. But several important Irgun men in Italy were arrested, including Epstein. Epstein tried to escape but was shot by an Italian policeman just as he slipped out of the building in which he had been detained. Begin first learned of Epstein's death from a radio news bulletin. He mourned his friend, for whom he could not even recite memorial prayers at the synagogue because it was not safe for him to be seen in public. But there was no time to lament the dead. There was work to be done on behalf of those who still lived.

A month later, in December, 1946, there occurred an incident that roused Begin to fury. It had long been the custom of British officials in the colonies to use the cane or the whip to punish troublesome "natives." Now the British introduced that punishment also into Palestine. Two Irgun boys, one named Katz, the other Benjamin Kimhi, both of them 17 years old, were arrested under British emergency legislation for carrying arms. They were tried and sentenced to fifteen years' imprisonment and eighteen lashes of the whip.

For centuries, Jews had been caned and flogged in Poland, Russia, Germany and other lands of persecution. Begin himself had never forgotten how, as a boy of seven, he himself had been forced to look on while Jews were publicly whipped in the park of Brest-Litovsk for supposed pro-Bolshevik sympathies. Would the Jews be unable to escape the cat-o'-nine tails even in their own homeland? Begin wondered. This time, if Jews were to suffer humiliation, he would not stand by quietly.

Almost immediately after the British had announced the sentence, warning posters in both Hebrew and English sprouted on walls and kiosks almost wherever one looked in little Palestine. Begin's written English at that time was still rudimentary, but it adequately conveyed what he intended to say:

> WARNING!
>
> A Hebrew soldier, taken prisoner by the enemy, was sentenced by an illegal British Military "Court" to the humiliating punishment of flogging.
>
> We warn the occupation Government not to carry out this punishment, which is contrary to the laws of soldiers' honour. If it is put into effect — every officer of the British occupation army in Eretz-Yisrael will be liable to be punished in the same way: to get 18 whips.
>
> HaIrgun Hazvai Haleumi b'Eretz Israel

One of the posters was later found embellished with a postscript, scrawled by a British soldier who had added his full name, rank and serial number: "Please, Mr. Irgun, don't forget about my sergeant major."

The Irgun's warning was flashed around the world by the press and radio, but the British did not heed it. On the evening of December 27, 1946 — a Sabbath eve — Kimhi received his eighteen lashes. Two days later, Irgun men seized several British officers and "noncoms," each in a different town, gave each of them eighteen lashes, then sent them back to their units. To make sure that the British authorities would get the point and at least keep their hands off Katz, Kimhi's companion in adversity, the Irgun issued a new communiqué, threatening that "if the oppressors dare in the future to abuse the bodies and the human and national honour of Jewish youths, we shall no longer reply with the whip. *We shall reply with fire.*"

The warning served its purpose. Katz's flogging was cancelled and, exactly as the Irgun had intended, the British authorities in Palestine became the laughing stock of the world press. The result was that the British not only stopped flogging Jews in Palestine but, two weeks later, officially abolished flogging in India as well. This incident won the Irgun new recruits who believed that positive action would yield more dividends than soft talk.

As was to be expected, the British did not remain passive when their prestige was at stake. The wholesale massacre of Palestinian Jews so greatly feared by leaders of the Jewish Agency did not take place. It was as Begin had insisted all along: the authorities knew they could not afford to antagonize liberal public opinion in the free world by killing Jews. But house to house searches became routine, and in January, 1947, Dov (Bela) Gruner, who had been wounded and captured at Ramat Gan nine months before, was tried and sentenced to the gallows. As in the case of the two Sarafand raiders, the Irgun again asserted that Gruner, as a freedom fighter, had the right to be treated not as a common criminal but as a prisoner of war, and that the execution of a prisoner of war was deliberate murder. When the British stood firm and set the last Tuesday in January, 1947 as the date for the execution, the Irgun once again resorted to the method it had used to save the two Sarafand men. They kidnapped a British army major from his home and, eighteen hours later, a British judge from his court bench in Tel Aviv. The British authorities at once declared a curfew for Tel Aviv and for large parts of Jerusalem and Haifa. Next, they threatened to impose martial law. The Jewish Agency and Chief Rabbi Herzog sent urgent appeals to Begin to release the two Englishmen in order to avert catastrophe, the Agency hinting it had word that Gruner's sentence would not be carried out after all.

This time Begin acceded to the pleas of the official Zionist leadership and set the Englishmen free. The Jewish Agency then sent a lawyer to Gruner, who told him that the Irgun wanted him to sign a petition to the Privy Council in London asking for a reprieve. Gruner, however, said he would not do that, not even if Begin himself were to request it of him. To appeal for a reprieve, he insisted, would imply that he accepted the authority of the British courts in Palestine when, in fact, the British, by their conduct, had forfeited their moral right to be there.

Petitions on Gruner's behalf were sent to London nevertheless, first by his uncle, an American, and then by the city of Tel Aviv. After some debate, the Privy Council granted him a reprieve, probably in consideration of Gruner's distinguished service in the British army during the war and the wounds he had suffered in the Ramat Gan raid. In the House of Commons, Winston Churchill, as leader of the opposition, criticized the Labor government for capitulating to the "terrorists." But at the same time he praised Gruner for his bravery. Never before in the history of the British empire, said Churchill, had a man condemned to death refused to sign an appeal for clemency.

However, the reprieve was only temporary. On April 16, 1947 Dov Gruner, along with three other Irgunists who had been arrested at the time of the flogging incident the previous December, was hanged at the prison fortress of Acre. Forty-eight hours before his execution, he wrote a letter to Begin, which was later smuggled out of the prison. In the letter, he reaffirmed his loyalty to Begin personally and to the aims of the Irgun:

> . . . Of course I want to live. Who does not? But if I am sorry that I am about to "finish," it is mainly because I did not manage to do enough. I, too, could have "let the future fend for itself," taken the job I was promised, or left the country altogether and lived securely in America. But that would not have given me satisfaction as a Jew and certainly not as a Zionist . . .

> The right way, to my mind, is the way of the Irgun, which does not reject political effort but will not give up a yard of our country, because it is ours. And if the political effort does not have the desired result it is prepared to fight for our country and our freedom — which alone ensures the existence of our people — by all means and in all ways. That should be the way of the Jewish people in these days; to stand up for what is ours and be ready for battle even if in some instances it leads to the gallows . . . .

> Your faithful soldier,
> Dov

About a week after Gruner's hanging, another Irgunist, Meir Feinstein, and his cellmate Moshe Barzani of the Stern Group, both of them awaiting execution in Jerusalem's Central Prison, managed to get two hand grenades smuggled into their cell by their underground friends. They placed one of the hand grenades between them, put their arms around each other and blew themselves up in order not to suffer the indignity of dying at the hands of British hangmen.

Throughout the early part of 1947, the Irgun's operations against British installations had continued without letup. On March 1, 1947 alone — a month before Gruner's execution — Irgun units had carried out sixteen acts of sabotage; the most impressive of these was the blowing up of an officers' club deep inside a British security zone.

The day after that explosion, the British authorities imposed martial law and a 24-hour curfew on most of the Jewish areas of the country. For fourteen days all government services, including mail deliveries, were cancelled. Except for motor transports of British security officials, no vehicles, public or private, were permitted in the streets. Food was distributed by the army. Civil courts were suspended and replaced by military tribunals. Soldiers were given authority to shoot anyone disobeying their orders.

The fourteen days of martial law were not only a military siege but also an attempt to strangle the economy of Palestine Jewry. The shutdown of the port of Tel Aviv alone threw hundreds of men out of work. Evidently, the British hoped that the threat of economic ruin would frighten the Jews of Palestine into informing on the underground fighters in their midst.

But these hopes proved illusory. Of the 78 Jews arrested during the two weeks, only 12 were ultimately identified as Irgunists and 15 as Stern Group members. Moreover, the Irgun carried on its activities apparently undisturbed by the restrictions. Irgun men executed 20 operations including attacks on oil pipelines in Haifa and elsewhere, on British military transports, and on British army camps.

Menahem Begin spent the days of martial law at the home of a Jew who served in the British police but whose sympathies lay with the resistance movement. Earlier that year, Begin had ceased being Rabbi Israel Sassover and made his third and last change of identity. The house on Joshua Bin-Nun Street, into which the Begins had moved over two years before, had been sold to a Jew from Egypt who wanted the space for himself after the lease (signed by Begin's friend Meir Kahan) had expired. Now that the lease was running out, the new landlord made plans to build a hotel on the site of the garden of the house. But most important, and dangerous, of all, the British had been paying too much attention to the neighborhood for Begin's comfort.

Accordingly, "Israel Sassover" shaved off his beard and, with Aliza, Benny and Hasia, moved into a different neighborhood. The Begins' new home was a small apartment at 1 Rosenbaum Street in midtown Tel Aviv, not far from the old Habimah Theater. The family was to live in this apartment for next 30 years.

Like the house on Joshua Bin-Nun Street, the Rosenbaum Street apartment, too, had been found and rented by Meir Kahan. Kahan had chosen it because it was on the ground floor and had a separate entrance so that the Begins could stay clear of the staircase used by other tenants. Again it was Kahan who signed the lease, explaining that the apartment was for his brother-in-law, an invalid too sick to settle the formalities himself. "Israel Sassover" had become Dr. Yonah Koenigshoffer. Begin had taken the name from a passport which had been picked up by accident in one of the city's public libraries. He liked the name because it sounded German. German refugees had a reputation for being quiet, law-abiding citizens whom the British were not likely to suspect of complicity with "terrorists."

Clean-shaven, Begin looked years younger than he had as "Sassover." When Benny first saw his father without his beard, he did not recognize him; only the voice was familiar. The boy thought that his father had gone away and that an uncle had come to visit. As for the baby, Hasia, she was still too young to notice the difference.

The one problem was the Begins' new landlady. When she first met Begin, he had just removed his beard and his newly-shaven face looked unnaturally pale. The woman was convinced that Begin was suffering from tuberculosis. Afraid that he would infect the entire house, she suggested to Kahan that his "brother-in-law" either go to a doctor or else find a new apartment. Begin did neither of these things. In fact, he made no attempt to scotch the rumors about his illness. The result was that the landlady and everyone else in the building kept clear of him, an ideal setup for a man in Begin's situation.

During the year that followed, Begin continued to disregard Dr. Zondek's advice about exercise and fresh air. He hardly ever left the apartment during the day. When he had to meet with anyone on the outside he would be picked up by car at night. If the meeting, as often happened, ended very late, he would spend the next day at the house where the meeting had been held and return home by car only after dark. His wife hardly ever left the apartment at all. Her social circle consisted of Irgun members who came to see her husband. Groceries were sent in by Meir Kahan; her personal shopping was done by wives of Irgun men or by a girl known only as Ruhama, who served as secretary to her husband and to chief of staff Hayim Landau. Aliza's only relaxation was to sit on the secluded porch and knit. Begin helped with household chores such as washing Hasia's diapers; he insisted that housework provided him with all the exercise and relaxation he needed. He might be bathing, dressing or feeding the children — Benny was four, Hasia not yet a year old — while discussing future operations and vital policy decisions with members of the Irgun command.

Journalists from Europe and America were making contacts with the Irgun, and some of them were taken to Begin's home. With a few of them, he formed personal friendships. He felt particularly drawn to Lorna Lindsley, a newspaperwoman whose daughter had joined the Free French forces and had been killed the day before the war ended. Begin, having lost his own family in the Holocaust and a growing number of comrades in the struggle against Britain, sympathized with Mrs. Lindsley, who in turn gave maternal compassion and understanding to Begin and his young friends.

In one interview, which first appeared in March, 1947 in the Paris edition of the *New York Herald Tribune,* Mrs. Lindsley got Begin to state his conception of Irgun's role after the establishment of the independent Jewish state. He emphatically denied suggestions that the Irgun was only biding its time until the day it could overthrow the Zionist establishment and impose a militarist, Fascist-style regime on the Jews of Palestine.

"We strongly oppose any totalitarian structure within our state," Begin said.

> Our only aim is to free our country from foreign rule. We are educating our members in the tenets of individual freedom and social justice; they are being taught the principles of democracy in preparation for their future responsibilities.

For the moment, the Irgun's most pressing responsibility was to help ensure the survival of the Jewish people by fighting for Jewish independence:

> We know that the only means of safeguarding our people here in Eretz Yisrael and those still abroad is to give them a state, and an army to defend it.[1]

World events were taking an interesting turn. After fourteen days of siege had failed to crush the Jewish underground, Winston Churchill, speaking from the opposition bench in the House of Commons, wanted to know how long it would take the Attlee government to understand that it was incapable of putting an end to Jewish resistance in Palestine. "One hundred thousand Englishmen," he said, "are being kept away from their home and work for a senseless, squalid war with the Jews. We are getting ourselves hated and mocked by the world . . ."

As early as February 18, 1947, the British government had announced its intention to refer the "Palestine problem" to the fall session of the United Nations General Assembly. But the Assembly did not wait until September. On April 27, 1947, it met in special session at Lake Success, New York, to appoint a United Nations Special Committee on Palestine (UNSCOP). The chairman of this committee, which included representatives of eleven nations, was Emil Sandström, a Swedish jurist. Sandström was assisted by an American, Ralph Bunche, who was then director of the UN Trusteeship Division.

While the United Nations debated the future of Palestine, the Irgun engineered what the British press described as one of the most ingenious prison breaks in modern history. On May 4, a week after the opening of the special UN session, 34 Irgun men, traveling in four trucks and led by Dov Cohen, a former member of the British commandos, broke into the prison fortress of Acre, a solid mass of rock which not even Napoleon's armies had been able to penetrate. Working in broad daylight, the Irgun raiders, aided by powerful explosives — and by comrades incarcerated inside — blew open a wall of the medieval citadel, where Dov Gruner and his comrades had gone to the gallows 18 days before. According to newspaper reports, a total of 251 political prisoners — 131 Arabs and 120 Jews — were able to escape. Of these, 40 had been members of the Irgun and the Stern Group. Twenty-four hours later, some 190 of the escapees, including 21 Jews, were still reported at large. The personnel on duty inside the prison at the time of the raid had consisted of four British soldiers (two officers and two sergeants), four policemen and 132 Arab guards. They had been taken completely by surprise. But by the time the Irgunists were ready to withdraw, British reinforcements had arrived, there was a gun battle, at least seven of the raiders were killed, and a number captured. On June 16, 1947, three of the captured Irgunists — Avshalom Haviv, Yaakov Weiss and Meir Nakar — were sentenced to death. They were hanged the next month, on July 23, 1947. Eleven days before the hanging, the Irgun had captured two sergeants of the British intelligence service to keep as hostages for the three Jews. The day after the Irgunists went to the gallows, the Irgun hanged the two British soldiers.

The raid on Acre, followed by the execution of the two British sergeants, caused an uproar in England. In the House of Commons a member exclaimed that there had "never been anything like it in the history of the British empire."[2] Two years later, a high British official publicly admitted that the hanging of the two British sergeants, more than anything else, had persuaded the British that, unless they were ready to unleash their full military might against the Jews, they had no other choice but to withdraw from Palestine.[3]

On June 16, 1947, the day the British military court passed its sentence on the three Irgunists captured in Acre, the UNSCOP arrived in Palestine for five weeks of intensive study and conferences. Justice Sandström, the chairman, conferred with a delegation of Haganah, then made it known that he wanted to meet with spokesmen of the Irgun as well. A meeting with Begin was arranged through Carter Davidson, an Associated Press correspondent who had been in touch with Shmuel Katz, head of the Irgun's "English Department."

In the evening of June 24, eight days after his arrival in Palestine, Sandström, accompanied by Ralph Bunche and Victor Hoo, chief secretary of UNSCOP, were driven from their Tel Aviv hotel to the apartment of the poet Yaakov Cahan in the center of the city where Begin, Katz, and chief of staff Hayim Landau were already waiting. The meeting, which began a little after 8 o'clock, lasted for over three hours. Throughout the evening, Bunche took copious notes which were read and approved by Begin before they were recorded in their final form.[4]

Begin sat at the head of the table in Cahan's living room, flanked by Katz and Landau. Facing them were Sandström, Bunche and Hoo. Begin launched into a lengthy exposition of the Irgun's history, its ideals and its determination to put an end to British rule in Palestine. As he spoke of the treatment meted out to Irgun prisoners by the British, Begin allowed himself a public display of emotion, rare for him in those days; he raised his voice slightly. Sandström worriedly urged Begin to lower his voice because people outside might hear him. Begin apologized and continued his presentation. He explained the Irgun position that Transjordan, as part of Biblical Palestine, was part of the Jewish homeland despite the fact that the British had detached it in 1922 from the Jewish National Home envisioned in the Balfour Declaration. But at the same time Begin emphatically rejected the proposal made by the British Labor party in the enthusiasm of the 1944-45 election campaign that the Arabs now living in Palestine should be encouraged to leave and go elsewhere. "There is enough room in Palestine for all, both Jews and Arabs," he said, just as Vladimir Jabotinsky had declared ten years earlier. Transjordan, Begin pointed out, was still absolutely empty, with only four people for every square kilometer of land.

The visitors asked Begin to state his position on two specific solutions for the Palestine problem which were then being discussed at Lake Success; the federalization of Palestine on the pattern of Switzerland with cantons based on ethnic lines, or the partition of Palestine — as it was now, without Transjordan — into two states, one Jewish and one Arab.

Begin rejected both solutions, the former on the basis of the principle that Palestine was a Jewish state, and the latter on practical grounds as well.

> We cannot give up any part of our country, which has been defended for generations by Jews who hope to come back to it. Thus, we reject partition first of all on the basis of principle.

Also, partition in his view was not feasible:

> Allegations have been made in United Nations meetings that Jews and Arabs cannot live together, that their aims and aspirations are irreconcilable, and therefore partition is necessary. But actually, if these allegations are true, then partition is impossible, since no line of demarcation can actually provide for the peoples of this country living apart from each other.

Transfers of population, either Arab or Jewish, which had been suggested to implement the partition plan, were unacceptable to Begin. It was not moral, he said, to take people from their homes against their will.

As for the immigration of Arabs from non-Jewish territory into the Jewish state, that would be a matter for the government of the state to decide, just as any other state was free to decide its own immigration policy. The Irgun had no fixed prejudice against anyone, no matter what his religion, who might apply in good faith for a visa to the Jewish state.

The matter of most immediate urgency, Begin continued, was to bring into Palestine all the Jews who wanted to settle there. This process could be supervised by a Jewish provisional government such as he had proposed again and again since 1944. Once the resettlement was completed, elections would be held to choose a permanent government for the Jewish state. Arabs would be eligible to vote and to hold public office. In fact, the government of the Jewish state could include Arab cabinet ministers and perhaps even an Arab vice-president.

When questioned about the place of his underground organization in the future Jewish state, Begin replied that once the British left Palestine and the Jewish state had attained independence, the Irgun would be dissolved. But, Sandström pressed further, Begin had just said that the Irgun wanted all of Palestine. What would the Irgun do if a partition proposal were passed by the United Nations and imposed upon the Jews? To this, Begin answered that none of the Irgun members would accept a "carving up" of the territory which they considered part of the Jewish homeland. However, he felt it would be premature to discuss the forms which resistance to partition might assume.

Sandström, the jurist from liberal Sweden, seemed impressed with Begin's presentation. "I am sorry," he said, "that the other members of the Committee were not able to come and hear you." Dr. Hoo, whose father had once been China's ambassador in Moscow, parted from Begin with the words, "Au revoir in an independent Palestine." Ralph Bunche, the black American, stopped in the doorway and said: "I can understand you. I am also a member of a persecuted minority."

Other members of UNSCOP, anxious to give a fair hearing to all sides in the Palestine controversy, were also interested in talking with the leadership of the Irgun. Soon after the meeting with Sandström, Hoo and Bunche, Begin met with the South American members of the Committee, Dr. Jorge Garcia-Granados of Guatemala and Enrique Fabregat of Uruguay. Yoel, the Irgun's chief of intelligence, escorted the two Latin Americans to the apartment of Israel Waks, another Irgun friend in Tel Aviv. Once again, Shmuel Katz was with Begin, but this time Landau was not present; instead, there was Begin's old friend Meir Kahan. Since Fabregat knew little English, he spoke in Spanish, a language Begin did not know, with Garcia-Granados acting as interpreter.

The atmosphere at this meeting was more informal and cordial than it had been at the conference with Sandström because the two

South Americans had themselves spent time in exile and in the underground, fighting against repressive governments in their own countries. Thus, Begin from the outset regarded them as comrades in arms. When Begin first told his visitors his name, Garcia-Granados shouted excitedly, "So you are the man!" and enveloped him in a bear hug. Begin was particularly impressed with Fabregat, who won his heart by asking whether the children in the town of Natanya, which was then under martial law, were getting enough food and milk. Begin believes that the ability to love children is a reliable indication of basic human kindness.

Begin said nothing about Transjordan now, but he urged Garcia-Granados and Fabregat to insist on a Jewish state in all of Palestine as it had been since 1922 and to oppose any plan to partition the country again between Jews and Arabs. Garcia-Granados replied that if he and Fabregat were to constitute themselves a minority advocating a Jewish state in all of Palestine, there might not be enough votes to give a majority to the partition proposal. In that case the Jews might not get their state at all. Besides, Garcia-Granados gently reminded Begin, the Jewish Agency was apparently willing to settle for part of Palestine if that would be the only way of obtaining Jewish independence. "We can't be more extreme than the Jewish Agency, you know," he said.

Meanwhile, at the United Nations, the Palestine debate continued. The Zionist case was brilliantly presented at Lake Success by Dr. Abba Hillel Silver of Cleveland, Ohio, one of the most eloquent orators in the American Reform rabbinate of his day and one of the few outspoken activists within the official Zionist establishment. Begin had met Silver in Tel Aviv during his "Israel Sassover" period, in the room of his friend Meir Kahan near the seashore. Instead of the usual criticisms of "dissidents" and "terrorists," Silver had given Begin words of encouragement. American public opinion, he had told Begin, was sympathetic to Palestine Jewry's struggle for freedom, because the American people, too, had once fought the British "by extralegal means." Begin, who by his own admission is not easily carried away by personalities whom others may consider outstanding, allowed that Silver was, as he put it, "a personality."

In July, 1947, public opinion throughout the world was shocked by the fate of the 4,500 refugees from Europe's DP camps who had set sail for Palestine aboard the S.S. *Exodus*. The British intercepted the *Exodus* on the open sea, boarded the boat and towed it into the harbor of Haifa. There, members of UNSCOP witnessed the sight of the hapless refugees setting foot for the first time on the soil of Palestine, only to be seized by British soldiers and shoved aboard three British boats that took them back to Europe.

Now not only the "dissidents" but also Haganah went into action. While the Irgun and the Stern Group stepped up their raids on British communications and on police and military installations, Haganah made two attacks on British radar stations near Haifa and sank a British boat in Haifa harbor. On August 8, Ben-Gurion called for the liquidation of the British regime in Palestine. Three weeks later, the UNSCOP published its report, recommending the partition of Palestine into two independent states, one Arab and the other Jewish, with Jerusalem placed under international control.

On November 29, 1947, the United Nations General Assembly, by a two-thirds majority, passed a resolution accepting the UNSCOP recommendation. The Arab nations represented in the UN — Egypt, Iraq, Lebanon, Syria, Saudi Arabia and Yemen — opposed the resolution. Iraq and Saudi Arabia made a point of declaring that they regarded the resolution as invalid and reserved the right to take appropriate action in order to prevent its execution.

But to most of the Jews in Palestine, all that mattered was that a majority of the world's nations, as represented officially at Lake Success, had been willing that the Jews should have their state. The results of the final vote reached Palestine at about midnight. Jews turned off their radios and rushed into the streets, shouting and dancing: "We have a Jewish state! Long may it live!"

The only Jews in Palestine who felt unable to share wholeheartedly in the general rejoicing were Begin and his supporters. Beyond their basic ideological objections to any partitioning of the Jewish homeland, they feared that such an arrangement would not even guarantee a peaceful existence to the Jewish state about to be born. Begin, who had known Jew-hatred in Poland from his earliest childhood and had witnessed the beginnings of the Nazi Holocaust, did not believe that mere territorial concessions would persuade avowed foes to accept the existence of a Jewish state.

Long before the Palestine vote at the UN, Begin had consistently predicted that the Arabs in the part of Palestine allocated for the new Arab state would take no action to set up a government of their own. They would become playthings in the hands of King Abdullah, the so-called "moderate" ruler of neighboring Transjordan, who would do what he could to prevent the implementation of the Palestine partition plan. As an Arab ruler and a protegé of the British to boot, Abdullah would not want to stand accused even of indirect cooperation with the Jews. Therefore, instead of using his influence to assist in the birth of the Palestinian Arab state, he would send his British-trained Arab Legion into battle against the Jews to make sure that the Jewish state would never see the light of day. Begin's fears were well founded; in the war which Israel had to fight for her survival, Abdullah annexed the entire "West Bank" of the Jordan, the sector which the United Nations had intended for the new Arab entity. As a matter of fact, it was Abdullah's cherished dream to expand his kingdom to include all of Palestine, including the Jewish sector.

On the day the partition plan was adopted by the United Nations, Begin said that if and when the Arab world made war on the Jewish state, the Jews would have to be prepared to defend themselves alone. The United Nations might have sanctioned the founding of a Jewish state, but would not be able to assure its establishment and survival.

> The dream of an international force being created to impose partition in the name of the UN is evaporating, even as we warned months ago it would. In the war that is surely coming, we shall have to stand alone — while the UN Assembly issues academic calls for peace . . .

Begin was convinced, too, that the Britsh would do everything in their power to encourage the outbreak of war between Jews and Arabs in Palestine.

"It will be a war for our very existence and future," he said. "And in that war, all the Jewish forces will be united . . ."[5]

10. Deir Yassin, Jaffa and Independence: December, 1947 — May, 1948

The day after the adoption of the UN resolution, Arab violence, which had been almost non-existent for a decade, erupted throughout Palestine almost as if by prearranged signal. Organized bands of Arabs roamed the country, robbing, looting and burning Jewish property and killing Jewish men, women and children. Arab snipers took aim at Jewish buses on the highways. Arabs left their villages, crept toward neighboring kibbutzim and opened fire on them. Arab mobs attacked the Jewish quarter in Jerusalem's Old City. Jews were wounded and killed in Haifa and in the border area between Arab Jaffa and Jewish Tel Aviv. The raiders were joined by Arabs from neighboring Lebanon, Syria and Transjordan.

The mastermind behind the undeclared Arab war on the Jews was not in Palestine but in Cairo. He was Hajj Amin al-Husayni, Mufti of Jerusalem, who had directed the Arab riots of 1936. He had spent the World War II years in Berlin as a fervent and effective supporter of Adolf Hitler, had been interned by the French after the war but had been allowed to "escape" to Egypt, from where he now labored tirelessly to inflame Arab minds against the Jews.

The British authorities, who were scheduled to leave Palestine on May 15, 1948, did nothing to defend the Jews or to stop the Arabs, nor did they make arrangements for an orderly transfer of authority. They had no desire to see the UN partition plan translated into reality. They made sure that all the 50 police fortresses in the country, even those in the areas allocated to the future Jewish state, should be occupied by Arabs. As a matter of fact, Englishmen occasionally abetted the Arabs in their attacks on Jews. In Jerusalem, British soldiers disarmed four Jews and turned them over the Arabs, who mutilated and murdered them. On February 1, 1948, two British deserters, one soldier and one policeman, acting on Arab orders, parked an explosive-laden truck in front of the *Palestine Post* building, then made a fast retreat. The truck blew up, and the *Post* building went up in flames.

The Irgun from the very beginning urged the Arabs to ignore incitements from the outside and to live in peace with the Jews. On December 3, 1947, four days after the UN vote for partition, the Irgun broadcasting station, "Voice of Fighting Zion," went on the air with an appeal to the Arabs: "Arab neighbors . . . Hands off the Hebrew citizens of the country! Do not disturb the peace between two peoples . . . In this country we shall live together, and together progress to a life of freedom and happiness. Do not reject the hand that is stretched out to you in peace."

At the same time, the Irgun made it clear to the Arabs that it had the strength, and the will, to fight those who would not accept the Jewish state. "We shall grip the hand of a good neighbor in friendship," the broadcast concluded, "but the hand of murderers we shall cut off without mercy."

Also in December, 1947, the Irgun issued a call to the Jewish community of Palestine, warning the Jews of the hardships that lay ahead and announcing the measures the Irgun would take to prevent a massacre of Jews after the British had left Palestine:

> The greatest danger facing us is that we should not understand in time the magnitude of our immediate peril. The people must know the truth, for only this knowledge can avert the catastrophe.
>
> The [British] blockade at sea will continue for another five months. The British will permit no reinforcements either of men or of war material. Jewish blood will be shed . . . And arms will be taken away, and ammunition consumed. Jewish fighters and defenders will be arrested, or will be murdered by incited rioters. Our economy, if not destroyed, will be undermined. Communications will be disrupted.
>
> All this will continue for five whole months. Then, on the night of the 15th of May, 1948, with the end of British rule, the land frontier-posts of our country will fall. The frontiers will not be manned by any Jewish guards, because most of these frontiers are in the areas allocated by the ruinous partition plan to the "Arab State." Through these frontiers . . . will come thousands of murderers equipped with British arms.

The Irgun was not going to wait until May 15 to go into action:

> We must . . . prepare while there is yet time. First and foremost, we must end our defensive situation. We must take up the offensive. We must attack the murderers' bases.
>
> What we have to prepare is not local defensive plans, but broad strategic plans for repulsing attacks and for preparing the offensive of the liberating Hebrew army. Preparations must be made abroad. New cadres of experienced fighters must be organized.
>
> All this will be done by united forces. All of us, without exception, will face the same dangers. The situation is terribly grave. The war will be difficult and costly in sacrifices. But there must be no panic. If we all understand what we have to do, we shall smite the enemy hip and thigh.[1]

The Irgun leadership was faced with the formidable task of making a complete turnabout in its military tactics. The struggle against the British had to be waged underground, guerrilla-fashion. But the war against Arab marauders and invaders would call for fighting largely in open terrain. Chief of operations "Giddy" Paglin and his helpers set up camps sheltered by the citrus groves of Ramat Gan, just outside Tel Aviv, where large numbers of old-timers and new recruits could be trained — or retrained — in regular army-style warfare. At that time — late 1947 and early 1948 — the Irgun still had no more than a few dozen men on full-time service, but it was able to draw on a reserve of 5,000 members who, though engaged in everyday civilian employment, were subject to call on short notice.[2]

The Irgun launched a crash program of arms procurement. Haganah's equipment and war materiel were funded by the Zionist establishment, but the Irgun was financially dependent on private donations and on the Revisionist party. Irgun representatives worked in Europe, particularly France, to obtain funds and small weapons. In Palestine, the Irgun set up a small plant for the manufacture of Sten guns and hand grenades.

During the second week of December, 1947, after two weeks of ceaseless Arab attacks, Irgun units went into action against the bases from which the Arabs operated within Palestine. During the morning hours of December 11, an Irgun party moved into the village of Tireh, not far from Haifa. After warning the women and children of the village to leave, the Irgun men blew up the main building there, leaving 13 Arabs killed and six wounded. Simultaneously, three other hotbeds of Arab activity came under Irgun attack: the village of Yazur near Tel Aviv, Shaafat near Jerusalem and Yehudiyeh on the highway linking Tel Aviv and Lod. Bombs were planted in the Arab market in Haifa and in front of Jerusalem's Damascus Gate: both these sites were known as gathering places for Arabs plotting atacks on Jewish transports, towns and settlements.[3]

Begin pointed out that this series of above-ground Irgun operations represented the first counterattack by an organized Jewish armed force since the days of the Romans. Ben-Gurion, chairman of the Jewish Agency, anxious not to forfeit the good will of the United Nations, still kept Haganah under restraint. But there were some within the Agency who felt that it was time for Haganah to reach an agreement with the Irgun. There was no need for a long-term political settlement between the two fighting organizations, for Begin had already made it clear that once the British had gone and the Jewish state had been officially launched, he would dissolve the Irgun. But considerations of economy and effectiveness demanded an operational agreement under which the two bodies would be able to cooperate in an atmosphere of mutual trust while the Irgun was still in existence.

To this end, the Jewish Agency made contact with Begin, and on December 15, 1947, Begin, accompanied by Hayim Landau and Shmuel Katz, went to the Tel Aviv apartment of scholarly David Zvi Pinkas, who represented the Mizrahi (religious Zionist) party on the Agency Executive. In addition to Pinkas, four other representatives of the Agency were there: two more Mizrahists, Rabbi Judah L. Fishman (Maimon) and Moshe Shapira; the General Zionist leader Itzhak Gruenbaum, whom Begin had offered to coopt for an investigation of the King David Hotel disaster, and David Remez, a leader of the Mapai party in Labor Zionism, who acted as chairman of the Va'ad Leumi. Also present was a longtime friend of the Irgun from South Africa, Rabbi Louis I. Rabinowitz, chief rabbi of the United Hebrew Congregations of Johannesburg, who had served in the British army during the war as senior Jewish chaplain in the Middle East.

The negotiations dragged on through the winter. Finally, on March 8, 1948, the operational agreement materialized. Irgun defense bases would come under Haganah command, but in order to ease the process of integration, Haganah's commands would be transmitted to the Irgunists through Irgun officers. Raids on British installations for the purpose of acquiring needed weapons would be executed jointly by Haganah and Irgun units. All Irgun plans for operations against the Arabs or reprisals against the British would be subject to prior approval by Haganah. In addition, the Irgun would agree to carry out whatever operations it would be assigned by Haganah. At the same time, Irgun would be permitted to retain a measure of independence; it would continue to resist any attempts by the British to disarm its men, and would be permitted to continue raising its own funds. (On March 12, 1948, four days after the formulation of the agreement, *The Answer,* the organ of the Revisionist party in the United States, published an appeal from Irgun headquarters "to our friends, wherever they are," for at least $1 million within the next three months. The appeal was signed with the initials "M.B."".) The Haganah-Irgun agreement was not ratified by the Agency's advisory body, the Zionist General Council, until a month later.

On April 9, 1948 there occurred the second in a series of tragic events — the first had been the King David Hotel bombing — which happen often enough in warfare but which unhappily for years cast the Irgun and Begin in a role of villains which they deserved no more than the leaders and men of any other fighting force. Even more unfortunately, this event was, and still is, portrayed by the Arab propaganda machine as an act of "Zionist terrorism," which sent masses of frightened Palestinian Arabs into headlong flight, turning them into homeless refugees.

On April 9, 1948, the world was told, the peaceful Arab village of Deir Yassin, just west of Jerusalem, was overrun by a military unit of 100 Jews, members of the Irgun and the Stern Group, who looted the village and wiped out its entire unarmed civilian population. Initially, Arab propagandists set the number of Arab civilian dead at 240. Over the years, the number was inflated to 1,000 and more. What was more, some Jews themselves joined in condemning the Irgun operation. On the day after the event, the Haganah commander in Jerusalem, Colonel David Shaltiel, who originally had approved the attack, declared that the village had been of no military value and denounced the raid as a "premeditated act which had as its intention slaughter and murder only."[4] Almost a quarter-century later, in 1971, Begin had to write a reply to Louis Heren, deputy editor of the London *Times,* who equated what happened at Deir Yassin in 1948 with the My Lai massacre of the Vietnam war in the 1960's.[5]

Actually, Deir Yassin in 1948 had been anything but a "peaceful" village. It was, in fact, one of the two key Arab military bases on the road to Jerusalem. The thrust of Arab strategy, directed by the Mufti in Cairo, had been to starve Jersualem into surrender. From Deir Yassin, Arab irregulars kept the only access to Jerusalem under constant fire and made frequent incursions into the western suburbs of the city. The Irgun and the Stern Group, both of which had contingents in Jerusalem, were eager to participate in Haganah's Operation Nahshon, intended to relieve the beleaguered city. (The code name was taken from a Biblical figure, Nahshon, son of Aminadav, the first Jew to walk into the Red Sea after Moses had ordered the waters parted.) All three fighting organizations agreed that the occupation of Deir Yassin, in particular, was vital to keep the road to Jerusalem open for Jewish convoys bringing food and water to the city. The Irgun and Stern Group asked Shaltiel for permission to clear the enemy out of Deir Yassin.

Colonel Shaltiel, who detested the Irgun and had helped plan the "open season" back in 1944, decided to put aside his loathing for the "dissidents" for the moment and formally sanctioned the operation in identical letters addressed to Mordecai Raanan, the Irgun commander in Jerusalem, and to the commander of the Stern Group in the area:

> I learn that you plan an attack on Deir Yassin. I wish to point out that the capture of Deir Yassin and its holding are one stage in our general plan. I have no objection to your carrying out the operation, provided you are able to hold the village. If you are unable to do so, I warn you against blowing up the village, which would lead to the flight of the inhabitants and the occupation of the destroyed and empty houses by foreign forces.

If regular Arab forces were to move into the ruins of Deir Yassin, Shaltiel said, the village would have to be reconquered in fighting that would probably entail heavy losses for Haganah. Furthermore, Shaltiel pointed out, the occupation of Deir Yassin by "foreign forces" would upset "our general plan for establishing an airfield."[6]

(The airfield mentioned by Shaltiel was duly set up by Haganah at Deir Yassin following the Irgun's capture of the village. For a time, it served as the only link between Jerusalem and the Mediterranean coast.)

Early on April 9, 1948, a task force of about 120 men, Irgunists and Sternists, set out for Deir Yassin. The entire operation, in line with the Irgun's traditional principles set forth by Begin, was planned so as to avoid harm to noncombatants. In his impressive historical account, *Genesis, 1948,* Dan Kurzman notes that Mordecai Raanan, the Irgun commander in Jerusalem, then a young man of 25, made a point of warning his men that he would not tolerate any wanton looting or killing of Arab civilians in the capture of Deir Yassin. When one of the Irgun youngsters sarcastically wanted to know whether the Arabs would be equally considerate if they were to capture a Jewish settlement, Raanan replied, "If a dog bit you, you as a man should not act like a dog. I would not expect you to bite the dog."[7]

The Irgun planned to approach the village from several directions, but leave the western access clear, to enable inhabitants of the village to escape. An armored truck equipped with a loudspeaker was to precede the attacking force, warning all civilians to leave at once because their village was about to be attacked. By broadcasting this advance warning, the attacking force deliberately sacrificed the all-important element of surprise.

As in the case of the King David Hotel, everything seemed to go wrong for the Jewish fighters at Deir Yassin from the very start. The original plan had been for the Irgun's loudspeaker truck to penetrate into the center of the village ahead of the attacking force and from there call for the surrender of the village and the immediate departure of all civilians. But the truck never made it that far. It plunged into a primitive tank trap on the edge of the village and could not be freed, so that the voice from the megaphone could be heard only in the outermost row of Arab dwellings. Under the circumstances it was surprising that as many as 120 of the civilian population — including women and children — escaped. These Arabs, who had taken shelter behind the slopes of surrounding hills, were placed on trucks, transported to the border of Arab-held East Jerusalem, and released. Many other noncombatants, however, remained trapped in their huts, either because they never heard the warning, or because they relied on the local Arab irregulars — abetted, as it turned out, by troops from Iraq who were also stationed in the village — to fend off the Jews. It seems, too, that the villagers of Deir Yassin were victims of an oft-used Arab ploy to exploit Jewish concern for civilian lives — and perhaps the propensity in anti-Jewish circles to look for "evidence" of Jewish brutality — by placing their military strongholds in civilian population centers.

At any rate, the Irgun-Sternist force was met by Arab gunfire from every house, so savage that neither the Irgunists nor the Sternists could get close enough to the buildings to use their guns effectively, much less to notice whether or not there were any civilians among the Palestinian and Iraqi fighting men inside. It took the Jewish fighters two hours to reach the center of the village, and by the time they arrived there, many of their men had gone down. Altogether, the Jews suffered 41 casualties, including four killed. Among the wounded was their leader, Ben-Zion Cohen. In the end, Yehuda Lapidot, who had taken over from Cohen, decided that under the circumstances house to house fighting had become too costly in Jewish lives. He therefore sent word to Raanan at nearby Kibbutz Givat Shaul to send up hand grenades and other explosives to throw into the windows from which the firing came. Toward the end of the fighting, a unit of Palmach men, equipped with two-inch mortars, came to the aid of the Irgunists.[8]

By the early afternoon, the battle was over and Deir Yassin was in Jewish hands. But the Jews were shocked to find, side by side with fallen Palestinian and Iraqi soldiers, the bodies of Arab civilians. Probably about 200 had been killed, including 90 Arab irregulars who had defended the village.[9] (The total population of the village had been about 1,000.)

The fact that, despite all the precautions taken, civilians had been killed, was a source of real distress to the Irgun leadership, particularly Begin. "It was tragic and painful," he was to write in his letter to the London Times in 1971.

Haganah and the Jewish Agency, on learning that Arab civilians had lost their lives at Deir Yassin, reacted much as they had after the explosion at the King David Hotel two years before. They still regarded the Irgun as terrorists even as they did the Stern Group and were prepared to assume the worst about them. Thus, when they heard a hysterical broadcast over the Arab radio reporting the slaughter of hundreds of Arab civilians at Deir Yassin, they did not dismiss it as enemy propaganda but gave it credibility by denouncing the "terrorists" for the "massacre" they had perpetrated. On the day after the battle, David Shaltiel, who had officially endorsed the operation as important for Haganah's own strategy, hastened to dissociate Haganah from the capture of Deir Yassin and denied that he had ever viewed the village as an object of strategic value. The Jewish Agency and David Ben-Gurion, still cherishing hopes of coming to terms with King Abdullah, felt called upon to apologize to the world on behalf of the Jewish community, and hastily put out a statement expressing "horror and disgust" at the attack; on the following day they repeated the substance of this statement in a telegram to King Abdullah.

The charges of premeditated murder were augmented by accusations of looting, and atrocity stories diligently spread by Arab leaders frightened thousands of Palestine's Arabs into fleeing from their homes. Actually, the only loot amassed by the Irgun in Deir Yassin consisted of large amounts of weapons of various makes, including many British submachine guns which the British had taken from the Irgun and turned over to the Arabs. As for the mass flight of the Arabs, much of it had been abetted by Arab leaders calling on their people in Palestine to clear the way for the Arabs to throw the Jews into the sea, after which they would be able to return and take possession of the wealth the Jews would leave behind.

On the fifth anniversary of the capture of Deir Yassin, Yunes-Ahmed Assad, an Arab survivor of the battle, who had resettled in Jordan, gave a more balanced summation of the events at Deir Yassin, and it is interesting to note that his words were published in a Jordanian daily, *Al-Urdun:*

> The Jews never intended to harm the population of the village, but were forced to do so after they encountered fire from the population which killed the Irgun commander. The Arab exodus from other villages was not caused by the actual battle but by the exaggerated description spread by Arab leaders to incite them to fight the Jews.[10]

As for Begin, he ended his reply to Heren's "My Lai" analogy with the words:

> Whoever fought in a populated area and never caused, inadvertently, casualties among noncombatants, let him make his misleading analogies. Or let him admit that most of the battles, if not all of them, that he ordered or waged, were one chain of repeated massacres. No hypocrisy, please.

Not until 1969 did the Israeli Foreign Ministry issue a full factual report on what actually took place at Deir Yassin.[11]

Two weeks after the capture of Deir Yassin, the Irgun launched what was to be the largest military operation in its brief history. In the course of that operation, Begin was to make his first public appearance before the rank and file of the Irgun, and to have his first meeting with Yigael Yadin, the soldier-archeologist who was to play a key role in his political career thirty years later. This operation was the capture of Jaffa, today a part of Tel Aviv, but then an Arab city. For some time the Irgun had suspected that the Arabs, abetted by the British, were planning to use Jaffa as a base for an army to be sent to Jerusalem, cutting off the Negev, splitting the territory allotted to the Jews under the UN plan, and so putting an end to all hopes for a Jewish state even before that state could officially be brought into existence. In addition, Arab snipers had been active in Jaffa's Manshiyah Quarter for months, shooting at civilians in the all-Jewish city of Tel Aviv. As a consequence, Begin came to regard Jaffa in Arab hands as a direct threat to the survival of Tel Aviv itself.

On April 21, 1948, Begin met with the Irgun command and drew up plans to attack and occupy Jaffa with 600 men under the command of "Giddy" Paglin. The equipment — vehicles, Bren guns and ammunition — would be of British make, recently "confiscated" by Irgun raiding parties from a British army camp and a British military train. The men and the materiel were assembled at Camp Dov — named after Dov Gruner — in Ramat Gan, outside Tel Aviv. The date for the march on Jaffa was set for April 25, 1948.

At two o'clock in the morning of April 25, Begin arrived at the camp to address the men before they went to battle. Perhaps for the first time in his life, Begin admitted to suffering from stage fright. Most of the men he was about to address had never seen him before; to them, he had been only a name and a symbol. Besides, eight years had passed since he had last spoken in public. That speech had been in the main synagogue in Kovno to eulogize Vladimir Jabotinsky. Now he stood in the middle of a square formation of young men to send them off into a battle from which many of them might not return.

Begin's entire speech takes up just eleven lines of one page in his memoirs of the underground years. In it, he said all the things a commander ordinarily tells his men about the purpose of their battle, the nature of their enemy, and the importance of swiftness and valor. But he concluded it with a command to accord decent treatment to those Arab men who would surrender, and to all women and children in the city. Intellectually, he had accepted the civilian deaths at Deir Yassin as an inevitable consequence of warfare, but the memory still plagued him. "In battle, show no more mercy to the enemy than he shows mercy to our people," he said, "but spare women and children. Whoever raises his hands in surrender has saved his life. You will not harm him."[12]

Begin accompanied his men as far as Tel Aviv, where they set up headquarters in a dilapidated former school building. From there, Begin watched the men go off to fight, singing a battle song, and he offered a silent prayer for their victory and their safe return.

On May 13, after long and heavy fighting, Jaffa fell to the Jews and Haganah moved in to take over. Irgun yielded place to the Haganah troops, but insisted on an official receipt. Written on a page torn from the notebook of the Haganah commander, it read: "Received from Irgun Zvai Leumi: One Jaffa."

The Irgun's losses in the battle for Jaffa were 42 killed and 400 wounded, or one-third of the nearly 1,500 men who participated in the operation.[13]

It was during a critical point in the battle, when the Irgun was contemplating a temporary suspension of the operation, that Begin first met Yigael Yadin. Yadin, at the time head of Haganah's operational branch, and Israel Galili, the deputy commander in chief, conferred with Begin to discuss the continuation of the attack under the terms of the operational agreement between Haganah and Irgun. After the fall of Jaffa, Begin arranged a meeting between Yadin and Yadin's Irgun counterpart, "Giddy" Paglin. Begin recalls that the two young men took an instant liking to each other. "He knows what he wants and is full of energy," Paglin said. "He is like one of us."

In the meantime, May 15 was approaching, the day when Britain was to withdraw from Palestine and leave it to the Arabs and the Jews. As early as April 6, 1948, the Zionist General Council, convened in Tel Aviv by the Jewish Agency, had set up a provisional government — a cabinet of 13 members and a council of state of 37. The office of prime minister and minister of defense was assumed by Ben-Gurion. By early May, the Jewish community, preparing for the departure of the British, had taken over many of the administrative functions formerly carried out by the British authorities. But one important question remained: Would the provisional government proclaim an independent Jewish state when the time came for the British to leave, or would it make the fate of Jewish Palestine subject to a temporary United Nations trusteeship? The latter alternative had been advocated on March 19 at the UN General Assembly by the United States, which had become apprehensive at the possibility that it might have to send troops to Palestine to help enforce the partition plan once the British had gone. In fact, as the weeks went by, the U.S. Department of State under Secretary George C. Marshall had brought considerable pressure to bear on the Jewish authorities in Palestine, urging them to accept a truce under which neither the Arabs or the Jews would proclaim their state but each would preserve peace in the areas under their control until a permanent settlement could be worked out. Moshe Shertok (Sharett), head of the Jewish Agency's political department, had been disturbed by warnings from the United States that if the Jews would declare their independence, they would not be able to count on American assistance against their enemies. Secretary Marshall told Shertok he did not think a Jewish state would be able to withstand an invasion from neighboring Arab states. Shertok was also impressively warned that, by becoming involved in a war with the Arab states, the Jews of Palestine might trigger off a third world war, and it was even hinted that if the Jews insisted on going ahead with their state despite American misgivings, the United States might place an embargo on funds sent to Palestine by American Jewish individuals and organizations.

Begin was becoming increasingly worried, and impatient with the Jewish Agency's indecision. Early in May, he wrote that if the Jewish provisional government were to proclaim the independent Jewish state on schedule, the entire Jewish people, including his own followers, would "rally and fight shoulder to shoulder for our country and people." But if, instead, "a declaration of shameful surrender is published, if the leadership succumbs to the tactics of the enemy and Hebrew independence is destroyed before it comes to life — we shall rebel. There will be no surrender except by 'Vichy' leaders. The Hebrew government will certainly be established."[14]

Begin was gratified to learn that, unlike the cautious Shertok, Ben-Gurion, the acting prime minister, was among those leaders who favored the proclamation of Jewish independence despite the Arab menace and American preachments of "gloom and doom." The advocates of independence on May 15 believed that if the Jewish state were not officially announced on the day the British left Palestine, it might not materialize for years to come, if indeed it ever would.

Ben-Gurion's reaction to the Irgun's demands for independence was to send one of his trusted lieutenants, the writer Eliezer (Liebenstein) Livneh, who was then editor of *Eshnav*, Haganah's underground weekly, to call on Begin. Livneh began the conversation by conveying Ben-Gurion's appreciation for Begin's efforts; the Irgun's pressures for the proclamation of the state, he said, were most helpful to Ben-Gurion in overcoming opposition from various dovish quarters. However, Livneh suggested that in future statements in the Irgun paper *Herut* and elsewhere, Begin emphasize the positive point, namely, the Irgun's pledge of full support to the government of the Jewish state, rather than what the Irgun would feel called upon to do if the Jewish Agency waffled before Arab threats and American pressures.

A few days after the talk with Livneh, Begin published a new statement:

> The Hebrew government will certainly arise. There is no "perhaps." It will arise. If the official leaders set it up, *we shall support it with all our strength.*

Still, he insisted on adding this note of warning:

> But if they surrender to threats or allow themselves to be cajoled, our strength and that of the majority of the fighting youth will be behind the free Government which will arise from the depths of the underground and which will lead the people to victory in the war for freedom.[15]

Begin had no plans for setting up a rival government, but the Irgun made preparations for unilateral action just in case Ben-Gurion should have a change of heart, succumb to pressures and defer independence after all. Since May 15 fell on a Sabbath that year, the proclamation would have to be made the day before, Friday, May 14. If it was obvious that no proclamation would be forthcoming from Ben-Gurion, the Irgun would declare the Jewish state on its own in Jerusalem, at the Edison Cinema, then the largest motion picture theater in the country.

As things turned out, the Irgun did not need to take matters into its own hands. On May 12, 1948, ten of the thirteen leaders who comprised the provisional cabinet (three were unable to attend, two because they could not leave Jerusalem and one because he was in the United States) met and, by a vote of 6 to 4, decided to proclaim the Jewish state on schedule.

Haganah sent an emissary to notify Begin of the decision. Begin told the Haganah man that he and the Irgun would give their unqualified support to the government of the new Jewish state, no matter who its members were. At the same time, Begin made no attempt to minimize the seriousness of the military situation. "If the Jewish Government is proclaimed on Friday, May 14," he told his visitor, "the first enemy planes will be over Tel Aviv on Saturday morning."

At four o'clock in the afternoon of Friday, May 14, the members of the provisional council of state met in special session at the Tel Aviv Museum. Standing under a huge portrait of Theodor Herzl, David Ben-Gurion read aloud the declaration of independence proclaiming the Jewish state. In a quavering voice, Rabbi Judah L. Fishman (Maimon) recited a blessing of thanksgiving. Then one by one, the members of the council stepped up to the platform to sign the document. No representatives of the Irgun had been invited to sign the declaration, or to attend the ceremony.

The next day, Saturday, May 15, was a quiet Sabbath for the Begins. The whole family — including the latest addition, a second daughter, Leah, born several months earlier — emerged from the apartment on Rosenbaum Street to visit Doris Katz, whose husband, Shmuel, was then in France on Irgun business. Actually, this was not the first time that the Begins had left their hideout in broad daylight. For some months now, on the urging of Doris, who had been concerned about Begin's pallor, which she attributed to lack of outdoor exercise, they had been taking regular Sabbath walks on the banks of the Yarkon River. But this was the first Sabbath when such excursions no longer carried any risk of arrest or worse.

In the afternoon, Doris and the Begins went out together to visit other friends, the wife and two children of Yaakov Meridor, Begin's deputy commander who had been arrested by the British and deported to Kenya. Meridor had escaped from the British internment camp and had been in Paris for a month now. Suddenly the older of the Meridor children, 11-year-old Rachel, walked to the window. "Mother! There's Father!" she said. It was indeed Yaakov Meridor, and with him was Shmuel Katz. Both of them had arrived home in time to celebrate the birth of the new Jewish state.

That night, after the appearance of three stars in the sky had signaled the end of the Sabbath, Begin and a few close associates walked through the dark streets of Tel Aviv to the house in the heart of the city where the Irgun kept its secret radio transmitter in a crowded little room. There, in the stifling heat, Menahem Begin went on the air at 8:30 sharp; it was his first broadcast in all the four years that he had been the Irgun's commander. It was a long speech, but its most important point could be summed up in a few short sentences: Begin would not cease to hope and work for the establishment of a Jewish homeland in all — not just part — of Palestine. However, he declared himself ready to carry out what he had consistently pledged to do once there was a Jewish state: he would initiate steps to disband the Irgun and have its active members inducted into the official army of the State of Israel. The "Hebrew underground" was no longer needed. Begin and the Irgun would accept the authority of the provisional government of the State of Israel.

> The Irgun Z'vai Leumi is now leaving the underground within the borders of the independent Hebrew state. We went down underground — or better, we went *up* underground — under a foreign regime of oppression, to beat it and to liquidate it. And we beat it. We beat it good and destroyed it forever. Now we have Hebrew rule, [even if] for the time being it is only in part of our homeland. In this part of our homeland . . . there is no [longer any] need for a Hebrew underground. In the State of Israel, we shall be soldiers and builders. We shall abide by its laws, for they are our laws. We shall respect its government, for it is our government.[16]

He urged the Ben-Gurion government to remain firm against political and military pressures designed to shrink the boundaries of the Jewish state even further. Appeasement could buy only one kind of peace, "the peace of the graveyard, the peace of Treblinka." As he had in his proclamation of revolt four years earlier, Begin now ended his salute to the newly-created State of Israel with an appeal to Divine aid:

> O God of Israel, keep Thy soldiers and bless their sword which gives a new birth to the covenant that Thou hast sealed with Thy beloved people and Thy chosen land. Forward to the battleground! Forward to victory![17]

Some of the jurists and political leaders who, under Ben-Gurion's guidance, had helped compose the text of Israel's declaration of independence had similarly wanted to end their document on a religious note. But they had met with resistance; an agnostic in the group had pressed for the elimination of the phrase "with trust in the Almighty" from the final paragraph. In the end, the framers of the declaration had reached a compromise; the Hebrew text contains a reference to *Tzur Yisrael,* "the Rock of Israel," a term vague enough to satisfy everyone.

The sword and the battleground of which Begin had spoken materialized almost immediately after the ceremony at the Tel Aviv

Museum. The member nations of the Arab League declared war on the State of Israel. Egyptian planes dropped bombs on Tel Aviv, and Egyptian troops crossed Israel's borders from the south. The armies of Syria, Iraq and Lebanon marched into Israeli territory from the north, while the Arab Legion of Transjordan (the Hashemite Kingdom of Jordan) moved swiftly to annex all the land originally allotted for the new Arab state in Palestine, and prepared to overrun the new Jewish state as well.

After he had finished his broadcast, and his friends had locked up the "radio station," Begin went out into the night. The streets of Tel Aviv were empty and blacked out; early that morning, three British-made Egyptian planes had swooped low over the city and discharged their load of bombs. It was now close to midnight, and the two days just past had left Begin emotionally spent. But his day was not yet over. He still had an appointment that night with Israel Galili and two other representatives of Haganah. This midnight meeting had been arranged at Begin's request to discuss certain developments that were taking place at a seaport on the southern coast of France. It was the beginning of a chain of events which, a month later, led to what Begin had sought so desperately and consistently to prevent: Jews shooting not at their enemies, but at one another.

11. Failures in Communication: The Tragedy of the S.S. *Altalena*

To this day in Israel the mention of the S.S. *Altalena* in a speech at the Knesset or in the course of casual reminiscences among friends in a living room is enough to turn a calm exchange into a heated debate.

The basic facts about the tragedy of the S.S. *Altalena* are these: On June 20, 1948, a month after the establishment of the State of Israel and during the first Arab-Israeli truce imposed by the United Nations in Israel's War of Independence, the *Altalena,* a 4,000-ton tank landing craft purchased and manned by the Irgun and its friends, approached the shores of Tel Aviv. She carried 900 Irgun-recruited trained volunteer fighters from Europe along with a cargo of arms and ammunition sufficient to equip several thousand fighting men. When the boat landed and began discharging its passengers and weapons, it was attacked and sunk by units of Tzahal (*Tz'va Haganah L'Yisrael*), Israel's newly organized official army, direct successor of Haganah. The battle between the Irgunists and the Tzahal men resulted not only in the loss of weapons desperately needed by Israel's underequipped fighting forces but also in human casualties. Fourteen Irgunists and two Tzahal men were killed, and 69 Irgunists and six Tzahal men wounded.[1] Perhaps for the first time since the Roman siege of Jerusalem, Jewish fighting men spent precious time and strength battling each other instead of standing united against enemies seeking to put an end to Jewish independence.

Beyond that, the explanations of what happened, and why, diverge. For almost 30 years, the world at large had tended to accept without much questioning the official account given by Ben-Gurion and his associates and subsequently picked up by the world press. According to that version, the boat with its weapons and volunteers had been brought to Israel without the knowledge of the provisional government and in direct violation of the UN truce, which forbade the introduction of new weapons and military personnel into the war zone. Ben-Gurion, the prime minister, and Israel Galili, who was then acting as deputy minister of defense, assumed that the landing of the *Altalena* with its volunteers and armaments was part of a conspiracy by the Irgun "dissidents" to topple the government and to seize power for themselves. In order to prevent a breach of the truce and to make it clear to the "terrorists" that the government would not tolerate any infringement on its authority, Ben-Gurion demanded that the boat and its contents should be turned over to the government and placed under the control of the United Nations. The Irgun, however, had not only rejected the government's ultimatum, but had opened fire on the lawfully constituted army of the State of Israel. Finally, in order to avert reprisals from the UN and to save the country from anarchy, the government felt it had no other alternative but to sink the ship. During the election campaign of 1977, Begin's opponents would trot out the *Altalena* story to show that at one time Begin had been willing to start a civil war in order to become the leader of the Jewish state.

Begin's version of the story differs radically from the "official" Ben-Gurion-Galili account. According to Begin and his associates, the provisional government, through Deputy Minister of Defense Israel Galili and others, had been told about the *Altalena* — and her contents — long before she had set sail from her port in southern France. This had been the purpose of Begin's clandestine meeting with Galili in the small hours of the night between May 15 and 16. Following the Arab-Israeli truce, Begin had attempted to keep the boat from sailing; unable to do so, he had immediately informed the government of the boat's departure and its impending arrival in Israel. He did not agree with the foreign policy of the provisional government, and he viewed the truce with distaste, but, having accepted the provisional government as the supreme authority in the State of Israel, he would not take the law into his own hands. As for the reaction of the government to the news about the *Altalena*, Begin says that at no time in his negotiations with Galili and other representatives of the provisional government prior to the ship's arrival had he been given reason to believe anything else but that the government — notwithstanding the UN truce — had approved the landing of the boat with its arms and volunteers. The government had even promised to help in the unloading and distribution of the weapons. The government's ultimatum, delivered after the *Altalena* had landed, and then Tzahal's armed attack on the boat, came to

Begin as such a profound emotional shock that, for months and even years thereafter, he was incapable of attempting a coherent interpretation of what had caused Ben-Gurion to make a turnabout and give the order to attack and sink the *Altalena*. Eleven years later, Begin was to confront Prime Minister Ben-Gurion on the floor of the Knesset and call on him to admit that, in fact, the *Altalena* had come to Israel with the full knowledge and consent of the government. Ben-Gurion refused to enter into a debate with him and all but cut him off. Some who reject Ben-Gurion's account have suggested that he had indeed originally authorized the landing but had suddenly experienced a change of heart because it had dawned upon him — or else one or more of his associates had led him to believe — that Begin might use the volunteers and the weapons aboard the boat to start an Irgun revolt against the Labor Zionist-controlled government. Others, less sympathetic to Ben-Gurion, say he could not have been so utterly irresolute or gullible. They maintain that Ben-Gurion's actions had been part of a carefully orchestrated plan. Ben-Gurion, disturbed by the growing popularity of Begin and the Irgun among Israelis, had only pretended to approve the landing in order to lure Begin and the Irgun into a trap and provoke a shootout. Begin and his men would then stand exposed before Jewish and international public opinion as irresponsible, dangerous firebrands. If anyone were to cast doubt on Ben-Gurion's story that the *Altalena* had sailed without his knowledge and authorization, it would be the word of David Ben-Gurion, former chairman of the universally respected Jewish Agency Executive and now the acknowledged leader of the Jewish state, against that of Menahem Begin, the leader of dissidents who had always been outside the world Zionist organizational framework and who had already shown their lack of responsibility and statesmanship by their actions at the King David Hotel and in Deir Yassin.

Now, thirty years later, historians are attempting to reconstruct the sequence of events which, in fact, began almost a year before the establishment of the Jewish state and ended with gunfire on the seashore of midtown Tel Aviv on June 22, 1948.

The S.S. *Altalena* had been bought in the spring of 1947 from American World War II surplus stock by the Hebrew Committee for National Liberation, one of the activist organizations that had been formed in the United States with the help of such Irgun emissaries as Hillel Kook and Arye Ben Eliezer. The boat was renamed *Altalena*, after the pseudonym used by Vladimir Jabotinsky in his early writings.[2] Originally, the boat had been set aside for a large transport of immigrants, because it could have accommodated more than 5,000 passengers without luggage. But now that the Jewish state was fighting for its very survival against its Arab neighbors, it was decided that the boat should transport to Israel able-bodied volunteers from all over Europe to augment Israel's fighting forces, along with weapons which the French government had promised as a gift, without strings attached, to the Irgun representatives in Paris. The crew of the boat was to be made up of Jewish volunteers from the United States under the command of Monroe Fein of Chicago, who had served as a naval officer in the Pacific during World War II. Fein's services had been procured in the United States by the veteran Revisionist Abraham Stavsky, who had settled in the United States and was operating a shipping company from New York. The volunteers aboard the boat were to be under the command of Eliahu Lankin, who, it will be remembered, had been a member of the Irgun command in Palestine until his arrest by the British. He had been deported to Africa, but, like Arye Ben Eliezer, had escaped and reached Paris. There, both men had become part of the "diaspora command" set up by the Irgun for the recruitment of volunteers and the procurement of military supplies in Europe. Another officer aboard the *Altalena* was Palestine-born Yitzhak "Mike" Ben-Ami, who had been among the Irgun emissaries in the United States. His function was to be that of chief political officer, responsible for conducting whatever negotiations might be required on the *Altalena*'s behalf with international factors, meaning the United Nations. As things turned out, Ben-Ami's services as negotiator were never used. Stavsky was also to be aboard; after many years in America, he wanted to go home to Israel.

Early in May, 1948, the *Altalena* moved to an anchorage off the coast of southern France to wait for the arrival of the Irgun fighters and the French arms she was to take to Israel. However, the boat was not yet able to leave port, because funds for such essential things as fuel and for the purchase of weapons to supplement the French arms were not available. Had it not been for that difficulty, the boat would have been ready to sail much earlier in the war, and the story might have had a happier ending. The postponement of the sailing due to lack of funds helped set the stage for the tragedy which befell the S.S. *Altalena*.

When Begin learned of the financial problems that were keeping the *Altalena* in France, he sought the aid of Israel's provisional government, because the men and the arms to be brought in by the *Altalena* would benefit the army of the Jewish state about to be formed. Hence the meeting between Begin and Galili on the Saturday night following the establishment of the State of Israel. The conference took place at the Freud Hospital, a small health clinic near Tel Aviv, which the Irgun had been using as its headquarters. Begin was accompanied by Shmuel Katz, chief of staff Hayim Landau, and Yaakov Meridor. Galili, the provisional deputy minister of defense,[3] had brought with him two other men who, like himself, had been leaders in Haganah: David Hacohen, a liaison officer with the Ministry of Defense, and Levi Shkolnik, Haganah's chief financial administrator and one of its arms procurement specialists, who was going to be named director general of the Ministry of Defense. This was Begin's first official meeting with the man who, as Levi Eshkol, would succeed David Ben-Gurion as prime minister of Israel fifteen years hence.

Begin informed the three Haganah leaders of the *Altalena*'s existence and proposed that the provisional government, of which Galili was a member, should supplement the Irgun's funds to permit the purchase of additional arms and to pay all the other expenses which had to be met before the boat could sail. Shmuel Katz recalls that the amount of financial assistance Begin requested was about $250,000.[4] As for the volunteers aboard, Begin pointed out, they, like the weapons, would become part of the official army which would be created by the government to succeed Haganah. Galili and his two colleagues were also informed that Haganah could place aboard the boat an additional 2-3,000 men of its own[5] (Haganah, too, had been active in postwar Europe, gathering recruits and training them for military service in Israel) along with whatever weapons Haganah might purchase in Europe with Jewish Agency funds. Once the *Altalena* reached Israel, the Irgun would present the boat, which was in good condition, as a gift to the provisional government. Katz remembers, too, that his group informed Galili of negotiations which the Irgun had been conducting in Canada for airplanes, and offered to hand those planes over to the government as soon as they arrived in Israel.[6] Galili promised to relay the Irgun's proposals to Ben-Gurion, who, as already noted, was not only prime minister but also minister of defense in the provisional government. (Hence, Galili, as deputy minister of defense, reported directly to Ben-Gurion.)

On Monday, May 17, Landau received discouraging news from Galili: Ben-Gurion wanted no part of the Irgun's proposals.

Begin's broadcast two days earlier, declaring his loyalty to the provisional government, had not been sufficiently convincing to overcome Ben-Gurion's deep-seated dislike and mistrust of the Irgun, which many Labor Zionists tended to regard not only as reactionary but also as somehow intellectually and morally inferior to the socialist elite. Probably, too, Ben-Gurion resented Begin's allusions in his broadcast to tendencies of appeasement on the part of the government. However, Galili gave no indication to Landau, or to Begin, that Ben-Gurion or the provisional government would take action to keep the Irgun ship from leaving France whenever it would be ready to do so, or from landing on Israel's shores.

At any rate, seeing that funds were forthcoming neither from the provisional government nor from Haganah, Katz flew back the very next day to his post in Paris, from where he continued his intensive efforts at fund raising and arms procurement.

On May 19, two days before the negative reply from Ben-Gurion, the French government informed the Irgun representatives in writing that it was now ready to release the promised weapons.

There was no doubt that Israel's defenders were urgently in need of every soldier and every piece of equipment they could get. The reports from the battlefront were not joyful. True, the Arab armies had not been able to overrun the Jewish state as they had boasted they would do within a matter of days, but they certainly had the edge on the Israelis in the fighting. In the north, Syrian forces had made some progress along the river Jordan. In the south, two Egyptian columns had been advancing in the Negev. The Egyptians had been repulsed at two villages on the way to Tel Aviv, but by the end of May, by-passing the villages on the route orginally mapped out, they had reached a point just north of Ashdod, 20 miles south of Tel Aviv. After heroic fighting, the Etzion bloc of kibbutzim in the Judean mountains between Hebron and Jerusalem fell to the Jordanian Arab Legion. (The Etzion bloc area was to remain in Jordanian hands until it was recaptured by Israeli forces during the Six-Day War of 1967). On May 28, the Arab Legion occupied the Old City of Jerusalem. Only after heavy fighting had the Egyptians been driven back from Kibbutz Ramat Rahel, the southern gateway to the rest of the Holy City.

Until the end of May, 1948 there still was, in effect, no official Israeli army. Haganah continued as before, taking orders from Ben-Gurion and the provisional government as it had done previously from the Jewish Agency under Ben-Gurion. The Irgun and the Stern Group still fought independently of the others. The

Irgun would go it alone until Ben-Gurion would establish a new non-political army to replace Haganah, which for so long had projected the image of an organization virtually controlled by the Labor Zionists.

Finally, on May 31, 1948, the provisional government issued an order creating the Israel Defense Forces — *Tz'va Haganah L'Yisrael*, or Tzahal. Now Begin set about his self-imposed task of disbanding the Irgun as an underground organization and integrating its fighting units into the newly-created Israeli army. Underground organizations do not usually dismantle themselves of their own accord, but Begin insisted on doing just that. From the very early days he had envisioned the eventual role of his "fighting family" in the new Jewish state not as perpetual revolutionaries but as law-abiding citizens, still continuing to fight for the ideals of Jabotinsky and Betar on which he, Begin, had reorganized the Irgun in 1944, but doing so in a legitimate, democratic manner — as a political party, perhaps — within the framework of a democratic system of government.

However, the integration of the Irgun into Tzahal could not be completed by fiat from one day to the next. Though many Irgun fighters were inducted directly into Tzahal units containing former Irgunists as well as ex-Haganah men, many other Irgun people were reluctant to give up their separate organizational identity. Especially those who had undergone the experience of being interrogated by Haganah or turned over to the British by Haganah informers during the "open season" were understandably loth to entrust themselves entirely to the command of former Haganah officers. There was resentment on both sides; stories were circulating of Irgun men on the battle lines turning to Haganah units for arms or reinforcements only to be met with insults and obscenities.[7]

It seemed that the higher-level Haganah commanders understood the problems involved in the transition, for on June 1, 1948 Haganah and Irgun signed an agreement whereby the changeover could be made gradually, over a period of weeks. Irgun people, if they so desired, were permitted to take the oath of allegiance and join the Israeli army as separate units, retaining their own middle-echelon officers and also their own weapons.

The newly-established Israel Defense Forces, it should be noted, did not extend their authority to the New City of Jerusalem, which the UN partition plan had left in a state of legal limbo, assigned neither to the Jews nor to the Arabs but theoretically envisioned as an international city. There, Haganah (under the command of David Shaltiel), the Irgun (under Mordecai Raanan) and the Sternists continued to maintain themselves as separate units, cut off from the rest of the country, cooperating whenever possible but preserving their organizational independence.

These complex Tzahal-Haganah-Irgun-Sternist relationships were to be a dominant factor — if not *the* dominant factor — in the fate of the S.S. *Altalena*.

The day after the signing of the agreement between the Irgun and Haganah brought an added though not unexpected complication. On June 2, the provisional government of the State of Israel and the governments of the Arab states both announced their acceptance of a 28-day truce imposed by the United Nations Security Council, to take effect on Friday, June 11. For the duration of the truce, neither side was to import volunteers or armaments into the war areas. This provision was intended to maintain the *status quo* between the two fighting sides, but in fact it worked only to discomfit the Israelis. It did not prevent the landing of British weapons in Transjordan (the Hashemite Kingdom of Jordan), Iraq or Egypt, whose seaports were properly remote from the fighting zones. The only effective check on the import of arms and men was from the Mediterranean Sea to the Jewish forces in Israel.

On Tuesday, June 8, French army trucks, driven and manned by French soldiers, arrived at the port of Sète, where the *Altalena* had been riding at anchor. It was the same port from which the ill-fated S.S. *Exodus* had set sail the year before. At the dock, the French soldiers proceeded to unload the trucks. Though the Irgun representatives had specified the kinds and quantities of supplies they wanted they had no way of knowing whether they would actually receive everything they had requested until they had checked the deliveries at the pier. Yitzhak Ben-Ami recalls the thrill and awed surprise he and his friends felt as they watched first the long procession of trucks moving toward the pier and then the seemingly endless succession of crates and cases being transferred from the trucks onto the dock. The shipment included 5,000 rifles, 300 Bren guns, 150 Spandaus, five caterpillar-track armored cars, four million rounds of ammunition, several thousand bombs, and miscellaneous other military supplies.[8] At two o'clock the next morning, stevedores started to move the precious cargo from the pier onto the boat. And then trouble came: one of the shipping cases broke open, revealing its contents. The stevedores, many of whom were Algerians and hostile to the State of Israel, were furious and promptly went on strike.

Now that, through the strike, the nature of her cargo had become a matter of public knowledge, it was essential that the *Altalena* should leave port as quickly and quietly as possible. Fein, Lankin and the others feared the possibility of Arab sabotage. Dr. Shmuel Ariel, the chief political representative of the Irgun in France, hastily rounded up Irgun volunteers and French soldiers from the area to complete the loading at top speed. By noon on Friday, June 11 — the day the truce was to come into force — all the weapons were aboard the boat. The 900 volunteers were brought to the pier in trucks from the two camps nearby where they had been waiting for orders to board the ship. At 8:30 that evening, the *Altalena* finally set sail. Her destination, in accordance with instructions from Israel, was a beach at the foot of Frishman Street, in midtown Tel Aviv.

Oddly, it seems that no one had thought of informing Begin — who, after all, was the Irgun's commander — that the boat was about to sail. Begin, who originally had been eager for the *Altalena* to move as soon as possible, was in fact relieved at having no further news from her. He assumed this meant she was still waiting in port, and it was just as good she was still there, because her arrival in Israel with her cargo of weapons and volunteers once the truce had become operative could cause real trouble. He did not know of the broken case that had given away the secret of the *Altalena*'s cargo and had made it, in effect, impossible for the *Altalena* not to sail.

The first word Begin received that the boat had sailed was not from the *Altalena* herself but from a BBC news report late in the evening of June 11. That report was followed by an announcement that the Arab-Israeli truce had begun, and that its terms included agreement by both parties not to import additional troops or weapons into the fighting zone while the truce lasted.

Begin was stunned. "Whatever our attitude to the truce might be," he wrote, "we were not entitled to bear the responsibility for the possible consequences of a breach . . . This was no longer an underground partisan-political fight. This was a fight in the open field and the consequences of defeat might be destruction for our people."[9] He clung to the hope that perhaps the *Altalena* had not yet sailed after all, that the BBC report had been only a British hoax, designed to alert United Nations truce observers and frighten the ship's crew into remaining in port. He therefore cabled to Katz at Irgun headquarters in Paris: "Don't send the boat. Await instructions." Katz received the cable the next day, Saturday, June 12, and attempted to make radio contact with the *Altalena,* but was unable to do so. He then cabled to Begin in Tel Aviv that the *Altalena* had left and that Begin should try to communicate with her directly. From the Irgun radio station, Begin had the secretary of the Irgun office radio the boat: "Keep away. Await instructions." Aboard the *Altalena*, Eliahu Lankin, commander of the 900 volunteers, heard a faint, garbled message and recognized the voice just before the transmission faded out. Monroe Fein, the captain of the boat, tried to acknowledge the message and ask Tel Aviv to repeat the instructions, but nothing more came through except static.

In the meantime, Begin in Tel Aviv, not knowing whether the *Altalena* had received his message, contacted Galili and requested an urgent meeting at the Freud Hospital. At this meeting Galili once again had with him Hacohen and Shkolnik. Also present was a new face, a Defense Ministry official named Pinhas Vaze.[10] Begin told the four men that the *Altalena,* which he had discussed with them a month earlier, had sailed from France and would arrive in Israel in five days' time. He also informed Galili and his colleagues of the exact number of volunteers and the quantity of arms aboard — the 900 volunteers, each with a clean bill of health certified by the Irgun's physician in Paris, and the weapons, which were enough to equip ten battalions. When Galili and the others heard these details, they were thunderstruck. Not in all the years of its existence had Haganah been able to amass the quantities of weapons which the Irgun had apparently managed to obtain for that one shipment. For some moments, no one spoke. Then Begin broke the silence. "But there is the problem of the truce," he began. He did not want to take upon himself the responsibility for breaking the truce terms. "You, gentlemen, are the representatives of the government," he said. "It is you, not I, who must decide whether, under the circumstances, the boat should be permitted to come here, or whether she should be diverted."

Galili made a quick assessment of the situation as he saw it. On the one hand, the weapons about to arrive could be a godsend for the hard-pressed Israeli forces; therefore, he felt he had no right simply to refuse them. On the other hand, he was unable to set aside his suspicions about the Irgun's motives. What if the Irgun were to use these weapons, and the volunteers, not against the enemy but in a *putsch* against the provisional government?

Galili stalled for time. "Get in touch with the *Altalena*'s captain," he said to Begin, "and tell him to slow down a little while we figure things out." Immediately after the meeting, he gave Ben-Gurion a report of what he had heard.

On Tuesday, Galili and Shkolnik informed Begin and his colleagues that the government had come to a decision. Despite the truce, the *Altalena* was to proceed to Israel as quickly as possible. Ben-Gurion had told Galili and his staff to work out the details of the landing of the ship, the unloading of its cargo, and the distribution of the weapons.

Begin was delighted. The weapons aboard the *Altalena* were badly needed. For instance, a large part of Tzahal's meager equipment had been put out of action for lack of the proper type of British-made ammunition; an ample supply of that ammunition was now in the hold of the *Altalena*. Also, Begin was relieved that the government had reacted as he hoped it would. The provisions of the truce had turned out to be clearly one-sided in favor of the Arabs; the Arabs kept receiving supplies by devious routes beyond the eyes of UN observers, while the Israelis, with the minuscule size and geographic position of their country, plus their political isolation, had no recourse to such help. Accordingly, Begin did not view an Israeli violation of the truce as a question of ethics, as he had, for example, the question of his leaving the Polish army without an official discharge. But Israel now had a legitimate government which had the ultimate authority to decide questions of war, peace or truce. Israel could not afford the luxury of an underground movement, a private army working at cross-purposes with that government. Consequently, if the government had ordered Begin to stop the *Altalena*, he would have done so. Now he was gratified that the government had apparently understood the needs of the army as he had seen them, and that it had taken upon itself the responsibility for circumventing the terms of the truce. Begin now sent a new order to the *Altalena:* "Full speed ahead."

In Paris, an overjoyed Arye Ben Eliezer said to Shmuel Katz: "There are now no internal problems. Galili has promised that Haganah will send trucks to help us unload the ship as quickly as possible so as to reduce to a minimum its exposure to possible UN intervention."[11]

In Tel Aviv, Begin believed that everything about the *Altalena* had been settled in principle except the manner in which the arms aboard the *Altalena* should be allocated to the Israeli fighting units. In view of what had appeared to be Galili's cooperative attitude, he was convinced that these details, too, would be agreed upon with dispatch.

Initially, Begin's plan had been that 20 per cent of the weapons aboard the *Altalena* should be turned over to the Irgun unit in Jerusalem, which was seriously short of materiel and which, as already noted, had retained its independence even as had its Haganah and Sternist counterparts in the isolated city. The remaining 80 per cent were to go to the Irgun units on all fronts which had joined Tzahal but which Begin believed were being discriminated against by former Haganah officers when it came to the distribution of needed weapons.

To Begin's pained surprise, Galili seemed to agree that 20 per cent of the weapons should go to the Irgun contingent in Jerusalem but refused to entertain the notion that the other 80 per cent should go only to Tzahal units composed of ex-Irgunists. Begin could not understand Galili's attitude.

Had the boat come several weeks earlier, as the Irgun had planned, he said to Galili, the Irgun would have had all the arms, because then there had been only Haganah, and not an official Israeli army to which the Irgun would have felt in any way subordinate. "Wouldn't you agree that our boys should come into the Army at least fully armed and equipped?" Begin continued. "You yourself demanded that in view of the gravity of the situation all arms and equipment in the possession of the Irgun should be issued to the Irgun boys who were going into the Army. What has changed? These particular arms were merely late in arriving. Our boys are already in the Army or will be within a matter of days. It would only mean that they will be mobilized with the full equipment which we in any case would have given them. What is wrong with that? Why can't you agree?"[12]

The reason why Galili could not agree was that the men who claimed Irgun identity now numbered not hundreds, but thousands. True, the Irgun people had taken the oath of allegiance to Tzahal, but Galili, along with Ben-Gurion, feared that if they would be allowed control of the weapons, they would pose a threat to the unity of the army and to the survival of the government. But Galili did not communicate these apprehensions to Begin.

Hearing of Begin's talk with Galili, Hillel Kook, who had returned to Israel after having served with the Irgun mission in the United States, advised Begin not to insist on the 80 per cent. "If you do, it might provide Tzahal [meaning the ex-Haganah leaders now holding similar positions in Tzahal] with an excuse later on to discriminate against Irgun men under their command. Keep the 20 per cent for the Irgun boys who are on their own in Jerusalem, but let the other 80 per cent go to Tzahal for distribution wherever they are needed — with no strings attached."

Kook's argument convinced Begin, Landau and Meridor that the demand for the 80 per cent should be withdrawn. According to one report, however, Begin suggested that each Tzahal unit receiving the weapons should be addressed by a former Irgun man, who would tell the soldiers that the arms had come to them by courtesy of the Irgun.[13] Begin wanted to make sure that the rank and file of Israel's new army would know about this final accomplishment before the Irgun became a thing of the past.

Begin once again contacted Galili and informed him that he was now willing to forego the 80 per cent and would be satisfied as long as 20 per cent would be sent to the Irgun contingent isolated in Jerusalem. Galili replied that this could be worked out; 20 per cent, he said to Begin could "go to Jerusalem." He said nothing about the Irgun but Begin took it for granted that Galili meant the Irgun unit in Jerusalem. Begin did not insist on having Galili "dot his i's" or put the agreement into writing. This was not typical of Begin, but Begin subsequently pointed out that he and the Irgun had not suspected the government of any hidden motives because the Irgun for its part had been straightforward about its own intentions. This failure in communications on both sides was the next act in the *Altalena* tragedy. The fact was that Galili and Ben-Gurion had already decided between themselves that the 20 per cent should not go to the Irgun but to the Haganah detachment which was also holding out in Jerusalem.

Begin's next meeting was with Pinhas Vaze from the Ministry of Defense to decide on the place where the *Altalena* should land. Vaze said that the boat could not very well land anywhere off Tel Aviv, where it would obviously attract the unwanted attention of UN observers. Rather, said Vaze, the *Altalena* should dock at Kfar Vitkin, an agricultural settlement just to the north, near Natanya, where she would be able to discharge her cargo with a minimum risk of detection. When Lankin aboard the ship received Begin's radioed instructions to head for Kfar Vitkin, he was more than pleased. He explained to Monroe Fein, the American, that Kfar Vitkin was a stronghold of Labor Zionists, loyal to Ben-Gurion and frankly opposed to the Irgun, Hence, if the government had chosen Kfar Vitkin as the landing site for the *Altalena,* it must mean that the government had agreed to cooperate fully with the Irgun in the landing and unloading of the boat. "All our troubles are over," Lankin exulted. Fein, the former naval officer, was not quite so optimistic. He was worried, not so much about possible lack of cooperation — or outright opposition — from the provisional government as he was concerned about the chances of being detected and bombed from the air by enemy planes. He therefore mounted 22 guns and 30 machine guns as anti-aircraft weapons and trained the volunteers to use them in case the need arose.[14] Ben-Ami, the chief political officer, still recalls how he watched the proceedings with trepidation, fearful that the recruits would be unable to manage the machine guns and fire the bullets into each other instead of into the sea. For the rest, Ben-Ami remembers that the journey to Israel had many aspects of a pleasant Mediterranean cruise. The weather was fine, the sea calm, and the men were in excellent spirits.[15]

Meanwhile, in Tel Aviv, the talks between Begin and Vaze continued. Vaze had one more stipulation to make in the name of the government. After the arms had been unloaded at Kfar Vitkin, they were to be placed into government warehouses. Begin agreed, but asked that while the arms were in the warehouses, they should be guarded jointly by regular Tzahal men and ex-Irgunists who had joined Tzahal.

Vaze then telephoned Galili and arranged for another meeting between Galili and Begin, this time not at an Irgun site but at Tzahal headquarters in the garden city of Ramat Gan, just outside Tel Aviv. At that meeting, Galili struck the first note of alarm for Begin. He conveyed to him a blunt warning directly from Ben-Gurion: Begin and his associates would have to comply with all the government's terms relevant to the landing and unloading of the *Altalena*, or else they would have to "bear full responsibility for the consequences, and the responsibility would be very heavy indeed." Then came Galili's parting shot. Unless Begin changed his mind, Galili said in the name of Ben-Gurion, "we will wash our hands of unloading the arms."[16]

Begin was relieved. The talk about "responsibility for the consequences" had taken him by surprise and worried him. But if the sole "consequence" of his failure to agree to the government's terms would be that the Irgun would have no help from the government in unloading the weapons, that problem could be overcome. It might make things a little more difficult, but it would be no cause for concern. Also, as Begin later noted, Galili had said nothing about the government's not wishing the boat to land in Israel. So, apparently, despite Galili's strange statement, nothing had really changed and all would be well.

Hayim Landau, hearing of the conversation, did not even think Galili had been serious about the government's refusing to lend a hand in the unloading. He telephoned David Hacohen, the liaison officer, and requested him to arrange for help. The next day, Friday, June 18, Hacohen told Landau that Tzahal would indeed send trucks to Kfar Vitkin.

But Galili's words, though vague, had been in fact far more ominous than either Begin or Landau suspected at the time. The two Irgun leaders thought that if the worst came to the worst, there always would be Irgun men available to do the unloading. What they did not realize was that such an unsanctioned unloading operation was the very thing neither Galili nor Ben-Gurion would tolerate. The provisional government would regard the Irgun's going it alone as an act of defiance of government authority, requiring stern action on the part of the government. This, and not the work of unloading, was what Galili meant when he had spoken of Begin's bearing "full responsibility for the consequences." Here was yet another communications breakdown in the story of the *Altalena*.

Plans had called for the boat to arrive early Saturday evening and unload during the night. However, the *Altalena* did not come within sight of Kfar Vitkin until just before dawn on Sunday, June 20. Fein had had some difficulty pinpointing the small harbor because he had avoided moving too far north of Tel Aviv; he was unwilling to risk coming too close to the port of Haifa, where the UN had established an outpost.

The *Altalena* stopped about 40 yards from the two red lights at the end of the Kfar Vitkin pier, which extended about 100 yards from the shore. Begin had come to the pier to meet the ship. The arrival of the *Altalena* was to him a moment of high emotion, indeed, a historic occasion. To him, the landing of the boat with its arms and men aboard was a dramatic event, an appropriate finale as the Irgun prepared to pass into history. As he waited for the boat to land, Begin was somewhat taken aback to note that no government personnel had come to the shore to receive the men and the weapons from the ship.

Fein was unable to land his cargo at Kfar Vitkin that morning. At first, the sea was too rough for the recruits to be transferred to the shore; most of them had never made a sea voyage and were not swimmers. Also, the contingent aboard the ship included a sizable number of women. By the time the sea became calmer, it was already morning and, for obvious reasons, Lankin did not want to start unloading in broad daylight. The boat therefore pulled back out to sea, beyond the sight of United Nations observers, and waited until after dark Sunday evening to return.

On that Sunday afternoon, liaison officer David Hacohen called at Irgun headquarters at Freud Hospital, where he found Bezalel Amitzur, of the Irgun command. Amitzur informed him that the *Altalena* had arrived, but that the boat had come later than scheduled and that, therefore, the landing and the unloading would not take place until the evening. Hacohen repeated his promise that Tzahal would assist in the unloading of the weapons and that, if necessary, he personally would round up additional help from the vicinity. Begin even remembers a report that Hacohen had commented favorably on Lankin's decision to delay the operation until after dark. "Of course you're right," Hacohen had said. "I'll tell Israel about it."[17] "Israel" was Israel Galili.

The trucks promised by Hacohen never materialized; neither did Hacohen himself, nor Galili, nor any of the other government representatives who had been present at the meetings with Begin.

A little later that afternoon, Israel's provisional cabinet met in Tel Aviv to decide what to do about the *Altalena*. Moshe Shertok (Sharett), formerly head of the Jewish Agency's political department and now Israel's first foreign minister, summed up the situation. To Shertok, the important question was not whether the arrival of the *Altalena* had violated the Arab-Israeli truce. Rather, the issue was one of principle: The Irgun had not accepted the government's terms for the distribution of the weapons. Therefore, he explained, the government was not going to help in the unloading. But under the circumstances, could the Irgun be allowed to do the unloading on its own authority without reference to government approval? And if not, should force be used either to prevent the weapons from landing, or to seize them? Shertok suggested that 500 Tzahal men should be sent to Kfar Vitkin to disperse any Irgunists who might come to watch the unloading, and to arrest anyone getting off the boat. Among those present at the meeting was Yigael Yadin, formerly head of Haganah's operational branch and now chief operational officer of Tzahal, who had first met Begin during the battle for Jaffa and for whom the Irgun's chief of operations, "Giddy" Paglin, had expressed particular admiration. Now Yadin reported that he already had 600 men in the Kfar Vitkin area but that he did not know whether these soldiers would obey orders to use force against the Irgunists.

Ben-Gurion was all for using force. Whether and to what extent he had been informed about Begin's plans for the allocation of the weapons and for the induction of the 900 volunteers into Tzahal is still to this day a subject of allegation and counter-allegation. In any event, Ben-Gurion's mistrust of the Irgun was so strong that he was ready to imagine the most sinister motivations behind the coming of the *Altalena*. He already visualized the Irgun swelled by 900 new members and in complete control of the weapons from the *Altalena*. He pictured the underground organization, its popularity in Israel bolstered by the *Altalena* tour de force, not dissolving as Begin had promised but remaining as a dangerous rival of Tzahal and of the government, taking independent and drastic action to vitiate any agreement he, Ben-Gurion, might be able to make with the Arabs. Things could not be permitted to come to such a pass.

In the end, the cabinet gave the Tzahal command blanket authority to do whatever might be necessary at Kfar Vitkin. In effect, this meant that, in order to assert its authority, the provisional government was willing to risk the outbreak of civil war.

In the meantime, Galili had learned, probably through David Hacohen, that the *Altalena* was within reach of Kfar Vitkin. Galili immediately contacted Brigadier Dan Even (Epstein), commander of the Alexandroni Brigade and also of the Kfar Vitkin area. In his foreword to a history of his brigade, Even was to recall in detail the briefing Galili gave him on that Sunday, June 20, 1948, in the presence of Yigael Yadin. This briefing was altogether different from the government's subsequent allegations that it had not been given advance information about the existence, the contents and the purpose of the *Altalena*. "The Irgun Zvai Leumi," Even quotes Galili as telling him, "has brought a boat filled with arms and ammunition to the shore of Kfar Vitkin. We knew the arms were due to arrive and reached an agreement whereby we and they were to unload the arms together. The Irgun Zvai Leumi has broken the agreement. They did not inform us of the date of the boat's arrival nor where it was going to anchor."[18] To this day, no one has come forward to refute Even's account of what Galili had said to him.

It was on the basis of this briefing that Brigadier Even prepared an armed attack by Tzahal on the *Altalena* and the Irgun.

At nine o'clock on Sunday evening, the *Altalena* returned to the mooring position it had left in the early morning hours. Begin, who had been waiting on the beach all the time, boarded the boat and received an enthusiastic welcome from the passengers and crew. Within two hours, all but 50 of the 900 volunteers aboard the *Altalena* had been taken ashore by motor launch. Begin remembers seeing many of the young people jubilantly falling to their knees and kissing the cold, damp sand of the beach. Then they climbed aboard trucks which took them to a camp in Natanya for a rest. They did not take any weapons with them. The 50 who remained with the boat got to work helping the crew unload the weapons. Before long, Irgun sympathizers from the area were making their way in the dark to the beach, ready to lend a hand. The unloading continued all through the night. In his broadcast following the sinking of the *Altalena*, Begin said that about 15 men from Palmach, the shock troops of the Israel Defense Forces, turned up in a small boat and offered their services. Begin was surprised, for most of the Palmach's members were considerably to the left of Ben-Gurion. When he thanked the leader of the group, the Palmach officer replied, "I had no orders to do this, but my men and I are happy to assist you in this job."[19] The Palmach men worked for a while, then asked Lankin to give them a guided tour of the *Altalena,* and subsequently withdrew.

Some of the Irgunists who had come to the beach had noticed Tzahal troops setting up road blocks on the way, but they had not given the matter any further thought at the time. Also during the night, two boats had taken up positions not far from the *Altalena;* later, they were identified as corvettes of the fledgling Israeli navy.

Meanwhile, Monday, June 21 was dawning. It had become clear that the unloading was going to be a very slow process. If the work would go on only after dark, Begin feared, it might take as long as a week to complete, increasing the chances of detection by the Arabs or by United Nations observers. Begin therefore instructed "Giddy" Paglin to have the unloading continue throughout the day. Paglin, however, did not think this was safe. He had heard reports that the Tzahal had the beach surrounded and was closing in fast. He therefore radioed Begin aboard the ship, urging him to have all the people and arms already on the beach moved back to the *Altalena*.

Begin was shocked by Paglin's report, but he was more worried about the possibility of UN observers reaching the scene than he was about the Tzahal's maneuvers. He left the boat, stepped ashore and tried to persuade Paglin that the work would have to go on. When Paglin would not listen, Begin dismissed him and ordered Yaakov Meridor to take over. Paglin walked away from the beach and headed for the house of a friend in Natanya.

Before long, a Tzahal officer appeared on the beach. He walked up to Begin and handed him a note. It was an ultimatum signed by Brigadier Dan Even, demanding that all the weapons aboard the *Altalena* be turned over to Tzahal. If Begin refused, Tzahal, in the name of the government, would use force. Begin was given ten minutes to reply. Begin protested that such matters could not be decided within ten minutes. The officer withdrew.

Begin, now on the beach, gave Meridor permission to leave the area to contact leaders of the town councils of Kfar Vitkin and Natanya; these officials promised to intercede with the government. Meanwhile, Begin sent a messenger to Even with a request for an interview. In his broadcast afterwards, Begin said that at this point he heard the motor of an airplane overhead; he looked up and saw it was a UN plane. The *Altalena* had been discovered, but now the ship and its cargo were past the point of retreat. Soon, two UN observers appeared; Begin remembered that one of them was French and the other American. "They wanted to know what was aboard the ship and asked for permission to board her. We told them that this could not be so at that moment. They understood and saluted us. They left and we continued unloading."[20] The sooner the work would be completed, the better. The men worked under the blazing sun, without a break for so much as a drink of water.

In the afternoon, Meridor returned. He agreed that, after the surprise visit from the UN, time was running out for the *Altalena* and her cargo. He and others insisted that the boat should leave Kfar Vitkin and proceed to Tel Aviv, as originally planned. There would be more stevedores and Irgun supporters in Tel Aviv than at Kfar Vitkin to speed the operation. Besides, if the government really considered using force, it would think twice before starting a civil war in the middle of Tel Aviv, a center of Irgun activity.

At first, Begin would not hear of leaving Kfar Vitkin. The government might interpret such an act as an attempt to escape, and he, for his part, considered that dishonorable. Besides, what would become of the weapons that already had been unloaded? Surely, placing them back aboard the boat would only lose additional time. No trouble, said Meridor. He and some of the men would stay behind on the beach to guard the weapons. In the meantime Begin, in Tel Aviv, would be able to communicate directly with the government, clear up what Begin still insisted could only be a dangerous misunderstanding, and come to an agreement with Tzahal about arrangements for the removal of the weapons. Finally, Begin was persuaded that, under the circumstances, the best thing to do was indeed to head for Tel Aviv and to land at the pier at the foot of Frishman Street originally marked on Monroe Fein's map.

At five o'clock in the afternoon, Begin ordered the exhausted men to stop unloading and explained to them that the boat would proceed to Tel Aviv.

It was precisely at this moment that Tzahal chose to attack. Mortar and machine gun fire came from all sides, raking the beach and hitting the *Altalena*. Fein's first thought was that the Arabs had pulled off a sneak attack; he could not imagine that Jews would shoot at one another. His next thought was that he would have to head out to sea if the stores of ammunition aboard the ship were not to explode, causing the loss of the weapons and ammunition, and perhaps also disaster in Kfar Vitkin itself.

Begin's instinctive reaction was to throw himself flat on the sand to keep from getting hit. His first thought was that he could not leave with the *Altalena* now. Misunderstanding though it might be, this was a battle; Tzahal was shooting at unarmed Irgun men. Throughout the years of the underground, Begin had never participated personally in any of the Irgun's operations, but now he was right there, in the midst of the fighting, and for him to withdraw would be tantamount to deserting the men under his command. However, Meridor insisted that Begin go with the ship. Moreover, Begin was given no time to think. While others on the beach dived for cover from the rain of bullets and shells, Lankin, Abraham Stavsky and several members of the crew grabbed Begin and, together, they dragged him to the motor launch that had been used to unload the volunteers. Fein headed the *Altalena* south toward Tel Aviv, weaving and turning this way and that to avoid fire from the corvettes, which were following her.

Meanwhile, on the beach of Kfar Vitkin, the shooting continued through the evening and the Irgun men fought back with whatever small arms they were able to grab from the *Altalena*'s cargo. Six of the Irgun men were killed and eighteen wounded, while Tzahal lost two killed and six wounded on the beach. Eventually Meridor saw no point in continuing the unequal struggle; he particularly feared that Tzahal's bullets might hit the explosives unloaded from the *Altalena*, set off a raging fire and turn the fighting on the beach into a catastrophe for innocent civilians in the village as well. Meridor arranged for a cease-fire; Tzahal collected the weapons on the beach — about a fifth of the *Altalena*'s total load — and placed the Irgunists under arrest.

It was after midnight when the *Altalena* reached Tel Aviv. She ran in at full speed and was grounded at the foot of Frishman Street. At once, gunfire started from shore and the two corvettes which had been following the *Altalena* took up positions nearby to trap her. When dawn came — it was now Tuesday, June 22 — Begin and the others aboard the ship saw that the entire shore area was surrounded by Tzahal men.

While the *Altalena* was still on the way to Tel Aviv, Hayim Landau called on Itzhak Gruenbaum, who had become minister of the interior in the provisional government. Six months before, Landau and Gruenbaum had met when Begin and the Jewish Agency Executive had started negotiations for cooperation between Haganah and the Irgun. It was Gruenbaum's name that had been mentioned by the representatives of the provisional government when they had given Begin what had seemed to be the government's approval for the *Altalena's* coming to Israel.[21] Now Gruenbaum appeared genuinely surprised to hear that the government had been negotiating with Begin and other Irgun representatives prior to the boat's arrival. As far as he, Gruenbaum, knew, the government had never been informed about the *Altalena* before she landed at Kfar Vitkin. Ben-Gurion had only told his associates that the Irgun had sprung a surprise on the government by bringing in a boat loaded with arms which Begin and his colleagues now refused to surrender to Tzahal. In other words, Ben-Gurion had flatly announced that the Irgun had launched a revolt which would have to be crushed. Gruenbaum promised to go to Ben-Gurion at once, with a proposed compromise for the unloading and storage of the weapons until a mutually satisfactory arrangement could be worked out for their distribution. Landau never heard from Gruenbaum again. (Gruenbaum, then in his late 60's, did not remain in Israeli political life much longer; he eventually retired to resume a distinguished literary career.)

As for Ben-Gurion, he did not want an agreement with the Irgun, but a showdown before as wide an audience as possible to finish off Begin and the Irgun. The *Altalena* at the foot of Frishman Street had hoisted the white flag of surrender, but Tzahal seemed to be paying no attention. Although the men aboard the boat did not return the fire, Tzahal guns kept right on taking potshots at the *Altalena*.

The action aboard the *Altalena* and the scene at the seashore began to look and sound like a sad melodrama. From the ship, Begin was shouting through a loudspeaker, appealing to the people of Tel Aviv to help unload the weapons from the boat. Meanwhile, on the terraces and balconies of beachfront hotels, foreign correspondents were enjoying open-air breakfasts as they kept an eye on the events. Other reporters, more enterprising, followed the crowds of curious onlookers who were flocking to the seashore to join in the excitement. And all the while, on the terrace of the Kaethe Dan Hotel, directly opposite the *Altalena,* United Nations observers looked on and did nothing. A motor launch laden with crates full of weapons was lowered from the *Altalena* and chugged toward shore, where the men jumped out and dumped the crates onto the beach. Watching quietly some 60 feet away, a group of Tzahal men stood, unmoving.

A few of the Irgun men from the motor launch remained on the beach as the craft returned to the *Altalena.* Since the first unloading had gone smoothly, Fein ordered the little boat back to the beach with a second load of arms. It was now one o'clock in the afternoon of Tuesday, June 22.

As the motor launch moved toward shore on its second trip, it ran into a sudden volley of gunfire from the beach. The shooting seemed to come from everywhere all at once. The crew of the launch raised a white flag, but the firing continued. The pilot was hit in the chest; however, the launch managed to reach shore. From the *Altalena,* Begin radioed Hayim Landau at Irgun headquarters to try to arrange a cease-fire with Tzahal. He then ran back to the loudspeaker, appealing to the Tzahal troops ashore to stop shooting. "The weapons we're unloading are for you and us both!" he shouted.[22] Moments later, the *Altalena* herself came under heavy fire, and the loudspeaker was knocked off its mounting. On deck, men fell dead and wounded. Among the fatally wounded was Abraham Stavsky. The heavy bombardment of the *Altalena* continued and seemed to intensify every time Begin appeared on the bridge. Later, at least one of Begin's followers was to insist that the Tzahal had been deliberately pursuing Begin, that Ben-Gurion had wanted to see Begin trapped and killed.

Throughout that morning, hearing that their comrades were under attack, ex-Irgunists who had joined Tzahal left their posts and moved in the direction of Tel Aviv. They attempted to get through the Tzahal cordon that surrounded the beach, but could not do so. A reporter from *HaAretz,* Israel's only morning paper not affiliated with any political party, saw the men trying to get through two different intersections near the beach, and he noted that in each instance they neither used force nor opened fire on Tzahal.[23]

Begin and Fein contacted Tzahal headquarters at the Ritz Hotel, where Yigal Allon and Itzhak Rabin, commander and deputy commander, respectively, of Palmach, were in charge.[24] Begin and Fein asked for a cease-fire so that the wounded could be removed from the *Altalena*. After forty-five minutes Allon agreed to a cease-fire which was to go into effect at four o'clock that afternoon. Then Allon noticed some Irgun men setting up a machine gun on the *Altalena*'s deck; the gun, it seemed to him, was aimed at the Ritz Hotel.[25] He telephoned Ben-Gurion for permission to use artillery fire against the *Altalena*, first as a warning and then to sink the ship. Ben-Gurion gave his approval. At about that time a delegation of notables, led by Israel Rokach, the mayor of Tel Aviv, who enjoyed the respect of the entire Jewish community in Israel, appeared at Ben-Gurion's office, urging him to order a cease-fire. Ben-Gurion said he was in no position to do that. He could not, he explained, interrupt military operations on his own, without the approval of the cabinet.

Fein expected the cease-fire to go into effect as scheduled. Instead, a large gun located on the seashore to the north of Tel Aviv began to fire at the *Altalena*. The gun fired three shells, all of which passed over the boat and exploded in the water. These were Allon's warning shots. The *Altalena*, not knowing what the firing meant, radioed the Ritz Hotel to inquire whether the cease-fire order was still in effect and, if so, what had been the reason for the three shots. The reply was that the cease-fire order still held good and that the gun would be silenced at once. There was no more shooting for the next fifteen minutes. Fein urged Begin to make sure that the *Altalena*'s men, too, would continue observing the cease-fire; once again, he warned Begin of what might happen if the *Altalena* were to receive a direct hit so close to land with her cargo of high explosives.[26] Begin was in full agreement with Fein. He was just about to give the appropriate orders when the heavy gun resumed firing. A shell tore through the deck of the *Altalena* and exploded in the ship's hold. One after another, the ammunition cases in the hold exploded. The crew did their best to put out the flames, but with little success. Fein's first thought was to get the wounded men off the boat. Then, he ordered all the men aboard to abandon ship. Begin declared that Fein and his American crew, who were not members of the Irgun but had merely volunteered "to serve the people of Israel," were free to leave, but that he, Begin, and the Irgun men still on board would not surrender.[27]

Fein hoisted a white flag, then radioed Rabin and Allon at the

Ritz Hotel, asking once again whether the cease-fire was still in force. The answer was: "There is a general cease-fire, but the order has not reached all the units of the army." By that time the main deck of the *Altalena* was in flames. Fein and the others began to abandon ship. The wounded went in rafts; the others jumped into the water and swam toward shore. Some of them were waving white handkerchiefs; nevertheless, Fein and the others who were still aboard saw that the men in the water were being shot at from rifles and machine guns on the beach.[28] Irgun men from the beach paddled out on surfboards and rafts to rescue the survivors from the *Altalena*. When only seven men were left aboard the ship, Fein and Lankin both insisted that Begin jump into the water, but he refused to do so. As commander, he said, he could not leave until everyone else was off. Fein then commanded two men of the crew to grab Begin and toss him over the side into the water.[29] The last two men off the boat were Fein, captain of the ship, and Lankin, commander of the 900 volunteers.[30]

The agony of the S.S. *Altalena* went on throughout the evening, as the ammunition and bombs stored within her hold continued to detonate, enveloping the blazing ship in a cloud of smoke. The Irgun people no longer cared about the boat and its cargo; what mattered now was to help the survivors, particularly the 69 who had been wounded. The 14 Irgunists killed in the tragedy are still remembered at memorial services each year. In the summer of 1977, when Begin delivered the memorial address, it was the first time that a prime minister of Israel paid public tribute to the fallen of the *Altalena*.

Begin's first tribute to the fighting men aboard the *Altalena* came over the Irgun's own radio station on the evening of June 22, 1948. He was driven by the thought that he had to tell the people of Israel the truth about what had happened to the *Altalena* while each little detail of what he himself had heard, seen and experienced was still vivid in his memory. Already, the *Palestine Post* (later the *Jerusalem Post*), Israel's only English-speaking daily, which had a world-wide audience, had carried a large headline, "Breach of Truce Foiled by Israel."[31] Though exhausted from his sixty-hour ordeal, Begin would not permit the official communiqués issued by the provisional government to go unchallenged. Unfortunately he did not realize that he was in no condition to go before the public, even if it was only on the radio. His speech was unprepared, long and rambling. Several times, he did something which until then he had never permitted himself to do in public: he wept. He was right, perhaps even more than he himself knew at the time, when he said: "My beloved brothers in Zion, there are many conclusions to be drawn from what has happened at Kfar Vitkin, and in Tel Aviv today. But at this moment I am incapable of drawing conclusions."[32] He was bitter in his accusations against the provisional government and Ben-Gurion. But there was one emotion even stronger within Begin than his anger against those who had caused the tragedy of the *Altalena:* his determination that the new Jewish state must not be torn apart by civil war. "Raise not your hand against your brother," he pleaded, "Not even today."[33] He ended his speech with these words: "The people of Israel is not Mapai [i.e., Ben-Gurion's Labor party] . . . We shall continue to love Israel, the good and the bad, the misled and the mistaken. We shall continue to love Israel and to fight for it."[34]

To many who listened to him that night it seemed that, politically, Begin was finished. The unsentimental *sabras* of the time were not accustomed to public displays of emotion and considered tears a sign of weakness. Some of them had viewed Begin as a serious contender against Ben-Gurion for political power; now they were not so sure. Some Irgun elements called him naive for ever having believed that the provisional government had been honest with him when it had given him its consent to bring the *Altalena* to Israel. Shmuel Katz later said that Begin should have realized what was afoot when the provisional government ordered the *Altalena* to land at Kfar Vitkin, the stronghold of Labor. Instead of interpreting the order as a sign of approval from Ben-Gurion, Begin should have realized that this was a trap to maneuver him and the Irgun into an impossible position. But then Katz himself points out that this naiveté had been more than shared by Arye Ben Eliezer, Eliahu Lankin and other Irgun leaders to whom — unlike Begin — it apparently never even occurred that the government might not welcome the landing of the *Altalena*.[35] The simple truth is that in those days Begin and his friends in the Irgun were idealistic young freedom fighters, not seasoned politicians.

As for Ben-Gurion, he came in for his own share of criticism. At an emergency meeting of the provisional council of state — forerunner of the Knesset — on June 23, the day after the tragedy, he had given his and Galili's version of what had happened. The *Altalena* had to be destroyed, he concluded, because it was bringing ruin to the State of Israel. "Blessed be the gun that set the ship on fire," he declared. Not all those present at the meeting accepted Ben-Gurion's explanation. Two of the ministers — Rabbi Judah L.

Fishman (Maimon), Minister of Religious Affairs, and Moshe Shapira, Minister of Immigration and Health[36] — resigned from the cabinet in protest. Several members of the council asked questions to which neither Ben-Gurion nor his associates could give logical answers. First: If the Irgun had indeed planned to start a *putsch* against Ben-Gurion, why should its leaders have agreed so readily to change their original plan and to bring the *Altalena* to Kfar Vitkin, whose population was known to side actively with Ben-Gurion against the Irgun? Secondly: Immediately after landing at Kfar Vitkin, the volunteers were taken away by Irgun trucks to a rest camp, and not one of the recruits had carried so much as one revolver on his or her person. Was such behavior typical of fighters imported to launch a revolution against a government known to be favored by a large part of the population and supported by a capable army? And finally, why had Tzahal soldiers continued to shoot at the boat after it had run up the white flag of surrender, and at the survivors who had abandoned the ship and were swimming toward shore unarmed?

Yet, Ben-Gurion emerged victorious from the meeting, so much so that a motion for the naming of a committee to investigate the *Altalena* affair was defeated on the spot by a vote of 22 to 3. Apparently, the shock and confusion that had taken hold of the general public, the manner in which the government had presented the *Altalena* story, on the one hand, and Begin's uncharacteristically incoherent portrayal of the Irgun's side, on the other, had worked in Ben-Gurion's favor.

Nevertheless, the debate around the *Altalena* continued. In 1956 Monroe Fein, who was then living in New Jersey, discussed the *Altalena* with a visitor from Israel. Captain of the *Altalena* though he had been, he had never been asked to join the Irgun or to participate in its secret deliberations. Yet, he said he was convinced that the weapons he had helped bring to Israel could not have been intended for an Irgun *putsch*. "Does one start a revolution with arms unscrewed into parts and oiled and packed into cases?" he demanded. "If we [had] intended to fight [the provisional government], we could have unpacked the cases, armed our people within half an hour, and occupied Kfar Vitkin, where we landed first. But you don't make revolutions with arms packed in cases." Also, he said he had been able to see at first hand that the bringing of the *Altalena* had been endorsed by Haganah, "because all the while we were loading the ship in France, two official Haganah representatives — a man and a woman — were coming on board daily to conclude with us all the necessary arrangements."[37]

In January, 1959, memories of the *Altalena* set off a shouting match between Ben-Gurion, then still prime minister, and Menahem Begin, who was speaking as leader of the opposition. In a heated reply to Begin's motion for a vote of non-confidence in the government, Ben-Gurion accused Begin's Irgun of refusing to disband after the establishment of the State of Israel and of having brought in the *Altalena* without informing the provisional government. In reply, Begin went over the whole ground, starting with the negotiations begun by the Jewish Agency and the Irgun at the end of 1947 and ending with Galili's declaration that Haganah would not participate in the unloading of the *Altalena*. When Begin recalled that Galili had not said one word to indicate that the government would oppose the coming or the unloading of the ship, Ben-Gurion shouted, "That's a lie!" The prime minister called on members of the Knesset who had been members of the provisional government in 1948 to come forward and tell whether they had ever had the question of the *Altalena* put before them. When none replied, Begin said that Ben-Gurion had probably kept the truth from them. Ben-Gurion retorted that the first time he, Ben-Gurion, had ever heard about the coming of the *Altalena* had been on Saturday, June 19, the day before she had actually landed. No one, Ben-Gurion said, had ever negotiated with Begin on his, Ben-Gurion's, behalf. It was not Galili who had negotiated with Begin or with the Irgun but some other person who had had no authority to do so. No, Ben-Gurion would not divulge the name of the person. When asked why not, the prime minister brusquely replied, "Because I don't want to. Finished."[38]

In later years, there were rumors afoot that Ben-Gurion was no longer so sure he had done the right thing in having the army attack and sink the *Altalena*. After Ben-Gurion's death in December, 1973, statements were heard here and there to the effect that Ben-Gurion had been deliberately misled by his associates who had wanted to see him "finish" Begin and the Irgun. In 1977, soon after becoming prime minister, Begin quoted a well-known and widely respected member of the Labor Zionist movement in the same vein. However, Begin added that this individual did not wish to be identified.

Doris Katz recalls that during the days immediately following the sinking of the *Altalena* Begin was in a state of deep depression. He went to the Katz home in Ramat Gan for a few days of quiet recuperation.[39] Shmuel Katz, who returned to Israel from Paris on the day after the tragedy, found him haggard and tense, but as determined as ever to remain in control of the situation. The shooting had faded away after the *Altalena* had been left to its fate, but Katz found the mood in the Irgun "explosive."[40] Begin was determined that there must be no civil war. He emerged from seclusion, accompanied by Katz, to address a meeting of 200 ex-Irgun officers in Tel Aviv. Within two weeks, he told his audience, the truce with the Arabs would be over and it was vital that Israel stand united against her enemies. The Irgun would settle its accounts with Ben-Gurion not with guns, but with votes. It would cease to be a military organization, but it would set up a political party. In the meantime, Begin urged the men to join Tzahal because Tzahal was the army of the State of Israel, not just of David Ben-Gurion. No one in the room protested against his appeal. There would be no civil war.

That meeting marked the beginning of Tenuat Herut, the "Freedom Movement," which under Begin's leadership entered Israeli politics as the Herut party.

Soon after the *Altalena* incident, Begin made his first public appearance in the New City of Jerusalem, where the Irgun still held out as a separate entity and would continue to do so until September. Begin went to visit the wounded in the hospitals, the ultra-Orthodox community in Mea Shearim, and the neighborhoods populated mainly by Jews from Oriental countries. He even visited the training schools of Palmach. No one in the city had ever seen him before, but wherever he went, he seemed to be surrounded by cheering, yelling crowds. During the late afternoon he addressed a mass meeting in Zion Square; his audience numbered thousands. The crowds were so great that he could barely make his way to a restaurant for a hasty supper.[41]

The next day he participated in a ceremony by which, officially, he ceased to be commander of the Irgun. He grasped the banner of the Irgun — it bore a gold emblem of a hand grasping a rifle against a background of blue and white silk — and handed it over to Mordecai Raanan who, as commander of the Irgun in Jerusalem, was the leader of the last remaining Irgun unit. Shortly thereafter, Raanan was succeeded by Shmuel Katz, who proudly recalls that he was the "last commander of the Irgun."[42] Begin returned to Tel Aviv with a full guard of honor including a motorcycle escort composed of Irgun men from Jerusalem. But he was now no longer the commander of a splinter army; he had become the leader of a political party.

Back in Tel Aviv, the Begins' neighbors were surprised to learn that the nondescript-looking man they had known only as Dr. Koenigshoffer or "Benny's father" had been the commander of the notorious Irgun. Benny Begin, now five years old, first heard about it from the children in the neighborhood. Benny had not exactly understood what the Irgun was. He had only known, as did all the children in the neighborhood, that everyone seemed to "belong" somewhere. Begin once overheard a conversation between his son and Yefet, a little Yemenite boy who lived in the same apartment building.

"Benny, what do you belong to?" Yefet had asked.

"I belong to LEHI," Benny promptly replied.

"The Stern gang? Aw, Benny, they're no good!"

"Okay, okay! So I belong to Haganah," said Benny.

"Haganah? They're worse! Listen — I belong to the Irgun. They're real good! They beat 'em all."

Now, Benny's first reaction to the reports about his father's job in the Irgun was not to believe them. Newspaper in hand, he shyly walked up to his father, pointed to a picture captioned "Menahem Begin" and asked, "Is that really you, *Abba*?" Begin let Aliza handle the task of telling their son the whole long story.[43]

One of Begin's worries over the years had been that the secrets and untruthfulnesses of underground life — the visitors with two and sometimes three different names ("*Abba*, where is Uncle Moshe who is called Yeruham?") and his own changing identities ("Didn't you once have a beard, *Abba*?") — would have an adverse effect on Benny, who, unlike his little sisters, Hasia and Leah, was old enough to sense that odd things were going on at home. How, Begin had wondered, would it affect the future relationship between himself and his son? "It is a bad thing for a son not to be able to tell his father the truth," Begin was to write. "It is even worse when a father cannot tell his son the truth." It was one of the unseen but painful sacrifices he had had to make for his work.[44]

While Begin made plans for the formation of his political party and superintended the Irgun's gradual integration into Tzahal, the war for Israel's independence continued. On July 9, the truce between Israel and her Arab neighbors ended, and the fighting resumed at once on all fronts, to be interrupted again by a short-lived cease-fire eight days later. As the weeks passed, the tide of battle began to turn in Israel's favor. Thanks to systematic mobilization, thorough training, the long-delayed arrival of arms from Europe, ingenious strategy and sheer determination, Israel's little army was able to bring its powerful enemies to a standstill. But many months were to pass before Israel was able to inflict on the Arabs losses sufficient to bring the war to an end.

During the summer of 1948, Count Folke Bernadotte, a member of the Swedish royal family, who had been appointed United Nations Mediator for Palestine, submitted a new peace proposal to the Israelis and to the Arab nations. This plan called for major changes in the territoral arrangements made under the United Nations partition plan the previous November. The entire city of Jerusalem, along with all or part of the Negev in the south (which today comprises almost two-thirds of Israel's area), was to be turned over to the Arabs; in return, the Israelis were to receive all or part of the western Galilee. Lydda and Haifa were to become free ports. The status of Jaffa was to be determined at a later date. Initially Bernadotte had also proposed a political and economic union between the Israelis and the Arab sector of Palestine, but he later dropped that proposal. The Bernadotte plan was rejected, not only by the Israelis but also by the Arab nations; what the Arabs wanted was not a truncated Jewish state but no Jewish state at all in the Middle East. In addition, Egypt and Saudi Arabia did not want a situation created that would enable Abdullah, ruler of the Hashemite Kingdom of Jordan, to fulfill his long-cherished dream of seizing all of Palestine.

On September 17, 1948, Bernadotte was assassinated while on an inspection tour in the New City of Jerusalem. Responsibility for the shooting was claimed by a splinter group which called itself Hazit HaMoledet (Fatherland Front). The assassins were never caught, but it was generally believed that they had represented an offshoot of the Stern Group. Based on this assumption, the Israeli provisional government (as it still was then), concerned about the international reaction to the murder of a peace envoy, immediately outlawed the Stern Group and began to arrest its members.

Actually, this time the Stern Group was not to blame. In fact, though Bernadotte clearly had been no promoter of Israeli aspirations, most of the Sternists were shocked by the assassination. As opposed to the case of Lord Moyne four years earlier, most Sternists did not consider Bernadotte important enough to kill. Former Irgun members, too, regarded the killing as pointless and counterproductive. At a press conference, Begin paid tribute to Bernadotte's memory, expressed sympathy for his widow and children, and firmly declared that there was no connection between Hazit HaMoledet and the Irgun remnant in Jerusalem. "No Irgun soldier in Jerusalem," he said, "ever joined Hazit ranks." He said that, indirectly, the United Nations was to blame for Bernadotte's death, for though that international body had been instrumental in the emergence of the State of Israel, it had done nothing "to help the new state and its struggle against unprovoked aggression." He was "appalled" at the tragedy and was just as anxious as the Ben-Gurion government to have the murderers brought to justice. But he regarded the drastic measures of the government against the Stern Group as undemocratic. "This is no time for mass arrests, secret police and concentration camps," he said. "The government has no right to arrest people just because they belong or had belonged to some opposition party."[45] Years later he was to take the same position when Ben-Gurion wanted his support for the peremptory expulsion of all Communists from Israel's parliament.

On September 20, 1948, three days after Bernadotte's assassination, Ben-Gurion, bent on eliminating every trace of "dissidence" from Israeli political life, presented Begin with an ultimatum signed by Chief of Staff Yigael Yadin, ordering the immediate disbandment of the Irgun remnant in Jerusalem. Begin already had been negotiating final arrangements toward that end with the Minister of the Interior, Itzhak Gruenbaum. He was not interested in provoking a conflict with Ben-Gurion or Tzahal by prolonging the negotiations. On Tuesday, September 21, Shmuel Katz, at a press conference in Jerusalem's Eden Hotel, announced the end of the Irgun.

Irgun representatives in Europe, however, were not yet ready to give up their image as revolutionaries. Though the Irgun had ceased to exist in Israel, they visualized its continuation in Europe as an expatriate organization. But Begin insisted that there was no more justification for an underground movement when the Jewish state had a stable government of its own. He began pressing the "diaspora command" to give up all its plans for future underground operations and to turn over to the Israeli government all the arms and aircraft they had acquired in Europe. Eventually, Begin himself went to Paris to put things in order. On January 12, 1949, the Irgun diaspora organization dissolved, and its Paris headquarters became the official European bureau of the Herut movement, a supporter of the Herut party in Israel even as Israel's other political parties had the support of like-minded organizations in diaspora Jewry.

The platform of the Herut was strongly nationalist. It protested against the emergency laws which the Ben-Gurion government had promulgated for dealing with dissenting parties, and called for a vigorous capitalist approach in domestic affairs as opposed to the government's socialism. Herut's foreign policy orientation was not neutrality in the "cold war" but an emphatically pro-Western line. And of course the platform reiterated the thesis of Jabotinsky and the Revisionist movement of which Herut considered itself the ideological heir: that the original historic Jewish homeland included the territory on both sides of the Jordan which had been the Biblical Palestine. Herut questioned the legal basis of the United Nations decision to divide Palestine into two states, amputating, as Herut saw it, yet another segment from the Jewish homeland after most of it had already been ceded to Abdullah's Kingdom of Jordan almost three decades before. The United Nations had made no provisions for implementing its partition plan; indeed, some of its own members in good standing were attempting to nullify the UN resolution by putting an end to the Jewish state, and the world body was taking no action to stop them.[46] Hence, the facts of life for the State of Israel were based not on resolutions passed by a United Nations unable or unwilling to enforce its own decisions, but on Israel's own ability to secure her survival. Prime Minister Ben-Gurion himself publicly acknowledged these truths in the late fall of 1948. "A new reality has been created in Palestine," he said, answering a question in the Provisional Council of the State on November 11, 1948, "and Israel's government is fully aware that Israel's present borders have been determined by Israel's armed forces."[47]

By the end of December, 1948, Tzahal had driven the Egyptians out of Israel and was pursuing them into the Sinai desert; the Egyptian forces in the Gaza Strip were all but trapped. It was only due to heavy political pressures from two world powers, the United States and Great Britain, that Tzahal withdrew from Sinai and the Gaza Strip. (In 1956, after she had all but defeated the armies of Gamal Abdel Nasser, Israel was to be forced to make the same withdrawal, this time by crude threats from two superpowers, the Soviet Union and, once again, the United States).

In January, 1949, Egypt, her dream of a swift victory over Israel shattered, entered into negotiations with the Jewish state, and a month later an armistice agreement was signed between the two countries. The next country to conclude an armistice with Israel was Lebanon, on March 23, 1949; the Hashemite Kingdom of Jordan followed suit on April 3. Syria held out the longest; she did not agree to an armistice with Israel until July 20, 1949. The negotiations were conducted under the guidance of Ralph Bunche, who had expressed his understanding for Begin's views when the two men had met in Tel Aviv and who had now succeeded Count Bernadotte as United Nations Mediator.

Thus, after twenty months of fighting and at the cost of over 6,000 men and women killed, Israel's War of Independence came to a close. It was only an end to outright warfare; none of Israel's enemies had expressed readiness to sign a peace treaty with the Jewish state whose very existence they still refused to acknowledge. Still, the absence of war enabled Israel to turn her full energies to the political and economic necessities of sovereign statehood.

On January 25, 1949 Israel held elections to choose the Constituent Assembly which became Israel's legislative body, the Knesset, with 120 members. In that election, the Ben-Gurion government coalition consisting of Mapai, the United Religious Front, Progressives, Sephardim and the Arab Democrats received a total of 72 seats.[48] Herut obtained 14 seats. The delegation which the Herut party sent to Israel's first Knesset included Jabotinsky's son Eri, one woman, Esther Raziel-Naor (sister of David Raziel), Arye Ben Eliezer, the poet Uri Zvi Greenberg, Shmuel Katz, Hillel Kook, Eliahu Lankin, Yaakov Meridor and, as the leader, Menahem Begin.

12. Leader of the Opposition

At four o'clock in the afternoon of February 14, 1949 the newly-elected Constituent Assembly of the State of Israel met in the Jewish Agency building in downtown Jerusalem. The choice of this location in Jerusalem's New City, which Jordan's Arab Legion had been unable to conquer, signalled to the world that Israel considered the New City an integral part of the Jewish state. The UN resolution to internationalize Jerusalem had been intended to safeguard the holy places of the three great religions there. But the world body had been unable to implement also that part of its 1947 resolution, and now Jordan's annexation of the Old City, where most of the holy places were located, had invalidated the entire purpose of internationalization. And so, as Israel was to state in an official proclamation later that year, the Ben-Gurion government saw no reason to conceal the fact that in the eyes of the Jewish people the city from which the kings of Judah had reigned in the days of old was the historic capital also of the modern Jewish state.

The session of the Assembly was opened by Chaim Weizmann, formerly president of the World Zionist Organization and shortly to become the first President of the State of Israel. There had been times when Weizmann had wondered whether the Jewish "national home" promised in the Balfour Declaration could ever become the independent Jewish state envisioned by the founders of political Zionism. Now old and ill, he had lived to see the Zionist dream fulfilled. "This is a great day in our lives," he said. "Let no one think us arrogant if we add that it is also a great day in the history of the world. At this hour a message of hope goes forth from this place and from this holy city to the persecuted and oppressed the world over who are struggling for freedom and equality. A struggle for a just cause is never in vain. If we, the people of sorrows and affliction, have been given to see the event which is taking place here today, then, truly, there is hope for all those who long for justice."[1]

Two days later, on February 16, 1949, the Constituent Assembly passed the Transition Law by which it became Israel's first Knesset. Twenty days later, on March 8, 1949, the Knesset approved the country's first official government, headed by Ben-Gurion as prime minister. Since no single party had succeeded in obtaining an absolute majority of Knesset seats, the Ben-Gurion cabinet represented a coalition of parties with a mixed bag of political and religious ideologies but under the control of Ben-Gurion's Mapai. Because of the multiplicity of political parties in the Knesset, all of Israel's subsequent cabinets have been coalitions including middle-of-the-road liberals and leaders of Orthodox religious parties but until 1977 dominated by the Labor movement. By notable contrast, except for a brief span of three years from the eve of the Six-Day War of 1967 until the summer of 1970 the right wing, led by Menahem Begin, was consigned to the role of perennial opposition party until May, 1977.

It is Begin's remarkable achievement that he was able not merely to survive as a member of the Knesset for almost 30 years without interruption but also, despite Herut's eight succesive electoral defeats, to remain his party's uncontested leader. It was also his singular good fortune that, at a time when many observers in Israel and elsewhere were ready to write him off as a "has-been," he led his party to victory and made a successful transition from leader of the opposition to leader of his country.

Begin's three decades in the Knesset gave him ample opportunity to learn the workings of government in depth. He was a member of the Knesset committees on foreign affairs and security and on law and constitution. In addition, he traveled widely on behalf of his party, addressing mass rallies in Europe, the Americas, South Africa and Australia. And even where the established Zionist leadership showed no great enthusiasm for Begin, ordinary Jews who were largely innocent of intra-Zionist politics flocked to see and hear the leader of the underground movement which they associated with the liberation of the Jewish homeland from British rule.

Begin's first trip abroad since his arrival in Palestine as a refugee in 1942 came in the late fall of 1948 when Israel was still in the midst of her War of Independence. He paid the first of many subsequent visits to the United States, stopping in Paris on his way there, and again on his homeward journey a month later.

The announcement of Begin's impending arrival in the United States to tour the eastern half of the country and to raise funds for

Herut was received with distaste by the leaders of the American Zionist establishment who regarded him as a dangerous "dissident." The American Zionist Emergency Council planned to issue a statement urging its constituents to boycott Begin's visit. According to Begin, the reason why the statement never materialized was the adamant opposition of Dr. Abba Hillel Silver, honorary president of the Zionist Organization of America, who had met with Begin during the underground period near the seashore of Tel Aviv and had shown sympathy for the Irgun's position. Silver refused to have anything to do with the Emergency Council's proposed statement. In a heated discussion with other Zionist leaders, he said, "The Irgun will go down in history as a factor without which the State of Israel would not have come into being."[2]

Begin's first arrival in New York by air on Monday, November 22, 1948 went almost unnoticed. He did not stay in the city but immediately proceeded to Washington, where he spent one day. But at three o'clock the next afternoon, November 23, when he returned to New York from the capital, landing at LaGuardia Airport aboard an American Airlines plane, he was given a hero's welcome. The *New York Times*[3] reported that over 500 people had turned out at the airport for the occasion. Jewish observers who were there that day claim that this was a conservative estimate, influenced, perhaps, by the *Times'* cool attitude toward Zionism, regardless of party label. They recall that the crowds which received Begin were out of all proportion to the small and not always very effectual membership of the Revisionist party, Herut's sister organization outside Israel.

Paul O'Dwyer, a long-time active supporter of the Irgun whose cause he equated with that of the Irish revolutionaries, stepped forward to greet Begin on behalf of his brother, William O'Dwyer, then the Mayor of New York. There was an official reception committee of 40, including rabbis and other Jewish dignitaries, and a band of Jewish war veterans struck up "The Star-Spangled Banner" and *Hatikvah*. One aged Orthodox rabbi approached Begin with a Scroll of the Law in his arms, in keeping with a time-honored Jewish welcome usually accorded only to great scholars or powerful rulers. Among the others present were Dr. Louis I. Newman of New York's Temple Rodeph Shalom (he was perhaps the only American Reform rabbi to belong to the Revisionist party in those days), Stella Adler of the Yiddish theatrical family, and finally, one who perhaps meant more to Begin than all the others: Johanna Jabotinsky, the widow of Vladimir Jabotinsky, who had arrived in the United States after her husband's death and had settled in New York.[4] Deeply moved, Begin embraced and kissed the woman whom he and his followers revered as the "mother of Betar."

After the greetings were over, an automobile procession escorted Begin to the Chatham, a quiet hotel on East 48th Street in midtown Manhattan just off Fifth Avenue. At the hotel, he found the press waiting for him and he held his first press conference in the United States. The newsmen commented on his fluent English, his aplomb, and the sense of humor with which he handled their questioning. When they inquired what he had been doing for a whole day in Washington, he replied with a gentle smile that he had merely gone underground for 24 hours, out of sheer habit. On a more serious note, he explained that he had come to the United States "to tell Americans of all faiths about Israel's fight for freedom" and in answer to a question he stated that while he was opposed to the internationalization of Jerusalem he favored extraterritorial status for the Christian and Moslem shrines in the city.

On Friday, November 26, he received New York City's official welcome at City Hall from Mayor O'Dwyer, who had been briefed on the visitor by his brother Paul. The mayor compared Menahem Begin to the Irish patriot Michael Collins. Begin said all the right things. In his response he declared that if "a son of the great Irish people and a son of the Hebrew people" who had both won their freedom in revolutionary wars could shake hands on the free soil of America, it was "an assurance that liberty will live as long as there are men ready to die for it." Perhaps at the moment he recalled how, 10 years earlier, at the 1938 Betar congress in Warsaw, he had urged an Irish-style Jewish revolt in Palestine.

Begin had scheduled no public engagements for the Sabbath. On Friday night he attended Sabbath eve services at New York's patrician Spanish-Portuguese Synagogue, the oldest Jewish congregation in the United States, whose beginnings date back to the 17th century. The next morning, November 27, he worshipped at the Jewish Center, a well-known Orthodox synagogue on the West Side, most of whose members, like those of the Spanish-Portuguese congregation, were anything but radical in their Jewish or Zionist politics. Begin heard the Center's rabbi, Dr. Leo Jung, preach an impressive sermon extolling him as "the man who defied an empire and gained glory for Israel."

The following Monday, November 29, Begin was guest of honor at a dinner given by the Revisionist party at the Waldorf-

Astoria Hotel, with Prof. Fowler Harper of Yale University Law School acting as toastmaster. With Mrs. Jabotinsky seated at his right, Begin, wearing a tuxedo, heard the noted painter and illuminator Arthur Szyk propose a toast to David Ben-Gurion and — perhaps significantly — to succeeding prime ministers of Israel. In his response, Begin told an audience of 2,000 that, contrary to their possible expectations, he would not criticize Ben-Gurion anywhere outside Israel. "Abroad," he said, "I'm an Israeli citizen and the Israeli Premier is my Premier. From this podium I will not utter a single word against him or his government."

The next day there was another dinner, this one across the Hudson River, in Newark, New Jersey. On Wednesday, December 1, Begin visited Philadelphia, where he laid a wreath at the base of the Liberty Bell and heard Mayor Bernard Samuel liken the fighters of the Irgun to the soldiers of the American Revolution. The following day he went to Chicago; this was a far west as he would go on that first visit to America. In Chicago, too, there was a City Hall welcome, and also a warm reunion with Monroe Fein, captain of the *Altalena.*

On Sunday, December 5, Begin was back east in Philadelphia, to attend yet another dinner in his honor. On Monday, he returned to New York to address an audience of almost 3,000 at Carnegie Hall. He went uptown to visit Yeshiva University, where students may take rabbinic and secular undergraduate and graduate studies under one roof. Begin addressed an assembly of 1,000 students in Hebrew and Yiddish, recalling the role played by synagogues in the underground struggle in Palestine and picturing the future of Jerusalem as a center of Hebrew learning and culture.

He managed two more days in Washington, where he paid his respects at the Israeli embassy, only to find that Ambassador Eliahu Elath was out of town. The reception on Capitol Hill was somewhat warmer. Begin was entertained by Senators Claude Pepper of Florida and William Langer of North Dakota, both of whom had been isolationists prior to World War II. Also in the party were a number of Congressmen. Begin's background of legal studies drew him to the U.S. Supreme Court. He attended one of its sessions; his host was Associate Justice Wiley B. Rutledge.

On Sunday, December 12, he had his first television interview on *Meet the Press.* He said he would never use force against any "Hebrew government," no matter what its composition. When questioned on reports that he was a Communist agent, he jokingly replied, "The pro-Fascists call me a Communist; the Communists call me, as you have all heard, a Fascist. I can only conclude that I am either a Communistic Fascist or a Fascist Communist."

Begin concluded his month's stay in the United States with an appearance at New York's Manhattan Center. In keeping with the season, his address, in Yiddish, was entitled, "The Miracle of Hanukkah." It dealt with the Maccabean uprising in ancient Palestine against Hellenist tyranny.

On Monday, December 20, he left New York by plane, stopping in Paris for several days of meetings with the Irgun's "diaspora command," gently but firmly informing his "fighting family" there that he would oppose any effort to continue the Irgun as an expatriate organization.[5]

In Paris he was given a warm reception by the French press and French political leaders. "The French press," the London *Jewish Chronicle* noted with a touch of irritation, "has placed a halo around Menahem Begin's head — a glittering halo to match the price of £10,000 alleged to have been placed on this same head by the British authorities in Palestine." The *Chronicle* attributed Begin's success in France to lingering French resentment over the expulsion of France from Syria.[6] In numerous press interviews Begin reiterated his principal theses: that neither he nor the party under his leadership would ever go underground against the government of the State of Israel but would seek to attain power solely by legal, democratic means; that Jerusalem must be the capital of Israel even as Rome was the capital of Italy; and that the partition of Palestine was unworkable since the Arabs in the territory allocated to them had proven incapable of setting up an independent state of their own. Other Arab countries, he stressed, had no right to take over that sector of Palestine. A dinner was given in Begin's honor, at which he was praised by two prominent public figures, M. René Capitant, a close associate of General Charles De Gaulle, and Robert Briscoe, a member of the Irish parliament and staunch supporter of the Irgun who was to become the first Jewish mayor of Dublin. Like O'Dwyer in New York, Briscoe drew an analogy between the struggle of the Jews and that of the Irish against British imperialism.

Returning to Israel, Begin settled down once again with his family in their Tel Aviv apartment on 1 Rosenbaum Street, then took his seat in the Knesset. As opposition leader, he spoke out against the Ben-Gurion government's foreign and domestic policies. On May 3, 1949, the eve of Israel's first Independence Day, he attacked the austerity program which had been intended to cope with the burdens of defense expenditures, immigrant absorption and economic development. Austerity, including stringent food rationing, had been an attempt to distribute the country's limited resources equitably, to save currency and to encourage foreign investments by reducing both prices and consumption. Begin, however, argued that an austerity program was not the way to achieve these ends; it would only lower the country's standard of living without improving the economy. Also, the government's plan to standardize production was not compatible with Israel's effort to attract investors from other countries.[7]

In December, 1949, the Ben-Gurion government issued a proclamation declaring the New City of Jerusalem the capital of the State of Israel. On January 2, 1950, Begin urged the Knesset to follow up that proclamation with another, announcing that the New City and the Old City were "one and indivisible." The State of Israel, he argued, could have obtained both sectors of Jerusalem, and probably all of pre-1947 Palestine as well, had it not been for what he called the "muddled" foreign policy conducted by the Jewish leadership and subsequently by Foreign Minister Moshe Sharett (who had officially Hebraized his original surname, Shertok).

In the spring of 1950, Begin left Israel again; this time he visited Latin America — first Mexico and then Cuba — where he was studiously ignored by the Zionist establishment but nevertheless found responsive Jewish audiences. On the way back to Israel that summer he briefly stopped in New York, where a report that he might appear at a memorial service for Jabotinsky sent thousands to the East Side funeral chapel where the gathering was held.[8]

He published his first book, his reminiscences of the underground period. Originally published in Hebrew, the book was subsequently translated into English as *The Revolt*,[9] and has gone through a number of English printings. (Begin gave the money from that book to Irgun veterans in need of financial assistance.) It opens with a brief account of Begin's imprisonment in Russia, but it primarily covers the period from his arrival in Palestine to the establishment of the State of Israel, including his somewhat sketchy and emotional version of the *Altalena* affair a scant two years after the event. By Begin's own admission, *The Revolt* was not an attempt at an objective historical or autobiographical work. It was still too early for that. In his introduction to the first English edition, he explains that he wrote the book primarily for the Jewish people after the Holocaust ("lest the Jew forget again — as he so disastrously forgot in the past — this simple truth: that there are things more precious than life, and more horrible than death").

Concomitantly, *The Revolt* was meant to serve notice on the Gentile world that the Nazi Holocaust had produced "a new specimen of human being, a specimen completely unknown to the world for over eighteen hundred years, the 'Fighting Jew,' " who would never again resign himself to the role of unresisting victim. "It is axiomatic," Begin states, "that those who fight have to hate — something or somebody." However, he goes on to explain, the feelings of hatred which inspired the Jewish freedom fighters in their underground struggle had nothing to do with the British people. Rather, the hostility was directed against the former defenseless position of the Jewish people, a situation which Begin called "inexcusable" and a "standing invitation" to persecution and massacre; against the idea that the Jewish people in their own land should be ruled by an alien power which barred "the gates of our own country to our brethren, trampled and bleeding and crying out for help in a world morally deaf;" and against those who, "equipped with modern arms [as well as with] the ancient machinery of the gallows," denied the Jewish people the means of self-defense and of attaining national independence and self-respect.

Feelings of hatred, in Begin's view, are not condemnable if they spring from love, which is the highest human emotion. If you truly love what is good and right, then, conversely, you must hate all that is evil. If you truly love freedom, then you must hate slavery, and if you truly love your land and people, you cannot help hating those who seek to destroy either of the two. The hallmark of a decent human being is that he has ideals for which he will be ready to fight and, if necessary, to lay down his life. This was what Begin meant when, in selecting a title for the fourth chapter of *The Revolt*, he chose to recall Descartes' classic statement, "I think, therefore I am," with his own widely-quoted dictum, "We fight, therefore we are." This phrase has often been cited out of context to portray Begin as an exponent of terrorist ideology. But that is not the philosophy of Menahem Begin. His belief is that the level on which any man can truly be said to exist as a human being must be gauged not solely, as Descartes put it, by his intelligence but just as much by his ability and willingness to defend his ideals and to go to battle against evil — in short, by what Begin considers elementary self-respect. It is Begin's own variation on Jabotinsky's theme of *hadar*.

From the day Begin first made his pledge of allegiance as a

member of the Knesset, his concept of *hadar* was evident in his conduct on the Knesset floor and on speakers' platforms elsewhere. When he spoke from the opposition bench, his style was correct, in strict accordance with the forms of parliamentary etiquette. His words were sharp, but compared with the utterances of some of his old-style Labor colleagues who had little use for courtesies they considered meaningless, his language was dignified, even elegant. There was only one occasion when he allowed his emotions to get the better of him in public debate. This happened in January, 1952. The issue was a moral one which triggered a bitter dispute unparalleled in the history of Israel to this day and which drew from Begin an outraged appeal for the overthrow of the Ben-Gurion government — by force, if necessary.

As early as September, 1945, almost three years before the establishment of the State of Israel, Chaim Weizmann, on behalf of the Jewish Agency, had requested the governments of Great Britain, the United States, the Soviet Union and liberated France, to include in their own demands for reparations from Germany the claims of the Jewish people. In September, 1951, the government of the German Federal Republic (West Germany) in Bonn, led by Konrad Adenauer, had declared itself ready in principle to negotiate directly with the State of Israel and with representatives of Diaspora Jewry on the payment of reparations for the destruction of Jewish communities and for the losses of Jewish life and property in the Nazi Holocaust.

This declaration from West Germany brought the leaders and the people of Israel face to face with an agonizing question: Could the State of Israel decently enter into direct negotiations with the government of Germany, a country which only a few years earlier had been responsible for the murder of six million Jews and which had, in fact, named a number of former Nazis to positions of official leadership?

Large segments of Israel's population felt that it would be morally wrong for Israel as a state and also for Jews as individuals to accept what they considered "blood money" from the Germans. Most of the people in Israel had experienced various aspects of the Holocaust themselves, or had lost their families in German ghettoes and death camps. The trauma was still too fresh for them to consider the matter in rational terms. For Jews to negotiate with the Germans, in their eyes, was tantamount to certifying that the land of Adolf Hitler, by the simple act of laying down a specified amount of cash, could pay its debt to society and make itself eligible for membership in the family of civilized nations. It would appear as if the Jewish people were ready to extend the hand of forgiveness to Germany in return for a financial indemnity, and that would be a desecration of the memory of the millions of Jews who had died in the Holocaust. In this view, direct negotiations with a German government would have been morally justifiable only if the German people themselves had overthrown the Hitler regime instead of waiting until after the Allied victory to voice their disgust with Nazism.

Among Israel's elder statesmen who opposed negotiations with the German Federal Republic on these moral grounds were such leaders as Itzhak Gruenbaum, the former minister of the interior, and Rabbi Judah L. Fishman, who had Hebraized his name to Maimon and was now minister of religious affairs in the Ben-Gurion Cabinet.

Also opposed was the Mapam party, *Mifleget Poalim Meuhedet* or "United Workers Party", which was considerably to the left of Ben-Gurion's Mapai and was then not part of the government coalition. The leaders of Mapam rejected contacts with the German Federal Republic partly out of moral considerations but partly also out of political motivations. In their eyes West Germany, as opposed to the "German Democratic Republic" in the east, could do no right. They viewed the German Federal Republic as a puppet of Western imperialism, whom the Western powers were eager to show off in the best possible light, the easier to rearm the Germans and use them as spearheads for an "imperialist" attack on Soviet Russia.

The main opposition, and the most active resistance, to the projected dealings with the West German government, however, came from Menahem Begin and the Herut party. His heart and mind seared by the Holocaust, Begin, whose own life-style bordered on the ascetic — a friend once said that all Begin knew about money was how to give it away to those in need of help — was unreceptive to the weighty argument that the payments received under a reparations agreement with West Germany would shore up Israel's economy, already strained to the limit by defense expenditures, rampant inflation, and mass immigration. To rebuild the Jewish state with the help of "blood money" paid by Germans as atonement for lost Jewish lives, he declared, would be a *hillul ha-Shem*, an outrage against the good name of the Jewish people. In speech after speech he hammered home his conviction that turning to any German government for reparations would deprive the

Jewish people of whatever respect they might have acquired in world opinion after Israel's successful struggle for independence and Jewish national dignity.

Ben-Gurion himself had gone through no little soul-searching before making the decision to negotiate with the West German government for financial restitution, but as prime minister his thinking had to be guided in large measure by the harsh realities of Israel's critical economic situation. The three and a half years that had passed since the establishment of the state had been marked by a costly war, followed by the doubling of Israel's Jewish population. During the first three years of her existence, Israel had received over half a million immigrants from 70 countries — survivors of the Nazi Holocaust and refugees from social and economic oppression in Arab and other Oriental lands. Nearly all the newcomers had arrived in Israel destitute. At one point, over 200,000 of them lived in *ma'abarot,* transition camps consisting of tents, wooden shacks or tin huts set up near places where employment might be available. The crowded, primitive conditions brought incredible hardship during the rainy winter season and during the months of summer heat. Already, the Israelis had accepted stern austerity measures; by the summer of 1950 not only food but also clothing was rationed, there were critical shortages of raw materials and the country's meager foreign exchange reserves were exhausted. This state of affairs could not endure much longer.

Ben-Gurion's view, which he took pains to make clear also to others, was that if Israel were to meet with the representatives of West Germany and to accept reparations from them, she would not regard the money as Germany's atonement for what Hitler had done to the Jews. She would accept the indemnity as a financial infusion to help her fulfill one of the basic purposes for which the Jewish state had been created: to accept and absorb Jews who had no place of refuge except the ancient homeland of the Jewish people.

Israel's claim to German reparations was based on the fact that the overwhelming majority of Jewish displaced persons within West Germany's borders at the end of World War II had chosen to go to Israel, and that Israel had assumed the social and economic responsibility for rehabilitating these victims of the Nazi Holocaust. Legally, too, the State of Israel, as the independent political entity created by the Jewish people, considered itself the natural heir of the Jewish communities that had been wiped out in the Holocaust, and of individual Jews who had lost their lives in the horror without leaving any families. These were the considerations which Ben-Gurion cited when the question of direct negotiations with the German government was placed before the Knesset for approval on January 7, 1952.

The debate was to be the stormiest in Israel's brief history. The opponents of negotiations with West Germany had been making their voices heard in the press and on public platforms. *Ma'ariv,* a politically independent afternoon daily, polled more than 10,000 readers and claimed that 80 per cent had reacted negatively to the idea of direct talks with the German Federal Republic.[10] On the Sabbath preceding the Knesset debate, rabbis in numerous synagogues delivered sermons urging their congregations to oppose any direct contact with the Germans. Zivia Lubetkin, who nine years earlier had been a leader in the Warsaw ghetto revolt, exhorted an audience of Mapam members not to insult the memory of the Six Million by allowing the government to approve the negotiations.

Meanwhile, in Tel Aviv, Begin mobilized his party and, in an impassioned speech at a mass rally, called for a Herut "march on Jerusalem" to protest against the talks with Germany.

Begin's followers throughout the country — along with many who did not support him on other issues — heeded his call. On Monday morning, January 7, hours before the Knesset session began, Jerusalem's Zion Square and the streets running into it were black with humanity; the crowd was estimated at about 15,000. Standing on a balcony of the Zion Hotel which overlooked the square was Menahem Begin. Near him was a venerable, bearded figure — Professor Joseph Klausner, a widely-respected scholar in Hebrew history and literature who had been the Herut candidate for the presidency of Israel against Chaim Weizmann in 1949. Now in his late seventies, Klausner, a veteran Zionist from the days of Theodor Herzl, had been asked to lend the aura of his presence to Begin's emotional appeal for revolt.

During the "open season" in the days of the British mandate, Begin had ordered the Irgun not to retaliate against the Haganah informers. After the shelling of the *Altalena,* Begin again had pleaded tearfully with the members of his "fighting family" not to raise their hands against their brothers who now constituted the government of the Jewish state. But at this point, when it seemed to him that the Ben-Gurion government, by considering talks with a government in Germany, had violated the very foundations of Jewish dignity, Menahem Begin appeared to have abandoned one of his own cherished definitions of *hadar,* of stating his convictions firmly and effectively but with self-restraint.[11]

"When you fired at us with your cannon," he shouted, his words aimed at the members of the Ben-Gurion government who were already assembling in the Knesset hall 500 yards away, "I ordered our comrades to hold their fire. But today I shall give the order, 'Yes!' This will be a war of life and death. We know they will grant us no mercy, but we shall have no mercy on wholesalers of the blood of our mothers and fathers . . !

"That blood which was poured out in German concentration camps gave us courage to rise and overthrow the British . . . That sacred blood gave us a state, and the premiership to Ben-Gurion. How shall we face the world after trading that blood for [German] marks?

"I call on Ben-Gurion to hold back. I tell him there will be no negotiations with Germany. For this we all are ready to give our lives and there is no sacrifice too dear . . . I would rather die than see my own son ashamed of being a Jew . . . The government which negotiates with the Nazis is not a Jewish government but a tyranny which is supported by bayonets . . ."

Finally, close to tears, Begin left Klausner to continue the proceedings. He himself disappeared from the balcony, walked out of the hotel and toward the Knesset hall. All but four of the 120 members of the Knesset were on hand for the debate. Begin's old comrade Arye Ben Eliezer, who had been seriously ill, insisted on being brought into the chamber on a stretcher to cast his vote. The year before, a new Knesset had been elected and the Herut party had lost 6 of its original 14 seats. Each one of the party's remaining 8 votes was precious.

Ben-Gurion took half an hour to explain the government's viewpoint. The Jewish state, as he saw it, was the rightful heir of the property of Jews and Jewish communities destroyed in the Holocaust. "Let not the murderers of our people be their inheritors!" he pleaded.

Begin's speech on the Knesset floor was mild compared to the near-hysterical oration he had delivered to the protesters on Zion Square, but it left no uncertainty about his attitude.

As far as he was concerned, there was not one German who was not a Nazi, because the Germans had either voted for Hitler or else had done nothing to keep him from becoming Germany's leader and remaining in power for twelve years. Accordingly, it would be a "national sin," as he put it, for a Jewish government to deal with Germany on the question of reparations.

> In what savage tribe will you see the son of the victim go direct to the man who killed his father and ask him for compensation? But you, orphaned children bereft of your parents, would go directly to the murderer . . . In what primitive tribe have you ever seen an abomination like that? Into what would you turn the people of Israel, which has been the bearer and teacher of civilization for 4,000 years? . . .
>
> The Gentiles not only hated us . . . first and foremost, they despised us. And in this generation, which we call the last generation of slavery and the first of redemption, the generation in which we have achieved dignity . . . you, for the sake of a dirty few million dollars . . . would impair the bit of dignity we have acquired . . .

Begin appealed to Ben-Gurion's personal pride as a Jew:

> I am turning to you not as one opponent to another . . . [but] as the son of an orphaned people, the son of a people of mourners: Stop! Do not do this thing! It is an abomination of abominations in Israel!

The government, he said, could still retreat from what he considered an intolerable position; it could hold a referendum and withdraw from the negotiations, citing widespread popular opposition.

His speech ended on a note of martyrdom:

> We will leave our families, say goodbye to our children, and there will be no negotiations with the Germans . . . I know you will throw us into concentration camps . . . But there will be no "reparations" from Germany.

Before returning to his seat, Begin made a swift changeover from fiery orator to disciplined parliamentarian. He announced that, as of four o'clock that afternoon, he waived parliamentary immunity for himself.[12] He felt that this was only fair. Even while he had been speaking in the Knesset hall, the people whom he had stirred by his oration outside had begun a full-scale riot. Begin, though, he was not with them physically, regarded himself as one of the demonstrators, and he thought it only proper that if they would be arrested, he should share their fate.

Despite the efforts of the police, which used clubs, water jets and tear gas, thousands of demonstrators got past the police line surrounding the Knesset and hurled rocks through the windows of the building. Several Knesset members were cut by flying glass. Dozens of civilians and policemen were also injured. Ben-Gurion castigated Begin for the activities of the "hooligans" outside. Begin forgot the courtesy with which he customarily addressed the premier and called him a "hooligan" in return. (The word has been taken over into the Hebrew language.) The Knesset session broke up until a semblance of order was restored.

Two days later, the Knesset approved negotiations with West Germany, but the margin was narrow: 61 to 50, with five members abstaining; of these five, four had been absent from the session. The vote reflected the large number of Israelis, irrespective of party affiliation, who wanted no truck with the Germans so soon after the Holocaust. Perhaps the one argument that had carried the day for negotiations was Ben-Gurion's plea that the nation which had been responsible for the murder of six million Jews should not be permitted also to inherit the property of its victims.

Over 400 of the Herut demonstrators were arrested in Jerusalem, many of them at bus stations where they had been waiting to return to their homes. Begin was not arrested, but he was suspended from the Knesset for a period of three months. He took the punishment with good grace. He had lost what he considered the first round in the battle, but he was so sure of his cause that he did not think a revolt against the Ben-Gurion government would be necessary. "I believe," he told a *New York Times* correspondent after the Knesset debate, "that the negotiations will be frustrated by our people, both here and abroad."[13] He was convinced that once the Jewish people in Israel and in the Diaspora realized the implications — as he saw them — of the Ben-Gurion government's decision, they would take some action to prevent Israel from committing what he called the "national sin."

The talks between Israel and Germany opened at The Hague on March 12, 1952. In Tel Aviv there was a mass demonstration at which Begin appealed to the government to withdraw its representatives from the negotiations. But this time the crowds were orderly and Begin did not talk of revolution.

While negotiations between Germany and representatives of Israeli and world Jewry continued, Begin left Israel on a tour of two continents to arouse world Jewish public opinion against negotiations with Germany and the purchase of German goods. This journey, which began in May, 1952 and continued into the late summer, took Begin to Paris, New York, Canada, Mexico, Brazil and Argentina.

In Paris, where he spent 10 days, he urged an audience of 700 to agitate for a worldwide Jewish boycott of all German products. "These products," he said, "are made in the same factories that prepared the arms of death with which our fathers and mothers were burned, and perished in the gas chambers."[14] Also in Paris, Lucien (Lazar) Rachline, a wealthy Jewish industrialist, arranged for him to meet General Charles De Gaulle. The two men had something in common: each had been the leader of an underground movement during World War II, but in 1952, neither of them was in the seat of power in his country. Begin and De Gaulle spent over an hour together at De Gaulle's party headquarters on 5 Solferino Street. Begin was accompanied into the general's office by Ben Zion Chomsky, veteran Revisionist and member of Jabotinsky's Jewish Legion who was then living in France. De Gaulle insisted that Begin speak to him in Hebrew; Chomsky acted as interpreter. During the interview, De Gaulle asked Begin whether the Israelis regarded Jerusalem as their capital. "Would the French ever agree that Paris should not be their capital?" Begin asked De Gaulle in reply. When they parted, the French leader said to him, "Give my greetings to the young State of Israel and to the brave men of the underground."[15]

From France, Begin proceeded to the United States, where he arrived on May 12 and launched what he described as a public enlightenment campaign. On the day after his arrival, he spoke at New York's Town Hall. In his address, he called for a worldwide Jewish plebiscite to decide whether the State of Israel or Jewish organizations in other countries should continue negotiating directly with Germany for reparations. As regarded the political scene in Israel, he asserted that the country needed a free enterprise system, a "complete separation between the power of the ruler and the power of the employer," which would serve as a "guarantee of civil liberties and human dignity."[16] The New York audience was impressed with Begin's sincerity and his views on free enterprise, but showed little enthusiasm for his opposition to accepting reparations from Germany.

In June, Begin went north to Canada. It was his first visit to a member nation of the British Commonwealth. The Canadian Jewish Congress and United Zionist Council had urged all Canadian Jewish organizations to boycott Begin's appearances in

Montreal and Toronto because they considered his views "destructive of the unity of Canadian Jewry." Nevertheless, when Begin landed at Montreal airport, in a summer rainstorm, a crowd of thousands was waiting there to greet him. He addressed a mass meeting in the Monument National Auditorium in Montreal and then a great public gathering at Massey Hall in Toronto, where, alternating between Yiddish and English, he discussed a worldwide Jewish plebiscite on German reparations, the boycotting of German manufactured goods, and the dangers inherent in the rearming of Germany.[17]

In July and August, Begin addressed a meeting sponsored by the Revisionist party organization in Mexico City, then traveled on to Rio de Janeiro and Buenos Aires.

Meanwhile, in Jerusalem, the Zionist General Council, the supreme governing organ of the World Zionist Organization, had rejected by an overwhelming majority a resolution introduced by its Herut representatives for the worldwide plebiscite proposed by Begin.[18]

On September 10, 1952, an agreement on German reparations payments was signed in Luxembourg by Chancellor Adenauer for the German Federal Republic, Foreign Minister Moshe Sharett for the State of Israel, and Dr. Nahum Goldmann for the Conference on Jewish Material Claims against Germany, representing 23 Jewish organizations in other countries. In Israel, the reparations paid by Germany in cash and capital goods were to become a major factor in priming the economy of the Jewish state. They were to help mechanize Israel's agricultural production, increase diversification and production capacity in Israel's industries, build up an Israeli merchant marine, provide modern rolling stock to replace the sadly obsolete trains that had made up Israel's railroad system, and improve the country's telephone service which had been incredibly neglected by the British authorities. In addition, thousands of Jews in Israel along with hundreds of thousands of Jews in other countries were materially aided by indemnities for loss of educational opportunities, deprivation of income and livelihood, and damage to physical and mental health suffered as a result of the Holocaust.

But for many survivors of the Holocaust it was still too soon to accept the idea of dealing with Germany. Following the Luxembourg agreement, the Herut party declared that it would continue its fight against the acceptance of "blood money." Protests kept coming also from other circles in Israel even while Foreign Minister

Sharett publicly reiterated his government's official position in claiming and accepting German reparations. The Israeli government, Sharett explained, as he had many times before, would not regard the payments as atonement for the Nazi Holocaust. However, by pledging to make restitution to Hitler's victims, and by honoring her pledge, Germany would have an opportunity to make her contribution to the establishment of law and justice in human society.[19] The Germans understood what was at stake; despite Arab threats to boycott West Germany, the West German parliament ratified the agreement in March, 1953, and the pact went into operation on April 1.

In 1953 Begin published the second volume of his personal memoirs, *BeLeilot Levanim,* the story of his arrest in Vilna and his deportation to Siberia. Four years later, the book was to appear in an English edition entitled *White Nights: The Story of a Prisoner in Russia.* In 1953, too, Begin went abroad once again in behalf of his party. This time he toured the Union of South Africa, where Vladimir Jabotinsky had also visited 16 years before and had won influential and enthusiastic followers for the Revisionist philosophy. Begin and his wife arrived in South Africa in October, 1953 and remained there until early in January, 1954. During that period, Begin traveled over 25,000 miles by train, plane and automobile, visiting 20 cities and towns, delivering some 50 addresses in Hebrew, Yiddish, English and French. He also met Prime Minister Daniel F. Malan. He was warmly received by his South African friends, notably the Union's chief rabbi, Dr. Louis I. Rabinowitz, who had been present at the negotiations between Begin and representatives of the Jewish Agency in December, 1947. Rabinowitz reported that the Boer elements hailed the visitor as the hero who had managed within a scant few years to do in Palestine what the Boers had not been able to accomplish in decades of struggle: to throw off the yoke of British domination. As Begin entered his hotel in Rhodesia, a British policeman greeted him. "I'm glad to see you here, Mr. Begin," he said, then explained that he had been stationed with the British police force in Palestine and had enthusiastically participated in the search for Begin, hoping to get part of the prize that had been placed on Begin's head. "Well, if that's the case, I am also glad to see you here," Begin replied.[20]

While Begin was in South Africa, Ben-Gurion announced that he was resigning from the premiership and retiring to Kibbutz Sde Boker. He was succeeded by Foreign Minister Sharett, who retained the portfolio of foreign affairs as well and who seemed to believe that Israel could best assure her survival by lying low and doing nothing to offend "world opinion." Yet, half a decade after the signing of the armistice, Egypt and the other Arab states still considered themselves in a state of war with Israel. Israel's outlet to the Red Sea, the port city of Elat, was blocked by Egyptian guns at Sharm el-Sheikh, which, at the southern tip of the Sinai peninsula, commanded the Strait of Tiran and the Gulf of Elat. Egypt was deep in negotiations with Britain about Britain's planned withdrawal from the Suez Canal, likewise blocked to Israeli ships and cargo bound for Israel. Also, Britain and the newly-elected Eisenhower Administration in the United States were vying with one another in arming the Arabs. Secretary of State John Foster Dulles had announced his intention to "redress the balance" in American Middle Eastern policy in favor of the Arabs. Meanwhile, Arab infiltrators were raiding Israel's border areas, inflicting losses of life and property.

In the face of these threats, Begin considered Sharett's foreign policy too passive, and not adequate for the preservation of Israel's independence. In mid-August, 1954, he told a crowd of 7,000 gathered in Jerusalem's Zion Square his ideas about a military and diplomatic strategy that would avert the danger threatening the Jewish state. Israel, he said, was faced with two alternatives: either to accept the Arab guerilla raids until the regular armies of the Arabs, equipped by the United States and Britain, felt powerful enough to launch an all-out attack, or else to prevent such an attack by limited action, destroying the bases from which the infiltrators had been operating. He concluded his lengthy speech with an appeal to his audience to break with what he regarded as a passive ghetto mentality developed over centuries of persecution:

> These, then, are the alternatives before you today, citizens of Israel: fatalistic acceptance of fatal developments, or a policy of planned strategic action, an independent state moving towards its historic destiny, or a besieged and attacked ghetto. Yours is the choice.[21]

On the Knesset floor, Begin declared that Israel was not faced with a choice between peace and war, but with the problem of stopping a war which was already in progress. In his opinion, the risk that a limited Israeli action against the infiltrators' bases would bring on a massive Arab counter-attack was minimal, since the Arabs knew that Israel's army was strong. It was on this account that the

Arabs had refrained from starting a full-scale war against Israel but were seeking instead to sap the country's strength and morale by constant guerilla raids. By its inaction in the face of this steady Arab blood-letting on all of Israel's borders, Begin said, the Sharett government was, in effect, telling the people of Israel to resign themselves to a war of annihilation.[22]

Meanwhile, in America, many members of the U.S. Congress were expressing opposition to the pro-Arab tilt of the Eisenhower Administration. In October, 1954, Begin addressed a personal letter to each member of the Senate and House of Representatives in Washington, "as a member of [the Israeli] Parliament to a member of the [U.S.] Congress," protesting against U.S. arms shipments to the Arab nations. Appealing to the United States as the one nation that had saved the free world from Nazism and Communism, he pleaded with each American Congressman and Senator to examine his own conscience on the specific issue of rearming the Arab states at Israel's expense. He stated that while, as a citizen of a foreign country, he had no right to decide what was in the best interest of the United States, he felt he had the right to protest against the American arms policy because it posed a threat to the survival of the Jewish state which had been born of incredible suffering:

> This is the reason why I permit myself, with respect, to address to you the question whether, in America, too, expediency, or what seems to be expedient, is to overrule moral values, the real bulwark of the free world.

This letter was Begin's first public appeal to the morality and basic sense of fairness which he had long attributed to the American people. But he made it clear that his letter was not intended as a desperate plea for mercy.

> This appeal, Sir, is not written in panic . . . This generation of Jews does not, and will never again, rely on the world's pity . . . It is a fighters' generation.

> But our people are still bleeding from the horrible wounds inflicted on them by the German exterminators and by the Arab aggressors. Should their blood flow anew, this time by means of arms made, or paid for, by the United States of America?

> The tragedy may still be avoided . . . And as a freely chosen

representative of your people, raise your voice, Sir, to avoid doing wrong to an ancient, renascent nation which has bled enough.

Yours sincerely,
M. BEGIN
Menahem Begin
Member of the Knesset[23]

In Israel, Begin and his party were gaining popularity among the new immigrants, many of whom had come from Arab lands and did not share the Sharett government's hopes that a soft attitude on Israel's part would bring peace with the Arabs. During the fall of 1954 Begin toured the *ma'abarot,* the transition camps where thousands of newcomers were still living, many of them blaming the Labor government for the fact that they still had no permanent homes. They received Begin with enthusiasm. When Begin visited Shikkun HaMizrah, near Petah Tikvah, a settlement consisting mainly of immigrants from Egypt and Iraq, he was swept from the ground and borne shoulder high by a crowd of admirers.[24]

Begin's rising popularity was reflected in the elections to the Third Knesset, which were held on July 26, 1955. From only eight seats in the Second Knesset, Herut jumped to 15 seats, one more than it had won in the first elections of 1949, making it the second largest party in the Knesset.

The months directly preceding the 1955 elections brought back poignant memories to Begin. During Passover week, he and 1,500 other former underground fighters assembled in the yard of Jerusalem's Central Prison, where hundreds of Irgunists and Sternists had been jailed during the period of the revolt. The occasion for the rally was the seventieth birthday of the saintly Rabbi Arye Levin, known throughout Israel as the "father of the prisoners." During the underground years "Reb Arye," who had settled in Palestine as a young man, had acted as the unofficial chaplain to Irgun and LEHI fighters arrested by the British. An unworldly man, he himself had never mixed in politics, but his tender heart had gone out to the freedom fighters. He went in and out of the prisons, visiting prisoners, carrying messages back and forth between the prisoners and their families (sometimes committing the messages to memory), and interceding with the British authorities to have harsh sentences commuted. When the date for an execution had been irrevocably set, "Reb Arye" would comfort the prisoner during his last hours. Afterwards, he would go to the man's family and weep together with the mourners. His kindliness and compassion earned him the respect and affection even of those who were far from Orthodox in their own religious behavior. Now, veterans of the "fighting family" met again at the prison to honor their rabbi. Flanked by Begin and a guard of honor "Reb Arye," who had shunned publicity all his life, was handed a parchment scroll and a silver medallion to mark the occasion. The celebration ended with the daily afternoon service. It was an emotion-filled day for Begin and his comrades in arms.

In June, Begin revisited the Savoy Hotel where, eleven years earlier, he and his family had narrowly escaped being arrested by the British. Now he came to the hotel to honor Prof. Aage Bartelsen, leader of the Danish underground during World War II, who had saved 6,000 Jews from death at the hands of the Nazis. As a gesture of gratitude, the Israeli government had invited Bartelsen as its honored guest. The Herut party arranged a reception for him at the Savoy. Begin greeted him as a "brother in arms," and Bartelsen replied that he felt completely at home with his fellow freedom fighters. "We feel here a bond of friendship of Undergrounders," the Dane said. "In Denmark, we fought not only for the freedom of our country but also for a free world. I understand now that you did the same."[25]

In the meantime, Israel's political and military situation continued to deteriorate. Arab guerillas stepped up their attacks on the border settlements, and Jewish casualties multiplied. In September, 1955, Egypt signed a Soviet-sponsored agreement with Czechoslovakia, under which Egypt was to be supplied with sophisticated weapons from the Communist bloc. In the United States, the Eisenhower Administration continued its efforts to demonstrate its friendship for the Arab nations, and whenever Israel retaliated against an Arab raid, Secretary Dulles did not show much understanding for Israel's predicament. On October 18, Begin in the Knesset branded as "hypocritical" a speech by Dulles expressing concern over the Egyptian-Czech arms deal when in fact the Middle Eastern arms balance had already been upset much earlier by Western arms shipments to Arab lands, notably the British Centurion tanks sent to Egypt and America's own agreement to supply Iraq with $100 million's worth of weapons. In the debate on Israeli foreign policy, Begin called for the expulsion of Egypt from the Gaza Strip, a narrow piece of land projecting into Israel at the south, which Egyptian-trained *fedayeen* fighters were using as a strategic advance base for hit-and-run guerilla attacks against settlements within Israeli territory. The Gaza Strip had become part of the Second Jewish Commonwealth during the Maccabean era and in 1947 had been assigned to the modern Jewish state. During the War of Independence it had been occupied by Egyptian forces and formally came under Egyptian control under the 1949 armistice agreement. But Egypt had never claimed political sovereignty over the Strip; consequently, there was a legal basis for Begin's argument that the area from which the *fedayeen* were launching their raids was in fact part of the historic Jewish homeland.

"If Egypt is getting more and more powerful, and in only a few years it will be many times stronger than we in Stalin and Centurion tanks," Begin said in the Knesset, "then, first of all, we must eject the Egyptian invader from Eretz Yisrael so that he cannot strengthen his base of attack near our homes and children."[26]

But even while he was concerned about Israel's political and military problems, Begin directed his thoughts to the moral aspects of Jewish statehood. He urged his fellow citizens not to lose sight of the humanitarian purposes which the State of Israel was meant to fulfill. In an address before a mass rally in Jerusalem he encouraged the government's efforts to initiate steps for the systematic transfer of all North African Jewry to Israel. The Jews of Tunisia, Morocco and Algeria were suffering from persecution by aggressively nationalist Arab majorities and had already begun to move to Israel in large numbers.

"Israel was born to be a haven for persecuted Jews," Begin said. "Our strength to fight and die for the homeland comes mainly from the knowledge that our struggle is not only for the continued existence of the nation, but to rescue our brethren as well." He proposed that an IL200 million fund earmarked for the development of the country be diverted to the mass evacuation of the Jews from North Africa. "Rescuing Jews precedes development," he insisted.[27]

Ben-Gurion's retirement to Kibbutz Sde Boker had been short-lived. At the beginning of 1955 he had rejoined the Israeli Cabinet as minister of defense, replacing the controversial Pinhas Lavon. In November, 1955 he took the premiership from Sharett, leaving Sharett in his old post as foreign minister. Before long, however, basic disagreements developed between the two men, with Ben-Gurion now insisting that, in the absence of peace, Israel's foreign policy had to be subordinated to the needs of the country's defense. In June, 1956, Sharett was to be replaced as foreign minister by former Minister of Labor Golda Meir.

The year 1956 began with still more acts of Arab terror, yielding an ever-growing list of Israeli victims. Now the Egyptian army, too, was preparing for an onslaught against Israel. In February, 1956, an Egyptian division commander issued a training directive to his men: "Every officer must prepare himself and his subordinates for the inevitable struggle with Israel with the object of realizing our noble aim — namely, the annihilation of Israel and her destruction in the shortest possible time . . ."[28]

In the Knesset and from public platforms Begin accused the government of offering no real policy which would remove the threat of annihilation from Israel. He argued that a swift, incisive Israeli military operation to destroy the bases of the Arab aggressors before the regular Arab armies launched a massive first strike against Israel could not be construed by world opinion as a "preventive" war.

> A preventive war is possible only between states which are at peace. There is no peace between us and our enemies, who openly claim that there is a state of war. If during a state of war which finds expression in continuous bloodshed, the victim of aggression launches a military operation . . . this is no "preventive war" nor an "initiated war," but an operation whose practical aim is to put an end to warfare which [already] exists and despoils us; and its moral significance is defense.[29]

In March, 1956, Begin briefly turned from the gloomy political scene to a joyous occasion in his family. His son Benny had reached the age of 13 and celebrated his *bar mitzvah*. The boy was called at a synagogue service to read from the Scroll of the Law for the first time to mark his passage to Jewish manhood. A family picture[30] taken at the subsequent festivities shows Begin in a happy, relaxed mood, proud of his family and looking younger that his 42 years, having removed the mustache he had sported ever since his underground days.

In July, 1956, Egypt's dictator, Gamal Abdel Nasser, proclaimed his intention to nationalize the Suez Canal; it was another step closer to war. Begin understood that under Egyptian jurisdiction the Canal would not be opened to Israeli shipping, that the great powers would do nothing to make Egypt open the Canal to Israeli boats and that, in fact, Egypt's seizure of the waterway and the departure of the British forces which had served as a buffer between Egypt and Israel presented a grave danger to the Jewish state. To an American journalist, Begin put forward a peace plan which in his opinion could serve as a basis for negotiations between Israel and Egypt and prevent the outbreak of war. His proposal consisted of four points: 1) The evacuation of the Gaza Strip by Egypt; 2) the opening of the Gulf of Elat (Aqaba) and the Suez Canal to Israeli shipping; 3) cessation of guerilla raids and 4) negotiated reparations for damage to Israeli life and property caused by Arab infiltrators from Egypt. But Begin frankly admitted to the reporter that he considered the chances of Egypt's agreeing to peace talks with Israel slim, to say the least.[31]

In mid-September Begin was in France, which had all but become Israel's ally against Egypt, supplying Israel not only with tanks, fighter jets and other war materiel, but also with staunch moral and political support. When Begin arrived in Paris, he was received more like a visiting statesman than as the leader of an opposition party in the parliament of a tiny young nation. Waiting for him and Aliza at the airport was a guard of honor composed of units of the Republican Guard in gala uniform. This time he did not meet with De Gaulle, who was out of the city, but he was invited to address a group of about 40 members of both houses of the French Parliament, representing all of France's political parties except the Communists. The meeting took place in the hall of the Chamber of Deputies, and the opening sentences of Begin's address were in Hebrew. It was the first time that Hebrew had ever been spoken within the walls of the Palais Bourbon. During his stay in France Begin met several times with leading French statesmen, including Foreign Minister Christian Pineau.[32]

In Israel, during the first week of October, the Herut party held a national convention. In his opening speech to the delegates at Tel Aviv's Habimah Theater, Begin projected his vision of a future coalition government under the leadership not of Labor, but of Herut. "The day is drawing near," he said, "when the disciples of Jabotinsky will be summoned to the President of Israel and will be requested to form, together with other national elements, a government replacing the Mapai regime."[33]

This new government was not to become a reality for another 21 years. Indeed, 11 years were to pass before Begin was even asked to join a Labor-led coalition as a minister without portfolio. But a scant three weeks after the week-long Herut convention had adjourned in Ramat Gan, he was invited, for the first time, to the home of his political adversary, David Ben-Gurion. On October 28 the prime minister, ill in bed with a high fever, summoned Begin, along with leaders of other non-coalition parties in the Knesset (except for the Communists) to obtain their endorsement for the course to which he and the Cabinet were about to commit the country. The situation had deteriorated to a point where the Ben-Gurion government had come to regard prompt military action as the only way of assuring Israel's survival. Israeli settlements were now raided not only by *fedayeen* guerillas from the Gaza Strip but also on a large scale by infiltrators from Jordan. Ominously, Jordan had become a base for Iraqi troops. On October 24, Jordan, Syria and Egypt had established a joint military high command directed against Israel. Now, four days later, Ben-Gurion informed Begin and representatives of other non-government parties of plans for a military operation designed to clear the Gaza Strip of *fedayeen* raider bases and to thwart Egyptian-led plans for an all-out attack on Israel. Begin had the grim satisfaction of seeing his own views, to which he had adhered with such dogged determination, vindicated.

On October 29, 1956, Israel's armed forces, under the command of Chief of Staff Moshe Dayan, began to move. Within one week the Sinai Operation had attained its main objectives: the Egyptian *fedayeen* bases were destroyed, the Egyptian blockade of the Gulf of Elat at the Strait of Tiran was broken, and the Sinai peninsula, along with the Gaza Strip, was occupied. At the same time, by prearrangement, France and Great Britain attempted to seize the Suez Canal. Egypt's utter ruin was prevented only by intervention from the United Nations, threats from the Soviet Union, and the United States working strangely in collusion with the Soviets against Britain, France and Israel. On November 5, 1956, a cease-fire imposed by the United Nations took effect.

Two days later — in the afternoon of November 7 — the Knesset met in a mood of celebration to hear the official report of Israel's victory. Begin, as a member of the Knesset's Foreign Affairs and Security Committee, rose to pay tribute to the army and to its chief of staff, who in the underground days had praised Begin and the Irgun for proving that it was possible to attack the British authorities with some success. Next, Begin congratulated the Ben-Gurion government for having planned the operation, waged it successfully and now refusing to retreat from the territories the army had occupied.

"I know that if our teacher and master, Vladimir Jabotinsky, were alive today," Begin declared, "he would say [that] no matter what our differences past or future, with the [Labor] government, let us congratulate the Prime Minister and his associates for having made the wise and right decision the Sunday before last. More power to them!"[34]

The session ended with the exuberant singing of *Hatikvah*. Many in the Knesset chamber that afternoon hoped that, after almost nine years of independence, Israel had come a step closer to normal relations with her Arab neighbors. But Egypt's Gamal Abdel Nasser, abetted by the United Nations, willed otherwise.

13. Peace and War: 1957-1967

E ven while the Egyptian forces were retreating in headlong flight from the advancing Israelis, Israel came under intense international pressures to relinquish her gains promptly and unconditionally. Faced with Soviet threats of armed intervention, including hints of nuclear attack, the United States joined the Soviet Union in forcing Britain and France to quit the Suez Canal zone and in coercing Israeli forces to withdraw from the Sinai peninsula and the Gaza Strip without any Egyptian promises of future peace.

Initially, the Israeli government took a firm stand against any Israeli retreat, but it soon was forced into ordering a phased withdrawal from Sinai. However, despite a steady barrage of threats from the two superpowers, working through the United Nations, Israel refused to leave the Gaza Strip, from where the *fedayeen* had staged their raids on Israel, and the western shores of the Gulf of Elat, including Sharm-el-Sheikh, from where Egypt had blockaded Israel's port of Elat for seven years. On January 23, 1957, the Knesset passed a resolution declaring that Israel would occupy and administer the Gaza Strip on a permanent basis.

Ben-Gurion's anger at Soviet Russia was reflected in his sharp remarks about the small Communist minority in Israel. On one occasion he used the terms "hooligan" and "contemptible" to describe the person and the conduct of one of the six Communist members of the Knesset. Begin, whose hatred for Communism was well known, leaped at the opportunity to rebuke the prime minister for language unbecoming his high office. "We have no need to repeat our attitude toward the Communists," said Begin. "They are agents and slaves of a foreign government . . . But nevertheless, it is my conviction that a citizen who performs the function of a prime minister should not demean himself by using such terms as 'contemptible' and 'hooligan' about a fellow citizen. Such [name-calling does] not injure the Fifth Column but only the values which we should cherish particularly during these difficult times."[1]

In January, 1957, Begin announced that he would visit the United States for a month's lecture tour, primarily to mobilize American public opinion against the Eisenhower Administration's efforts to dislodge Israel from the territories her army had taken in the Sinai Operation.

Before his departure in February, Begin, accompanied by Yaakov Meridor, was again received by Ben-Gurion for a discussion of political developments and came away with the feeling that the prime minister was still resolved to have Israeli troops remain in Sharm-el-Sheikh and the Gaza Strip.[2]

On his way to America, Begin stopped briefly in Belgium and France. Speaking at the Diamond Exchange in Antwerp, he discounted the promises of international guarantees which were then under discussion in return for Israel's withdrawal from the remainder of Sinai and from the Gaza Strip. He reminded his audience that, twice within a quarter-century, similar guarantees had proven ineffective in saving Belgium from invasion. In France, Begin met with General De Gaulle, who was still over a year away from his return to power and who urged Israel to stay firm in her policy of no further retreat.

On February 28, 1957, Begin arrived in New York. The press correspondents who met him at the airport wanted to know his reaction to the latest news: Ben-Gurion had announced that, on the basis of specific "assumptions" about her future security from blockade and guerilla attacks, Israel was going to withdraw from Sharm-el-Sheikh, from the rest of Sinai, and from the Gaza Strip. Begin refused to comment. The next morning, March 1, he sat in stunned silence in the gallery of the U.N. General Assembly hall as Foreign Minister Golda Meir walked up to the rostrum to announce Israel's decision. Israel forces would leave the disputed area, to be replaced by a United Nations Emergency Force (UNEF) which would keep Sinai clear of Egyptian troop concentrations and prevent infiltrators from resuming their activities from the Gaza Strip.

After Mrs. Meir, Henry Cabot Lodge of the United States took the speaker's rostrum. What particularly disturbed not only Begin in New York but also Ben-Gurion in Jerusalem was Lodge's failure to state clearly Israel's right to self-defense in case of renewed Egyptian encroachments at Gaza or at the Strait of Tiran, and to specify that only the UNEF and no Egyptian military presence would be permitted in the Gaza Strip. The Israelis felt that, after all manner of privately discussed undertakings from the United States, they had been double-crossed. Begin's mood was somber and pessimistic. "The day Israel lowers its standard in the ancient city of Gaza and in Sharm el-Sheikh will be a day of mourning for every Israeli soldier," he told a newspaper reporter.[3] Afterwards, he was spotted by Enrique Fabregat of Uruguay, who had been a member of the United Nations Special Committee on Palestine and had met with Begin in Tel Aviv. With Latin American exuberance, Fabregat rushed up to Begin, embraced him, and said, "You must hurry back home and inject that good old Irgun spirit into the people."[4]

Begin had the same idea. He stayed in the United States only long enough to attend a welcome dinner given him at the Roosevelt Hotel in midtown Manhattan on March 3, with Paul O'Dwyer as chairman, and some 800 guests present. The next day he flew back to Israel.

At home, Begin immediately started a campaign to have the Knesset dissolved and call special new elections. If Ben-Gurion were to remain minister of defense, he said, it would destroy whatever morale was still left in the Israeli army; if he were to remain prime minister, it would destroy whatever faith was left in Israel's future. On March 7 he addressed a crowd of approximately 10,000 in Tel Aviv's Mograbi Square, declaring that "not Nasser but the United States" with its threat of economic sanctions had brought about Israel's withdrawal from Sinai and the Gaza Strip.[5] He made similar speeches to audiences of thousands in Ashkelon, Rishon Lezion, and in Rehovot, where the soccer stadium was the only place large enough to accommodate the crowd.

There was considerable bitterness among Israelis of all political shadings at what was considered Israel's humiliating "surrender" to crude foreign pressures. Within days after Israel's withdrawal, Egypt announced that, despite President Eisenhower's publicly stated "assumption" to the contrary, the Suez Canal would continue to be closed to Israeli and Israel-bound shipping. Next, Egypt resumed military control of the Gaza Strip, not expelling the United Nations Forces, but appointing an Egyptian general as military governor.

But despite the widespread mood of dissatisfaction in the country, the Knesset neither forced the Ben-Gurion cabinet to resign, nor did it vote for its own dissolution. Eventually, for want of another alternative, Israel resigned herself to the fact that, although she had given up all her bargaining counters without any sign that the Arab world would abandon its belligerent attitude toward her, she had been able to record some tangible gains from her victory:

border raids from the Gaza Strip had ceased, and Elat, free from Egyptian blockade thanks to the UN presence in Sharm el-Sheikh, was fast becoming a major seaport for trade with Asia and Africa.

Late in April, after the Passover holidays, Begin flew westward across the Atlantic to start the lecture tour he had cancelled so abruptly the month before. His first stop on the American continent this time was Canada, where he told a press conference in Montreal that the only real and durable solution to the Middle East issue "would be to reunite both parts of Eretz Yisrael under the Israeli flag;" the part of Palestine which the Kingdom of Jordan had annexed during the 1948 war should become part of the Jewish state.[6] Also in Montreal, he was honored at a dinner at which the main address was delivered by the French consul general. In Toronto, he addressed an audience of 3,000 and was interviewed on television. From Canada, he went on to the United States.

On May 2, he helped celebrate the ninth anniversary of Israel's independence at New York's Manhattan Center, where he had extolled the "miracle of Hanukkah" during his first visit to America in 1948. This time, his address to an audience of 4,000 was a plea to the free world, and particularly the United States, to change its attitude toward Egypt and her dictator Nasser, who had thrown open "the door into the Middle East and the gateway to Africa to Communist penetration and expansion." He also reiterated his argument that the Gaza Strip was a part of the historic Jewish homeland. Egypt, he pointed out, had occupied it by an act of military aggression in 1948 and "turned it into a base of permanent attack against Israel."[7] Begin then turned to Israel's future. As long as Israel was heavily dependent on philanthropic funds from abroad, particularly the United States, she would continue to be vulnerable to every sort of foreign political pressure. One of Eisenhower's threats which had compelled Ben-Gurion to order the Israeli withdrawal from Sinai and the Gaza Strip had been that embargoes could be imposed on private as well as public financial aid to Israel from American organizations and individuals. Begin declared that Israel would have to cease being a "charity economy" and strive to become economically self-sustaining. With the port of Elat open to international commerce, he said, it should be possible to attain this objective. But in addition, Israel would have to furnish proper incentives for foreign investors; this would best be accomplished by a new Israeli government which, unlike the Labor regime, would be "pledged to free enterprise."[8]

In Washington, Begin met with the Senate minority leader, the

Republican William Knowland, and the Senate majority leader, Lyndon B. Johnson, both of whom had openly opposed the Administration's threat of sanctions against Israel.

In Boston, he addressed a session of the Massachusetts State Legislature.

In addition, he visited Pittsburgh, Chicago, Cleveland, and, for the first time, traveled as far west as San Francisco and Los Angeles.

After a short few weeks at home in Israel, Begin went abroad again, this time to support the Herut party fund raising campaign in South Africa. Arriving on August 14, with Aliza and Hayim Landau, the Irgun's former chief of staff who was now a member of the Knesset, Begin traveled through the country. Speaking at a rally in the Johannesburg City Hall, he attacked the "confused policy" in Washington which had prevented the overthrow of Nasser and had failed to take the opportunity to stop Communist penetration in the Middle East. When he learned that Chief of Staff Moshe Dayan was about to visit South Africa, he called on his audience to welcome the "great guest from Israel" with the warmth and enthusiasm due the "gallant soldier and commander."

The year 1958 marked the tenth anniversary of Israel's independence. On April 8, Begin led a parade of 14,000 Irgun veterans from Tel Aviv to Jaffa, retracing the route on the highway which the "fighting family" had taken in its march on Jaffa ten years earlier. Among the guests of honor at the mass rally that followed the anniversary parade were a non-Jew, Jacques Soustelle, a member of the French parliament who had fought in the French underground during World War II, and Aaron Zvi Propess, who, back in the 1930's in Poland, had first picked the young Menahem Begin for a position of leadership in the Betar youth movement.[9]

In June, Begin returned from these memories of the past to the arena of sharp parliamentary debate in a controversy which caused a crisis in the Ben-Gurion government and the resignation of two Cabinet members. This time the issue was a religious one: Who, or what, was a Jew? Under Israeli law, every permanent resident of the State of Israel carries, for purposes of personal registration, an identity card, on which there is one space for "citizenship" and another for "national (or ethnic) identity." In Israel, just as in many European countries since World War I, a clear distinction has been made between these two concepts. An individual may be an Israeli by citizenship, and a Jew, Arab, Druze or member of any other ethnic group by national identity — a distinction which, however, in no way affects his personal rights as a citizen. According to the minister of the interior, Israel Bar Yehuda, an avowed secularist, any person who declared in good faith that he or she was a Jew had to be registered as Jewish by "national (or ethnic) identity" with no other proof required. The government ratified this ruling on June 22, 1958. The result was vehement opposition from religious Jews not only in Israel but also in other countries. Under Jewish religious law a Jew can only be one who was born to a Jewish mother or who has been converted to Judaism by a recognized religious authority. And now Bar Yehuda had ruled that it was not necessary for the Israeli authorities to demand such proof of eligibility in order to register an individual as a Jew by "national identity." Under this ruling, a child born of a mixed marriage could be registered as a "national" or "ethnic" Jew on the mere say-so of his parents even if the mother had not been converted to Judaism prior to the birth of the child. And this meant that the personal status of Jew "by national identity" could be assigned to someone who under Jewish religious law was not a Jew at all. The Orthodox objected: they said that while one did not have to be Jewish to be an Israeli citizen, one could not be a non-Jew and claim Jewish "national identity." Most Jews nowadays agree that in Judaism, as distinct from other religions, religious heritage and ethnicity are one and the same. But religious Jews add one more qualification: whether a person is a Jew or a non-Jew is not for that person, or his parents, or even the Israeli government to decide. Only Jewish law, and its authorized rabbinic interpreters, can do that.

In the Knesset debate of Bar Yehuda's ruling, the representatives of the religious parties stood firmly grounded in the authority of Rabbinic law. The membership of the Herut party included religious and non-religious Jews alike, but Begin supported the religious parties' stand against the secularists with an impassioned plea which would have done credit to any spokesman of Orthodox Judaism. His speech reflected his own feelings about the relationship between Jewish religious values and Jewish national identity:

> Other nations started out as savages, living in jungles and caves, in fear of thunder and lightning, and in star-worship. Foreign nations came and forced *their* religion upon them; later, other foreign rulers came and forced another religion upon them.
>
> Our nation arose differently. It began with a divine promise —

and with this promise it has lived ever since. This promise lived with our people when it went down to Egypt, and it lived with them even in slavery. With this promise the Jewish people left slavery and wandered in the wilderness; with this promise, it accepted the Divine Commandments and with it, too, they conquered the Promised Land . . The promise still lived with them when they fell, were exiled [to Babylonia] and then restored; it was with them when they once again revolted [this time against Rome], when they were suppressed and dispersed among the nations. And it was by this promise that they returned to Eretz Yisrael. Thus did our nation arise and thus it has lived for many generations.

Begin and the representatives of the religious parties in the Knesset argued that if now the Israeli government would ignore the criteria of religious law when it came to the question of Jewish "national identity," it would create confusion and eventually a schism in world Jewry, whose concept of Jewish ethnicity was based on the bond of a common religious heritage. To Begin, it was a matter of simple logic: Citizenship and religion should be two separate concepts in Israel, and Israel must guarantee equal rights to all her citizens regardless of religion or nationality group. But for Jews there could be no separation between their religion and their "national identity":

> Does the government truly believe that, with regard to Jews, one can differentiate between religion and national identity? If it does so believe, then I must ask: Can a member of the Jewish nation be a Catholic? Can a member of the Jewish people be a Calvinist, Anglican, Baptist, Anabaptist?

Already, the government's ratification of Bar Yehuda's ruling had brought about the resignation of two ministers, both members of the religious Mizrahi-haPoel HaMizrahi party. Even more unfortunate, it had become the subject of heated discussions in Jewish circles, religious and secularist alike, in Israel and Jewish communities the world over. "For the sake of our nation," Begin concluded, "our country, our children and the future of the nation which is only a remnant today, let us not sever the bond — that simple and great, obvious yet mysterious, abstract yet concrete, deep and heavenly bond — which is the foundation and the secret of our national existence — that everlasting bond between our nation and the God of our forefathers."[10]

Eventually, the government made a temporary compromise: in cases of doubt, the space for "national (or ethnic) identity" on the registration card would be left blank.

Later in the year, Begin was again on the road for Herut. In the summer he went to France. He received a medal from the mayor of Paris, M. Jean Louis Vigier, a veteran of the French underground, who embraced Begin as a fellow fighter for freedom. An alderman named Moscovitch, who attended the ceremony at the Paris city hall, was overheard saying, "Next year we hope to receive Menahem Begin in our midst not as the great Herut leader but as Menahem Begin, Prime Minister of Israel."[11] The Paris alderman was looking ahead to the elections for Israel's Fourth Knesset, to be held in 1959.

Begin launched his party's election campaign soon after his return to Israel. In September, 1958, discussing his views on Israel's domestic and foreign policies, he called for an end to the anomalous system which enabled Histadrut, Israel's national federation of labor, to act not only as a labor union but also as the owner of profit-making enterprises employing tens of thousands of workers. This "identity between political ruler and economic provider," he said, not only endangered individual freedom but also created "great monopolies and trusts" which placed obstacles in the way of the private investments Israel badly needed. To correct the world's still-lingering image of his party as a sworn enemy of the official Zionist leadership, Begin declared that Herut would not wage its campaign against the Ben-Gurion government in a spirit of hostility. "There must be no hatred between parties, and especially no hatred based on the past. We do not regard Mapai as our enemy but as our political opponent." The enemy was still Egypt's dictator, Nasser, whose vision of a pan-Arab empire could not become reality without the destruction of Israel. Begin equated the Western world's efforts at placating Nasser with British and French attempts to appease Hitler two decades earlier. It was "a dangerous illusion" to believe that perhaps "if Nasser becomes really strong . . . it may be possible to talk peace to him." Unlike many of his colleagues, Begin had experienced in his own life where appeasement could lead. "Many intellectuals and statesmen, including leaders of great powers, were deceived with exactly the same argument. The consequences are history."[12]

The Herut election platform characterized the hoped-for coalition under Begin's leadership as the "National Liberal Government" of Israel. Its eight-point program included a warning to the Arabs: if the Arabs would continue telling the world that they were in a state of war with Israel, then Israel's right to defend herself would include the right to take "defensive initiatives." A Herut government would maintain friendship with Asian and African nations and seek alliances with friendly powers, particularly France. But while it would seek to maintain "regular relations" also with the Soviet Union and its satellites, it would "leave no doubt that it is our belief that the spread of Communism is a danger to all values of freedom and justice in which Israel believed from the day it became a people."

In the elections, which were held on November 3, 1959, the largest gain went to Mapai; the vote for the incumbent leadership reflected the country's rising prosperity and the peace on Israel's borders which had been achieved during the tenure of the Ben-Gurion coalition. Herut increased its Knesset strength by only two seats (it now had 17 as against the 15 it had received in the 1955 elections). Some post-election analysts claimed that Herut had lost many potential votes because of an unfortunate gaffe in Begin's campaign style. One evening's schedule had called for appearances by Begin at four rallies, each in another part of Tel Aviv. In order to convey Begin from one rally to the next as rapidly as possible, one of his enterprising followers had conceived the idea of organizing a motorcycle escort for Begin's car. As it passed through the city's neighborhoods, the impromptu parade was joined by other enthusiastic motorcyclists until the car bearing Begin was surrounded by a phalanx of roaring motorcycles. For many voters this display, plus Begin's practice of delivering speeches from balconies, revived unpleasant memories of Mussolini's appearances in Fascist Italy, and Herut had to pay the price in votes. Begin did not have to be told twice: after this, there were no more balcony speeches and mass motorcycle escorts.

The Fourth Knesset lasted less than two years. Ben-Gurion himself brought about the dissolution of the Knesset, because of a dispute between himself and members of his own cabinet. The quarrel concerned a so-called "security mishap" for which the blame had been placed on Pinhas Lavon, a former minister of defense. Late in 1954 an Israeli intelligence unit operating in Egypt had deposited explosive charges in certain Cairo public buildings; the intention had been to destroy American and British government property in the naive hope that the United States and Great Britain would blame the damage on Egyptian instigation and reassess their friendly relations with the Nasser government. However, the plot was discovered, and two of the accused were executed by the Egyptians. Lavon himself resigned from his post. But the question whether the orders for the unfortunate action had indeed come directly from Lavon continued to agitate Israeli politics. Late in 1960 a cabinet committee exonerated Lavon from any responsibility for the "mishap." Ben-Gurion, resentful of the verdict, resigned, and on March 28, 1961, the Knesset passed an act for its own dissolution. The special elections, held on August 15, 1961, brought no change in parliamentary strength for Herut. Ben-Gurion returned to office with a new coalition which no longer included the extreme left Mapam and the middle-of-the-road Liberals. For Ben-Gurion, who was then in his seventy-fifth year, this challenge to his personal authority spelled the beginning of the end for his long political career. Two years later he was to resign and retire once again to Kibbutz Sde Boker, this time for good.

Sometime during that special election year, Begin completed the publication of a four-volume collection of his speeches, articles and "wall newspaper" communiqués from the underground period. The anthology, which is available only in the original Hebrew, was appropriately entitled *BaMakhteret* (In the Underground).

The early part of 1962 saw Begin taking sides again in a religious debate in the Knesset — on the permissibility of keeping and raising pigs in a Jewish state when the basic dietary laws of Judaism forbade not only the eating of pork, but also the raising and keeping of pigs. In February, 1962, a group of six Knesset members — three from the religious parties, two from Mapai and one from Herut — introduced the so-called "Pig-raising Bill," which banned the raising and keeping of pigs except in specified places with a predominantly Christian population. The opposition to the bill was led by Mapam and the Communists, who did not approve of religious tradition being made the subject of a secular law. But to the supporters of the bill, including many who themselves did not keep kosher homes, this was more than a matter of religion; it was a question of Jewish national honor. Forcing Jews to eat, or to touch, the flesh of pigs had been one of the weapons used by Gentile oppressors for centuries to undermine Jewish dignity. The pig had become the symbol of efforts to degrade the Jew. Begin championed the bill in a highly emotional speech, invoking the memory of Jewish martyrdom down to the era of the Nazi Holocaust. To him, and to others of like mind, it was self-evident that no matter how one might feel about observing the Jewish dietary laws, there could be no place for the pig in a land that symbolized the rebirth of the Jewish spirit.[13] The bill was passed.

In 1963, Begin visited the one continent he had not yet touched on any of his previous journeys: in April, he and Aliza flew to Australia, where Begin was scheduled to visit the Jewish communities of Melbourne, Sydney and Brisbane. In Melbourne, he addressed an audience of 7,000 who had gathered to celebrate the fifteenth anniversary of Israel's independence. But he was unable to carry out the rest of his program, because he received an urgent call from his party to return home as soon as possible. All signs pointed to an imminent Arab onslaught on Israel. Egypt, Syria and Iraq had signed a manifesto calling for an expanded "United Arab Republic" to include all three countries, and the proposed constitution of the new entity included a statement on the duty of all Arabs to help bring about the "liberation of Palestine" from the "Zionist peril." Begin cut short his tour of Australia and returned to Israel where Ben-Gurion was demanding joint American-Soviet guarantees for Israel's borders or an alliance between Israel and the United States. The prime minister seemed to be panic-stricken. Abba Eban, in his memoirs, recalls that Ben-Gurion sent desperate letters to over 100 heads of state, including President John F. Kennedy, Charles De Gaulle (now President of France) and Britain's Prime Minister Harold Macmillan, expressing doubts about Israel's ability to survive in the future.[14]

Fortunately, the expanded Arab federation did not move beyond the drafting stage, and war did not come to Israel for another four years, but on June 16, 1963, Ben-Gurion abruptly announced his retirement. He was succeeded as prime minister by Levi Eshkol, whom Begin had first met in the late spring of 1948 at Irgun headquarters in the Freud Hospital to discuss the financial plight of the S.S. *Altalena*. Eshkol, by then in his late sixties, had served in Israel's previous cabinets as minister of agriculture and, from 1952 on, as minister of finance. Eshkol, who had been the Haganah's expert on arms procurement, also became minister of defense.

The months that followed this start of a new era in Israel's history brought two milestones in Begin's personal life as well. That summer he turned fifty. His birthday was marked by congratulations from Herut branches throughout the world, and by a special issue of *Herut*, the party's Hebrew-language organ in Israel, filled with interesting personal reminiscences from Begin's friends and followers. In October, his son Benny, barely 20 years old, married

Ruth Shoer, a girl from Natanya. The wedding took place at the Jabotinsky Center in Ramat Gan.

Begin still maintained close personal contacts with friends and supporters of his old "fighting family" throughout the world. In April, 1964, he flew to New York expressly to attend the funeral of Ben Hecht, the author, playwright and stormy petrel of Zionism who during the 1940's had been a leading and highly vocal supporter of the Irgun's cause in the United States. By his own description, Hecht had started out as an "indifferent Jew," but the rise of Hitler had brought Hecht's Jewishness to the surface. In the days before Pearl Harbor, Hecht became outraged at the reluctance of some American Jews, particularly his acquaintances in Hollywood, to "rock the boat" in the still-neutral United States by speaking out on behalf of the oppressed Jews in Hitler's Europe. He came under the influence of Peter Bergson (Hillel Kook), who had come to the United States to find friends and financial supporters for the Irgun. Joining Kook's Committee for a Jewish Army, Hecht had applied his talents and his prestige in the theatrical and movie world to the task of making propaganda and raising funds for the Irgun on a large scale. Following the Nazi Holocaust, he condemned both the American government under Franklin D. Roosevelt and the official Zionist establishment under Weizmann and Ben-Gurion for not having taken drastic action to save more Jews from extermination. Roosevelt, Hecht said, had had a share in the guilt because he had not permitted the transfer of funds for bribing Nazi bigwigs who were ready to save Jews in return for a monetary reward, and because he had refused to authorize the bombing of the railroad lines that led to the Nazi death camps. The official Zionist leaders, too, had been remiss because, as Hecht saw it, they had concentrated on the material development of Palestine and the immigration of Jewish pioneers into the country instead of attempting to protect the lives of Jews also in the diaspora. Now Hecht had died at the age of 70 and Menahem Begin, as former commander of the Irgun, paid his final tribute to the American Jewish activist for having done "so much for the Jewish people and for the redemption of Israel."

By the 1960's the bitter memories of past strife between the Zionist establishment and the "dissidents" of Irgun and the Stern Group had mellowed. Matured by years of joint struggle for the survival and development of the State of Israel, each side had come to acknowledge the contribution made by the other in the emergence of the Jewish homeland as an independent nation.

Not long after Eshkol had taken office as prime minister, Begin brought to his attention a provision in the last will and testament of Vladimir Jabotinsky. At odds with the official Zionist leadership until the end, Jabotinsky had requested that if he died outside Palestine, his remains should be buried wherever he died and not be transferred to Palestine except by express orders from the government of an independent Jewish state. Accordingly, Jabotinsky in 1940 and his wife nine years later had been buried in Pine Lawn, New York. Ben-Gurion, Begin told Eshkol, had known about Jabotinsky's last wish, but had not seen fit to do anything about it. Now, Begin said to the prime minister, it was high time that the State of Israel paid its debt of gratitude to Jabotinsky.

Eshkol listened to Begin with some surprise. He had not known about this stipulation in Jabotinsky's will. He himself had been far from a Revisionist sympathizer, but in his youth he had been an avid reader of Jabotinsky's early writings and had admired the man and his idealism, if not all the aspects of his Zionist ideology. He, Eshkol, had never blinded himself to the fact that Jabotinsky's ideas, even those which the Zionist establishment had rejected, had been an important influence in the development of Zionism and the rise of the Jewish state. Begin did not have too much difficulty convincing Eshkol to act. In the spring of 1964 Eshkol announced that the Israeli government would arrange to have the remains of Vladimir and Johanna Jabotinsky brought to Israel. They would be buried on the summit of Mount Herzl, where the remains of Theodor Herzl had been reinterred in 1949, and where space had been reserved for other revered leaders of the Zionist movement and the State of Israel. "We have lived to repatriate our spiritual father to our homeland!" Begin exulted.

Starting with the arrival of the coffins of Jabotinsky and his wife in New York City for the flight to Israel and ending with the solemn rites on Mount Herzl, the reinterment bore all the marks of an occasion of state and a triumphant homecoming. The main streets of New York's Upper West Side were filled with people and all but closed to traffic as the caskets, in an old-fashioned hearse drawn by two white horses and preceded by an escort of mounted police, were moved first from a funeral parlor to an Orthodox synagogue on West 91st Street and then to the airport. En route to Israel, the El Al plane bearing the two coffins stopped briefly at Orly Airport in Paris, so that Eshkol, who was then visiting Paris, could pay his respects. The prime minister and the plane were greeted not only by Jewish notables but also by a detachment of French troops and a fanfare from a French air force band.

When the plane touched down at Lod Airport in the late afternoon of July 7, Begin and the leaders of the "fighting family" were there, but so were thousands of others, representing every shade of Zionist ideology. A representative of the President of the State of Israel and the senior officers of the Israel Defense Forces stood at attention as Yaakov Meridor, Begin's immediate predecessor as commander of the Irgun, came forward to place Jabotinsky's officer's sword upon his coffin. Then, with Begin joining the pallbearers, the coffins of Vladimir and Johanna Jabotinsky were taken first to Ramat Gan, where some 100,000 people lined the streets to watch the procession, and then to lie in state overnight in Tel Aviv, where over 200,000 came to pay their respects. From Tel Aviv, the coffins were escorted to Jerusalem with an honor guard led by Aaron Zvi Propess, the former commander of Betar, and Isaac Remba, Jabotinsky's personal secretary. While the members of the Knesset met in special session to hear the Speaker, Kaddish Luz, an old-time Labor Zionist leader, deliver an impressive eulogy in tribute to the founder of Revisionist Zionism, the coffins lay in state surrounded by a new guard of honor, led by Eliahu Lankin, commander of the volunteers aboard the *Altalena*.

On July 9, President Zalman Shazar, the members of the Cabinet and the Knesset, the Supreme Court, the two Chief Rabbis of Israel, and representatives of the World Zionist Executive, followed by tens of thousands of less exalted men and women, escorted the cortege from the city to Mount Herzl for interment with full state honors. David Ben-Gurion had pointedly stayed away, but nearly all the other leaders, politicians and fighters — rightwing, left-wing and moderate, religious and secularist, old-timers from Haganah mingling with veterans of the Irgun and the Stern Group — were at the graveside. A unit of young parachutists who had known about Jabotinsky only from their teachers or youth movement leaders stood at rigid attention. Jabotinsky's son Eri recited the Kaddish. Then the mourners, one by one, stepped up to fill the graves with handfuls of earth from the Mount of Olives, from the graves of Jabotinsky's mother and sister in Tel Aviv and from the grave of Joseph Trumpeldor in Tel Hai. Among the first to join Menahem Begin in this final act of reverence were "Reb Arye" Levin, the "prisoners' rabbi" from the underground days; President Zalman Shazar; Shazar's wife, known in her own right as the Labor Zionist writer Rachel Katznelson; Mrs. Rahel Yanait Ben

Zvi, widow of Israel's second President, Itzhak Ben Zvi, and Foreign Minister Golda Meir.

The next year brought two joyous events to Menahem and Aliza Begin. In March, 1965, their elder daughter Hasia left the apartment on Rosenbaum Street to marry Matityahu Milikovsky, a young engineer. In October, Benny and Ruth presented the Begins with their first grandchild, a girl.

Nineteen sixty-five was another election year. The elections to the Sixth Knesset were marked by a shifting in political party alignments. In April, just before Begin left for a visit to Canada, the leaders of the Herut and Liberal parties agreed to form a parliamentary bloc. The Liberal party, the result of a merger between General Zionist and Progressive parties several years earlier, represented a moderate platform in domestic matters. While they acknowledged the "cooperative" sector of Israel's economy, the Liberals demanded equal status for private initiative, greater consideration for the needs of the professional and middle classes, less government intervention in economic affairs, and the safeguarding of individual liberties. In the new bloc composed of Herut and Liberals, known by its Hebrew acronym Gahal (from *Gush Herut-Liberalism*), each party retained its own independent organization, but accepted the overall leadership of Menahem Begin. The next month, Mapai joined forces with another socialist party, Ahdut Avodah-Po'ale Zion (United Labor Zionist party) to form the *Ma'arakh* or Labor Alignment. The response of former Premier Ben-Gurion and six Mapai members of the Knesset, including former Chief of Staff Moshe Dayan, was to bolt and form a party of their own, *R'shimat Po'ale Yisrael* (Israel Workers' List), more popularly known by its initials, Rafi. Begin did not rejoice in the split within the party of his old political foe. According to his long-time friend, Rabbi Louis I. Rabinowitz of South Africa, Begin said to a Christian theologian who was visiting Jerusalem's Hebrew University at the time, "It is a sad thing to see those who were such staunch comrades for so many years engage in a bitter slanging match. It is just as sad to see what was once a united party break up. Anything which makes for unity, even if we disagree with it, is to be welcomed; anything which destroys unity is to be deplored. For the sake of the State, I take no pleasure in it."[15]

In the elections held that November, the new Labor Alignment was able to form a coalition government under Prime Minister Eshkol. Begin's Gahal, in the the opposition, now had 26 seats and, just as Herut alone had been for ten years, was the second largest party in the Knesset.

By that time some circles in the official Zionist leadership outside Israel were willing to grant Begin a measure of respectability. In the summer of 1966, the official organ of British Zionism wrote of him: "He is no longer described . . . as a rabble rouser. Today, he is listened to, both for what he says and because of the way he says it, with a rare elegance of form and rhetoric."[16]

But meanwhile, in Israel, Begin was confronted with a mutiny of sorts within the leadership of Herut. As one of the insurgents put it, the revolt was "not over ideology but over system." There were elements within the party who, tired of being perpetually in the opposition, blamed Begin for the party's six consecutive electoral defeats and felt that, after 18 years with him, they might do better under a new leader. Not wishing to be the cause of a split within his party, Begin took the initiative and, at the party's eighth national convention in July, 1966, announced that he would not run for reelection to the chairmanship of Herut's Central Committee. In his speech, he said he was resigning because he did not want to be an obstacle to continued close relationships with Gahal's other component, the Liberal party, and to a possible rapprochement with Rafi. But though he stepped down as the party's chairman, he still had his seat in the Knesset and was regarded as the moral and political leader of the right-wing opposition.

That fall, the London *Jewish Chronicle* published Begin's views on the role of a "loyal opposition" in the unique framework of Israeli politics. "Opposition," Begin wrote, "is not an aim; it is a necessity:"

> If under a multiparty system, all the political groups should wish to be no more than satellites of the ruling party we would in fact have, not by force but by willing surrender, a "one-party democracy." The greater the shame. To avoid it, we need, whether under a bi-party or multi-party system, an "alternative". And . . . if by free ballot, an opposition becomes the Government, as it always wants to, and a Government takes over the opposition benches, as it never wants to, this is the proof of working democracy.
>
> Israel has not yet had this experience. For 18 years we have had the same Party in power, with varying junior partners. People used to say that under . . . a coalition system there is no stable government. We are . . . an exception to the rule. We have had

one of the most stable governments in the world. But it is in fact not only stable; it is perhaps the most entrenched in the non-totalitarian part of the world . . .[17]

In February, 1967, Begin agreed to return to office and the following month the Herut executive, by an overwhelming majority, voted to restore him as chairman of the party.

The year 1967 had opened on an ominous note for Israel. Already at the end of the preceding year, an era of relative prosperity had given way to an economic slump. By December, 1966, 30,000 Israelis were unemployed. Many young native-born Israelis complained of a lack of incentives and challenges and left the country.

Almost as if by design, Israel's hostile neighbors chose that time for renewed activity. Since 1957 Israel's border with Egypt, patrolled by the United Nations Emergency Force (UNEF), had been relatively quiet, and Israeli shipping through the Strait of Tiran to the Gulf of Elat had gone unhindered. But sabotage and infiltration across the Syrian and Jordanian borders by Arab guerillas had continued. Now these attacks, particularly from Syria, increased, and kibbutzim in the north of Israel came under Syrian gunfire from the Golan Heights. Syria's leftist government was receiving vigorous support from the Soviet Union. Instead of acceding to repeated Israeli requests to help curb guerilla raids from Syrian territory, the Soviet Union not only abetted Syria but also incited Egypt by spreading reports that Israel was about to invade Syria, with which Egypt had entered into a mutual defense agreement. When Prime Minister Eshkol invited the Soviet ambassador to accompany him to the border to see for himself that the Russian allegations were baseless, the ambassador refused the invitation.

On May 15, 1967, Israel celebrated the nineteenth anniversary of her independence. Even as Israel's leaders reviewed the Independence Day parade in the Israeli sector of Jerusalem, there were reports of huge concentrations of Egyptian tanks and infantry units in the Sinai peninsula close to the Israeli border.

On May 18, Egypt's President Nasser sent a request to U Thant, secretary-general of the United Nations, for the immediate withdrawal of UNEF troops from their positions along the Israel-Egyptian border. To Israel's dismay — and Nasser's surprise — U Thant promptly acceded to Egypt's request. The following week, Nasser blockaded the Gulf of Elat by closing the Strait of Tiran to all shipping to and from the port of Elat. Israel, Nasser said, now had the choice between a swift death if she made war, and slow economic strangulation if she did not. Many remembered the warning which Menahem Begin had sounded in Tel Aviv ten years earlier, after Israel had withdrawn from the Sinai peninsula and the Gaza Strip in return for the promise of a United Nations Emergency Force to be stationed between Israel and Egypt. At the outdoor mass meeting in Mograbi Square that day in March, 1957, Begin had told 10,000 listeners that "we have with our own hands assisted in the long run in the closing of the free passage to Elat and from Elat of ships flying the Hebrew flag."[18] Now, ten years later, it had become clear that this had been no exaggeration.

The United States and a number of other maritime nations reiterated their view that the Strait of Tiran was an international waterway and could not be blockaded by any country, but it soon became evident that Nasser would not be swayed by diplomatic action from the non-Communist world. Nasser openly proclaimed that he would regard any attempt to break the blockade as an act of war. He dared Israel to fight and, his confidence bolstered by huge amounts of Soviet armaments he had been receiving over the years, predicted that a war would be the end of Israel. Meanwhile, mobs in the Arab capitals clamored for a war that would "drive the Jews into the sea."

Israel's leadership seemed at a loss for a response to Nasser's threat. Foreign Minister Abba Eban visited Paris, London and Washington, bringing back with him a warning from Israel's erstwhile ally, General De Gaulle, now President of France, not to "make war," and not much more encouraging advice from Britain and the United States.

In the Knesset, Begin called upon the Government to be as explicit as possible in making known the line beyond which Israel would not permit Nasser to proceed without a war. He demanded a clear-cut statement from Israel insisting upon an immediate withdrawal of Egyptian troops from the border and freedom of navigation to and from Elat. He rejected out of hand the possibility of a UNEF presence on Israel's own territory to protect Israel from attack. "That force saved Nasser from final defeat at the hands of Israel [in the 1956 war]. Israel has no need of any foreign army to protect it. Israel is no puppet state. The soldiers of Israel and not UNEF will destroy the enemy."[19]

It became increasingly clear that Israel's Prime Minister Levi Eshkol was not adequate to the situation. His much-respected talent for compromise and temporizing would not help here. On May 24, 1967, the day after Nasser announced the blockade of the Strait of Tiran, Begin paid a visit to Eshkol, suggesting that Ben-Gurion be returned to office as prime minister and minister of defense, with Eshkol remaining as deputy premier in charge of domestic affairs. Whatever shortcomings Ben-Gurion might have had, Begin felt that hesitancy and lack of experience in foreign policy were not among them. Eshkol categorically rejected the suggestion. "We're two horses," he said in the homey way he had of expressing himself, "that can't pull together."[20] Begin said he knew about the differences Eshkol had had with Ben-Gurion and the harsh words that had passed between the two men. But, Begin reminded Eshkol, he himself had had much sharper tensions with Ben-Gurion in the past. In fact, Ben-Gurion had even made it a habit to walk out of the Knesset chamber whenever Begin got up to speak. But at the hour of danger the time had come to put these bitter memories aside and to work together for the sake of the country.[21] Eshkol, however, remained adamant. Ben-Gurion, he pointed out, was too old; he was past his eightieth birthday. He no longer saw things in their proper perspective. In "B.G." 's younger days, one of his outstanding qualities had been his talent for objective analysis; now, he tended to base his political judgments on personal prejudices. Also, Eshkol pointed out, Ben-Gurion had never established a relationship of confidence with an American President such as Eshkol had been able to build between himself and Lyndon Johnson.

Meanwhile, Israeli public opinion kept pressing for a "government of national unity," a wall-to-wall war cabinet which would place Israel's defense into the hands of the strongest, most experienced and most capable men in the country, irrespective of political affiliation.

As Arab mobs continued to shout threats of massacre and annihilation, Israel quietly mobilized. Her army swelled from a little over 70,000 to 230,000. Streets emptied as vehicles and their owners were drafted into the Defense Force. Schools closed, and some factories shut down for lack of manpower. Schoolchildren acted as postal clerks, mailmen and trash collectors. Since Egypt now had a large air force, supplied by the Soviet Union, it was expected that Israeli population centers would be bombed, with tens of thousands of civilian casualties. Hotels were converted into emergency hospitals and some parks were consecrated as emergency cemeteries. Still, the army was confident that in the end, Israel would be victorious, if only the country's leadership would take the proper action at the right time.

Begin still had not given up hope that Ben-Gurion might be brought back to power. He was certain now that war was inevitable, and that Ben-Gurion would be the best qualified to direct it, if not as prime minister, then perhaps at least as minister of defense. On Saturday evening, May 27, Begin, accompanied by Arye Ben Eliezer, paid a call on Ben-Gurion at his Tel Aviv home. They found the former prime minister with two of his associates who had left Mapai with him and had helped form the Rafi party — a former minister of housing, Joseph Almogi, and a former deputy minister of defense, who had headed Israel's naval service during the War of Independence: Shimon Peres.

It turned out that Begin and Ben-Gurion did not see eye to eye on Israel's response to Egypt's threats. Begin believed that time was of the essence and that war should be launched at once with a large-scale attack on Egypt before Egypt would have a chance to land a first strike. Ben-Gurion, on the other hand, had taken a more cautious position and did not favor an immediate preventive war on Egypt; he felt it was too late for that. Now, the "Old Man" proposed a limited military action confined to the area of the blockaded Strait of Tiran. But he stressed that he was not going to be a candidate for the post of minister of defense.

After leaving Ben-Gurion, Begin, Ben Eliezer, Almogi and Peres sat down at a table in the restaurant of the Yarden Hotel to pick another candidate as minister of defense. Their choice fell on former chief of staff Moshe Dayan, the *sabra* hero of the Sinai Campaign.

In the meantime Prime Minister Eshkol had been receiving cables from various heads of state, including President Johnson, urging Israel not to declare war. Also, Eshkol was frightened by the specter of Soviet military intervention on the Arab side. Accordingly, on May 28, the prime minister decided to address the nation over the radio, announcing that Israel had decided to wait, and explained why. A text was hurriedly drafted for him; he made some last-minute changes but had no time to read the second draft over. As a result, the speech was a disaster. He stammered into the microphone, turning the typed text in his hands this way and that, not knowing where to continue reading.

Instead of bolstering their morale, Eshkol's radio address threw the people of Israel into despair. They took the prime minister's mumbling and stammering for a sign of irresolution.

Soldiers who listened to the broadcast at their camps and bases felt frustrated to the point of tears. They were not afraid of battle and were ready to make whatever sacrifices the defense of their country might demand of them, but after hearing Eshkol, they felt that they had no leader.[22]

On May 30, the full extent of the danger and isolation in which Israel found herself became plain to the world. On that day, Egypt and Syria formed a military alliance with Jordan, under which King Hussein's armies were placed under Egyptian command. A similar agreement was signed with Iraq. In 1956 Israel had only Egypt to contend with, and she had had support from Britain and France. Now in contrast, it seemed that the principal Arab countries were politically and militarily united, supported mainly by the Soviet Union, while Israel stood alone. True, Israel received unprecedented moral and financial support from Jews and non-Jews throughout the free world, but the governments of that free world seemed powerless to help and were, for the most part, ready to mourn Israel's demise.

Two days later, on June 1, the very last evening news broadcast finally brought to the people of Israel the announcement they had been waiting so desperately to hear: a "Government of National Unity" had been formed. Eshkol remained prime minister, but Moshe Dayan had become minister of defense. The Gahal bloc was represented in the new Government by two ministers without portfolio: a former leader in the moderate General Zionist party, Joseph Saphir — *sabra,* veteran member of the Knesset and one-time minister of transport and communications — and the leader of the Herut party and the Gahal bloc, Menahem Begin.

The leader of the opposition had been asked to join a government which he had challenged without letup ever since the State of Israel had come into existence.

Among Begin's colleagues in Israel's Cabinet were two men of whom he had sad memories from the *Altalena* tragedy: Yigal Allon, former commander of Palmach, and Israel Galili, who had been deputy minister of defense in the Provisional Government of 1948. Now Allon was minister of labor, and Galili, a minister without portfolio. The army's chief of staff was Itzhak Rabin, former deputy commander of Palmach, who, together with Allon, had been in charge of Tzahal headquarters at the Ritz Hotel during the *Altalena* battle off the shore of Tel Aviv. Now, almost 20 years after the

Altalena, Begin and these men were officially comrades in arms in the struggle for Israel's survival.

After learning that he had been appointed to the Cabinet, Begin made two pilgrimages: one to Jerusalem's Orthodox Mea Shearim quarter to receive the blessings of "Reb Arye" Levin, and one to the grave of Vladimir Jabotinsky.

Four days later, Israel and her Arab neighbors were at war. For the first few hours of Monday, June 5, Arab radio stations featured reports of glorious Arab victories. But by the late afternoon, Nasser learned the truth which, until then, had been carefully withheld from him: in the morning hours Israeli bombers had attacked Egypt's military airfields and most of the combat planes of the Egyptian air force had been destroyed on the ground. Simultaneously, Israeli armored columns advanced into the Sinai peninsula. On Tuesday, June 6, Israeli forces had occupied Sharm el-Sheikh, the Egyptian position which Israel had evacuated after the previous war and from which Nasser had planned to enforce the blockade of the Strait of Tiran. By the end of the third day of fighting, Israel's army was in control of the Sinai peninsula, and on June 8, Egypt agreed to a cease-fire.

At the outset of the fighting, Israel had sent a warning to King Hussein of Jordan to stay out of the war. But Hussein, apparently taken in by reports of Egyptian victories, chose to ignore the warning and made war on Israel. Jordanian forces captured United Nations headquarters in Jerusalem and began to shell the Israeli sector of the city. But within hours Jordan's air force, too, was destroyed and within three days Israeli forces had captured most of the West Bank area of the Jordan river, which Jordan had annexed during the fighting in 1948. Jordan's defeat was so devastating that she accepted the United Nations call for a cease-fire on June 7, one day before Egypt did so.

The only enemy still adamantly rejecting the cease-fire was Syria. Israel now concentrated her forces against the strongly fortified Syrian positions on the Golan Heights from where the Syrians had been shelling Israeli border villages. Given the terrain and the massive fortifications the Syrians had built with Russian help, the fighting was fierce and costly, but there, too, Israel accomplished her military objective and, on June 11, 1967, Syria at last joined Jordan and Egypt in accepting a cease-fire with Israel. In less than six days Israel, fighting alone, had routed three of her hostile neighbors who had been supported by powerful countries, including the Soviet Union. Israeli forces had occupied the entire

Sinai peninsula, from which Egypt had sent out her troops against Israel and had planned to strangle the Jewish state by blockading the port of Elat; the Gaza Strip, center of Egyptian espionage and training base for Ahmed Shukairy's "Palestinian Liberation Army;" the West Bank area of the Jordan, from where Arab guerillas with Jordanian approval had carried out sneak attacks on Israeli territory; and the Golan Heights, from which Syrian guns had forced kibbutz children in the north to spend each night in air raid shelters. Faced with odds which most of the world had considered insuperable, Israel had fought for her life and won the battle.

Following Israel's victory in what almost immediately became known in the press and in "quickie" histories as the Six-Day War, it was assumed that, after three unsuccessful wars against Israel in less than 20 years, Israel's Arab neighbors would finally accept her existence in their midst and sign official peace treaties with the Jewish state. But as this book goes to press, over a decade and another war later, peace treaties and normal relations between Israel and all the nations that fought to destroy her still lie in the future.

The one event in Israel's Six-Day War which perhaps had the greatest psychological impact not only on Jews but also on non-Jews the world over was the entry of Israeli forces into the Jordanian-held Old City of Jerusalem. Under the original United Nations plan for the partition of Palestine, Jerusalem was to have been part of neither a Jewish nor an Arab state, but a separate entity under international control. This, it had been felt, would be the best assurance of equal protection for the holy places cherished by Judaism, Christianity and Islam and located in that city. Painful though it was for them to contemplate giving up Jerusalem, the city which Jews for thousands of years had revered as the heart of their homeland, the founders of the Jewish state initially had been willing to live with this arrangement. But during the fighting in 1948, the Old City, site of most of the holy places, was captured by Jordanian troops and annexed by the Hashemite Kingdom of Jordan. The armistice agreement of 1949 (which did not sanction Jordan's annexation of the Old City) stipulated that the Jordanian government was to allow the Jews free access to the holy places in territory occupied by Jordan. This meant that Jews were to be permitted to continue visiting and using the cemetery on the Mount of Olives, the most hallowed Jewish burial ground from ancient times, and to worship at the Wailing Wall, the last remaining part of the Holy Temple. The Jordanians never honored this agreement. Many of the tombs on the Mount of Olives were destroyed; tombstones were used as building and flooring material, and buildings were erected on the cemetery grounds. The Wailing Wall, where Jews had wept and prayed for centuries, was barred to Jewish pilgrims. For 19 years this state of affairs had been allowed to continue without protest or action from the United Nations and world public opinion.

Now, when Jordan entered the war against Israel, the Israeli government quickly decided that one of its objectives in the struggle should be the expulsion of the Jordanians from the Old City. The initiative for the decision came from two members of the Cabinet; one of them was Menahem Begin.

As soon as the Jordanians began to shell Jerusalem, Begin turned to Yigael Yadin, whom Eshkol had coopted as one of his military advisors, and said to him, "We must take Jerusalem." Yadin readily agreed. The two men talked to Minister of Labor Yigal Allon, who was in full agreement and, together, they went to put their views before Premier Eshkol. Eshkol, in his usual understated way, allowed that this was not a bad idea. Meeting in a small air raid shelter — the new Knesset building, dedicated only the year before, was under bombardment from Jordanian guns — the Cabinet discussed the strategy to be used for capturing the Old City. The main obstacle to overcome was the fact that, unlike other military objectives, the Old City, with its historic sites and holy places, could not be bombed or shelled. As a consequence, it would have to be taken in hand-to-hand combat. The problem was how to do that at at minimum cost in Israeli lives. It was not an easy thing to decide, and the discussion continued through the next day, June 6.

Very early on Wednesday morning, June 7, the third day of the Six-Day War, Begin awakened Eshkol from his sleep. He, Begin, had been listening to the British Broadcasting Company news report before dawn, as was his custom, and had heard an announcement that the United Nations in New York had issued a call for a cease-fire. Once the cease-fire went into effect, the chance of taking the Old City of Jerusalem would be irretrievably lost. A decision, one way or the other, would have to be made at once. Eshkol said he would have to telephone Moshe Dayan, the minister of defense. Begin undertook to call Dayan himself. At 7:30 A.M., the war cabinet met and the army was given the go-ahead signal. Several hours later, Israeli forces occupied the Old City, and Israeli soldiers, headed by Chief Army Chaplain Shelomo Goren sounding the ram's horn, prayed at the Western Wall — known for centuries as the Wailing Wall — for the first time in 19 years. Within hours, President Shazar, Prime Minister Eshkol, Moshe Dayan and other dignitaries made the pilgrimage to the Wall. Menahem Begin came, accompanied by Herut members of the Knesset and veterans of the "fighting family." At the wall, Begin recited several psalms, and a prayer he had composed especially for the occasion, ending with three verses from the thirty-first chapter of the Book of Jeremiah:

> Thus says the Lord:
> A voice is heard in Ramah . . .
> Rachel weeping for her children;
> She refuses to be comforted for her children
> Because they are not.

> Thus says the Lord:
> Keep your voice from weeping
> And your eyes from tears;
> For your work shall be rewarded,
> Says the Lord,
> And they shall come back from the land of the enemy . . .
> And your children shall return to their own border.[23]

Begin, who in those years rarely showed his emotion in public, wept openly, and so did most of the other men who had come with him to the Wall. Ten years later, recalling that occasion, he said: "We were not ashamed of those tears. They were men's tears . . ."[24]

A month later, Begin and Zerach Warhaftig, the minister of religious affairs, were called in by Foreign Minister Abba Eban to help draft a letter to United Nations Secretary-General U Thant, justifying the changes which had come about in the Old City of Jerusalem as a result of the Israeli takeover. "Where there had previously been strife, there is now peace. Where there had been sacrilege and vandalism. there is now a decent respect for the rights of all pilgrims to have access and free worship at the shrine which they revere." Also in that letter, the Ministers informed U Thant of Israel's attitude toward the status of the Christian and Moslem holy places in territory formerly occupied by the Kingdom of Jordan. Unlike other governments that had controlled these areas in the past, Israel was not going to claim "unilateral control or exclusive jurisdiction in the Holy Places of Christendom and Islam," and would be prepared to "give appropriate expression to this principle" in a peace settlement with Jordan.[25]

Twenty-three years had passed since Menahem Begin, in his "proclamation of revolt" against British rule in the Jewish homeland, first proposed that the future Jewish state "should declare extraterritorial status for the holy places of the Christian and Moslem faiths" within its borders.[26]

14. Minister Without Portfolio: 1967-1970

For three years after the Six-Day War, Menahem Begin was a minister without portfolio in the Labor-led "Government of National Unity." He was placed on six Ministerial Committees: the Committees for Jerusalem, the Holy Places, Legislation, Constitutional Law and — probably as a nod to his predilection for ceremony, learned during his days in Betar — the Committee for Ceremonies and Symbols. But, in the words of one noted Israeli journalist, Begin's most important function in the post-1967 Cabinet, as he saw it, was that of "watchdog against retreat without a true peace."[1]

Throughout the Six-Day War and the months that followed, Russia, the Communist satellites and the "unaligned" Third World had pressed Israel to withdraw from the territories she had occupied during the fighting. But this time, in contrast to the situation after the Sinai Campaign of 1956, the United States did not join Russia in forcing Israel to retreat to her former borders without concrete Arab assurances of peace and normal relations with the Jewish state. In August, 1967, two months after the war, the heads of Arab states, meeting at Khartoum, had adopted a series of adamant resolutions against the reality of Israel's survival in their midst: "No negotiations with Israel; no peace with Israel; no recognition of Israel." Nevertheless, Israel's adversaries in the United Nations, despite massive Soviet pressures, were unable to secure a resolution unequivocally calling for Israel's departure from the Sinai peninsula, the Gaza Strip, the West Bank and the Golan Heights. The oft-cited Resolution 242, passed by the United Nations on November 22, 1967, had been kept deliberately vague. True, there was a provision calling for the withdrawal of Israeli forces, but the drafters of the text had purposely avoided naming the territories to be evacuated or even specifying that Israel would have to leave all the areas she had occupied during the war. And even this loosely-worded statement was linked with a provision calling on the Arabs to make a just and lasting peace and to agree on secure and recognized boundaries with the State of Israel.

Nonetheless, there were many well-meaning people of influence who appealed to Israel to be "magnanimous in her victory" and make far-reaching concessions to the Arabs even before a guaranteed peace had been established. In the United States, mired in the hopeless Vietnam war, there were fears of a future Middle East conflict to which America might eventually have to send troops. Other advocates of Israeli "magnanimity" — in America and elsewhere — saw the Arabs not as well-armed adversaries waiting for another chance to destroy the Jewish state but as underdogs who had just come out as abject losers in a lightning war. Left-wing circles somewhat naively tended to class the Arabs as victims of "colonialist" designs. In Israel, too, there were elements who were thinking in terms of "magnanimity" to the Arabs. Some of these "doves" on the Israeli political and intellectual scene believed that, after losing three wars against Israel, the Arabs could be prevailed upon to make peace if only something were done to assuage their feeling of humiliation; others, less sophisticated, felt that "magnanimous" gestures to the Arabs would improve the image of the Jewish state in a not too friendly Gentile world.

It was against these tendencies, which they regarded as dangerously naive, that Begin and his Gahal bloc were on constant guard. Abba Eban recalls that while Begin was in the Cabinet, he, Eban, was called upon to report on Israel's diplomatic efforts toward peace in greater detail than he might have wished, primarily in order to allay Begin's apprehensions of imprudent "compromises." (Eban was opposed to Begin's political views but stresses that his personal relations with Begin over the years have been cordial and that he respects Begin's "constancy and sincerity as well as his record as a daring resistance fighter.")[2]

During the months that followed the Six-Day War, Begin frequently would invite visiting American statesmen and other public figures to a meal in the Knesset restaurant and seat them at his usual table next to a wide window giving them a magnificent view of the Jerusalem hills. He would then point out a hill from which, before the war, Arab guns had been within easy firing range of the Knesset building. "Would you agree to have Soviet guns stationed only a few kilometers away from your Capitol Hill in Washington?" Begin asked one visiting United States senator. "No, of course not," the senator replied. "Then why would you expect *us* to sacrifice our security and endanger our future?'' his host persisted. To this, the American visitor had no reply.

The euphoric postwar period had the effect of bringing Ben-Gurion closer to Begin. Although he had been unwilling to emerge from retirement, the former prime minister apparently had been touched by Begin's willingness to see him restored to power. Late in July, 1967, the two men made their first joint appearance on the same platform to discuss the same subject. They were addressing the Zionist Organization of America, which was holding its 70th jubilee convention in Jerusalem. Both Begin and Ben-Gurion urged the delegates to promote the large-scale settlement of American Jews in Israel.[3]

In December, Ben-Gurion happened to meet Begin at lunch in Jerusalem's King David Hotel and invited him to be a guest of honor at the convention of the Rafi party, for which he, Ben-Gurion, had come to Jerusalem. Begin accepted; it was the first time he had attended a Labor party convention. A picture taken at the convention shows him exchanging broad smiles with Ben-Gurion.[4]

Now that Begin was a member of the Israeli Cabinet, he was drafted for lecture tours by such "official" Jewish fund-raising organizations as the United Jewish Appeal and Israel Bonds. In November, 1967, he was in the United States and Canada, speaking for a Bond drive. He also visited Mexico and stopped in Zurich to put in an appearance at the European Herut Conference. In Montreal, he called on Israel's enemies to make a peace treaty with her, to "recognize forever the existence of the State of Israel." Israel wanted peace. "We do not want to kill any Arabs, nor do we want them to kill any Jews," he said.

There had been no historical precedent, Begin consistently pointed out, to indicate that a country which had fought and won a war of "national self-defense" should feel obligated to make advance promises of territorial concessions, let alone to yield all occupied enemy territory, before it could expect to start peace negotiations with its former enemy. In his address to the ninth convention of Israel's Herut party in May, 1968, Begin cited in detail the provisions of several twentieth-century peace treaties to prove his point. At the end of his address, he placed before the convention a ten-point "Declaration of the Rights of the Jewish People to Its Homeland, to Liberty, Security and Peace." Point 7 of the declaration specified that peace between nations after a war could be achieved only through direct negotiations between the belligerents and that peace treaties had to include security provisions which would prevent a defeated aggressor from starting another war at some future date. In the case of Israel, based on her past experience with hostile neighbors, these security provisions had to include Israeli "control over the areas which have served our enemies as bases for aggression." Begin did not accept the argument that a permanent annexation of the West Bank territory, with its large and prolific Arab population, might in the long run alter Israel's Jewish character by saddling the Jewish state with an Arab majority. In the face of a large Arab population element, Begin said, Israel would simply have to work harder to maintain her Jewish majority by fostering large-scale Jewish immigration and encouraging an increase in the size of Jewish families. "In a generation in which one-third of its sons were destroyed," he said, "the Jewish people has a right to encourage natural growth by available means in order to replace the cruel loss."

As for the status of Arab residents in territories ceded to Israel under a peace treaty, "the people of Israel believe in the sacred principle of equal rights for all citizens, without distinction of origin, nationality or religion." Israeli citizenship would not be forced upon Arabs, but "an Arab resident of the Land of Israel who applies for citizenship of the Jewish state and undertakes to be loyal to it — such loyalty is the condition for granting citizenship to any person in any State — shall receive it."[5]

In the spring of 1968, Israel celebrated twenty years of independence. Begin marked the occasion with a brief journey back into the past. He participated in a series of symposiums arranged by a leading Israeli journalist to acquaint a new generation of Israelis with the heroic days of the underground struggle for Jewish independence. The journalist was Geula Cohen, who, as a girl, had served as an announcer for the clandestine radio station operated by LEHI, the Stern Group, most extreme of the Jewish fighting organizations before the emergence of the State of Israel. Now a partisan of Herut and a staff member of *Ma'ariv*, a prestigious, politically independent afternoon daily, she had invited veterans of Haganah, Irgun and LEHI to join her for a round-table exchange of memories to be recorded verbatim in *Ma'ariv*.[6] The eight men who accepted Geula Cohen's invitation reflected Israel's political spectrum from the extreme right to the extreme left. A picture taken at one of the symposiums shows them sitting in an informal semi-circle, immersed in earnest but apparently not acrimonious discussion. There is Yaakov Riftin, a leader of the far-left HaShomer

HaTzair and former Mapam representative in the Knesset. Seen at his left is Nathan Friedmann-Yellin (Yellin-Mor), who had fled from Warsaw with the Begins and had been commander of LEHI. Since 1948, Yellin-Mor had made a complete ideological turn-about. After serving in the first Knesset as a one-man delegation representing a group of former LEHI members, he had startled Israelis by suddenly emerging on the other extreme, openly advocating a Jewish-Arab federation encompassing all of pre-1948 Palestine. Now his only link with LEHI was one of nostalgic memories. Seated next to this political maverick is Eliezer Livneh, philosopher-journalist of the Haganah, whom Ben-Gurion had sent to Begin shortly before the signing of Israel's declaration of independence. Since those days Livneh had become a controversial figure; he had left Mapai and had been writing articles sharply critical of Israel's political establishment. Next to Livneh is Moshe Sneh, the former Haganah commander of whom Begin had mixed personal memories. Shown on Sneh's left is Hayim Landau, former chief of staff of the Irgun and a member of Herut's Knesset delegation without interruption since 1949. Next to Landau is Menahem Begin. At Begin's left, completing the semi-circle, is Shimon Peres, the youthful Haganah veteran who, the year before, had been with Begin in the little group that had chosen Moshe Dayan as minister of defense.

For the most part, the representatives of Haganah and Irgun at Geula Cohen's symposiums explained and defended the philosophies which had guided them during the underground days. Yellin-Mor and Geula Cohen, the veterans of LEHI, apparently let the others, notably Begin and Sneh, do most of the talking. Begin went over the whole ground of the Irgun's history. He praised Haganah's work in the "illegal" transfer of Holocaust survivors to Palestine during the final years of British rule as "one of the most outstanding and important forms of opposition to the British regime" but stressed the military and propaganda aspects of the Irgun's activities, particularly the public information effort that had been carried on under his direction. "I believe there has never been an underground which elucidated its aims as we did," he said. On the whole, Begin's tone was calm and dignified, and as objective as it was possible for him to be. His language became sharp and emotional only when he discussed the *Altalena* affair. After 20 years, he still used the word "lies" for the Provisional Government's characterization of the *Altalena's* landing as an Irgun plot to seize power. Addressing himself to Livneh and Riftin, he said:

I repeat again. We did not fight to gain power over our people. We fought to liberate it. With all our hearts we said, "We do not ask who will rule in the Jewish State when it arises. That will be decided by democratic elections." [But] you disbelieved that.

In reply to a question from Geula Cohen, both Sneh and Livneh agreed in retrospect that it had been wrong of Haganah to cooperate with the British against the Irgun. Sneh said that the "open season" which Haganah had declared on the Irgun had been a "grave error" which "should not have happened." Peres, who had been too young to assume any role of leadership in Haganah during the underground years, volunteered that unfortunate phenomena such as the "open season" had occurred throughout history in every nation where more than one underground fighting force had been active for the same cause at the same time. "They clash more fiercely with each other than with the enemy," he commented.

Geula Cohen ended the proceedings with the hope that the recollections of her guests, despite some painful allusions to internal strife among those who should have regarded one another as comrades in arms, would prove an inspiration to the new generation that had grown up since the founding of the Jewish state. "We opened with a blessing on the life of the people of Israel," she said, "and with that same blessing let us conclude."

Early in June, Begin was back in the United States to promote the sale of Israel Bonds. During his visit Robert F. Kennedy was assassinated by a young Arab named Sirhan Sirhan. Begin attended Kennedy's funeral with Itzhak Rabin, formerly Israel's chief of staff, who had just been appointed ambassador to Washington.

Late in August, the free world was shaken by Russia's invasion of Czechoslovakia, where the Dubcek government had become too liberal for the Soviets. Together with Arye Ben Eliezer, who was then the chairman of the Herut executive, Begin appeared at a mass rally in Tel Aviv to protest against the subjugation of a small country by the Soviet superpower. In his speech, Begin urged the small nations of the free world to band together in a common front against the threat of Communist expansion.[7]

It was now over a year that Egypt, Jordan and Syria had signed a cease-fire with Israel through the United Nations, but, as Begin put it on the eve of the Jewish New Year, peace was still remote and Israel's enemies were clamoring for a new war.[8] The United Nations had appointed Dr. Gunnar Jarring, the Swedish ambassador to Moscow, as mediator between Israel and her hostile Arab neighbors, but his peace mission yielded no results. Rearmed by the Soviet Union but still unable to launch a full-scale military offensive against Israel, Egypt was waging a "war of attrition" at the cease-fire lines. These border battles took a steady toll of Israeli casualties and seemed to escalate every time a United Nations session or other announced diplomatic activity involving the Middle East conflict was expected. Meanwhile, Arab terrorists opened a new front in the Arab war on Israel. They started a wave of piracy and hijackings in the air; their targets were the planes of El Al, Israel's international air line. After each attack, the terrorists boasted of the personal hardship and human casualties they had inflicted. Following an attack on an El Al plane in Athens airport, the Israel Defense Forces retaliated in a manner reminiscent of the Irgun's sabotage acts during the underground days. A group of Israeli commandos raided Beirut airport and destroyed 13 planes on the ground without harming a single Arab. Beirut had been selected because Lebanon had become a base from which Arab guerillas launched their operations against Israel. Despite the fact that the Israeli raiding party had deliberately avoided causing Arab casualties, Israel came under strong international criticism for her act of retaliation.

The Israelis were outraged. As so many times before, they felt that, in the final analysis, the world would find the Jewish state deserving of sympathy only if it assumed the role of perpetual victim without protest. But Israel was not ready to pay that price for world sympathy. Begin made a televised address to voice these feelings in no uncertain terms. "When millions of Jews were led to slaughter, they had sympathy," he said, "but for years no action was taken to save them . . . We don't want sympathy for murdered Jews but understanding for Jews who fight for their national existence and freedom."[9]

The Arab "war of attrition" against Israel continued throughout the year 1969. The shooting in the Suez Canal zone intensified, and Israel retaliated with bombings and commando raids. Arab air piracy was stepped up; the El Al office in Athens was bombed and a non-Israeli plane — it belonged to Trans-World Airlines — was hijacked by Arab terrorists. Al Fatah guerillas terrorized their fellow Arabs in the Israel-administered Gaza Strip. Arab terrorist activity developed also within Israel proper. Bomb explosions at the Hebrew University in Jerusalem, at the central bus station in Tel Aviv and elsewhere caused injuries and loss of life. Stringent security measures were adopted. Inspections of hand-bags in movie theaters, at supermarkets and at the Western Wall, along with warnings to report all unusual objects to the police became part of daily life in Israel, just like the periodic casualty reports from the Suez front.

However, Israeli morale showed no signs of sagging. The economy flourished, tourists arrived and there was immigration from the free world, particularly the United States. There was also considerable activity on the political scene: 1969 was an election year.

In January, 1969, the Israel Labor party (product of a merger between Mapai, Rafi and Ahdut Avodah Po'ale Zion the year before) formed a parliamentary alignment with Mapam. Each of the two parties retained its organizational independence but formed a united bloc for electoral purposes. Moshe Dayan, the minister of defense, never a man to fit into a rigid political mold, gave signs of becoming restive in the Labor setup. He was said to have told leaders of Begin's Gahal bloc, "I regard myself as one of you."[10]

In January, a new Administration had taken office in the United States and it was expected that President Nixon and his secretary of state, William P. Rogers, would press Israel to an-nounce her stand on the future of the Arab territories she had been administering since the Six-Day War. In the Knesset, Begin proposed the setting up of new "Jewish quarters" in the Arab cities on the West Bank and in the Gaza Strip that had come under Israeli control. An arrangement whereby Jews would be settled per-manently in these cities, he said, would not only help the security situation but would also create an atmosphere of mutual trust between the native Arabs and their Jewish neighbors.[11]

On February 26, 1969, Prime Minister Eshkol, who had been ailing for some time, died of a heart attack. Initially, Begin had not regarded Eshkol as a strong leader, but during their work together in the Cabinet, he had come to respect the older man and realized, too, that Eshkol could be resolute when the need arose. "He gave his heart and his hand to the establishment of [the Government of] National Unity," Begin said on learning of Eshkol's death. "He knew how to withstand pressure and it is due to him that today we stand in all the places from where we expelled the enemy who sought to destroy us."[12]

Eshkol was succeeded by Golda Meir, who had retired from the government as Foreign Minister in 1965 and was now in her seventy-first year. Begin was pleased to see Mrs. Meir take a tough stand on policy toward the Arabs. The Nixon Administration had proposed talks among the "Big Four" — the United States, the Soviet Union, Britain and France — to explore possible solutions to the Middle East conflict. In view of the fact that, of these four, the United States was Israel's sole supporter, there was apprehension that if the "four-power talks" materialized, they would end in a Munich-type settlement imposed on Israel at the expense of her basic security interests. Begin, on the Knesset floor and elsewhere, insisted that a Middle East "Munich" could be averted if only the government and people of Israel did not lose their nerve.

The election campaign for the Seventh Knesset was now in full swing. Observers commented favorably on Begin's new, mature campaign style. There were no more motorcycle escorts and balcony speeches. Begin had always attached great importance to neat and proper attire; now his suits were not only neat but well-cut and stylish, worn with white shirts and polka-dot bow ties. His style of public speaking, too, had changed. During the underground period, he had acquired the habit of speaking in whispers. For a while, after his emergence into Israeli politics as leader of the opposition, he had swung to the other extreme, using flowery language and working up to a theatrical pitch. Now he spoke quietly, with the earnest but calm dignity of one sure of himself and his beliefs.

Herzl Rosenblum, editor in chief of *Yediot Aharonot*, a widely-read and influential evening paper, noted that Begin's campaigning differed from that of most other Israeli politicians in two basic respects: he never cast personal slurs on his opponents and he never attacked the government publicly while he was a member of it. According to Rosenblum, a cabinet member who did not foul his own nest, as it were, was something of a novelty in Israeli life. "Hitherto," Rosenblum wrote, "it has been customary to sit in the government — and yet to attack it like a member of the opposition and so to enjoy [the best of] both worlds. [But] Begin has stated that while he is in the Government he will not act as if he were in the opposition, because a minister who has any complaints about fellow ministers should enter these complaints within the Cabinet." If Begin continued in this fashion, Rosenblum wrily concluded, Begin "could be considered a reformer on the Israeli political scene."[13]

In the election, which was held late in October, Begin's Gahal bloc did not gain seats in addition to the 26 it had held since 1965, but the Labor bloc lost several mandates. According to *Le Monde*, an important Paris paper, the election had "revealed a clear trend to the right and will result in increased influence with the government for Menahem Begin, leader of Gahal, the right-wing alignment."[14] Some observers said that there was now a "new" Begin, less extreme than the "old one," and hence more popular and widely respected, but Geula Cohen, for one, disagreed. It was not that Begin had become less extreme, she said, but that the people had become more extreme.[15] Given the continued hostility of the Arab world and the "no-war, no-peace" situation in which Israel still found herself more than two years after the Six-Day War, this was not surprising.

Following the elections, Golda Meir formed a new cabinet based on a broad coalition, with four additional members from the Gahal bloc: Elimelech Rimalt and Leon Dultzin, both from the Liberal party, who became minister of posts and minister without portfolio, respectively; Hayim Landau, who was named minister of development; and Ezer Weizman, literally the father of the Israeli air force, who became minister of transport. For Weizman, the career soldier (unlike his famous uncle, Chaim Weizmann, he spells his last name with only one "n"), this was the first experience in civilian public office.

The year 1970 opened with personal sadness for Menahem Begin. Arye Ben Eliezer, his close friend and associate from the early days of the underground, died late in January after a long period of ill health. Begin, who was born in the same year as Ben Eliezer, wept at the funeral as he eulogized his "fellow brother."

In February, the Knesset once again took up the issue of "Who is a Jew," which had been left in quasi-abeyance twelve years earlier. This time the question of who, under Israeli law, might properly be defined as a Jew, was debated in the context of the Law of Return, which automatically conferred Israeli citizenship on any Jew who entered Israel as an immigrant and who did not expressly opt to retain citizenship in another country. The following month, the law was amended to define as a Jew a person who had been born of a Jewish mother or who had formally converted to Judaism, and was not a member of a different faith. Begin took the Knesset floor to support this amendment. At the same time he appealed to the Orthodox rabbinic authorities to ease the conversion process for Gentiles who had married Jews and had chosen to link their fate with that of the Jewish people. Begin had in mind particularly non-Jewish men and women who had saved their Jewish spouses during the Nazi Holocaust, and Soviet non-Jews who had agreed to leave the Soviet Union with their Jewish spouses and to settle in Israel.

In the spring of 1970, Begin spent several weeks abroad. First, he visited Argentina and Uruguay, where he participated in philanthropic campaigns to aid Jewish causes in both Israel and the diaspora. On the way home, he stopped in Switzerland to aid in the promotion of Israel Bonds.

Begin's position as a member of the Israeli Cabinet had brought no changes in his personal life style. He did not receive or demand any perquisites. His official car was still the one given him by the Herut party years before, and he still lived with Aliza and their unmarried daughter, Leah, in the old two-room apartment on Rosenbaum Street. (After Hasia's marriage, Leah had moved into the living room, while her parents moved from the living room to the bedroom.) "We pay lower rent because it is an old house," he explained late that year to an American radio audience.[16]

His relations with his colleagues in the cabinet were informal. He was on first-name terms with Yigal Allon, Israel Galili and Shimon Peres, who in 1969 had become yet another additon to the group of ministers without portfolio. But unlike his Labor colleagues in the Cabinet and in the Knesset, the courtly Begin could never bring himself to refer to his immediate superior as "Golda." to him, she was always "Madam Prime Minister" or "Mrs. Meir."

During the spring months of 1970 Egypt's "war of attrition" against Israel took a disquieting turn. Israeli war planes raiding the Suez area in retaliation for border incidents encountered Soviet SAM-3 ground-to-air missiles and, more ominously, Egyptian military aircraft flown by Soviet pilots. The United States, concerned about the growing Soviet involvement in the Middle East conflict, no longer sided with Israel's insistence on direct peace negotiations with her hostile Arab neighbors. In December, 1969, Secretary of State Rogers had announced a peace proposal which provided for an Israeli withdrawal from virtually all the Arab territory occupied in 1967, with a few insubstantial border rectifications to be agreed upon by Israel and the Arab states. What the Arabs would have to do in return was phrased in much vaguer terms. Rogers asked the Arabs to promise a binding peace with Israel, but did not specify that there would have to be direct negotiations between the two sides before Israel could be expected to make any troop withdrawals. In fact, the Rogers proposal left nothing of substance open for negotiation. The Israeli government rejected the proposal, which it viewed as an open appeasement of the Arabs and a threat to Israel's survival. In the end nothing came of the Rogers initiative because it was rejected also by the Arabs and their Soviet patrons. They could not accept even the idea that someday the Arabs might be expected to talk face to face with the Israelis.

But in June, 1970, the American secretary of state announced a new peace initiative. Like its predecessor, this "second Rogers plan" also did not specify face-to-face negotiations between Israel and the Arabs. Israel and Egypt were to agree to a cease-fire of at least 90 days during which the United Nations mediator, Dr. Gunnar Jarring, would supervise negotiations between the two sides. The cease-fire also entailed a bilateral military standstill; both Israel and Egypt would undertake not to introduce additional personnel or armaments into the border areas while the cease-fire was in force.

Initially Mrs. Meir rejected this new "Rogers plan." The opponents of the plan, including, of course, Begin and the Gahal bloc, declared that, promises of military standstills notwithstanding, the cease-fire would accomplish nothing except give Egypt a breathing spell to prepare for her long-proclaimed "fourth round" against Israel. But this time Egypt's President Nasser accepted the American proposal. As a result, Israel was given to understand that if she were to spurn the Rogers initiative, world opinion would consider her as an obstacle to the search for peace. The "war of attrition" would continue, with losses of Israeli lives and the constant threat of direct Soviet participation, and Israel would risk losing the support of the United States. At the same time, the Israelis received assurances from President Nixon himself that Israel would not be forced to withdraw any of her troops from the occupied areas without a contractual peace agreement and that her military position would not suffer as a result of the cease-fire.

Early in August, Israel's Cabinet decided to accept the Rogers initiative. The Knesset voted 67 in favor of the plan and 28 against, with nine abstaining. For the first time since it had won a place in the coalition cabinet, the Gahal bloc in the Knesset voted against the government. The Central Committee of the bloc met to decide whether or not, under the circumstances, Gahal could decently continue in the Cabinet. The committee was split down the middle: the Liberal party was willing to remain in the coalition while Herut felt, as Begin was to put it, that it could not be "united with a government which capitulates." The vote was close: 117 members of the Central Committee voted for leaving the coalition and returning to the opposition, 112 voted against. "We are not happy about the situation, but at least we are true to ourselves," Begin said. "It is Nasser who dictates the terms . . . What is asked of us is a Munich — a total surrender."[17]

On August 6, Golda Meir formally announced the government's approval of the Rogers initiative. After Mrs. Meir had finished speaking, Menahem Begin rose from his seat at the Cabinet table and read a note announcing the resignation of the six Gahal ministers. In a brief farewell speech he thanked Mrs. Meir "and all my former colleagues for their comradely and cordial attitude,"[18] then bent to kiss Mrs. Meir's hand. Golda Meir, with equal parliamentary courtesy, expressed "deep sorrow" at the resignation of her Gahal colleagues. "I hope our comradeship and mutual trust will continue," she said.[19] Begin walked away from the Cabinet table and took a seat in the section of the Knesset assigned to members of the Gahal bloc. Once again, Begin was leader of the opposition.

15. "I Have the Floor": 1970-1977

The cease-fire between Egypt and Israel went into effect on August 4, 1970. Israel's misgivings about Nasser's sincerity were confirmed almost immediately. Within days after the shooting had stopped, Israeli intelligence noted that Egypt had violated the military standstill by setting up new SAM-3 missile bases close to the cease-fire line on the Egyptian-held bank of the Suez Canal. When the Israeli government called this to the attention of the United States, the American government confirmed that violations had indeed taken place, but took no action to stop the Egyptian activity.

Begin, now no longer a member of the government, felt free to "go public" in protest against the government's "capitulation" to American pressures. In the Knesset, on August 12, he called on American Jews to take to the streets and demonstrate against the American-initiated cease-fire which had enabled Egypt to build new missile sites undisturbed and had put her in a position where she could effectively neutralize Israel's ground and air defenses in a new war. "Don't stay silent the way you did during the Holocaust of six million European Jews in World War II!" Begin cried. "The Americans are deliberately deceiving us. Accepting the American plan will mean for Israel either a settlement followed by war or a war with no settlement."[1] Addressing a conference of American Jewish leaders in Jerusalem, he pleaded with American Jewry to urge Nixon "not to go down in history as the man who traded the blood of Jewish children for material deals with the Arabs."[2]

Early in September, the Israeli government informed the United States that Israel would not enter into negotiations with Dr. Jarring under the terms of the Rogers plan until Egypt had moved her missiles back. The United States, admitting at last that Israel's complaints about Egypt's cease-fire violations were justified, did not press Israel to negotiate. The "Jarring mission" was briefly resumed early in 1971, but came to a permanent end when the

Arab governments insisted that there was nothing to discuss because they would accept nothing less than an Israeli withdrawal to the boundaries as they had been prior to the Six-Day War, boundaries that would make Israel indefensible against an Arab invasion.

On September 28, Nasser died suddenly. He was succeeded by Anwar el-Sadat, who announced that Egypt would "continue" her "preparations for the first electronic war in history,"[3] and Golda Meir warned the nation to be prepared for war. However, another three years were to pass before Egypt launched a full-scale attack on Israel.

In December Begin and his wife were in the United States. In New York Begin was the main speaker at the annual dinner of the Zionist Organization of America. Also in New York, a radio interviewer questioned him about his resignation from the government coalition and his return to the opposition benches. Begin assured the interviewer that relations between the Gahal bloc and the Labor Alignment were still friendly. As for his relationship with Premier Golda Meir, Begin said that despite the "difference of opinion" between them, he respected her "very highly indeed" and considered her a "very strong" head of state.[4] In Los Angeles, he was unpleasantly surprised to learn that bodyguards had been assigned to him and that he was best advised not to leave his hotel without them. He protested that he had never had personal bodyguards before — not even during his underground years. Was the Los Angeles police afraid that he might be manhandled by Arab demonstrators? The detective shook his head. What worried him, he said, was not Arabs. He showed Begin a leaflet that had been distributed by the left-wing HaShomer HaTzair and the Radical Zionist movement, equating Begin's "extremism" with that of the Arab Al Fatah guerillas and describing Begin as a representative of the "most reactionary" faction in Israel. Recalling the incident several weeks later, Begin wrote that it had left him "deeply saddened. What if Arabs had set up pickets and distributed leaflets? But to call out guards and policemen for my sake against Zionists, even radical Zionists . . ."[5]

Notwithstanding such strident attacks — largely from the radical left — Begin's public image, even now that he was once again in the opposition, was much different from what it had been in the early years of Israel's statehood. During his three years in the Cabinet, the freedom fighter and opposition leader had acted — surprisingly, as some of his opponents saw it — like a responsible statesman, careful (unlike some of his fellow ministers) never to leak information intended for the Cabinet only, and had been painstakingly loyal to coalition discipline. Many observers insisted that in matters of foreign policy, with Israel thoroughly disillusioned by the persistence of Arab hostility after three wars, there was no longer any basic difference between Begin's attitude and that of Mrs. Meir or Moshe Dayan, except in degree and expression. After he had become Prime Minister, Begin enthusiasts pointed out in retrospect that his tenure as a member of the Cabinet had removed the psychological barrier which until then had kept Israeli public opinion from considering him as a serious candidate for the premiership.

In February, 1971, Begin and former Prime Minister Ben-Gurion were in the delegation sent by the State of Israel to the Conference on Soviet Jewry which was held in Brussels. Attended by representatives of Jewish communities from 50 countries, this assembly had been called by two American Jewish umbrella organizations, the American Jewish Conference on Soviet Jewry and the Conference of Presidents of Major American Jewish Organizations, to consider ways of alleviating the political and religious plight of the Jews in the Soviet Union. Begin, still haunted by memories of his own imprisonment in Russia, delivered a scathing attack on the methods of the Soviet secret police. "They break bodies in order to destroy souls," he said. "They crush souls in order to turn persons into non-persons. There is no depth to which this machine, the most terrible on earth after the Gestapo, cannot descend to achieve its purpose."

Begin was greatly upset by one incident which occurred at the Brussels conference. Attendance at the sessions was by official invitation only, but Meir Kahane, leader of the militant Jewish Defense League in New York, demanded admittance to the conference hall. The Defense League's physical and noisy methods of fighting anti-Semitism in the United States and calling attention to the persecution of the Jews in Russia had become the subject of heated controversy among American Jews. The presidium of the Brussels conference, representing established institutions of world Jewry, enlisted the aid of Belgian police in barring Kahane from the conference on the grounds that Kahane was the leader of a group which "practiced and preached a philosophy of violence." An uproar ensued in the hall; Kahane was placed under arrest and was deported from Belgium. To Begin, and numerous others in the hall (including the author Elie Wiesel), the action of the presidium smacked of "informing," a contemptible violation of Jewish solidarity. Demanding the floor, Begin said that while he was not acquainted with Kahane and did not necessarily approve of his activities, he suggested that the conference should concentrate its energies on denouncing only one kind of violence — the kind practiced by the Soviet secret police. "The era in which Jews denounced other Jews to the police has passed forever," he declared.[6]

In March, Begin carried his fight for Soviet Jewry to the United States, where he participated in a mass solidarity rally arranged in New York by three major Zionist organizations to bring the plight of Soviet Jewry before a wider public.

In Israel's Knesset, Begin continued in his self-appointed role as watchdog against retreat without a negotiated peace. In May, Secretary of State Rogers visited Israel. He had come away from Cairo convinced that the only obstacle to peace negotiations between Israel and her Arab neighbors was Israel's refusal to leave the Arab territories she had taken in the Six-Day War. Premier Meir felt that Rogers had been overly credulous; she was not as certain as the American Secretary of State that Egypt was ready for genuine peace with Israel. On May 7, the Knesset committee on foreign affairs and security, of which Begin was a member, met with Rogers for over two hours, with the Israelis presenting their case against complete withdrawal to the borders as they had been before the outbreak of the 1967 war. A debate between Rogers and Begin ensued, with Begin lecturing the American visitor on the danger Israel would face if she withdrew to her old, indefensible borders:

> If we accept your plan, all our cities would be within range of the enemy's shells. For you, it may be an important issue —[but] for us it is a question of life and death. You were impressed by Sadat's consent to peace but we remember Hitler and Stalin speaking of peace and meanwhile preparing their tanks for conquests.

As for the hope held out to Israel that the Arabs would agree to peace negotiations once she had withdrawn from the Arab territories, Begin put it bluntly, "What actually do we have to discuss after you have, in your plan, given the Arabs everything?'

Rogers, with a touch of asperity, interrupted Begin several times. Finally, Begin's patience wore thin. "We are accustomed to parliamentary interruptions in our democratic House," he told Rogers, "but please, Mr. Secretary, I have the floor."[7]

In the summer and fall, Begin was on the road once more for his own party and for Israel Bonds. He visited Brazil, and then the Union of South Africa, as ever a strong Revisionist base, where he met with Prime Minister J.B. Vorster. Next came Venezuela, Canada, and — for the second time within one year — the United States, where he addressed a Washington dinner attended by 20 U.S. Senators to discuss the balance of arms in the Middle East.

In January, 1972, he made his first trip to England — a brief lecture tour of London — at the invitation of the Revisionist party of Great Britain. In England, which almost three decades earlier had put a price on Begin's head, the welcome was a good deal cooler than that accorded him in any of the other countries he had visited. Arab diplomats let it be known that they would spare no effort to get their hands on the man whom they labeled as the murderer of Deir Yassin. British Fascists and Arab Al Fatah agents both threatened to kill Begin, and the Jews of Great Britain were tense and anxious. The British press, including the London *Jewish Chronicle*, had little good to say about him. The only newspaper to soften its condemnation of Begin with a grudging tribute to his political tenacity was the house organ of the British Zionist establishment, in an editorial published two days prior to Begin's arrival:

> The Mandate ended 23 years ago, yet for the broad mass of public opinion [Begin] is still only a name from the past, associated with violent anti-British deeds . . . [However] Begin is not just a man from the past. He has been a prominent Israeli leader throughout the country's independent history. And although his party's policies were often hysterically divisive, they did not destroy the fabric of Israeli society but rather helped to season and strengthen it.[8]

When Begin, accompanied by his wife and by his right-hand man, Yechiel Kadishai, landed at London's Heathrow airport on January 9, he found only members of the Israeli embassy staff, some Herut members and a few cameramen there to greet him. He soon learned that two Scotland Yard detectives had been assigned to guard him day and night, and that the management of the two halls hired by the Revisionists for functions in his honor had decided to cancel their contracts because of bomb threats they had received. One of the two halls was in the Royal Garden Hotel, where the Begins themselves were staying. Begin took it all with philosophic calm. When he was asked how it felt to be so closely guarded by British police, he said, "Well, they smile at me and I smile at them." However, he asked the manager of the Royal Garden Hotel whether it might not be better if he and his party would move out and stay somewhere else. The manager, with typical British courtesy, protested, "Oh, no, I am proud to have you."⁹

Instead of the originally planned elaborate banquet at Westminster Central Hall, with 2,000 guests in attendance, there was only a dinner for some 250 guests at a kosher catering hall. Still, an effort was made at festivity and elegance, with Begin and his party in formal evening attire. Thanks to attacks in the British press and the *Jewish Chronicle,* Begin's visit turned into something of a sensation. While the dinner was in progress, members of the British branch of Mapam staged a demonstration outside, with shouts of "Begin, go home!" Begin shrugged it off with a wry smile. It seemed, he said, that his visit had brought "complete national unity" at least in Israel, where the counterparts of the British Mapamniks were now defending him against his unfriendly critics in England. At a press conference, he told 90 newspapermen that the enmity between his "fighting family" and the British was now a thing of the past. "The Irgun period," he said, "was the greatest in our lives, but the fight is now over. We must not dwell on the past, and the British are our friends." Recalling the hanging of the two British sergeants by the Irgun in the summer of 1947, he said that it had been a "tragedy," which "hangs on the heads of those who helped kill 10 Irgun members."

In view of the cool reception given him by the established institutions of both Great Britain and Anglo-Jewry, Begin was all the more touched by a letter he received from a British sergeant who had been stationed in Palestine during the final years of the British mandate. Sergeant Peter Dock, retired and living in Edinburgh, wrote to Begin to tell him "how deeply ashamed I am at your welcome in Great Britain" and to express his admiration for the Jewish underground and its leader:

> Let me say that I look back to the period of 1946-47 and 1948 with admiration at your exploits ... After all, this was a time when you were fighting for your homeland — and in my book all is fair in love and war. We all at heart regret the loss of life on both sides, but yours was a magnificent motivation ...
>
> Myself, I spent many an uncomfortable time, sleepless, looking for you and your men. But let me say if ever the British army had

a true adversary, it was you. After all, some of our tactics were not very good.

It has been with great interest that I have watched Israel grow into a great nation against all odds. Anyone who belongs to a race that has lost six million and could still come back and form a nation and a new homeland must be truly great. A truly magnificent conception . . .[10]

When Begin returned to Israel he faced reporters at Lod airport with a broad smile and declared that the days he had spent in England had been "the three most wonderful days of my life." Even in the worst days of the Irgun struggle, Begin had never felt hatred for the British people. Indeed, he had made a point of expressing his respect and admiration for British culture and the British tradition of parliamentarianism. The fact that he had been able to visit England as a citizen of the sovereign Jewish state which he had helped free from British rule gave him a sense of deep gratification, perhaps even of personal triumph. He would be glad, he told Israeli newspapermen at the airport, to visit England again any time the "comrades" — meaning the Revisionist party in Great Britain — would send him another invitation. In high spirits, he added that if the next invitation were to be extended by the British government, he would be more than happy to accept. Almost six years later, there really would be an invitation from the British government; it was addressed to "The Honorable Menahem Begin" as prime minister of the State of Israel.

In Jerusalem that summer, the Knesset met in special session to protest against the exorbitant emigration tax imposed by the Soviet Union on skilled professionals, which was aimed primarily at Jews seeking to leave the country. In effect, the tax deprived these unfortunates of the opportunity to emigrate or to join their families in the West or in Israel. Taking the floor after Golda Meir, Begin urged the Jews in the free world not to remain silent while their brethren in Soviet Russia were threatened with spiritual annihilation. Let Jewish students and young people hold round-the-clock vigils outside every Soviet legation in the free world, displaying copies of the United Nations Declaration of Human Rights, and let their elders call their governments to action. Begin addressed a special appeal to American Jews: march on Washington by the hundreds of thousands and urge the President of the United States to act on behalf of Soviet Jewry.

At the same time, he called upon the State of Israel to raise the issue of Soviet Jewry at the United Nations General Assembly and before the various agencies of the United Nations. Speaking at a conference of workers in Tel Aviv, he said, "Instead of the demand 'Let my people go,' we must revive the demand for the evacuation of the whole of Soviet Jewry — and be prepared to take in over two million of them within a short period."[11] It was the same proposal that he had first put forth nearly three decades earlier in his "proclamation of revolt" against British rule in the Jewish homeland.

Later that year, Begin crossed the Atlantic again to help in Israel Bond campaigns in the United States and western Canada. The United States had become the target of an all-out effort by Egypt's President Sadat to win American friendship. There had been reports of disagreements between Egypt and the Soviet Union on the nature, delivery and use of Russian weapons supplied to Egypt. Also, the conspicuous presence and activity of Soviet military advisors had become obnoxious to the Egyptians. Finally, in July, 1972, Sadat announced his decision to expel the Russian advisors from Egypt. Israelis feared that the United States, taking advantage of the opportunity to establish friendly ties with Egypt, might press Israel to accept a peace settlement favoring the Arab states at Israel's expense. Questioned in a radio interview about that possibility, Begin maintained that such pessimistic speculations, given sufficient currency in Israel's official leadership, would only be self-fulfilling. "Cabinet ministers' statements to the effect that we must be rid of Judea and Samaria" — he consistently refers to the occupied West Bank territory by its Biblical names — "practically at any price, actually invites pressures; the concession has thus been made and we shall be pressed to make further concessions for the sake of reaching agreement." Begin praised Foreign Minister Abba Eban for his declaration that the Gaza Strip would not be detached from Israel because it had been part of the historic Jewish homeland since antiquity. "This is an important historic reason," Begin said, "and I must therefore ask: did not Judea and Samaria belong to the Land of Israel in the same way?"[12]

In December, the Herut party held its 11th national convention in Tel Aviv. On this occasion, Begin's son Benny, 29 years old, delivered his maiden speech as an active member of his father's party. Father and son sat side by side in the convention hall, Begin, as usual, wearing a tie and jacket and Benny in shirt sleeves but with the same serious, scholarly expression on his face as his father. The chairman of the convention was Ezer Weizman, the former minister of transport, who had become chairman of the Herut party executive. For the eventuality of a Herut victory in the elections to the Eighth Knesset, which were due in October, 1973, Weizman presented to the convention a "shadow cabinet," with Begin as prime minister, Hayim Landau as foreign minister and himself as minister of defense.

The prize which Weizman really sought had been a higher one; he had hoped to replace Menahem Begin as the leader of the Herut party and so to put himself in line for the premiership. As he wrote in his autobiography, *On Eagles' Wings,* he respected Begin, but he and Begin were "poles apart in our characters, our viewpoints and our personal traits." Eleven years younger than Begin, Weizman was a *sabra,* born and raised in Israel, and endowed with the unquestioning self-assurance derived from a secure childhood in a well-known, highly respected family. The acknowledged head of that family had been his father's brother, "Uncle Chaim," the world Zionist leader and later first President of the State of Israel. During World War II Weizman had seen active service in the Royal Air Force. After the war he had spent some time in England to study aeronautics. Subsequently he had put his skills and experience to good use in organizing and later commanding the air force of the State of Israel. He had acquired a reputation for flamboyance of style; for years, he piloted his own vintage Spitfire which had its wings painted black and its propeller daubed a bright red. Unlike his uncle, Weizman was just as militant in his nationalism as Begin; in fact, after his return from England, he had served in the Irgun. However, he was impatient with what he considered Begin's old-fashioned diaspora style. "There was the friction you get between men who lack a chemical affinity," Weizman continues in his memoirs.[13] In the intra-party tug-of-war between the two men, Begin emerged as the winner. After the December convention, Weizman was no longer chairman of the Herut executive. Nevertheless, in January, 1973, Weizman, who after his resignation from the cabinet in 1970 had gone into business with Yaakov Meridor, agreed to take charge of the Herut election campaign, which, if it was successful, would make Begin prime minister.

The election year of 1973 was to be one of the most eventful years in the history of Israel since 1948. It opened on a note of prosperity and optimism, but closed in an atmosphere of shock, bewilderment and soul-searching such as the Jewish state had never known before.

The early months of 1973 saw a boom in Israel's economy and

the arrival of thousands of Jews from the Soviet Union. True, Israel was still officially in a state of war with her neighbors: Arab terrorist attacks and plane hijackings continued. In retaliation, Israel raided Arab guerilla camps in southern Lebanon, killing a number of top terrorist leaders. But that spring, as Israel celebrated the twenty-fifth anniversary of her independence, few Israelis believed that the *status quo* would be disrupted by a full-scale war.

In the Knesset that spring, Begin urged the government to take a more positive approach in demonstrating to American public opinion why Israel was well worth the military and economic aid she was receiving from the United States. Slightly altering the famous passage from John F. Kennedy's inaugural address, Begin said that the Americans should ask themselves not only what their country had done for Israel but also what Israel was doing for their country. Because Israeli troops were firmly entrenched on the east bank of the Suez Canal, Soviet transports of arms and other equipment destined for North Vietnam could not use the Canal but had to travel by roundabout routes. As a consequence, the Soviet shipments took 16 days longer to reach their destination than they would have, had the Canal been open. "Calculate the effect of that over five and one-half years to realize the amount of fire-power that did not reach the front line on time," Begin continued. "*That* fact should be brought to the notice of the American public." If the Israeli government refrained from acquainting the American public fully with Israel's military value to the United States, it was guilty of false pride motivated, in Begin's view, by "leftist snobbism."

A Mapam member of the Knesset objected to Begin's statement. He accused Begin of making it appear as if Israel had been taking the side of the United States in the Vietnam war. Begin indignantly denied that there had been any such intent on his part.

> Of course I did not say that. We were partners of neither side in the terrible Indo-China war. What I did say was an objective fact: that our position on the banks of the Suez Canal led to the continuous delaying of weapons of destruction intended to be used against American soldiers — whom all Americans wished to see return home alive and well.

If America sent modern jet fighters to Israel, Begin asked, "why should we not point out the mutuality of the aid? Would it be preferable, from the point of view of 'revolutionary socialism' for Israel to be regarded as an American 'client' receiving Phantoms as an act of charity? If the truth is helpful, why rest content with the harmful opposite of the truth?"[14]

Also during the spring months, Begin appealed to American Jewry not to remain silent while Soviet Jewry was faced with spiritual annihilation. Leonid Brezhnev was about to visit the United States; Begin urged the Jews of the United States to organize a one-day countrywide stoppage of work while Brezhnev was there, in protest against the Soviet Union's anti-Jewish policies. Begin did not accept arguments of Jewish leaders in Israel and elsewhere that such demonstrations in the free world would harm rather than help the Jews in the Soviet Union. The present generation, he said, had already had on its conscience the effects of its silence and inaction in the days of the Nazi Holocaust. "Let this proud demonstration of American Jewry — and its friends and sympathizers — make it clear to Mr. Brezhnev that not again in our time will we allow Jews to suffer through our inactivity."[15]

As the election campaigns moved into high gear, Israel's industries were hit by a wave of crippling strikes. Begin reiterated his party's view of the government's proper role in the elimination of poverty. "We are not in favor of an egalitarianism which does not acknowledge any economic differences. If that was the case, the social condition would stagnate. But what we insist on is that within a reasonable time a situation must be established in which the basic conditions of a reasonable existence in terms of housing, income, clothing and education are available to all.'" Then he added, "And if beyond that, there will be economic differences, that is no tragedy."[16]

Late in August, Begin's Gahal bloc opened negotiations with three smaller right-wing factions — the State List, the Free Center and the Land of Israel movement — to form a strong, united right-wing bloc for the coming elections. The driving force behind the negotiations was an army officer, Brigadier General Ariel (Arik) Sharon, a *sabra* in his late 40's who had begun his military career in the War of Independence and had commanded Israeli forces in the Sinai peninsula in 1956 and again in 1967. Sharon's fame as a fighting general worked to his advantage on the political scene. During the euphoric years following the Six-Day War, army officers enjoyed high popularity with the Israeli public, regardless of political party affiliation.

By September, Sharon had succeeded in welding the four right-wing factions together into the Likud (literally "consolidation" or "unity") bloc, under the leadership of Menahem

Begin. A common platform of four basic principles was hammered out. One: The Jewish people had an inalienable right to all of Biblical Palestine; hence, Likud would not accept an Israeli withdrawal from the West Bank territory. Two: Formal peace treaties between Israel and her Arab neighbors must acknowledge Israel's right to retain control over areas — more precisely, the Golan Heights and the Gaza Strip — which the Arabs had consistently used as springboards for attacks on Israel prior to the 1967 war. Three: The Israeli government had already established Jewish settlements in the Gaza Strip, the Golan Heights and the Sinai peninsula. Likud intended to promote the creation of additional Jewish settlements not only in those areas, but also in "Judea and Samaria," the West Bank territory. Four: All people living in the Jewish state, including the territories administered by Israel since the 1967 war, would enjoy complete equality, without distinction of race, religion, nationality or sex; at the same time, no inhabitant of territory under Israeli control should have Israeli citizenship forced upon him or her, or suffer discrimination because of his or her refusal to give up citizenship in another country.

The Jewish High Holidays in that election year came at the end of September, culminating on October 6 with Yom Kippur, the Day of Atonement. During this season of prayer and reflection, which opened on Rosh Ha-Shanah, the Jewish New Year, and concluded with Yom Kippur, the most sacred day in the Jewish calendar, election campaigning in Israel came to a temporary halt. When it was resumed, nothing in Israel was the same as it had been before.

On Yom Kippur, 1973, Egypt and Syria launched simultaneous full-scale attacks on Israel. In the south, Egyptian troops and tanks poured across the Suez Canal into the Sinai peninsula, while in the north mechanized Syrian forces crossed the ceasefire line in the Golan Heights. This time, in contrast to previous wars, Israel was caught off balance. The famous Israeli intelligence had not worked properly. When it finally became clear to them that an attack was imminent, Israel's top leadership decided to forego the option of a preemptive strike. Prime Minister Meir was convinced that preemptive action by Israel would alienate world public opinion and the United States; it was believed, too, that with the Sinai peninsula and the Golan Heights as buffer zones standing between the enemy and Israel proper, Israel could afford to absorb a first blow from the Arabs before striking back. Though shocked by the sudden renewal of all-out war, most Israelis, along with many of Israel's friends in other countries — including quite highly-placed military and diplomatic circles — persuaded themselves that this time, too, the war would end in a matter of days with Israel winning a smashing victory over her enemies as she had done twice before, in 1956 and again in 1967.

But in 1973 there was to be no lightning victory for Israel. It was as Begin had predicted three years earlier: The cease-fire and military standstill between Israel and Egypt imposed by the United States had served Egypt as a shelter beneath which to create a close missile network without having to fear counteraction from Israel. Now, when Israel's bombers were sent over the Suez area to stem the Egyptian advance, they were shot out of the air by Soviet-built missiles, permitting Egypt to transport troops, tanks and heavy equipment across the Suez Canal even in broad daylight. Meanwhile, in the north, Soviet-supplied Syrian tanks were rolling over the Golan Heights, causing heavy Israeli losses in lives and equipment and menacing the settlements in northern Israel. There was also the threat that Jordan would launch an attack on the West Bank and that Iraq would send troops to the aid of Syria. During the first week of the war, Israel's situation appeared hardly less critical than it had been in 1948.

Ten anxious days passed before the Israeli defense forces were able to bring their full strength into play. On October 16, an Israeli task force, led by General Ariel Sharon, crossed to the west bank of the Suez Canal. From then on, Israel's army, its material losses replaced by a massive arms airlift from the United States, performed in keeping with its past reputation for near-invincibility. In a matter of days, Israeli troops in the south were advancing into Egypt proper and had encircled the Egyptian Third Army of 20,000 men east of the Canal. In the north, after tank battles comparable in dimensions and fierceness to those between Germany and Russia during World War II, the Israelis were moving toward Damascus. On October 22, 16 days after the outbreak of the war, the United Nations Security Council passed a resolution (Resolution 338) calling for an immediate cease-fire and subsequent peace negotiations between the "parties to the present fighting." Egypt and Syria, reeling under the shock of Israel's devastating counterattack, readily agreed to a cease-fire. Israel, once again (as in 1956) under the combined pressure of the United States and the Soviet Union, had little other choice but to accept. Similarly, Israel, under threats of active Soviet intervention and, consequently, American pressure, had no other alternative but to allow the trapped Egyptian Third

Army to remain intact, to supply it with food and medical necessities and, in the end, to release it.

On November 11, 1973, the cease-fire agreement between Egypt and Israel was formally signed by representatives of the two armies meeting face to face at Kilometer 101 on the Suez-Cairo Highway. As for the Syrians, they were not yet ready for a direct meeting with anyone representing the State of Israel.

Mingled with the Israelis' natural relief that the fighting had come to an end, there was an undercurrent of resentment at the undue speed with which the United Nations had acted to stop the fighting when Israel had been on the verge of total victory over her enemies. It seemed that every time Israel won her fight for survival on the battlefield, the rest of the world stepped in to protect Israel's enemies from the full impact of their defeat.

From the strictly military point of view, the "Yom Kippur War" had ended in a near-miraculous victory for Israel. Despite initial reverses, Israel had been able not only to keep her borders intact but also to retain sufficient Arab territory to use as bargaining counters in eventual peace negotiations. But would the world ever permit Israel to hold out for direct negotiations with her enemies, without interference from nations which themselves were cool if not hostile toward the Jewish state?

The mood in Israel grew darker still when complete casualty reports were released. In 16 days of fighting, Israel had lost over 2,000 dead, and many more had been wounded; of the latter, hundreds had been maimed for life. There were young women who had lost a husband in the fighting in 1967 and had remarried, only to be widowed a second time in the Yom Kippur War. A new generation of Israelis, born and raised to maturity in an independent Jewish state, had seen Israeli soldiers led away by enemy troops as prisoners of war. For the first time, these *sabras,* who, unlike earlier generations, had taken the existence of a Jewish state for granted, had come face to face with the specter of defeat, of a return to the homelessness that had plagued the Jewish people for two thousand years before the rise of the State of Israel.

What, the people of Israel wanted to know, had gone wrong? How was it that Israel's intelligence service had overlooked, or misinterpreted, Egyptian and Syrian troop movements until the enemy was actually upon the country? And once the Prime Minister and her closest associates had been informed that an Arab attack was imminent, why had she not ordered preemptive military action, or at least an immediate call-up of reserves? Who had taken the decision not to launch a first strike, and not to mobilize? And why had these decisions been made without the assent of the full Cabinet?

In the Knesset, two days after the signing of the cease-fire agreement at Kilometer 101, Begin attacked the government for its "sins of omission and commission." Directly addressing Mrs. Meir, he said, "You knew well in advance of the massive Egyptian and Syrian preparations for an imminent attack, and yet you did not even admit this to your own government, and you overruled your own chief of staff when he wanted to stage a preemptive attack." Bluntly, he called upon Mrs. Meir and her cabinet to resign. "What moral authority do you have after this failure?" he demanded.[17] "I am compelled to say," he told the Herut executive, "not as a member of a party, and not as an active politician, but as a father and grandfather, that I can no longer depend on the Government as at present constituted to ensure the future of my children and grandchildren."[18]

Israel was isolated as never before in her quarter-century of independence. Under Arab and Communist pressures, emerging countries in Africa which had received generous aid from Israel broke relations with her. Led by Saudi Arabia, the Arabs had brought into play a new and potent weapon: an oil embargo against any country supporting the Jewish state. Many small countries, totally dependent on Arab oil for their economic survival, hastened to demonstrate their aloofness from Israel.

On November 22, Begin was in Paris, having flown there expressly to address a group of parliamentarians from nine countries of the European Economic Community who had opposed their governments' submission to the Arab oil blackmail. Hours later, he flew back to Israel to continue the Likud bloc's campaign for the elections which, due to the war emergency, had been postponed until December 31. What Begin wanted was not a cabinet of Likud loyalists, but a new "Government of National Unity" which, though under the leadership of Likud, would include "the strongest personalities and the best brains in Israel," even non-members of the Knesset, regardless of party affiliation, except, he stressed, for Communists.[19]

On December 1 David Ben-Gurion died at Kibbutz Sde Boker at the age of 87. On December 3, Begin went to the kibbutz to attend Ben-Gurion's funeral. In the final years of his life, the "Old Man" seemed to have developed a soft spot in his heart for Begin. In February, 1969, Ben-Gurion, writing to Begin as a member of the Cabinet, had added a warm personal note:

Permit me to add a few personal remarks. For some reason, my wife Paula was always an admirer of yours . . . I was very much opposed to some of your policies and actions, both before and after the establishment of the State. Nor do I regret my opposition, for I believe that I was right (anyone can err without realizing it). But on a personal level, I have never held a grudge against you, and the more I have come to know you in recent years, the greater has been my esteem for you — and my Paula was very happy about that.

With respect and esteem,

D. Ben-Gurion[20]

Four weeks after Ben-Gurion's funeral, the elections for the Eighth Knesset were held. The Labor Alignment suffered some losses, but still retained 51 seats. The right-wing bloc, as Likud, increased its Knesset strength from 26 seats to 39. In part, this gain was the result of Likud's having gathered in the smaller rightist factions. But it also reflected the dissatisfaction of many voters with a long-entrenched government which they held responsible for the near-disaster the country had suffered, and a growing tendency among Israelis to wonder whether Begin's tough stand in matters of war and peace was not more realistic than the softer line followed by the Labor government.

The end of 1973 and the year 1974 were marked by the "shuttle diplomacy" of Secretary of State Henry Kissinger, lightning back-and-forth trips between Israel and the Arab states to produce "progress toward peace." Begin feared that Kissinger would bend over backward to prove that, although he was a Jew, he could be completely objective about the fate of the State of Israel. On the Knesset floor, Begin said, as if speaking directly to the American Secretary of State:

> You are a Jew. You are not the first to achieve high office in the country of your residence. Remember the past. There have been such Jews, who, out of a complex of concern that they might be accused of acting for the benefit of their people because they were Jews, did the contrary . . . Let Dr. Kissinger beware of this distortion of what he calls "being objective."[21]

According to Begin, Kissinger, visiting Israel, had taken note of this warning "with the humor of which he was capable when he had the mind to use it."

"You gave me hell in the Knesset," said the Secretary of State to the leader of the opposition.

"Hell?" Begin quipped, pretending not to understand, "Oh no, I want you to go to paradise. That's why I want you to help Israel."[22]

Begin had harsh criticism for the "disengagements of forces" arranged under Kissinger's auspices at the cease-fire lines between Israel and Egypt, and between Israel and Syria. "Disengagement of forces," he declared, was merely a euphemism for unilateral Israeli troop withdrawals from enemy territory, an ingenious device for maneuvering Israel into giving up Arab lands without Israel receiving anything tangible in return. When the Knesset, in January, 1974, approved an initial "disengagement" in the Sinai peninsula, Begin turned angrily on Minister of Defense Moshe Dayan. "Whither are you leading this nation with your disengagement agreement, which provides for Israel's withdrawal without a concomitant Egyptian renunciation of the state of belligerency?" he demanded.[23]

In the spring of 1975 he cut short a visit to the United States to launch a campaign in Israel against the "disengagement of forces" in a sector of the Golan Heights which Israel had pledged never to abandon.

In April, Golda Meir, weary and heartsick, blaming her lack of foresight for Israel's reverses in the Yom Kippur War, resigned as Prime Minister. The Labor Alignment named Itzhak Rabin, formerly Israel's chief of staff and then ambassador in Washington, as her successor. Begin did not consider Mrs. Meir's resignation sufficient; he called for a dissolution of the Knesset and new elections. In Jerusalem, he addressed a mass rally of 8,000 citizens; afterwards, he was raised on the shoulders of enthusiastic supporters, who shouted, "Begin for Prime Minister!"[24]

Begin succeeded neither in preventing the "disengagement" on the Syrian front, nor in forcing a new election. On June 3, Rabin was sworn in as Prime Minister; Shimon Peres, formerly a minister without portfolio, was named minister of defense to succeed Moshe Dayan.

Two weeks after Rabin's installation, Israel received a visit from President Richard M. Nixon, who, bedeviled by trouble in southeast Asia and the Watergate crisis at home, was desperately anxious to redeem himself in American public opinion by achieving a peace breakthrough in the Middle East. Begin attended the banquet given for the President in the Chagall Hall of the Knesset building. He was seated directly opposite Nixon and took the opportunity to observe him closely. "I was able to see him as a melancholy man," Begin recalled. "There were times when he exchanged remarks with his neighbors that aroused smiles or laughter, but for most of the time he was silent, sunk in thought. The onlooker could not rid himself of the feeling that the President of the greatest Western Power was not really there, in Jerusalem — but wandering far across the ocean in his thoughts. Possibly he was even thinking about what might await him at home after all his wanderings were over . . ."[25]

Begin did not regard Nixon, or Gerald Ford, who succeeded to the Presidency in August, 1974, as enemies of Israel. Nevertheless, he was convinced that the American concept of "progress toward peace" — Israeli withdrawals from Arab lands without insistence on concomitant peace treaties between Israel and the Arabs — would leave Israel defenseless against the Arabs even as the Munich Agreement had left Czechoslovakia at the mercy of Nazi Germany 35 years earlier. In 1973, as in 1938, a small nation was told by well-meaning friends that it must make concessions to its enemy for the sake of world peace. In the case of Czechoslovakia, the result had been that the small nation lost its independence not as a result of defeat by the enemy but due to coercion from its friends. "It must be remembered," Begin wrote, "that the 'disengagement agreement' at Munich was not achieved by Hitler or Mussolini. It was prepared by Runciman and imposed by Chamberlain and Daladier, Czechoslovakia's great friends who stood surety for its security."[26]

Meanwhile, pressures were mounting on the Labor Alignment to set up a wall-to-wall coalition government under Rabin. In December, 1974 the executive of the Alignment met to decide whether Begin's Likud bloc should be invited to join the coalition. At the meeting, Rabin ridiculed Begin as an "archeological exhibit in our political life." Begin, he said, was in fact an asset to the Labor Alignment, for under his leadership it was certain that the Likud would never be more than an opposition bloc.[27]

Many Israelis — including opponents of Labor and its policies — were inclined to agree with Rabin's assessment of Menahem Begin. The younger generation tended to smile at his long, erudite speeches on the Knesset floor and at his quaint, non-*sabra* courtliness. And even among his admirers there were those who looked upon Begin, now past 60, as an old-timer, a relic from a heroic past, maybe, but with little chance of a future on the country's political scene.

Begin, however, was still far from a has-been. On January 12, 1975, his own Herut party made a point of holding its twelfth annual convention in the Israeli-occupied West Bank area. The 1500 delegates met in a flag-festooned factory hall at Kiryat Arba, the new Jewish settlement on the outskirts of Biblical Hebron. Among the guests of honor was President Ephraim Katzir, despite protests from the Labor Alignment — which had elected him — that, under the circumstances, the presence of the head of state might create the wrong impression about the Labor government's view on the future of territories taken by Israel in the Six-Day War. Another distinguished guest on the dais of honor was Rahel Yanait Ben Zvi, the 89-year-old widow of Israel's second president and a veteran labor leader in her own right.

In his keynote address, Begin proposed a three-year armistice period during which representatives of Israel and the Arab nations would engage in intensive negotiations, meeting alternately in Jerusalem, in Arab capitals and in neutral cities. To the Palestinian Arabs, he said: "We extend to you the hand not only of peace but of brotherhood also. We shall give you equal rights in our land, with cultural autonomy." Under a Likud government, Arabs of the West Bank who opted for Israeli citizenship would be given the right to vote as well as to be elected to public office. Those preferring not be become Israelis would also be accorded the full rights and privileges of citizenship, except those of voting or of running for elective office.[28]

Next, Begin turned to Israel's domestic problems — poverty and a decline in the idealism that had inspired the pioneers of an earlier generation. It was the duty of the government, he said, to provide rental housing for young Israeli couples who were faced with the choice of postponing marriage or moving in with parents because they lacked the cash reserves needed to buy an apartment. Large families should be subsidized, not as charity but as of right. To combat the frequent strikes that were plaguing the country, he proposed a trial period of two to three years during which "all elements of the economy" would "agree to refrain from strikes and lockouts and submit disputes to arbitration panels chosen by mutual agreement." He urged Israelis to adopt a simpler life style, to stop importing luxury goods so that foreign currency could be saved for the "real needs" of public and individual welfare. Finally, he called upon his fellow citizens to give greater heed to the standards of morality in personal, public and business life which had been the hallmark of the pioneer society. "Social peace and social justice" were just as much a part of the Begin ideology as his style of nationalism and foreign policy.

In February and March, 1975 Henry Kissinger continued his "shuttle diplomacy" campaign, now aimed at securing an Israeli withdrawal — without prior peace negotiations — from two locations in the Sinai desert: the Abu Rodeis oil fields and the strategic Mitla and Gidi passes. This time the American secretary of state met considerable resistance from the Israeli government. Premier Rabin declared that Israel would agree to this new withdrawal only in return for a solemn pledge of "non-belligerency" from Egypt. President Sadat's vague endorsement of the principle of "non-use of force," Rabin said, was not sufficient to warrant the military risk which Israel would assume in making the withdrawals proposed by the United States. Kissinger, making no secret of his frustration at being unable to produce further "progress toward peace," announced that his efforts to mediate between Israel and Egypt had ended in failure. After he left Israel, he implied that Israel was to blame for the impasse, and President Ford introduced an ominous note announcing a "reassessment" of American relations with Israel.

In April Begin, again in the United States, told television interviewers in New York that he considered the Ford Administration guilty of an "absolutely unfair" judgment and of "gross injustice" in blaming Israel for the breakdown of the Kissinger shuttle. One of the journalist-interviewers asked Begin why Israel was insisting on an Egyptian promise of non-belligerency before agreeing to evacuate the Sinai passes. Begin cited Sadat's vows that Egypt would continue her state of war with Israel not merely until Israel would agree to withdraw from part of the Sinai peninsula but until Israel would have retreated to her borders as they had been before the Six-Day War and paved the way for the formation of a Palestinian Arab state on the West Bank. Such an Arab state, Begin pointed out, would be taken over almost immediately by Yassir Arafat's Palestine Liberation Organization, whose charter called for the liquidation of the State of Israel. In other words, Begin said, Egypt would consider agreeing to renounce belligerency against Israel only after the Jewish state had been placed into a geographical and political position in which it would be defenseless against future attacks from its enemies. "[What] Sadat promises us [is] non-belligerency with a non-existent State of Israel," Begin concluded. "I don't think anybody will advise us to accept such a non-belligerency."

Another interviewer on the program challenged Begin to explain how he expected any of the Arab states to enter into peace negotiations with Israel when, in his party's frequently-stated view, Israel must not "give back one inch of the land of our fathers." Begin retorted that he himself had never made such a statement; then, he indicated that, in return for a genuine peace with her Arab neighbors, Israel could withdraw from some of the land she had occupied during the Six-Day War. A peace treaty with Egypt, with firm provisions for Israel's security, might stipulate Israeli withdrawals from part of the Sinai peninsula. "In Sinai, in the context of peace, we can find a border of peace between Egypt and Israel," he said. However, this reasoning could not be applied to the West Bank. As opposed to Sinai, the West Bank was not Arab land but "belongs as of right to the Jewish people inalienably," because it was part of Biblical Palestine. It had been annexed by the Kingdom of Jordan in 1948,illegally, in a war of aggression against Israel. However, he did not think that Israel's remaining in that territory would impede peace in the Middle East. "We believe we can live [there] with our Arab neighbors in peace and human dignity."

What of the political status of the Palestinian Arabs in the West Bank territory and in the Gaza Strip? These Arabs, Begin replied, were entitled to "cultural autonomy" within the Jewish state. What about the right of the Palestinian Arabs to self-determination? The Palestinian Arabs, said Begin, were part of a larger Arab nation which already enjoyed self-determination. "Those who call themselves Palestinians are Arabs. We recognize the great Arab nation, the Arab nationality. There are more than 100 million Arabs who possess 20 sovereign states, so their right for self-determination is [already] expressed in an unequalled, unprecedented form." One per cent of the people of that Arab nation live on the West Bank. Begin saw nothing wrong in having that one per cent live under the political jurisdiction of a Jewish state. The Arab people had 20 independent states of their own with a total area of 12 million square kilometers; the Jewish people had only Israel. "I think everybody should weigh these claims on the scales of justice, should draw the conclusion for themselves that ours is a just cause."[29]

The fall of 1975 was a bleak season in Israel's international relations. In September, the Rabin government, threatened with the loss of American military and financial aid, agreed to evacuate the oil fields and the passes in the Sinai peninsula without the hoped-for promise from Egypt to end the state of war with Israel. But this concession did not change the attitude of Israel's enemies. On November 10, in New York, the United Nations General Assembly passed a resolution condemning Zionism as a form of racism.

For the second time that year, Begin visited the United States, this time with a delegation from the Knesset, which had been invited to Washington by the U.S. Congress. After conferring with leaders of the Senate and the House of Representatives, the visiting legislators met with President Ford, Vice-President Nelson A. Rockefeller and Secretary of State Kissinger. Ford assured them that Americans condemned the anti-Zionist resolution passed at the United Nations, but this was scant comfort to the Israelis, who saw themselves increasingly friendless among the nations of the world.

Begin spent much of 1976 traveling. In January, he arrived in France with a Knesset delegation to attend a session of the Council of Europe in Strasbourg. He then crossed the Atlantic to tour Canada on behalf of the United Jewish Appeal. In February, along with former Prime Minister Golda Meir and others, he represented Israel at the second Brussels Conference on Soviet Jewry. Later in the year, he toured Latin American countries, stopping for a day in Switzerland on the way back to Israel.

In November, following Jimmy Carter's victory in the American Presidential elections, Begin went to New York. He was the featured guest in a "dialogue" sponsored by Congregation B'nai Jeshurun in New York, one of the oldest congregations in the United States. An audience of 2,000 listened to Begin refute charges that he and his followers were dogmatic and extremist and that the Irgun had been a band of terrorists. The Irgun's revolt against the British, Begin said, was necessary because the British had closed the gates of Palestine while Hitler was annihilating European Jewry. The Irgun had done it "to make it possible for the Jews to come home in conditions so that never again will a bloodthirsty, two-legged beast try to destroy a Jewish child. We had to fight for statehood, for national liberation, to insure the salvation of the Jewish people. Is this dogmatism? Or is this devotion to a just cause and the simple love for a people?"

To whom, he asked, did the term "extremist" apply more properly — to the Arab nation which already had 20 states in the

Middle East and wanted the Jewish people to have no sovereign state at all, or to the Jewish people, who, after 19 centuries of "dispersion, persecution and humiliation" could no longer live without an independent Israel? "Zion is the faith of our people throughout the centuries that the land of Israel should be the land of the Jews." That faith was based on the promise made to the Children of Israel in the Bible. "Is the Bible extreme?" Begin demanded.

He then proceeded to lecture his audience on the historical antecedents of "that horrible word, 'terrorism'." "Terror," he explained, was the Latin word for "fear." Then, as he had done in his book *The Revolt* a quarter-century earlier, he traced the first political use of the word "terrorism" to the Reign of Terror which followed the French Revolution, when "people were arrested or their heads fell in order to terrorize and instill fear among the French." By this definition, Begin explained, the Irgun could not be classed as a "terrorist" organization. "We never used terror. We never wanted to instill fear into anybody's heart . . . We never used personal assassination. In the Irgun, we carried out *military* operations against an overwhelming force of 100,000 British soldiers equipped with heavy guns, tanks and planes, and supplemented by 30,000 British policemen . . . Therefore, the term 'terrorist' doesn't fit us at all." If the Irgun's struggle was "terrorism," then all struggles for national liberation, including the American Revolution, would have to be described as "terrorist."

Begin rejected any comparison between the Irgun's underground fight for a free Jewish state and the operations of the "so-called Palestine Liberation Organization," whose aim to put an end to the Jewish state he equates with Hitler's "Final Solution." The Irgun, he said, "fought to save a people," while the PLO guerillas "shoot in order to destroy a people." The men and women of the Irgun had been fighting against Britain's military might; the PLO guerillas were "killers of women and children." The Irgun had done everything humanly possible to avoid civilian casualties, Jewish, British, or Arab. To this end, the Irgun fighters had often foregone the element of surprise and placed their own lives in jeopardy. Not so the PLO:

> What do they — the so-called PLO — do? They make the civilian population the target of their bloody attacks on men, women and children. They never express regret or sorrow when they have "succeeded" in killing an innocent Jewish man or

woman or child. On the contrary, they rejoice in it. And that is the difference between fighters and killers.[30]

Begin paid a visit to Zbigniew Brzezinski, President-elect Carter's advisor on foreign policy. The two men had already met once before, at Begin's apartment in Tel Aviv. Brzezinski, like Begin, had spent his formative years in Poland, and he had shared with Begin some personal reminiscences, mainly memories of his father, who had been the Polish consul in Leipzig early in the Hitler era. Sitting in the Begins' living room on Rosenbaum Street, Brzezinski had recalled his father's contempt for anti-Semitism and how, on one occasion, the consul had struck out with his cane at a group of students parading in the street with anti-Semitic posters.

Now with Carter elected and Brzezinski high in the councils of the President-to-be, Begin and Brzezinski met again, this time in New York City.[31] In the course of their conversation Begin asked Brzezinski to draw Carter's attention to certain "phraseology" which was commonly used by Israel's friends, including spokesmen of the American Jewish community, but which he, Begin, considered both wrong and "harmful," because it implied that, in the eyes of the world, the Jewish state, unlike other nations, had no right to take its independence for granted. One of these pat phrases was the constantly reiterated demand that the Arabs should acknowledge Israel's "right to exist." The other was the idea that the United States should regard itself "obligated" to Israel's survival.

Brzezinski wanted to know what was wrong with asking the Arabs to acknowledge Israel's right to existence. Everything, Begin retorted. When other nations declared their independence, world public opinion automatically took for granted their right to sovereignty and to normal relations with their neighbors. "Why should Israel be an exception among nations?" Begin wanted to know. "Our existence is our right . . . We received that right from the God of our ancestors, long before many other nations had even begun their separate existence." To speak of an American "obligation" to ensure Israel's survival, Begin said, smacked unpleasantly of patronage. If the American government were to acknowledge that the United States had an interest in Israel's security, it would bear no implications that Israel depended on the good graces of a mighty patron for her survival. Since Israel had already demonstrated her military importance to the United States, American "security assistance" to Israel was not an act of charity, but was in America's own best interest. "But responsibility for the continuance of our national existence is ours and no one else's" Begin told Brzezinski. "We, the representatives of our people, are responsible for its continued survival."

Israel's ability to see to the safety of her citizens even outside the country's borders had been demonstrated earlier that year, on July 4, 1976, in "Operation Thunderball," which had created a worldwide sensation. Two hundred Israeli commandos had descended on Entebbe airport in Uganda and rescued 105 Israeli victims of an airplane hijacking. The Israelis had been held as hostages in the airport by the hijackers, members of the Popular Front for the Liberation of Palestine, with the cooperation of Uganda's dictator Idi Amin; the price for the release of the hostages had been the release of convicted Arab terrorists held in Israeli prisons. Israel's government had been faced with the agonizing question whether it had the moral right to risk the lives of 105 Israelis because it would not permit the barter of Arab terrorists for Israeli hostages.

As leader of the opposition and a member of the Knesset's Committee on Foreign Affairs and Security, Begin was consulted and kept informed by Prime Minister Rabin on the Cabinet's deliberations. Begin pledged to Rabin the full support of the Likud bloc in whatever action the government would decide to take. When Rabin initially announced that the government favored entering into negotiations with the terrorists in order to gain time, Begin did not offer any resistance. "It is our duty to do everything to save our brethren from mortal danger,"[32] he said. Having been told by Rabin that there seemed to be no other way of saving the hostages, his first consideration, as it also had been in earlier years, was to prevent loss of lives, if at all possible. But when Israel's military leaders presented a daring plan for their commando rescue operation which the government felt would have a good chance of bringing the hostages back alive, Begin gave the venture his unqualified approval. At midnight on Saturday, July 3, he was at Rabin's Tel Aviv office with a small group of the nation's leaders, anxiously awaiting word that the rescue mission had been completed. When the news came that everything had gone according to plan and that the hostages were on their way home, Begin joined the others at Rabin's headquarters in a toast of *kiddush* wine and, close to tears, exulted over the Israeli radio, "Long live the Army! Long live Israel! Long live the nation that has such courageous sons!" Nor did he neglect to give Rabin his due for authorizing the operation.

"On this day, we shall say with all our heart, 'Well done, Prime Minister!' "

When the rescue plane landed at Ben-Gurion (formerly Lod) airport, Begin was there to help welcome the returning hostages and their rescuers and was raised high on the shoulders of emotional admirers. (The rejoicing was mingled with sorrow; three of the hostages and two of the rescuers had lost their lives. One of the two soldiers killed was the commander of the raiding force, Lieutenant-Colonel Jonathan (Yoni) Netanyahu, son of Begin's friends Ben-Zion and Zila Netanyahu.)

The success of "Operation Thunderball" had the effect of restoring Israeli morale and confidence in the army, which had been somewhat shaken by revelations about negligence and "oversights" among officers and men on the eve of the Yom Kippur War. Moreover, not many of Israel's military operations had received the unqualified plaudits and congratulations of the free world as had "Thunderball."

But the fact remained that, in addition to the ever-present threat of renewed Arab warfare and growing political isolation, Israel was beset with a domestic malaise she had not known before; many Israelis felt that all was not well with the leadership of their country. The moderate socialist Labor Alignment, the party of David Ben-Gurion and Golda Meir, had been accepted as the spiritual heir of the idealists who had come to Israel not only to build a Jewish homeland but also to pioneer a new social order. But over the years, the idealism had faded; the old leaders had gradually vanished from the scene and had been replaced by a new generation of pragmatists on the one hand and by a ubiquitous and much resented bureaucracy on the other. The conduct of some leaders of the Labor Alignment seemed to bear out the ancient truism that power, taken too much and too long for granted, can corrupt.

Israelis were shocked to open their newspapers to reports of scandal in the Labor elite. In the fall of 1976, Asher Yadlin, the director general of Kupat Holim, Labor's health insurance fund, was about to be appointed governor of the Bank of Israel when he was found guilty of bribery and sentenced to a term in prison. Several months later, Abraham Ofer, Minister of Housing, committed suicide after being charged with the misuse of official funds.

Itzhak Rabin, who had done well as a general in Israel's army and as Israel's ambassador in Washington, seemed to be under an unlucky star as prime minister, first abroad and later also at home. He had not been able to establish a rapport with either Kissinger or

Gerald Ford; photographs taken of Rabin and Ford together during Rabin's visit as Prime Minister showed both leaders somewhat ill at ease. Rabin's first meeting with Jimmy Carter at the White House in March, 1977, had been followed by a statement from Carter in Clinton, Massachusetts, about the need to establish a "homeland" for the Palestinian people, which Israelis interpreted as an implied endorsement of a PLO state. American newspapers began to describe Israel as "intransigent." And then an Israeli newspaperman revealed that Rabin and his wife had been violating Israeli foreign currency regulations: they had failed to close the dollar bank account which they had been entitled to keep in the United States while they had lived in Washington, but not after their return to Israel. The newspaperman had been tipped off by another Israeli, who said that he had seen Mrs. Rabin, during her visit to the United States as the prime minister's wife, transacting business at a Washington bank. Rabin did not attempt to justify his violation of the law. April 7, 1977, he resigned as prime minister. Minister of Defense Shimon Peres took over as leader of the Labor Alignment and as acting prime minister. He hoped that he soon would be confirmed as prime minister in his own right; the elections for the Ninth Knesset had been called for May 17, 1977.

The increasing dissatisfaction with Labor's long-entrenched leadership, the atmosphere of self-questioning that still lingered as an aftermath of the Yom Kippur War, reports of scandals in high places, and the steady deterioration of Israel's relations with her one trusted ally, the United States, moved many Israelis to wish for a basic change in Israel's political leadership. A new, small, middle-of-the-road party had made its debut on the political scene and was attracting intellectuals and professional people: the Democratic Movement for Change (DMC, or, in the Hebrew acronym, DASH), led by Yigael Yadin, the soldier turned archeologist, whom Begin had first met during the battle for Jaffa in 1948. This party had little new to offer in matters of foreign policy, but it had drawn up a program of electoral, economic and social reforms. However, Yadin had as good as no experience in politics, and the largest opposition bloc in the Knesset was Likud, so that the only candidate of consequence to run against Peres, the standard bearer of the Labor Alignment, was Menahem Begin. But when they contemplated the possibility of Begin's becoming prime minister, many Israelis, including some of Begin's admirers, considered the unsatisfactory but familiar situation safer than an excursion into the unknown under a leader with a reputation for extremist views in questions of war and peace. The truth was that by 1977 all of Israel's political parties except the extreme left were in agreement on certain basic issues of foreign policy — none of them favored a complete withdrawal to the borders erased by the Six-Day War of 1967, and none wanted to see international recognition of the PLO or the rise of a Palestinian Arab state in the West Bank and Gaza Strip regions. But due to a disadvantageous press, Begin's name evoked in many minds visions of a government run by war hawks and quasi-fascists. Perhaps in order to allay their own apprehensions, Israelis traveling abroad kept assuring foreign journalists and political pundits that while Labor might lose some of its Knesset majority, it still would win votes sufficient to continue its traditional control of the government.

It was in this mood that Israel anticipated the May elections, the results of which were to come as a surprise not only to the Israelis themselves but also, in a much greater measure, to Jewish and non-Jewish observers in the rest of the world.

16. Prime Minister: 1977

The Likud bloc had launched its election campaign during the first week of January, 1977 at the 13th convention of Begin's own Herut party. The delegates who filled Jerusalem's National Convention Center heard Begin set forth the platform on which Likud would run for election. If Likud were voted into power, it would promote private enterprise and private investment, enact measures to promote immigration and reduce emigration and unemployment, work for closer relations with the United States and a rapprochement with France. A Likud government would be willing to resume relations with the Soviet Union (which had broken diplomatic ties with Israel in the wake of the Six-Day War), provided the Soviets would stop persecuting their Jews and would permit them to emigrate to Israel. The plank that aroused the greatest interest was Begin's plan for a new initiative for peace between Israel and her neighbors. "We shall do so," said Begin, "not through the United Nations General Assembly, where the majority is hostile to us. We shall ask a friendly government, which has regular diplomatic relations with Israel and her neighbors, to transmit our proposal for starting negotiations for peace treaties."[1] Begin did not name the "friendly government"; it was that of Rumania, where Golda Meir as prime minister had gone secretly in May, 1972, at the invitation of the country's president, to meet a leader of the Arab world. But the Arab had never shown up.

The Likud election campaign was directed by Ezer Weizman, who had made his peace with Begin and was willing to see him become prime minister.

But for several weeks that spring, it seemed that even if Likud won the election, Begin might not be in a position to assume the office of prime minister.

In March, two days before leaving on a lecture tour of the United States and Canada, Begin suffered what was diagnosed as an attack of food poisoning. However, he started out on his trip according to schedule. In Detroit, he was taken ill again but insisted on continuing his tour.

Early one morning, several days after his return to Israel — it was in the latter part of March — Begin called in his secretary and close friend, Yehiel Kadishai, to deal with some correspondence. He casually informed Kadishai that his doctor, Eliahu Luria, wanted to see him at his office for a checkup. After completing his letters, Begin climbed into his car and drove to the doctor's office. After examining him, Dr. Luria permitted Begin to return home, but later that day quietly made arrangements to have him admitted to Ichilov Hospital in Tel Aviv for observation. Then he telephoned Begin. When Begin failed to appear at the hospital at the appointed time, Luria called him again, informing him that a private room had been reserved for him (complete with telephone so that he would be able to continue his work without interruption) and that he expected Begin to report to the hospital at once.

Dr. Luria issued a terse bulletin to the effect that Begin had "returned from abroad in a fatigued condition and tests showed constriction of the blood vessels in the region of the heart," and that he had been admitted to the hospital for further tests and treatment. Translated into layman's language, Luria had found that Begin was in imminent danger of suffering a heart attack.

After entering the hospital, Begin made certain rearrangements in his appointments schedule. On the Thursday following his admission to the hospital, he had been scheduled to receive former Defense Minister Moshe Dayan at the Rosenbaum Street apartment. That appointment had been for the early morning, but this was inconvenient for the hospital authorities because that was the time when the doctors were making their morning rounds. Dayan was therefore asked to come to Begin's hospital room at 12 noon.

While he was talking with Dayan, Begin suddenly took a turn for the worse and Dayan was told to leave the room. Almost immediately after Dayan's departure, Begin suffered a massive coronary thrombosis. Within an hour he was moved from his private room into the intensive care ward.

For several days his condition was listed as serious; his heart attack was complicated by pneumonia. But the full truth about his illness did not become known to the public until one day a photographer from the weekly picture magazine *HaOlam HaZeh* (This World) made his way into Begin's hospital room in the retinue of the son of Begin's revered friend, the late Rabbi Arye Levin. The photographer took a picture of the patient seated in an armchair and looking rather frail. Begin himself did not attempt to hide from the public how ill he had been. "There was just one step between myself and death," he said, "but thank God, I won the battle."

He had to spend the Passover holidays in the hospital. As soon as he felt up to working, he turned his hospital room into a political headquarters; he had conferences with Ariel Sharon, the organizer of the Likud bloc, and settled disputes among the various groupings within Likud. On April 5, about two weeks after his admission to the hospital, he was permitted to walk in his room. Eight days later, he was discharged from the hospital and moved into a hotel for two weeks of recuperation. Then he threw himself into the final round of the election campaign.

The campaign wound up on Sunday night, May 15, with a televised debate between Begin and his opponent, Shimon Peres. It was the first time that the TV debate had been used in Israel as an election campaign device. The 40-minute discussion had been taped late that afternoon in a small room in a Jerusalem theater. It was shown on television unedited. Peres seemed cool but somewhat disturbed by the cameras; Begin appeared more relaxed and gave the impression that he was enjoying every minute of his performance.

Tuesday, May 17, was a beautiful spring day. Almost 1,800,000 Israelis (or nearly 80 per cent of the country's eligible voters) turned out at the polls. Since election day was a legal holiday, and the weather was ideal, the beaches, swimming pools and picnic spots were crowded. Then, as evening came, the people went home to sit glued to their radios and television sets for the election returns. The Israel Broadcasting Authority had sent representatives to the United States and Great Britain to study the lastest methods used by the television networks there to cover elections. Empty minutes in between reports were filled by an entertainment trio who went by the name of *Gashash HaHiver*, literally, "The Searching Explorers."

As the evening wore on, it was clear that the Labor Alignment was suffering significant losses. Some of these losses were due to inroads made by the Democratic Movement for Change, which was running for the first time and won 15 seats. In the 1973 elections, Labor had controlled 51 out of the Knesset's 120 seats; now it lost 19 mandates, leaving it with only 32 places in the Knesset. Actually, Begin's Likud bloc won only four new seats, but with the 43 seats it now had, Labor's losses gave Likud a plurality in the multiparty structure of Israel's parliament. For the first time in Israel's history, the country's government was no longer in the hands of Labor.

Until the last, Peres had hoped that despite its losses, Labor would somehow manage to squeak through. But at 1:30 in the morning of May 18, he conceded defeat. "It is painful," he said, "but this is the verdict of the nation."

Thousands of Begin fans poured into the normally deserted pre-dawn streets of Tel Aviv, singing, dancing and cheering. When Begin put in an appearance in front of the Likud bloc headquarters in Tel Aviv, the streets around the building were full of cheering people who hailed the victorious candidate with chants of "Be-gin! Be-gin!" It was for him, Begin told them, the dream of a lifetime come true. When he had first learned that his party's victory was assured, he put on a yarmulka and pronounced the *Sheheheyanu,* the traditional one-sentence prayer of thanksgiving for having been permitted to live "to see this time." This was a new style for an Israeli prime minister. Previous holders of that office had not addressed God publicly in thanksgiving.

In his victory speech Begin stressed the unity of the Israeli people, regardless of party affiliation. After an emotional tribute to leading figures from Israel's recent past — including Chaim Weizmann, who had had little love for Begin's Irgun — he read the passage from Lincoln's second inaugural address, "With malice toward none, with charity for all . . ." and called for the establishment of a new Government of National Unity, headed by Likud but embracing "all Zionist parties loyal to the State of Israel." (He had no use for Rakah, the extreme Communist splinter group whose Zionist loyalties he regarded as questionable). Once that government was established, he said, he hoped to launch his peace initiative. He would call upon Sadat of Egypt, Assad of Syria and King Hussein of Jordan "to open negotiations, whether in the respective capitals or on neutral ground, like Geneva." In an interview with a correspondent of *Newsweek* magazine, he was asked whether he believed that he would be more successful than his predecessors in dealing with the Arabs. Begin's answer implied that peace with the Arabs could be obtained more readily by taking an extremist position than by starting out with too ready offers of piecemeal withdrawals from the lands Israel had occupied in the 1967 war:

I don't like to boast, but I can say that we will deal with [the

Arabs] on a realistic basis. Since the elections, I suppose all the Arab rulers and the great part of mankind have learned that they had some misconceptions. They talked about the *occupied* West Bank. We call it *liberated* Judea and Samaria. I think that this is a sounder policy than that of the previous government which promised withdrawals. They did not produce peace . . . So when we say that Judea and Samaria belong by right to our people, it's a sounder policy. It gives us security and a chance for peace, while a policy of partial withdrawals only invites pressure for more withdrawal, but it does not produce agreement with the Arabs. I therefore assume that ours is a sounder policy. Anyhow, let's give it a chance.[2]

Aliza Begin came in for her share in the celebrations. The family posed together for the press and television. In a later interview, Aliza was to say that politics was not "my line," that one politician in the family was sufficient.[3] Now she showed a matter-of-fact attitude about the impending change in her life. How, an Israeli reporter asked her, did she plan to adapt to her new role? "I imagine that I have already got used to everything in the 38 years I have been at my husband's side," she replied. "I have always been with him. I have always accompanied him and have always shared the hours of joy and sadness alike with him. Why make a whole business out of it?"[4]

The Labor Alignment, smarting from its defeat, spurned Begin's proposal of unity. As a matter of fact, there were some socialist circles in which Begin's victory set off shock waves hardly less turbulent than the shattering after-effects of the Yom Kippur War. Begin was sharply attacked even before he had an opportunity to announce his selections for his first cabinet. Anti-Begin snipes from certain left-wing groups became so vicious that former Prime Minister Itzhak Rabin, certainly no partisan of either Begin or Likud, went on the air urging the Israeli public to dissociate itself from what he bluntly described as "such slander."

Labor observers in Israel asked themselves what had "gone wrong" to bring about the Alignment's downfall. Some maintained that the Democratic Movement for Change had spoiled the election for Labor by attracting votes which otherwise would have gone to the Alignment. Others pointed to the vote of the generation of immigrants from the Oriental countries who did not believe in socialism and had long felt snubbed by the Labor bureaucracy, predominantly of East European origin. Some of these "Orientals" had served in the Irgun and probably remembered Begin's determination not to allow Irgunists from the Oriental countries to become victims of prejudice from European-born members of the "fighting family." Immigrants from the Orient had been inclined to admire the charismatic Ben-Gurion, whose authoritarian style appealed to them, but they had found his successors much less inspiring. Then, too, immigrants who had been limited to second-class citizenship in the Arab lands of their birth were impressed with Begin's oft-expressed policy of firmness toward the Arabs.

Laborites of an older generation blamed their party for not having been firm enough in the fight against corruption and crime. "We allowed corruption to grow," wrote 79-year old veteran Mapai leader David Hacohen. "We allowed crime to flourish, a mafia to establish itself and spread the use of drugs through our society, from schools up. The voters were fed up with the regime's inability to regain control over the deteriorating domestic situation."[5]

Begin had long been deeply disturbed by the increase of crime in Israel. This problem is not unusual in societies with a large component of immigrants, but the thought that it could happen in a sovereign Jewish state based on Jewish ethical norms came as a surprise and shock to Begin. "I am worried about three things in our country — murder, rape and narcotics," he was to tell an Israeli journalist that fall. "The people of Israel never had such crimes before. When did we ever hear of a Jew in the diaspora committing rape? In my opinion rape is second only to murder in brutality. It is also hard for me to accept the idea that among our own wonderful youth there should be some who indulge in narcotics which damage the human body and soul . . . We will have to take firm measures against all this, not just through the police and the courts, but above all through home training, the schools and Israeli society."[6]

Shortly after the election, Begin published a 26-point program of "basic policy guidelines" which, in addition to statements on foreign policy, included declarations on domestic reforms: maximum employment opportunities coupled with measures to encourage "pride of creativity and work morale," the eradication of poverty, and "respect for law and eradication of crime and violence." The guidelines called not only for freedom of conscience and religion for all of Israel's inhabitants, regardless of belief, but also for greater emphasis on the traditional values of Judaism in the government's schools.

Begin took a particular interest in settlements founded in the West Bank region by young pioneers who combined fervent Jewish nationalism with equally intense loyalty to the religious values of

Judaism, and who considered it their patriotic duty to establish Jewish settlements in the "Biblical" West Bank area. He visited one such settlement of the "Gush Emunim" (Bloc of the Faithful) which had been founded 18 months before. Wearing a yarmulka, with a tallith (prayer shawl) held over his head like a canopy, and a Scroll of the Law borne before him, Begin entered the settlement's synagogue, where he declared that more such settlements would be permitted in the region, but that it would be done only on previously uninhabited uncultivated land. No Arabs would be displaced from their homes by Jewish settlers. "We want to live with our Arab neighbors and in peace, in equality, in human dignity, in liberty and in progress," he said. "In this beautiful country there is enough room for all the Arabs living it it, for all the Arabs presently living here and for all the Jews who will come here to make the land of our ancestors fruitful again."[7]

Five days after his victory it appeared once again as if an unkind fate would intervene at the last minute to deprive Begin of his prize. He had spent several days at the Sharon Hotel in the seaside resort of Herzliya north of Tel Aviv, but he had been given no time to rest from the strains of the election campaign. There had been a steady stream of visitors to congratulate him and to discuss plans for the future. On Sunday, May 22, he drove from Herzliya to nearby Kfar Shmaryahu for lunch with Samuel W. Lewis, newly-appointed ambassador from the United States. That night at the hotel he felt ill. Fully dressed, he walked with Aliza to his car and was driven to Tel Aviv. Arriving at Ichilov Hospital at 2:45 in the morning of May 23, he was placed into the intensive care ward. At once, speculations became rife that Begin would be unable to serve as prime minister. Fortunately, however, the electrocardiogram showed no indications of a new heart attack. The doctors decided that Begin had pericarditis, an inflammation of the membraneous sac in which the heart is enclosed. It is an illness that sometimes appears following a coronary thrombosis, but it is not dangerous in itself. At the hospital, the patient slept soundly for several hours, then ate a hearty lunch. Dr. Luria said that the amount of work Begin had done during and after the election campaign would have been enough to make anyone ill, and that in his opinion there was nothing to prevent Begin from carrying out the duties of prime minister.

One of Begin's first official visitors in the hospital was Moshe Dayan. Soon after Dayan left Begin's hospital room it was announced that the former minister of defense, who had broken with the Labor Alignment and had remained in the Knesset as a member without party affiliation, had been appointed foreign minister in the new government. Begin and Dayan had first met during the underground period, and Begin had admired the *sabra* soldier first as one of the activists within Haganah and later as an able military commander. After a visit to the Suez Canal zone early in 1968, Begin had written him a note of appreciation: "Fortunate the nation that has a minister of defense like you in charge of the deployment of its armed forces."[8] Dayan had gained respect in the Arab world and on the international scene as a capable general. Unlike Begin, he had been in contact with Arabs from his earliest youth and felt at ease dealing with them; also unlike Begin, Dayan was not an unknown figure to foreign governments. Accordingly, Begin felt that Dayan was a good choice for the second most important position in the government he was about to form.

The post of minister of defense went to the man who had been assigned that place in the "shadow government" presented to the 1972 Herut convention: Ezer Weizman, who, like his former brother-in-law, Moshe Dayan (Reuma Weizman and Dayan's first wife, Ruth, are sisters), is a *sabra* and well-acquainted with Arab ways.

On May 28, Begin was discharged from the hospital. On June 8, he made his official call on President Ephraim Katzir to receive the president's charge to form a new government. He took Aliza with him. As they drove to the presidential residence, Begin spotted an old Irgun comrade on the street. He had his driver stop the car and leaped out to hug the veteran of his "fighting family." At the president's house, Begin was photographed bowing to Katzir and kissing Mrs. Katzir's hand. Begin's predecessors had not been so deferential in their conduct toward Israel's presidents. In their eyes, the president had been nothing more than a figurehead. Chaim Weizmann during his last years had complained bitterly that Ben-Gurion had never taken the trouble to inform him of the Cabinet's deliberations. Begin, unlike Israel's earlier prime ministers, sees the presidency as a valuable unifying force in the life of the country, and was to make a point of briefing the president on all important developments.

After his visit to Katzir, Begin read a tough foreign-policy statement to the press. The new government would not permit the establishment of a Palestinian state, it would not tolerate the presence of the Palestine Liberation Organization at a peace conference, and it would not agree to a withdrawal of Israeli troops to the indefensible borders with which Israel had been afflicted prior to the 1967 war. After the press conference, Begin proceeded to the Western Wall to pray. He opened a Bible and recited Psalm 4: "Answer me when I call, O God of my righteousness, Thou didst set me free when I was in distress; be gracious unto me and hear my prayer . . ." At the Wall, he was enthusiastically greeted by Oriental women ululating as Oriental Jews do at times of high emotion, and by yeshiva students who broke into impromptu song and dance in honor of the new Prime Minister.

From the Wall, he went to pay his respects to 88-year-old Rabbi Zvi Yehuda Kook, son of Israel's saintly Chief Rabbi Abraham Isaac Kook and spiritual mentor of the "Gush Emunim" settlers.[9]

On Tuesday morning, June 21, Begin was confirmed in office as prime minister. Wearing a neat, dark suit, he strode to the rostrum of the Knesset to seek the required vote of confidence. He read his speech from a prepared text, the first time he ever had been known to do so on the Knesset floor. He asked the Knesset and the nation to give his government a "year's moral credit" to effect the domestic reforms promised in the Likud election platform.

One of his government's fundamental foreign policy aims, he said, would be to deepen the friendship between Israel and the United States. Israel was "part of a free world which is shrinking under the assaults of totalitarianism. All free men should stand together to recognize this danger and protect the rights of man."

The government's main objective, he went on, was to avert a Middle East war. He appealed to King Hussein and Presidents Sadat and Assad to meet him, "either in their capital cities or on neutral territory, either in public or out of the flare of publicity. Too much Jewish and Arab blood has been shed in this region. Let us put an end to the bloodshed which we both abhor." Most of those who listened to Begin that day would have smiled incredulously if anyone had told them that, five months later, almost to the day, Begin would meet Anwar el-Sadat not in Cairo or in Geneva, but in Jerusalem. The other meeting, "out of the flare of publicity," was to come 15 months later, in the Catoctin Mountains, 75 miles away from Washington.

Turning to domestic affairs, Begin urged Israeli emigrants to return home. The government, he assured them, would not condemn them as so many other Israelis tended to do (the Hebrew term for an Israeli who has left the country to settle abroad is *yored*, literally, "one who has gone down") but would do its best to help them resettle in Israel.

In line with Likud's drive for greater efficiency in government, Begin announced the elimination of some ministries and the establishment of others to meet the country's changing needs. He abolished the Ministry of Police, which he pointed out had no counterpart in any other democracy; it was merged with the Interior Ministry.

To ensure his new government a comfortable parliamentary base Begin, like his predecessors, chose partners with whom to form a coalition. At the time of his first Knesset appearance as prime minister, he had already coopted the National Religious party (which had been part of all of Israel's previous governments) and the extreme Orthodox Agudath Israel (which had agreed to join the coalition in the Knesset for voting purposes but did not wish to take a place in the Cabinet). Begin was still negotiating with the Democratic Movement for Change, which was not to join his coalition until late October. When Begin named his first Cabinet, he held open several positions for the DMC; when the DMC joined the coalition, Yigael Yadin became deputy prime minister.

Begin's initial Cabinet was the first in which the majority were native-born Israelis; the non-*sabras* came from Eastern Europe and Morocco, and one, Joseph Burg, veteran of many previous cabinets and now named Minister of the Interior, was a refugee from Hitler's Germany. At 68, Burg was the oldest member of the Cabinet. The youngest, like Burg a member of the National Religious party, was 39-year-old Aharon Abu Hatzeira, a rabbi of Moroccan origin and former mayor of the town of Ramle, who became minister of religious affairs. Four of the ministers had been generals in the Israeli army: Moshe Dayan, Ezer Weizman, Ariel Sharon (who was named minister of agriculture; he had once engaged in farming), and Yigael Yadin. The other ministers classed themselves by profession as public servants, business executives, economist (one) and artisan (one). The artisan was 40-year-old David Levy, the minister of immigrant absorption, who had come to Israel from Morocco, was the father of 10 children and had started out as a construction worker.

After receiving a vote of confidence from the Knesset, Begin was welcomed to the Prime Minister's office by Itzhak Rabin (since Peres had served as acting premier only.) The two men toasted each other with glasses of wine. Rabin said he hoped that Begin would be able to "strengthen" Israel's relations with the United States. Begin thanked Rabin for the smooth transition of power and said that Rabin had earned a place in Israel's history as a soldier, diplomat and politician.

When Begin moved into the Prime Minister's office, he found the walls decorated with portraits of Israel's first four prime ministers: David Ben-Gurion, Moshe Sharett, Levi Eshkol and Golda Meir. To these, he added a portrait of Itzhak Rabin, and portraits of two others that also had not been there before: Theodor Herzl and Vladimir Jabotinsky.

The next day, June 22, Begin joined Ben-Zion and Zila Netanyahu at the Mount Herzl military cemetery to mark the first anniversary of the death of their son Yoni, commander of the paratrooper raiding force at Entebbe. According to the Jewish calendar, one year had passed since Yoni's death. As hundreds of paratroopers stood at attention at the graveside, Begin delivered the eulogy.

Begin's first official act as prime minister was to admit to Israel 66 Vietnamese refugees who had been rescued on June 9 by an Israeli freighter, the S.S. *Yuvali,* off the coast of Vietnam. These unfortunates, including children and adults of all ages, had been drifting about on the China Sea in a small flimsy fishing boat and were down to rations of three teaspoons of water a day for the children. Ships of four other nations had passed the refugees but had refused to help them. When the *Yuvali* sighted the boat, it was close to sinking. The *Yuvali* picked up the refugees and tried to put them ashore at various Asian ports, but they were turned back everywhere. Finally, Begin announced that Israel could not ignore the plight of these hapless people; it was too reminiscent of the history of Jewish refugees in the 1940's who sailed from port to port, only to be refused entry everywhere. When, the following month, President Carter commended Begin on his humane action in admitting the refugees to Israel, Begin told the President: "We have not forgotten the sufferings of our own people." The refugees were flown to Israel, where they were temporarily placed in the Ofakim immigrant absorption center near Beersheba and given the choice of settling in Israel or going elsewhere. (About half wanted to go to the United States). The government gave them work permits, pocket money, toys for the children, and ample supplies of the fish, rice and vegetables which Vietnamese regard as staple foods.

Begin's first official trip abroad as prime minister was to the United States, on the invitation of President Carter, who had written to the prime minister that he wished to join with him "in a partnership of principle leading to a just and peaceful settlement of the dispute between Israel and its neighbors." Referring to the fact that they both had in common a great attachment to their religious beliefs, the President had added, "We both are blessed with the historic opportunity to give substance to the religious meaning of our societies."

Before leaving for the United States, the Begins moved from the apartment on Rosenbaum Street in Tel Aviv to the official residence at 3 Balfour Street in Jerusalem, where Rabin had lived as prime minister. On their first Sabbath in Jerusalem (it was the Sabbath before their departure for the United States) the Begins held their traditional open house, a custom they had observed in Tel Aviv every Sabbath afternoon since 1948. Since the household help was off duty on the Sabbath, the Begin daughters, Hasia and Leah, served the guests orange juice and soda, while their parents moved among the visitors, greeting friends and well-wishers. The guests were led into the dining room where Aliza's two Sabbath candlesticks stood on a large table. The walls and bookcases were still bare of objects except for a *shofar* and a sketch of Jabotinsky. Some of the visitors brought along housewarming gifts — liquor, cakes, candy, and even Bibles. As it grew dark outside, Begin settled down in a raffia chair, talking to visitors and accepting their good wishes for his visit to the United States. When three stars appeared on the sky, a sign that the Sabbath had ended, a yeshiva student stepped forward, lit a braided candle (which he gave to one of the Begin granddaughters to hold) and pronounced the blessing separating "the holy from the profane", the Sabbath from the six days of the working week. For the first time, Israelis saw a prime minister observing the Sabbath at his home in the traditional manner.

During the five days that followed, Begin received a seemingly unending procession of American legislators and Jewish communal leaders who happened to be visiting in Israel and wanted to give the new prime minister advice on what to say and what not to say to the President of the United States.

Begin landed at New York's Kennedy airport in the morning of Friday, July 15, four days before he was to meet Carter in Washington. The Begin party included Aliza, Yehiel Kadishai, and, for the first time, a heart specialist. The Begins were met by Simcha Dinitz, Israel's ambassador to the United States, Chaim Herzog, Israel's ambassador to the United Nations, and Abraham Beame, the first Jew to hold the office of Mayor of New York. After the official greetings, the Begins were whisked away to the Waldorf-

Astoria Hotel, where an official suite had been reserved for them on the 35th floor. Begin spent that afternoon with Jewish business and communal leaders who had been eager to form their first-hand opinions of the man of whom most had known little except that three decades earlier, he had been a thorn in Ben-Gurion's eye and over the years had remained a controversial figure on the Israeli political scene.

The host at the Friday night dinner at the Waldorf (the food had come from a kosher caterer) was Ambassador Herzog, whose father had been Chief Rabbi of Israel from 1936 until his death in 1959. Herzog recited the traditional *kiddush* over wine and *hallah*, and Benny Begin, who had been studying geology in Colorado and had come east to meet his parents, led the gathering in the singing of *zemiroth*, the cheerful table hymns that are sung at traditional Sabbath meals. Someone remarked that the walls of the stately Waldorf had resounded to many kinds of music in their day, but never before to Sabbath hymns led by an Israeli prime minister and his family.

The Begins spent Saturday resting and meeting with friends. Because he was still tired from the plane journey, Begin decided not to go to the synagogue but to say his prayers at the hotel. In the afternoon, he played host to a group of Revisionist party leaders (the Revisionists are the diaspora counterpart of Begin's Herut party) who had come to New York from various parts of the United States to meet Begin. It was their day of glory. For the most part, the other prime ministers of Israel visiting the United States had given them short shrift, but the Begins welcomed them as their own.

On Sunday morning, July 17, Begin started his day with a visit from a delegation of the Conference of Presidents of Major Jewish Organizations. Most members of the "Presidents' Club" (as the Conference once had been popularly known) had not been quite sure what attitude to take toward Begin, whose ideology and personal style were so different from those of other Israeli prime ministers they had known. They came away from their meeting with Begin obviously reassured that all was still well with Israel and her government. They said they were impressed with Begin's "intensely Jewish" outlook and by his eagerness to promote closer spiritual, cultural and emotional ties between Israel and the United States.

Begin devoted that afternoon and evening to meetings with American Jewish religious leaders representing three distinct schools of Orthodox Judaism. First, he received in his hotel suite Rabbi Dr. Joseph B. Soloveichik, who combines profound religious belief and erudition with an impressive background of modern scholarship and to whom a younger generation of modern Orthodox rabbis and religious Zionists in the United States look for guidance in religious matters. Although Dr. Soloveichik is a number of years older than Begin, the two men had common childhood memories. Like Begin, Rabbi Soloveichik had been born in Brest-Litovsk, where his grandfather had served as chief rabbi while Begin's father had been secretary of the Jewish community.

After Rabbi Soloveichik's departure, Begin drove under heavy security to the Lower East Side to pay his respects to the ailing Rabbi Moshe Feinstein, a Talmudic sage of the old school and a revered mentor of the world Agudath Israel movement whose Israeli branch was now in Begin's government coalition.

At nine o'clock that evening, Begin emerged from the Waldorf again to drive to Brooklyn for a rather dramatic nighttime audience with Rabbi Menahem Mendel Schneerson, the "Lubavitcher Rebbe" who has built up a worldwide network of religious schools and has been waging a vigorous campaign to win non-observant Jews over to traditional religion. This Hasidic leader has followers throughout the world, including Israel, who travel to New York at regular intervals to seek his advice on a bewildering variety of business, religious and personal problems. One of his warm admirers was Zalman Shazar, Israel's third President, who would call on the Rebbe every time he visited New York.

The Rebbe met Begin on the steps of his headquarters and greeted him warmly. Begin told the Rebbe in Hebrew that he had come to consult with him and to ask his blessing before going to Washington. Begin translated his remarks into English for the benefit of the assembled newspaper reporters and TV men. The Rebbe replied in Yiddish; then, taking Begin's cue, he repeated his blessing in English.[10]

The next morning, Monday, July 18, Begin and his wife moved back into the arena of international politics. They boarded a United States Air Force plane for the flight from New York to Andrews Air Force Base, where they were greeted by Secretary of State Cyrus Vance. From there, they drove into Washington, directly to Blair House, guest house for royalty and heads of state who come to visit the President of the United States. Begin spent the remainder of the day with his aides, preparing for the next two days of meetings with Carter and other top officials.

On Tuesday, July 19, Begin and his wife received their ceremonial welcome from the President and Mrs. Carter on the White House lawn. During their first conference, Begin gave the President a capsule survey of the history of the State of Israel, its fight for independence and its struggle for survival. Carter told his visitor that he had read his book *The Revolt,* and could understand Begin's feelings. Begin produced maps to show Carter how Israel could be cut in half within minutes if the West Bank area were to be occupied by hostile Arabs. Carter asked Begin to halt the creation of additional Jewish settlements in the West Bank region — at least until the dormant Big-Power sponsored Middle East peace conference, which it was then thought could be reconvened in Geneva that October. Begin gently protested that it was neither possible nor logical that Jews should be forbidden to make their homes in such Biblical places as Bethlehem, Shilo, Hebron and Bethel, all of which were in the West Bank region. The two leaders amiably "agreed to disagree" on this subject and touched no more upon it that day. Carter, the "born-again" Christian, was impressed with Begin's thorough knowledge of the Bible. According to some reports, one of the things that had disconcerted Carter about Begin's predecessor, Rabin, had been that this prime minister of the land of the Bible had not shown much familiarity with Biblical literature.

After the meeting with the President, Begin drove to the State Department to confer with Secretary Vance, who was completing plans for a visit to the Middle East during August.

On Wednesday, July 20, Begin had a breakfast meeting with National Security Advisor Zbigniew Brzezinski, and gave him a gift: copies of four letters which Brzezinski's father, as Polish consul in Leipzig, had written in 1933 to the German authorities, protesting against the Nazi treatment of Jews in that city. Begin, remembering the story Brzezinski had told him in Tel Aviv about his father, had asked an aide to locate the letters in the Yad Vashem archives near Jerusalem, repository of documentary material relating to the era of the Hitler Holocaust. Brzezinski was deeply moved.[11]

There were additional meetings with Carter, with leading personalities of the U.S. Congress, and a "working dinner" at the White House. The menu was adjusted to meet the basic requirements of the Jewish dietary laws. In his response to Carter's ceremonial greetings, Begin said that the meeting between himself and Carter had been a manifestation of a Divine plan to join Israel and the United States more closely together in the quest for peace.

Before Begin's arrival in Washington, many observers both in Israel and in the United States had predicted that Begin, with his hard-line foreign policy, would find himself on a collision course with Carter. However, it turned out that, whatever disagreements there might have been — and still are — between Israel and the United States, Carter and Begin are drawn together by a mutual appreciation of each other's deep-felt religious convictions.

The American press gave Begin high marks for charm and personal magnetism and for handling loaded questions with an unmistakable air of authority. Even veterans on the Washington journalistic scene professed astonishment at Begin's quick sense of humor and his sharp recall of facts and figures. Congressional leaders declared themselves charmed by his wit, warmth and courtliness, and impressed with his ability to quote Shakespeare and Churchill with the same ease as he did the Bible. Apparently, after the bad and scanty press Begin had been receiving in America over the years, Begin in the flesh came to Americans as a pleasant surprise.

On Thursday, July 21, Begin flew back to New York, where he spent a long weekend before returning to Israel. That evening, he proclaimed to an Israel Bond drive dinner in New York that all had gone well between himself and Carter and that "the only confrontation we had in Washington was with the heat."

On Friday, July 22, he visited United Nations Secretary-General Kurt Waldheim. He expressed his dismay that while the European powers seemed to be exceedingly disturbed about the plight of the Arab refugees, none of them appeared to care about the thousands of Christians in southern Lebanon who were faced with annihilation at the hands of Moslem troops and Palestinian Arab "guerillas." Israel, he pointed out, was the only country which was sending aid to the Lebanese Christians to help them survive.

Later, at the Waldorf-Astoria, Begin addressed a meeting of United Jewish Appeal fund raisers, then received David Rockefeller, Mayor Beame and New York's Governor Hugh Carey. Afterwards, he and his wife returned to their suite to prepare for the Sabbath.

On Sunday, July 24, Begin observed the Fast of the Ninth of Av, a day of mourning in memory of the destruction of the First and Second Temples in Jerusalem, and the loss of Jewish political independence that followed these calamities. On the eve of the fast, he went to an Orthodox synagogue on East 85th Street, where he sat on the steps of the Holy Ark in the traditional Jewish posture of mourning and followed the reading of the Book of Lamentations. When he was interviewed Sunday morning on *Meet the Press*, he made a point of mentioning the destruction of Jerusalem, first by Nebuchadnezzar, King of Babylonia and again, six centuries later, by the legions of Imperial Rome. Begin does not share the feeling of many present-generation Israelis that the Ninth of Av has lost its relevance since the rebirth of the Jewish state. Aside from the fact that personally he observes the fast as a devout Jew, he views the destruction of Jerusalem as the initial link in a long chain of tragedies which befell the Jewish people and which culminated in Auschwitz.

Later that day, turning again to his official tasks, Begin conferred with former Secretary of State Henry Kissinger, then telephoned former President Gerald Ford, inviting him to visit Israel. Next, in a lighter vein, came a visit from movie star Elizabeth Taylor, who had converted to Judaism at the time of her marriage to the singer Eddie Fisher. Miss Taylor was received with a big smile from the prime minister and a hug and kiss from Mrs. Begin.

On Monday, July 25, Begin returned to Israel. When he and Aliza landed at Ben-Gurion airport, he was received with a warm embrace by U.S. Ambassador Lewis. According to all assessments, Begin's first visit to the President of the United States had been a success.

The next day the Israeli government announced that it had granted "legal status" to three "Gush Emunim" settlements in the West Bank area. This action brought a sharp rebuke from Secretary of State Vance; it was felt that Carter, after his talk with Begin about creating no additional Jewish settlements on the West Bank, would consider Israel's action as a slap in the face. But Begin rejected this interpretation. As so many times before, he stated his thesis that the West Bank area (which he insists on calling by its Biblical names of "Judea" and "Samaria") was part of Biblical Palestine. Then he assured the United States that, in fact, the conferment of legal status on the three Jewish settlements would have no bearing on the final political status of the West Bank area. In practical terms, the government's action meant simply that the inhabitants of these settlements were now eligible for government services formerly denied them. To clinch his argument, Begin took out his law books and cited an act passed by the Knesset immediately after the Six-Day War, permitting the government to apply the laws of the State of Israel to any territory occupied by Israel as a result of the war. That law, Begin pointed out, had been enacted with the approval of the Government of National Unity headed by the late Levi Eshkol.

Carter's reaction was not as negative as pessimists had feared. His response was a moderate one; it seemed as if he understood the complexities of the issues involved and did not want to turn them into a cause for confrontation between Israel and the United States.

In Jerusalem, Begin prepared to receive Secretary of State Vance, who was due to arrive in Israel on August 9. On August 8, addressing a conference of American and Canadian Israel Bond drive leaders assembled in the Knesset building, Begin once again said that public opinion in the United States and in the rest of the Christian world should be made aware that the aid supplied by Israel was all that stood between the Christians of southern Lebanon and "genocide." The day before, Begin had visited the Golan Heights and had promised Lebanese Christian soldiers that Israel would never desert them. The Jews remembered how they had felt as a persecuted minority. "We shall not stand by while the survival of the Christian minority in Lebanon is threatened," Begin said.

On August 9, Vance arrived in Israel and was honored by a state dinner in the Chagall Hall of the Knesset building. In his remarks that evening, Begin made reference to the various "trial balloon" statement that had emanated from U.S. State Department officials about the establishment of a "Palestinian homeland" and the possibility of negotiations with the Palestine Liberation Organization. Begin declared that he would never agree to negotiate with the PLO. He described the PLO Covenant, which calls for the destruction of the "Zionist state," as an Arab-style *Mein Kampf*. Events of the recent past, he suggested to the American Secretary of State, had taught that threats to destroy the Jewish state and the Jewish people should not be dismissed as idle rhetoric. It was his, Begin's, duty as "the man who bears responsibility for the future of his country to learn from the experiences of the past."

Begin candidly reiterated these views later that month at a state banquet tendered to him on August 25 in Bucharest, Rumania. Rumania's Premier Manea Manescu, in a rather infelicitous toast to the guest of honor, had urged an Israeli withdrawal from the West Bank and the Gaza Strip, the creation of a Palestinian Arab state, and the cooption of the PLO into the Geneva conference which it was then believed would be convened late in the year. In his response, Begin departed from his prepared text to tell his host, "It is my sad duty to inform you, Mr. Prime Minister, that the PLO wants to annihilate the Jewish state." How, then, could Israel be expected to negotiate with the PLO in Geneva, or anywhere else for that matter?

Later, Begin and Manescu issued a joint statement to the effect that even if Rumania and Israel differed on how best to reach a peace settlement in the Middle East, both were agreed that peacemaking efforts should be stepped up and that, in any event, such disagreements should not be permitted to mar the friendly relations between the two peoples.

Begin praised the Rumanian government for its policy of tolerance toward all religions and their practices. Manescu, in turn, made a point of telling Rumania's Chief Rabbi Moshe Rosen that Begin's own strict observance of his Jewish faith had inspired him, Manescu, with profound respect for the Israeli leader.[12] He had been deeply impressed by Begin's adherence to the Jewish dietary laws, and by Begin's moving, on Friday afternoon, August 26, from the Rumanian government's official guest house on the outskirts of Bucharest to a second-rate hotel in the city in order to be able to attend services at Bucharest's Choral Synagogue without having to travel on the Sabbath. (The streets though which Begin passed on foot that Friday night and again the next morning on the way to and from the synagogue were closely guarded by Rumanian police and security men).

Begin described his five-day visit to Rumania as "important, interesting and very moving." In Bucharest, he recalled how in the early months of World War II he had led a transport of 1,200 refugees from Poland to the Rumanian border, only to be turned back by orders from the British ambassador in Bucharest, who had not wanted these "illegals" to reach Palestine. Now, nearly four decades later, during Friday night services at the Choral Synagogue in Bucharest, he listened to a choir of young boys and girls dressed in blue and white, the colors of the reborn Jewish state, sing Israeli songs. When they broke into "Jerusalem of Gold," one of Israel's best-loved songs since the 1967 war, Begin, in his seat of honor next to Chief Rabbi Rosen, could not hold back tears. It was, he said, the most moving day in his life since the day Israel had declared her independence.

Begin found it equally moving, at a reception held by the Jewish community in his honor after the Sabbath, to see not only Christian prelates but also a Moslem leader, Regups Ali, the Imam of Bucharest.

Begin's most important achievement during his visit to Rumania was his talk with Rumania's President Nicolae Ceausescu. Begin told Ceausescu that he would welcome a personal meeting with Egypt's President Sadat. Several weeks later, Sadat, too, visited Rumania, and the two presidents discussed Begin. In an interview with *Time* magazine late in December, Sadat was to recall having asked Ceausescu whether he considered Begin a sufficiently strong leader to be able to make peace in the Middle East. Both presidents had agreed that Begin's predecessor, Rabin, had been "weak." But then, said Sadat, "Ceausescu told me what he discussed with Begin, and we reached the conclusion that [this] man is strong."[13]

A month after his visit to Rumania, Begin was hospitalized for the third time that year. Once again, the diagnosis was not a new heart attack, but pericarditis, and he was able to return home on October 11 after eleven days in the hospital. Five hours after his discharge from the hospital, Begin presided over a Cabinet meeting to approve an agreement made by Foreign Minister Dayan in Washington with President Carter over procedures to be followed in setting up the Geneva Conference of the Big Powers. There had been some anxious days both for Dayan and for Begin in his hospital room, because of the joint Soviet-Ameican statement signed by Carter on October 1 — the day after Begin had been taken ill — calling for an Israeli withdrawal from the lands taken in the 1967 war and for the establishment of a "Palestinian homeland." This was one of the seesaw moves in American policy toward the Middle East during the early part of the Carter Administration. Days later, Carter explained that, at least in the American view, the Israeli withdrawal would not be expected as a precondition for a Geneva conference or any other Middle East peace negotiations. "I would rather commit political suicide than hurt Israel," Carter was quoted as having said at one point.

Also in October, negotiations were finally concluded for the Democratic Movement for Change to join the government coalition. Initially Yigael Yadin, the leader of the party, had not been too anxious to join a Begin coalition. The DMC had not been set up to oppose the programs of the Labor Alignment or to develop new ideologies but primarily in order to press for better, more efficient government. This, Yadin soon realized, could not be brought about by a small, new party in the opposition. In order to make its voice count, the DMC would have to accept the opportunity to join the coalition that had taken over the country's government. Accordingly, the DMC, despite protests from within its leadership, joined the Begin coalition, raising the automatic support for the prime minister to a total of 78 of the 120 members of the Knesset, the most stable parliamentary base ever accorded a government in Israel.

That fall, too, Begin's wish, facetiously expressed as he left London in 1972, became a reality: he received an invitation to visit England, not from his Revisionist friends but from Prime Minister James Callaghan. Rumor had it that when Callaghan first proposed to invite Begin, he met with opposition from those in the British government who still remembered the Irgun revolt. But Callaghan was determined not to permit memories of the past to affect Britain's present-day policies. Accordingly, he invited Begin to visit England. Plans called for Begin to arrive in London on November 20, 1977 and to remain until November 23.

As things turned out, Begin had to postpone his departure for England until December 2, because of an unexpected engagement in Jerusalem which Callaghan agreed took precedence over his visit to London.

17. "Operation Gate:" 1977 and Camp David: 1978

On Wednesday, November 9, 1977 Egypt's President Anwar el-Sadat made an announcement to his parliament, the People's Assembly, which was received by his own people and the rest of the world first with disbelief, then with amazement. Four years earlier, Sadat had told his nation that he was willing to commit a million Egyptian lives to a war against Israel. Now he told his people that he was ready to "go to the ends of the world" in search of peace. "Israel will be astonished when it hears me saying now before you that I am ready to go to their house, to the Knesset itself, and to talk to them" so that there might be peace in the Middle East at last. He wanted no more Egyptian soldiers killed or wounded in battle.

The initial reaction in Israel, as well as in the United States, was to dismiss Sadat's announcement as another rhetorical flourish typical of the Middle East. Not so Begin. The day after Sadat's speech before the People's Assembly, Begin issued a public statement to make sure that Sadat was not coming to Israel under the illusion that Israel would be ready to capitulate to the Arab political and territorial demands for the sake of peace. "Israel categorically and absolutely rejects the conditions named by President Sadat; i.e., total withdrawal to the June, 1967 lines and the establishment of the so-called Palestinian state," he said, terms which would constitute a danger to Israel's very survival. On the other hand, Begin reiterated his dictum that in peace talks between Israel and her Arab neighbors everything was negotiable except the survival of the State of Israel. If the Geneva peace conference would be reconvened, Begin said, Sadat would be entitled "to put forward his country's position even as Israel would present her position." But "let no party turn its own stand into a prior condition for participating in the peace conference."[1]

On Friday, November 11, Begin delivered a radio address to

the people of Egypt. It was an eloquent plea for peace. "Four major wars have taken place between you and us," he said. "Much blood was shed on both sides. Many families were orphaned and bereaved, in Egypt and Israel." Egypt's attempts to destroy the Jewish state had been in vain. Israel was here to stay. The time had come for the peoples of Egypt and Israel to live together in friendship and ccoperation.

> There is no reason whatsoever for hostility between our peoples. In ancient times, Egypt and the Land of Israel were allies, real friends and allies, against a common enemy from the north. Many changes have taken place since those days. But perhaps the intrinsic basis for friendship and mutual help remains unaltered.

> We, the Israelis, stretch out our hand to you. It is not, as you know, a weak hand. If attacked, we shall always defend ourselves, as our forefathers, the Maccabees did — and won the day.

> But we do not want any clashes with you. Let us say one to another, and let it be a silent oath by both peoples, of Egypt and Israel: no more wars, no more bloodshed, and no more threats. Let us not only make peace. Let us also start on the road to friendship, of sincere and productive cooperation. We can help each other. We can make the lives of our nations better, easier, happier.

> . . . It will be a pleasure to welcome and receive your President with the traditional hospitality you and we have inherited from our common father, Abraham. And I, for my part, will of course be ready to come to your capital, Cairo, for the same purpose. No more wars — peace — a real peace and forever.

Begin quoted a passage (Surah 5) from the Koran, which, he explained, documented the right of the Jewish people to the Land of Israel: "Recall when Moses said to his people: O my people, remember the goodness of Allah towards you when he appointed prophets amongst you. O my people, enter the holy land which Allah hath written down as yours . . ." He concluded his address with *sulh* and *shalom*, the Arabic and Hebrew terms, respectively, for "peace."[2]

The Egyptian news media took due notice of Begin's appeal, commenting, however, that Begin should have included a promise to withdraw from all Arab lands and that he should not have addressed it only to the Egyptian people. The Egyptians were "part of the Arab world and had never been alone in their wars against Zionist expansionist plans."

Three days later, on Monday, November 14, Sadat told the veteran American journalist Walter Cronkite in a satellite interview that he would be ready to go to Israel within a week, provided he would receive a "proper" invitation from Begin. Begin thereupon requested U.S. Ambassador Lewis to see whether he, Lewis, could transmit the invitation to Sadat through the American ambassador in Cairo. The next day, November 15, Begin addressed an official invitation to "His Excellency, Mr. Anwar el-Sadat, President of the Arab Republic of Egypt, Cairo." In view of his planned visit to London, Begin initially suggested that Sadat arrange to come to Jerusalem the day after he, Begin, was due to return from Europe. If, on the other hand, Sadat wished to come earlier, Begin would postpone his visit to England in order to accommodate Sadat.

Sadat replied on the same day. He would prefer, he said, to make his visit to Jerusalem at the earliest possible moment; he was planning to land at Ben-Gurion airport on Saturday, November 19. Begin said that this would be acceptable, except that he did not wish Sadat to arrive before the end of the Sabbath. On Thursday, November 17, Ambassador Lewis conveyed to Begin an inquiry from Egypt's Vice-President Husni Mobarek as to when the Sabbath would end that Saturday evening. Begin answered that Sadat could land any time after 7:30 or 8:00 P.M.

When it became known that Sadat was really coming, Israelis received the news with a mixture of doubt, bewilderment and pure delight. Among the doubters was Lieutenant General Mordecai Gur, the army's chief of staff who, in an interview with the daily *Yediot Aharonot*, suggested that Sadat might be using the visit as a smokescreen behind which to launch a surprise attack in the Sinai peninsula, and that Israel should be on the alert while Sadat was there. Gur received a reprimand from his immediate superior, Defense Minister Ezer Weizman, but there were others in Israel's military intelligence who shared Gur's apprehensions, because Egypt had built new fortifications and set up new mine fields in the Sinai peninsula.[3]

People in the streets gathered in little knots, discussing the impending visit and trying to figure out what had come over Sadat. Was this a diabolically clever public relations stunt on the part of the Egyptian president to make the Western world place additional pressures on Israel at the Geneva conference? Those with a more optimistic turn of mind suggested that perhaps, after four unsuccessful attempts to defeat Israel, Sadat really wanted peace for his own people more than another try at destroying the Jewish state. A few religious souls exulted that Sadat's change of heart could mean only one thing: that the coming of the Messiah was imminent.

As the hours went by, the spirit of the optimists caught on among most of Israel's population. The Arabic-language program on Israel's national broadcasting station played Egyptian hit tunes, and newspapers bore banner headlines in Hebrew and Arabic: "Welcome, President Sadat." There was a rash of signs and poster reading "Sadat Shalom," a take-off on the traditional Hebrew Sabbath greeting "Shabbat Shalom" (A Sabbath of peace).

Meanwhile, Israel's government proceeded with preparations for Sadat's visit. Dozens of Knesset members and other dignitaries rushed back to Israel from trips abroad. Shimon Peres, the leader of the opposition, broke off a visit to the United States. So did former Prime Minister Golda Meir, who had gone to New York for the opening of the Broadway show "Golda," based on her life. Begin himself telephoned Rabbi Shelomo Goren, now the Ashkenazi Chief Rabbi of Israel, who was visiting in Vienna, and asked him to return home forthwith.

On Friday, November 18, a 60-man advance party, headed by the director of Sadat's office, flew in from Cairo to discuss security arrangements with the Israelis. Four Israeli Kfir fighter planes (*Kfir* is the Hebrew word for "lion cub") were dispatched to escort Sadat's presidential jet to Ben-Gurion airport. (The flight from Egypt to Tel Aviv would take about half an hour). In Jerusalem, 10,000 policemen and 2,000 security agents were placed on duty; so was a special anti-terrorist commando unit of the Israeli Defense Force, to protect Sadat from fanatical Arab terrorists who might now consider him a traitor for coming to Jerusalem. The King David Hotel, where Sadat was to spend his two nights in Israel, was cleared of its 300 guests and cordoned off. One Israeli security official declared that Sadat would be as safe in Israel as if he were at home in his own well-guarded palace. The places Sadat was scheduled to visit were painstakingly searched, and the procession route received a thorough inspection. Someone suggested that the procession from the airport to Jerusalem should include a military ambulance and a mobile cardiac unit because Sadat, like Begin, had a history of heart trouble. Jerusalem's only flagmaker was given a rush order to produce 500 Egyptian flags to display in the parts of the city through which Sadat would pass. The American embassy in Cairo had been contacted to supply the notes for the Egyptian national anthem, which would be played by an Israeli army band at the airport when Sadat's plane landed. When Cairo was slow in replying, Itzhak Graziani, conductor of the band of the Israel Defense Force, made a quick tape recording of the anthem from Cairo Radio, then transcribed the notes on paper for distribution to his men. He hoped that the music he had taped was really the national anthem, (Eventually the notes came through from the U.S. embassy in Cairo; Graziani had taped the right music).

The Israeli code name for Sadat's visit to Jerusalem was "Operation Gate — 1977." It aptly expressed Israel's hopes for the outcome of the visit: the Hebrew term for "gate" is *"sha'ar,"* which can be construed as an acronym for *"sha'at ratzon,"* or "time of good will."

On the day before Sadat's arrival one of Begin's aides relayed a special request to the official synagogue of Israel's Chief Rabbinate in Jerusalem: would the cantor at the Sabbath services the next day recite a special prayer for Divine assistance to Begin?

Begin himself spent the afternoon of Saturday, November 19, at his official residence, relaxing and playing with some of his grandchildren.

That evening, at 8:03 P.M., Anwar el-Sadat's white Boeing 707, with red trim and the legend "Arab Republic of Egypt," landed at a brilliantly floodlit Ben-Gurion airport. A blue and green ramp from El Al, Israel's national air line, was rolled up to the plane. As Sadat emerged, he was greeted by fanfares and a 21-gun salute. Begin and President Katzir were there to meet him. Onlookers blinked in disbelief as they watched Sadat, flanked by Begin and Katzir, stand solemnly at attention as the army band played first the Egyptian national anthem and then *Hatikvah,* the national anthem of the State of Israel, which expresses the Zionist dream of the Jewish people as a free nation with its own land. Escorted by Egyptian and Israeli officers, Sadat inspected a guard of honor composed of Israeli paratroopers and white-uniformed Israeli naval cadets. He briskly strode to the receiving line in which numerous dignitaries were waiting to greet him. He shook hands with Deputy Prime Minister Yigael Yadin, whom he had met almost thirty years earlier under vastly different circumstances; during Israel's War of Independence, the Egyptian army unit in which Sadat had then been a young officer in his late twenties had been surrounded by Israeli forces under Yadin's command. Sadat also greeted former Prime Minister Rabin, and Minister of Agriculture Ariel Sharon, who had led the spectacular Israeli crossing of the Suez Canal during the Yom Kippur War. He had a particularly enthusiastic handshake for Foreign Minister Dayan, and then bent to greet Golda Meir. Some said that he actually kissed the former prime minister, but it seems that this was only a rumor. The Speaker of the Knesset was on hand to welcome Sadat; so were both the Sephardic and the Ashkenazic Chief Rabbis of Israel, the Moslem clergy from Israel and the West Bank territory, and U.S. Ambassador Lewis.

After the welcoming ceremonies, Sadat, who, as a chief of state, outranked Prime Minister Begin, entered the official limousine of President Katzir for the 30-mile drive to Jerusalem. Begin followed in a second limousine.

That evening at the King David Hotel, Sadat had his first official meeting with Begin, Dayan and Yadin. Afterwards, Begin said to a radio reporter, "I had a personal, warm talk with President Sadat and I may say that we like each other. He has a sense of humor and I, too, sometimes have a sense of humor. We exchanged views. I think a fitting personal tie has been established between us."

Early the next morning, Sunday, November 20, Sadat, a devout Moslem, was driven to the Al Aqsa mosque to mark the Moslem feast of *Al-Adha,* which commemorates Abraham's taking his son Isaac to the sacrificial altar. Throughout the 45-minute service Sadat sat surrounded by a tight ring of Israeli and Egyptian security men. Afterwards, he walked across the Temple Mount toward the Dome of the Rock, which occupies the place of the Holy Temple. From there, he walked to the Church of the Holy Sepulcher, where he was greeted by Christian religious dignitaries, but also by young Palestinian demonstrators who protested against his betrayal of the Palestinian cause by visiting the land "under enemy occupation." He did not visit the Western Wall.

While Sadat was occupied with his ceremonial rounds, Begin and his cabinet spent the morning discussing detailed political proposals to be put to Sadat. After the meeting, Begin and his aides drove to the King David Hotel to call for Sadat and escort him to Yad Vashem, the memorial to the victims of the Hitler Holocaust. Escorted by Gideon Hausner, who had been chief prosecutor at the Eichmann trial in 1964, Sadat walked slowly through the exhibits and memorial halls. At the end of the visit, Sadat was taken to view

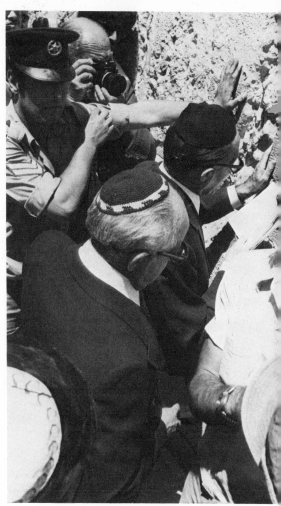

June 8, 1977: Begin (in black yarmulka) praying at the Western Wall after having been charged by Israel's President Katzir to form a new government.

Courtesy Israel Government Press Office.

O's: On one of his many journeys. Begin, in itreal, visiting with Ben Milner, President e Revisionist party organization of Canada.

February, 1978: Prime Minister Begin addresses a session in Jerusalem of the International Seminary on Soviet Jewry. At his left is Eugene Gold, President of the National Conference on Soviet Jewry.
Courtesy National Conference of Soviet Jewry.

December, 1977: A visit of good will. Begin, with Britain's Prime Minister James Callaghan, in front of the Prime Minister's residence at 10 Downing Street.

the "Hall of Names" which holds the names of 3 million Jews who were killed in the Holocaust. As he entered the hall, Begin offered him a yarmulka, explaining to him that this was the headgear donned by Jews when they entered a holy place, just as Moslems did not enter holy places with uncovered heads. Sadat put on the yarmulka but it somehow fell off. Before leaving the memorial, he wrote into the visitors' book in both English and Arabic, "May God guide our steps toward peace. Let us end all suffering for mankind."

At noon, there was a working luncheon attended by Sadat, Begin, Dayan, Yadin and two of Begin's aides.

Shortly before four o'clock that afternoon, Sadat arrived at the Knesset building to perform the task he had set himself: to speak to Israel's parliament about peace. The building flew an Egyptian flag in his honor. Before entering, Sadat inspected an honor guard of Israeli troops, then laid a wreath at the eternal flame honoring the men and women who had died in Israel's four wars of survival.

Inside the Knesset hall, Sadat received a standing ovation, was introduced to the Knesset members and mounted the rostrum to speak. Those in the hall, as well as those who viewed the proceedings on television, could not help noting that as he spoke, Sadat stood only a few feet away from the portrait of Theodor Herzl, father of modern political Zionism.

Sadat spoke for one hour, in Arabic, reading from a prepared text. "You would live with us in this region of the world," he said to the Israelis, "and I tell you in all sincerity that we welcome you among us with full security and safety." Israel had "become an established fact recognized by the world," the two superpowers had undertaken the responsibility for Israel's security and survival, and so, "since we seek true peace, we really and truly welcome you to live among us in peace and security." He made much of the need for eliminating the "psychological barriers" between Israel and her neighbors which, as he put it, constituted "70 per cent of the problem."

But then, in a tone which listeners in retrospect were to describe as "patronizing" and "menacing," Sadat warned that Israel could have neither peace nor international guarantees as long as she occupied any of the territory she had taken in the Six-Day War, including "Arab Jerusalem." All states in the Middle East had the right to live in peace inside secure frontiers, internationally guaranteed, he continued, and he claimed the same right on behalf of the Palestinian Arabs. If Israel, under the Balfour Declaration, had found "the legal and moral justification" to set up a national home on a land that "did not at all belong" to her, it was only fair that she should show understanding for the people of Palestine, who now wanted to establish an independent state "upon their land." Israelis, he suggested, would have nothing to fear from such an Arab state because "you will have all the international safeguards" and the new-born Arab entity would be dependent on outside support for its survival.

Sadat ended his address, which included numerous passages from the Book of Proverbs, the Psalms, the Prophet Zechariah ("Love righteousness and peace"), with a quotation from the Koran stating the Moslem belief in the Biblical patriarchs and in the revelations given to Moses and to Jesus of Nazareth.[4]

Unlike Sadat, Begin spoke extemporaneously. Speaking in Hebrew, Begin opened his address with a reference to the feast of *Al-Adha* which Sadat and his fellow Moslems were observing that day. At a time when other peoples still regarded human sacrifices as gifts most pleasing to their deities, Abraham, the common ancestor of the Jewish and Arab peoples, had taught that God did not desire fathers to sacrifice their sons upon His altars. Thus, Begin said, the Jewish people and the Arab people both had made an important contribution to the progress of mankind.

Begin praised Sadat's courage in coming to Jerusalem. "We, the Jews, know how to appreciate such courage," for courage was the character trait by which the Jewish people had survived through the ages. He recalled how Israel, in her Declaration of Independence, had offered "a hand of peace" to her Arab neighbors, only to be attacked on three fronts the next day. But Israel had no desire to remember past hostilities; she was now concerned with "the future, for our nation and for our children, our joint and common future, because we shall all have to live together in this area forever and ever — the great Arab nation in its various states and countries, and the Jewish nation in its country, the Land of Israel." History, Begin continued, had taught that war was avoidable, but that peace was unavoidable. "There are no such things as perennial enemies. After every war, the inevitable does come, and that is peace." He then outlined Israel's proposals for peace with her Arab neighbors, including a peace treaty between Israel and Egypt, the establishment of diplomatic relations, and economic cooperation between all the countries of the region.

We have wonderful countries in the Middle East. This is how

God created this part of the world. It is an oasis in the desert, but we have deserts, too. We can make those deserts flourish. Let us join hands in this respect. Let us develop our countries. Let us do away with poverty, overcome hunger . . . The combination of the Arab genius and the Jewish genius, together, can change this part of the world into a paradise on earth.

Begin invited President Assad of Syria and King Hussein of Jordan to follow in Sadat's footsteps, to open peace negotiations and sign peace agreements with Israel.

He refuted Sadat's characterization of the Balfour Declaration as the "legal and moral justification" for a Jewish homeland in a land that "did not at all belong" to Israel. The link of the Jewish people with their land went back unbroken to the dawn of humanity.

Here the kings of Judea kneeled before their God. This is where we became a people . . . And when we were expelled from our land, we never forgot this land even for one day. We prayed for the country, we longed to see this country. We yearned and spoke about our return to this country, since it has been written, "When the Lord will bring us back to Zion, we will be as dreamers. Our mouths will be filled with laughter and our tongues will speak of song and rejoicing."

The Balfour Declaration and the League of Nations Mandate merely recognized this age-old bond between the Jewish people and their land.

Reminding Sadat of his visit to the Yad Vashem memorial, Begin described the Holocaust as a direct result of Jewish homelessness. The world had kept aloof from the sufferings of the Jews, but now the Jewish homeland would stand on guard for the Jewish people. Israel would never permit herself to be maneuvered into a position of defenselessness against her enemies. "We shall never put our people, our wives and children in danger again; it is our duty to defend them, if need be, even at the cost of our lives. They will not be put within the range of fire for annihilation."

However, all the outstanding problems between Israel and the Arab peoples were open to negotiation. These differences would have to be solved not as a precondition to peace negotiations, as Sadat appeared to suggest, but as part of the negotiating process.

If there is a divergence of opinion between us, anyone who studied the history of war and what happened to peace treaties knows that all negotiations began with a difference of opinion, disagreement, and that in the framework of negotiations they reached agreement and consensus, which brought about the signing of peace treaties . . .

We shall conduct these negotiations as equals. There are no victors and no vanquished. All the people in this area, in this region, are equal. Let everyone treat his neighbor with due respect in the spirit of openness, of readiness to listen one to the other, to hear facts, explanations, reasons. With all the experience of convincing each other, let us conduct negotiations as I requested and suggested, to continue negotiations until we reach the happy hour when a treaty of peace is signed between us.

Israel was not only prepared to meet with her neighbors at a Geneva conference, but to meet with them even before, "Let us sit and go into each matter before Geneva, to clarify the problems. It is better to make [them] clear before we go to Geneva with open eyes and our ears ready to listen to all suggestions."

As for Jerusalem, Begin, addressing himself directly to Sadat, spoke of the Holy Places of Islam and Christianity.

"I feel good about Jerusalem," he said. Sadat, worshipping first at the Al Aqsa mosque and then visiting the Church of the Holy Sepulcher, had had an opportunity to see for himself that members of all faiths now had unrestricted access to their holy places, which they had not enjoyed prior to 1967. "We can assure . . . both the Islamic and the Christian world . . . that forever and ever access will be free without hindrance" to the holy places sacred to each faith. Israel would defend this right to free access, "because that is our belief. We believe in the equality of the rights of man and citizen, and respect and dignity for each faith."

Like Sadat, Begin concluded his address on a deeply religious note. He offered a prayer for "the wisdom required to overcome the difficulties and barriers, obstacles and difficulties, calumnies and slanders, incitements and attacks. May God Almighty grant that we reach that day we yearn for, that day all of our nations pray for — the day of peace. For indeed, verily so, the Psalmist of Israel says, 'Justice and peace have become one'[Ps. 85:11] and the Koran says, 'Love, truth and peace.' "[5] Perhaps as he uttered these words, Begin also recalled an apt commentary on that Biblical passage, not from Rabbinic literature, but from the address delivered by Theodore Roosevelt when he accepted the Nobel Peace Prize 71 years earlier:

Peace is generally good in itself, but it is never the highest good unless it comes as the handmaid of righteousness; and it becomes a very evil thing if it serves merely as a mask for cowardice and sloth, or as an instrument to further the ends of despotism or anarchy. We must bear in mind that the great end in view is righteousness, justice as between man and man, and between nation and nation.

That evening Begin gave a "working dinner" for Sadat, which was attended by about a dozen persons each from Israel and from the Egyptian delegation. Sadat seemed to have struck up an instantaneous friendship with Defense Minister Ezer Weizman, who had suffered a broken ankle and bruises in an automobile accident the Wednesday before Sadat's arrival but had come from the hospital in a wheelchair to hear Sadat address the Knesset.

On Monday morning, November 21, just as Sadat was about to leave the King David Hotel for a farewell call on President Katzir, Weizman was driven up to the entrance of the hotel. Sadat had already entered his limousine, but when he spotted Weizman, he jumped out, rushed over to him and kissed him on both cheeks.

At the presidential residence Katzir presented Sadat with a set of oil flasks dating back to Biblical times. Mrs. Katzir gave Sadat a book of "peace drawings" by Jewish and Arab children, and, as a gift for Sadat's wife, who had not accompanied her husband, a "peace rug" which had been executed by Israeli artists on two days' notice. Begin's gift to Sadat was a set of nine miniature oil lamps from the era of the Maccabean uprising against King Antiochus, and a copy of Begin's own memoirs, *The Revolt*.

On Monday afternoon, Begin and the entire cabinet saw Sadat off at Ben-Gurion airport. After broad smiles and hearty handshakes with Begin, Sadat climbed up the ramp into his jet for the brief homeward flight. As Begin turned to leave the airport, his face radiated the relief he felt that Sadat's forty-three hours in Israel had come and gone without a hitch.

During Sadat's visit, a schedule had been drawn up for an exchange of negotiating teams between Jerusalem and Cairo, and for another summit meeting between Begin and Sadat on Christmas Day, December 25, this time in Egypt. However, Begin would not be invited to Cairo, but to Ismailia, at the midpoint of the Suez Canal.

On Friday, December 2, Begin and his wife arrived in London for their belated visit. This time the welcome was not marred by bomb threats and hostile demonstrations. The Begins were greeted at Heathrow airport by Britain's foreign minister, Dr. David Owen, and by a large delegation of the Anglo-Jewish establishment, headed by Britain's Chief Rabbi, Dr. Immanuel Jakobovits. On Sunday, December 4, Begin was host at a dinner for Prime Minister Callaghan at London's Savoy Hotel. It was the first night of Hanukkah, and the two prime ministers, both wearing tuxedos and yarmulkas, watched the lighting of the first of the eight traditional Hanukkah candles in commemoration of the Maccabean bid for freedom.

On December 7, Begin returned to Israel. Four days later, he was host at another state dinner, this time at the King David Hotel, for Secretary of State Vance, who had come to Jerusalem to discuss the next move in the talks between Israel and Egypt. For the moment, there was no more talk of reviving the Geneva conference. The Sadat visit to Jerusalem had split the Arab world, and none of the parties — Israelis, Americans, or Egyptians, for that matter — relished the thought of a conference in which the Soviet Union would play a major role. The center of attention would be occupied by direct talks between Israel and Egypt, Israel's most formidable neighbor, without whose armed might the Arab world would be unable to defeat Israel in battle.

From the rostrum of the Knesset Begin sternly warned outsiders, particularly West European governments, not to seek to influence Israel in her negotiations for peace. Western Europe might be concerned about the continued flow of Arab oil, but Begin was haunted by the specter of a second holocaust within less than a half-century, unwittingly abetted by well-meaning friends who would urge Israel to be more flexible and willing to take unacceptable "risks for peace." His message was addressed primarily to the German Federal Republic and the Netherlands. "I remind the German people that it should be the last to give advice . . . which would endanger the security of our wives and children." The Dutch, too, were similarly told not to push Israel into taking steps "which would one day result in a little Israeli girl leaving a diary like that of Anne Frank."[6]

On the other hand, Begin was not blind to political realities. In mid-December, 1977, for the second time since becoming prime minister, he flew to Washington, seeking President Carter's endorsement of a 26-point peace plan he was going to take with him to Sadat in Ismailia. Begin's proposals went further than any of the ones drawn up by earlier Israeli governments. They dealt with the future of the Sinai peninsula, the West Bank territory and the Gaza Strip.

Before becoming prime minister, Begin had suggested that a "border of peace" between Egypt and Israel might be drawn somewhere in the Sinai peninsula. Now he was ready, in return for a binding peace treaty, to have Israel acknowledge Egyptian sovereignty over all of the Sinai peninsula, with a line of demilitarization drawn somewhere between 180 and 200 kilometers west of the international boundary that had existed before the 1967 war. At one point the Government of National Unity in which Begin had been a minister had been willing to give up most of the Sinai peninsula for peace, but it had visualized a peace treaty permitting Israel to remain in military control of a narrow strip of land between Elat and Sharm-el-Sheikh as an insurance against a third Egyptian blockade of the Gulf of Elat. As prime minister, however, Begin was willing — in return for a full peace resulting from direct negotiations — to have Israeli forces quit that area also, leaving it and the district of Yamit, a new town founded near the seashore several years earlier by Israeli settlers, surrounded by a United Nations zone.

The other aspect of Begin's proposal represented a basic ideological concession on Begin's part. Throughout the years since the Six-Day War, Begin and his followers had proclaimed that the West Bank and Gaza Strip must remain under Israeli sovereignty as part of historic Jewish Palestine. Now Begin announced a signal departure from this stand. He proposed that the question of the sovereignty of the two territories be kept in abeyance for the time being. However, for the sake of peace — as Begin was to put it — the Israeli government would think not in terms of geography, history or ideology when it came to "Judea, Samaria and the Gaza Strip," but in terms of the "individuals, the human beings"who were living there. The political status of their territory would be left "open," but the Arabs of the West Bank and the Gaza Strip would be granted civil and religious "self-rule." The Arabs would elect their own governing council to administer all their internal affairs. The Israeli presence would be restricted to specified military bases; Israel would assume responsibility for keeping the areas secure against attacks from without and against Fifth Column activity on the part of terrorist elements such as the PLO. But for all purposes other than security, the Arabs would enjoy a measure of independence that had never been theirs under Turkish, British, or, more recently, Jordanian occupation.

When Begin presented these proposals at the White House, Carter praised them a a "fair basis for negotiation," a long step forward and an expression of great flexibility. Begin came away with the impression that his peace plan now had the full backing of the United States. In a mood of high optimism, he went before the television cameras of *Face the Nation* on December 18 — a week before his meeting with Sadat in Ismailia — and told millions of American viewers that, once the peace treaty between Israel and Egypt had been signed, he would suggest a tripartite meeting between Carter, Sadat and himself:

> I have a suggestion to make to President Sadat . . . If we reach an agreement, as I hope we shall, then I would suggest that President Carter invite both President Sadat and myself to come to Washington, and then we shall be . . in a circle of friendship and faith — a Christian President, a Moslem leader and a Jewish prime minister, and announce to the world: *Pax vobiscum, Shalom Aleichem, Salaam Aleikum.* It means — all peace unto you. I think it will be quite an event in the annals of mankind in our generation.[7]

A Carter-Sadat-Begin summit meeting was indeed to take place, but not until eight months later and under circumstances somewhat different from those envisioned by Begin in his initial euphoria.

On Christmas Day, 1977, Begin made the flight from Ben-Gurion airport to Ismailia, where he presented his plan to President Sadat. Unlike Sadat in Jerusalem, Begin was not given an official reception in Ismailia. In fact, the welcome signs with which Ismailia was bedecked bore only Sadat's name. They made no mention of Begin, or of Israel, for that matter. It was, one Israeli observer noted, as if Sadat had come to Ismailia for a one-man summit meeting.[8] But Begin felt encouraged by his meeting with the Egyptian leader. Sadat had called him "my friend," had personally escorted him on a sight-seeing tour of the city,[9] and made no criticism of Begin's peace proposals.

Begin had been pleased, too, with reports of the welcome the Israeli peace delegation had been accorded on its arrival in Cairo. "They were received," Begin observed during a television interview, "with the warmest hospitality possible. This, too, is part of the peacemaking process; coming together, liquidating prejudice, seeing each other, seeing that we can live together, work together and make peace together."[10]

The first sign that the road to peace would not be smooth came when Egypt's minister of war and Israel's Defense Minister Weizman studied an Egyptian map showing the proposed demilitarization line in the Sinai peninsula. The Israeli proposal had placed the line somewhere between 180 and 200 kilometers west of the boundary between the peninsula and Israel's Negev region. But the line on the Egyptian map was only 40 kilometers west of the international boundary, putting Egyptian armed forces dangerously close to the towns and settlements of southern Israel.

Several days after his return to Israel from his meeting with Sadat, Begin was shocked to read in the government-controlled Egyptian press that he, Begin, had been behaving like Shylock, insisting on his pound of flesh, and that he should be grateful that he had not been thrashed within an inch of his life in Ismailia. These personal slurs on Begin were followed by openly anti-Semitic diatribes; "slanderous aspersions on the integrity and the dignity of the Jewish people," Begin called them. He and his colleagues, Begin later wrote, were appalled. He compared the insults in the Egyptian press with those that had been published in the 1930's in Julius Streicher's hate sheet, *Der Stuermer*. "Was this the 'new spirit' we had heard so much about?" Begin asked in genuine bewilderment.[11]

Still, for some days the negotiations between Israel and Egypt continued in Jerusalem and Cairo; in fact, they seemed to be making good progress, with the two sides apparently close to agreement on almost all the principal points under discussion. Then, without warning, on January 18, 1978, almost two months to the day since his journey to Jerusalem, Sadat recalled the Egyptian peace delegation. (Oddly, he did not expel the Israeli delegation in Cairo until July.) Begin was stunned. His proposals had offered Egypt concessions far beyond any offered by previous Israeli governments. Yet, Egypt appeared to be insisting once again on her original demands: no further talks with Israel until Israel would agree unconditionally to withdraw all her forces to the boundaries of June 4, 1967, and accept the creation of an independent Palestinian state on the West Bank.

Begin was angered by Sadat's public reversion from the role of peace emissary to that of an enemy presenting Israel with an ultimatum. Sadat, Begin wrote, had come to Israel fully aware of the Israeli position: once at the peace negotiating table, either side could present its maximum position, but it could not make that position its condition for coming to the peace table. In any event,

Israel would not bow to "the two utterly unreasonable demands" which, if Israel were to fulfill them, "would place the Jewish state in mortal danger."[12]

Sadat, for his part, insisted that by making the journey to Jerusalem, he had given Israel "everything," while Israel had given him "nothing" in return. Was the offer of the entire Sinai peninsula and of unprecedented Arab self-rule in the West Bank and the Gaza Strip "nothing", Israelis wanted to know, while Sadat's vague verbal acceptance of Israel's right to exist was "everything"? The euphoria that had gripped Israel during Sadat's visit was giving way to disillusionment and doubts. Some Israelis doubted Sadat's sincerity. Begin's political opponents, on the other hand, who had no patience with his Biblical and ideological claims to the West Bank territory (as opposed to military arguments for Israel's retaining part of the area) wanted to know whether Begin had been sufficiently forthcoming in his talks with Sadat. Their image of Begin as an extremist and a war hawk had persisted in their minds, and while hardly anyone in the opposition questioned Begin's patriotism or the selflessness of his motivations, many of his adversaries now proclaimed that they considered him a "disaster" for Israel.

The opposition's attacks on Begin received added impetus from the United States, where the Carter Administration now spoke no more of Begin's peace plan, but placed the blame for the breakdown in the negotiations on Begin's "intransigence" — a term which the U.S. government and American news media had also favored in describing the attitude of Begin's predecessor, Itzhak Rabin.

In the middle of March, 1978, for the third time since he had assumed the premiership, Begin flew to Washington for talks with President Carter. He made the trip several days later than originally planned: on March 11, the day before he had been scheduled to leave Israel, a band of Palestinian Arab terrorists from southern Lebanon had landed on the seashore of Tel Aviv in Soviet-built boats, killed a young girl, then massacred 36 passengers on a touring bus, injuring over 70 others. In response, Israeli forces struck deep into southern Lebanon where terrorist bases were concentrated. As Begin was to explain to the leaders of the American Jewish community, Israel had done this "not for retribution and certainly not for revenge" for the men, women and children who had been killed ("Not even Satan," Begin said, quoting the Hebrew poet laureate, Hayim Nahman Bialik, "could devise a way of exacting retribution for the blood of one little child"). Rather, "We sent our boys into southern Lebanon to eradicate the bases of evil, of those who call themselves the PLO" and who had turned southern Lebanon into a haven from which they could "strike at our heart, at our loved ones, at our children."[13]

Begin was to recall the three days he spent in Washington this time as "the most difficult of my life." At a news conference held at the National Press Club in Washington on March 23, he reviewed Israel's peace proposals in detail, then gave circumspect but open expression to his shock and disappointment at the complete turnabout in the positions of Sadat and Carter. "When I remember the Jerusalem and Ismailia meetings," he said, "I recall good days for President Sadat and for myself, for the Egyptian people and the Israeli people and for peace." He quoted Sadat as having told him in Ismailia, "We shall discuss our problems. We shall negotiate the Israeli proposal and an Egyptian counterproposal." Then, suddenly, had come the vilification campaign in the Egyptian press. "Names — bad names — were thrown into the arena. I am not impressed by name-calling — perhaps I am used to it. But when it besmirches the dignity of our people, well, we shall always defend their dignity. For too long have the Jewish people been vilified and humiliated. No more."

As for the Carter Administration, Begin cited the praise with which both the President and Secretary of State had welcomed the Israeli proposals only three months earlier, and contrasted it with the sudden chill in the American atmosphere. "It is with deep sorrow that I have to tell you that at a certain moment in recent weeks those good words of the past suddenly disappeared from the lexicon." He suggested that this had come about because of objections raised by Egypt to the peace plan. But, he went on, "Can such an objection to a plan that had been publicly and positively appreciated be enough to turn right into wrong, flexibility into intransigence, fair into unfair? Indeed, fairness and justice demand a different posture."[14]

At the National Press Club and later that day also at a meeting of the Conference of Presidents of Major American Jewish Organizations, Begin made his appeal for fairness directly to American public opinion, "because as a man of this generation, with all the experiences behind us, I do believe . . . in the moral greatness of America, proven time and time again, tested in many, many trials and ultimately always winning the day." He urged the constituent groups of the Presidents' Conference to publicize his peace plan in the American hinterland. The American public was not sufficiently informed on the Middle East issue, he said; if the American people knew the full story behind his peace effort, they would give Israel their support. "Ask for support," he said to his Jewish audience, "and you will have it. It will be given to you."

The main cause of the early misunderstandings between Sadat and Begin seemed to lie in the differences of personality and negotiating style that separate the two leaders from one another. Sadat, whose authority over his country is absolute, prefers to think and act in terms of sweeping decisions and grand gestures made on the inspiration of an impulse. But he has little patience with the details that are vital to all successful negotiations. By contrast, Begin, an elected public official, and a lawyer by training, applies both his legal and Talmudic backgrounds to the formulation of his decisions and agreements. He insists on spelling out every detail and on carefully examining all the "fine print." As a consequence, Sadat and Begin had difficulty communicating directly with each other. During their talks in Jerusalem and Ismailia, each misunderstood the other's statements on such crucial issues as Israeli troop positions and the future of the Jewish settlements which Israel had set up in the Sinai peninsula.

It seems that after his meeting with Begin in Ismailia, Sadat decided that he would be able to obtain more concessions from Israel if he stopped negotiating directly with Israel and went back to dealing only with the United States, the only great power in a position to put intolerable pressures on Israel by witholding military, economic and political support. Hence, during his meeting with Carter following the Ismailia talks, Sadat informed the President that Begin's peace plan — particularly Begin's silence about eventual Arab sovereignty over the West Bank and the Gaza Strip — was unacceptable and that if the United States were not successful in making Begin meet Egypt's conditions, there would be war. The Carter Administration, fearful of the consequences of a new war in the Middle East, then started portraying Begin to public opinion as intransigent and an obstacle to peace, and when Begin came to Washington in March, 1978, the President, in contrast to their previous meetings, was stern and cold to his visitor from Jerusalem. Aware that Labor Alignment partisans in Israel, along with many Jews in the United States, had not yet made their peace with the change in Israel's government, Carter Administration officials dropped hints that perhaps peace in the Middle East might be attained more readily if someone other than Begin were prime minister of Israel. The rumors about Carter himself wishing to see Begin removed from office were so widespread and persistent that Carter, on a visit to Brasilia that spring, felt called upon to deny publicly that he or any other high American official had ever suggested that America would be happier if Begin were no longer prime minister.[15]

Despite opposition from peace protesters in Israel and evidence of displeasure from the President of the United States, Begin adhered steadfastly to his peace plan and, upon his return from the United States, received a 64-32 vote of confidence from the Knesset. And Defense Minister Ezer Weizman told a youth rally of the Herut party in Tel Aviv, "I am sure Mr. Begin will be the one who will sign peace with our neighbors."[16]

In May, Begin was back in the United States, this time to help American Jewry celebrate the thirtieth anniversary of Israel's independence. Some of his close friends in Israel had attempted to persuade him not to make the trip; they were concerned about the reception he would get in the United States. The timing seemed all wrong for a visit from Begin. In Washington, the Congress of the United States was debating the sale of modern war planes to Saudi Arabia. Also, 36 American Jewish intellectuals and academicians, including some prominent figures in American Zionism, had signed a widely-publicized letter of support for "Peace Now," a highly visible peace movement in Israel, some of whose members somewhat naively suggested that, as a magnanimous gesture in return for Sadat's visit, Israel should withdraw from all Arab territory in advance of peace negotiations.* In view of the tensions between Washington and Jerusalem, and the Carter Administration's pressures on American Jewish leadership to make Begin "see reason," Begin's friends suggested, it might be wiser for him to postpone his trip until a more auspicious time. If he went now, they said, he might find himself subjected to unpleasantness and embarrassments.

But Begin refused to be deterred by these apprehensions. On May 1, he and Aliza arrived in New York for a one-week tour of the

---

*Former Premier Golda Meir, at a meeting of her party's central committee in Tel Aviv on May 21, 1978, was to call the members of "Peace Now" hopelessly naive. She said that while she, too, favored peace, it was not necessarily "now, and not with any deadline like a sword looming over any Israeli government." Could the members of "Peace Now," she demanded, promise that after Israel signed a peace on their terms, their children and grandchildren, too, would be able to live in peace and quiet?

United States which was to include stops not only in New York and Washington, but also in Los Angeles and Chicago.

The fears of Begin's friends that his visit to the United States would be marred by demonstrations of "Peace Now" supporters or embroilments with American officials did not materialize. Gauging the mood of American Jewry accurately, Begin this time soft-pedaled the differences between his country and the United States and, instead, chose as his main theme Israel's search for peace, her hopes for security, and the morality of Israel's cause. He appealed to American Jews to remain united in their support for the Jewish homeland. He spoke with deep emotion, but quietly and not without an occasional dash of humor.

Begin's tour of the United States opened on a positive note which was sustained throughout the week. In Washington, President Carter had invited 1,000 rabbis and Jewish communal leaders to a reception for the Begins on the White House lawn in honor of Israel's Independence Day. After a half-hour private meeting with Begin, Carter in his welcoming address pledged "total, absolute American commitment to Israel's security." In response, Begin called the President's speech "one of the greatest moral statements ever."

From Washington the Begins flew across the continent to Los Angeles, where Begin addressed a mass rally of 11,000 at the Los Angeles Forum and an Israel Bond luncheon at the Los Angeles Century Plaza, the hotel where he and his party spent their one night in the city. At the rally, he drew laughter when he said, "I bring you good tidings from Washington. I spent a whole day there and nobody asked me to resign." Then, as usual, he spoke of the sufferings of the Jewish people over centuries of homelessness which, he said, admitted of only one proper conclusion. "We must fight for our liberty, because if we do not, no one will give it to us." He also spoke of Israel's Biblical claim to "Judea and Samaria" — the West Bank — but this time, instead of the historical and ideological aspect of the West Bank problem, he stressed the practical importance of the area for Israel's military security. Begin made a profound impression on California's Governor Jerry Brown, who was young enough to be his son. Throwing his arms around Begin, Brown said he was "trying to send a message to Israel that peace will not come from making concessions before you even sit down at the bargaining table."

On May 3 the Begins flew to Chicago, where Begin addressed a United Jewish Appeal luncheon, was made an honorary citizen of the City of Chicago and the State of Illinois, and received and honorary doctorate of laws from Northwestern University, despite a vote of the University's student body (1,199 to 907) against honoring him because that would make the school seem to be taking sides in the Middle Eastern conflict. At the convocation, Begin heard the governor of Illinois, Jim Thompson, address to him an echo of John F. Kennedy's classic maxim with the words, "May you never fear to negotiate, but may you never negotiate out of fear."

Except for a few "Peace Now" protesters, the only hostile demonstration Begin encountered was that of several hundred Palestinian sympathizers (mostly from India and the Middle East) at Northwestern, who carried posters declaring that Israel Bonds would be used for the purchase of bombs. But these protests were offset by other Northwestern students bearing placards reading "We Love Israel."

Begin seemed to have won over the Jewish leadership of both Los Angeles and Chicago. Several Jewish communal leaders in Los Angeles who originally had told a *Washington Post* reporter that they would "speak frankly" to Begin about his government's foreign policy decided not to do so after they had heard him speak. It did not seem to be the right time and place, they later explained. In Chicago, a prominent Jewish communal leader who said he had some reservations about Begin's policies tuned down a chance to discuss his misgivings privately with the Prime Minister.[17]

On May 4 the Begins returned to New York, where they stayed at Gracie Mansion, official residence of New York's mayors, on the invitation of Mayor Edward Koch (who, like his predecessor, Abraham Beame, is Jewish). In the afternoon, Begin donned cap and gown to receive an honorary degree from Yeshiva University. When Begin came into view in the academic procession, the students and spectators assembled on the campus cast academic dignity to the winds and drowned out the processional music with a lively melody to which they chanted, over and over again, verse 11 of Psalm 97: "Light is sown for the righteous, and gladness for the upright in heart."

On Friday, May 5, Begin started his day at breakfast with a select group of editors and publishers at Gracie Mansion, and then was made an honorary citizen of New York.

Americans were eager to gauge Begin's response to the opposition among Israelis and American Jews to his policies. At a meeting with representatives of the Conference of Presidents of Major American Jewish Organizations Begin was questioned about his reaction to the "Letter of the 36" in support of "Peace Now" in Israel, which had been prominently featured in the American press. Begin replied that American Jews had the right to criticize his policies, but asked that henceforth such critics should first consider whether their way of expressing opposition to the Israeli government might not weaken Israel's position in her peace negotiations.

When television interviewers on the nationwide telecast *Meet the Press* wanted to know Begin's views on dissent in Israel and whether he felt that public opinion was turning against his position. Begin answered: "Not at all. I believe it's an expression of democracy. Everybody is entitled to his opinion . . . I accept it with complete calm. There are differences of opinion voiced in a free land, and so is the case with us." One reporter asked whether Begin considered the dissent within Israel "significant enough to change anything" in his foreign policy. Begin replied that his government's peace plan initially had been "declared to be a good one, and it doesn't become a bad one just because the other side doesn't accept it." He pointed out that he had never regarded his peace plan as the last word, or as an ultimatum to the Arab world. "We expected counterproposals. We did not get them — yet." He hastened to add that it was Sadat, not he, who had broken off the peace negotiations, and that both indirectly and in letters directly addressed to Sadat, he had pleaded with the Egyptian leader to resume the talks. After all, he said, "The essence of peacemaking is negotiation."[18]

On Sunday, May 7, Begin reviewed New York's Israel Independence Day parade, a major annual event featuring tens of thousands of marchers, and dozens of floats and bands. On the reviewing stand with Aliza, New York's Governor Hugh Carey, Mayor Koch and other dignitaries, Begin was clearly enjoying himself as he watched 200,000 paraders, representing a multitude of Jewish organizations, institutions and schools, marching, dancing and riding up Fifth Avenue. Following the parade, which took several hours to pass the reviewing stand, marchers and spectators — according to one police officer on duty that day, the overall crowd at the parade that afternoon was almost a million — turned off Fifth Avenue into Central Park to hear Begin speak from the park's bandshell. They cheered enthusiastically when Begin proclaimed, "The State of Israel lives and will live forever!"

For Begin, the afternoon on Fifth Avenue had been a brief but exhilarating change from the pressures of the months that had gone before. His friends noted that, despite the problems between Jerusalem and Washington, and efforts in some Administration circles to influence American Jewry against Begin, the Prime Minister's week in the United States had not only passed without trouble but had been a success from the public relations point of view. Begin had evidently discovered the right approach to the Jews of the United States.

During the months that followed, Begin was to be faced with stern tests of his ability to persevere in the face of harsh personal criticism. Unlike any of his predecessors, he would be challenged to convince his adversaries both in Israel and elsewhere that he was not a transient nuisance who could be wished away, but the duly appointed leader of his nation, who would tolerate no interference in carrying out the functions of his office.

Sadat, it seemed, was ready to lend a hand in efforts to topple Begin from power. Insisting that Begin was the sole "obstacle to peace in the Middle East," he attempted to secure the sympathies of Begin's political opponents in Israel. Early in July, he tried to up-stage the prime minister by agreeing to meet with the leader of the opposition, Shimon Peres, in Austria. The meeting was arranged within the framework of the Socialist International; the go-between was Austria's Chancellor Bruno Kreisky, who had little use for his own Jewish origins, had repeatedly declared his sympathy for the Arab cause and made no secret of his antipathy for Begin.

Begin was furious and grew even angrier when reports came out that Jordan's King Hussein also wanted to meet with Peres, in London. Begin refused to grant Peres a visa for that meeting, provoking an outcry from the opposition that he was suppressing dissent. (Actually, Begin was within his legal rights: Israeli citizens desiring to meet with statesmen of countries at war with Israel must seek the approval of the government). Someone eavesdropping on Begin chatting with supporters in the rear of the Knesset chamber claimed to have heard Begin use foul language to describe Peres. According to the same source Begin, still the old-style gentleman, apologized when he noticed that a woman had been listening.[19]

In yet another attempt to erode Begin's support inside Israel, Sadat met, also in Austria, with Defense Minister Ezer Weizman, whom he knew to have been a rival of Begin's. Implying that he found it much easier to deal with Weizman than with Begin, Sadat informally proposed to Weizman that, in response to his peace in-itiative in Jerusalem, Israel return to Egypt El Arish, the principal city of the Sinai peninsula, and Mount Sinai. When Sadat's proposal was brought before the Cabinet, Foreign Minister Dayan rejected such a unilateral concession. Begin publicly announced after the meeting that "nobody can get anything for nothing, and this is going to be the policy of Israel." Sadat, in a fit of anger, then expelled the Israeli peace delegation which until then had still waited in Cairo for the peace talks to resume.

Opposition leaders kept up their attack on Begin. One former Cabinet member was quoted in the Israeli press as saying that Begin's behavior was not that of a normal person. Others said that his "inflexibility" in matters of foreign policy was due to his impaired health, that the medication he had to take in order to survive was interfering with his mental functions. The press spread reports that he had blacked out at a Cabinet meeting and that he needed heart surgery but had refused it because he was unwilling to delegate his responsibilities as prime minister.

Finally Begin's patience wore thin, and he struck back. His counterattack, unlike his usual parliamentary thrusts, was not elegant, but frankly communicated his resentment and bitterness at what he considered grossly unfair treatment from his political opponents. He attacked the world press for "relying on the diagnoses of Dr. Peres and Dr. Allon" — former Foreign Minister Yigal Allon — who, he said, had characterized him as senile. "Did I ever refer to Golda Meir as senile, though she served as prime minister until she was 75, or to Ben-Gurion, who served till he was 80?" Begin protested. (Actually, Ben-Gurion had been 77 when he retired from the premiership.) As a member of the Government of National Unity, he recalled, he had known for months that the late Prime Minister Levi Eshkol was in failing health but he, Begin, had never said a word to anyone about it. (As for Begin himself, his physician explained that he was neither in failing health nor dependent on any medication that could have an adverse effect on his judgment.)

As for the charges that he was an "obstacle to peace," Begin retorted that he was an obstacle not to peace but to an Israeli surrender on Arab terms.

Begin accused the Labor Alignment leaders of being well-versed in the art of "character assassination." Their own former chief, Ben-Gurion, he said, had fared no better at their hands than had their arch-adversary, Jabotinsky three decades earlier. They had called Jabotinsky a fascist because he had opposed them, and when Ben-Gurion left Mapai, the main Labor party, to form his own Rafi splinter group, they had labeled him and Rafi as "neo-fascists."

But though the latter part of July was marked by bitter debates between Begin and his opponents on the Knesset floor, a no-confidence motion introduced by the Labor Alignment was defeated by a vote of 70 to 35, and alternative foreign policy proposals — actually not much different in essence from those of Begin — submitted by various opposition factions were rejected.[20] Begin had stood his ground and, to use one of his own favorite English expressions, had "won the day," at least in the Knesset.

Meanwhile, Begin's stock in Carter Administration circles rose slightly, in part perhaps because Sadat had displeased Washington by his public posturing: his slur on a highly respected American public servant and his refusal to resume negotiations with Israel except on his own terms. Sadat had stated that "we would not have suffered what we are suffering today" if Carter had been President in 1967, "without Arthur Goldberg, the Zionist." (Goldberg had been U.S. Ambassador to the United Nations during the Six-Day War.) In mid-July Foreign Minister Dayan had met with his Egyptian counterpart, Mohammed Kameel, at Leeds Castle near London, under the auspices of Secretary of State Vance, and it had been suggested that this meeting would soon be followed by other direct high-level talks between Israel and Egypt. But on July 30, Sadat announced that he would not agree to further negotiations with Israel unless Israel would agree in advance to the Arab demand that she evacuate all the lands she had taken in the Six-Day War.

Now it was Sadat's turn to be told that the United States was "very disappointed" by the hardening of his attitude. As a result, American public opinion temporarily shifted part of the blame for "lack of progress toward peace" from the Israelis to the Egyptian leader. In Israel, Sadat's categorical refusal to "bargain over land" had the effect of disillusionment to many who had believed Sadat would be ready to make peace at once if only Begin were more "flexible." The Labor Alignment was no more willing than Begin or Likud to submit to Sadat's demand for total, unconditional withdrawal. The one major point of disagreement between Likud and Labor was that while Likud, on historical and ideological grounds, refused to accept the idea that Israel, under the proper conditions, might relinquish part of the West Bank territory, and insisted on the right of Jews to establish settlements there, Labor was willing in principle to withdraw from those West Bank areas which were not essential to Israel's military security and was opposed to the establishment of Jewish settlements in a region whose political status had yet to be decided. But except for a few elements on the extreme left, no one in Israel — not even most of the "Peace Now" people, when pinned down for a straightforward stand —

was ready to see Israel retreat to the vulnerable borders to which she had been confined before the Six-Day War of 1967.

Meanwhile in the United States, the Carter Administration was becoming increasingly disturbed by the rapidly deteriorating prospects of peace in the Middle East. Sadat was receiving support in his new tough stand from Saudi Arabia, which was pressing him to restore Arab unity by ending his efforts to make peace with Israel. In fact, intelligence reports indicated that Egypt was mobilizing her armed forces. Something had to be done to revive the peace talks between Israel and Egypt and to save the Middle East from renewed warfare. Begin had been in office now for over a year and, despite opposition in Israel to his politics and rumors about his health, any hopes America might have entertained that Begin would either resign or be voted out of power in favor of someone more acceptable to Sadat showed no sign of materializing. For better or for worse, peace or war in the Middle East depended on whether or not Anwar Sadat and Menahem Begin could be brought together under conditions in which they would be willing and able to talk together.

On August 9, the White House released an announcement which astounded the world. President Carter had invited Menahem Begin and Anwar Sadat to join him in a summit meeting at Camp David, the secluded presidential retreat in Maryland's Catoctin mountains, and the United States would be a "full partner" in the talks between Israel and Egypt. Fourteen months earlier, in his inaugural address before the Knesset, Begin had suggested meetings between himself and Arab leaders in a setting removed from the "flare of publicity." Now the President of the United States was placing his hopes for peace on the chance that, living together for a few days in an informal, relaxed rustic atmosphere, protected from the intrusions of the news media and spared from the need for constant public rhetoric and posturing, the leaders of Israel and Egypt would develop a personal relationship making it possible for them to reopen their dialogue of peace. Begin and Sadat had both accepted Carter's invitation to the meeting, which was scheduled to begin on September 5, with no deadline set for adjournment. The object of the conference would be to arrive at a set of principles on which future peace negotiations between Israel and her Arab neighbor could be based.

Camp David is a 143-acre retreat on a 1,880-foot hill in the picturesque Western Maryland countryside, about 75 miles northwest of Washington. A recreation camp during the Depression-ridden

1930's, it had been bought by Franklin D. Roosevelt during World War II as a hideaway to which he would be able to retreat whenever he needed a brief rest or complete seclusion but could not travel far from Washington. Because the setting of the camp seemed far removed from the business and pressures of the nation's capital, Roosevelt had named his retreat "Shangri-La." It was here that he and Winston Churchill had met during World War II to plan the D-Day invasion of Western Europe. Dwight D. Eisenhower renamed "Shangri-La" in honor of his young grandson David, and the name remained unaltered through succeeding Administrations. Thus far, 20 leaders of foreign countries have stayed at Camp David as guests of Presidents of the United States. The summit conference between Eisenhower and the Soviet leader Nikita Khrushchev had made the camp's name a household word in world politics: the thaw in the Cold War which that meeting had achieved became known as "the spirit of Camp David."

In accepting Carter's invitation to Camp David, Sadat declared that this summit meeting would be the "last chance for peace." Begin did not take kindly to the pressure implied in Sadat's statement. In a radio and television address to his nation on Saturday night, September 2, the eve of his departure for the United States, he said that while he considered the summit conference "one of the most important events of our time," it was not necessarily the "last chance" for peace. "In life," he reminded his audience, "there are never last chances; there are always new chances." President Carter, too, was deliberately restrained in describing his expectations of the conference at Camp David.

On Sunday morning, September 3, Begin, accompanied by his wife, Moshe Dayan, Ezer Weizman and a team of top-level aides and advisors, took off from Ben-Gurion airport for New York aboard a regular commercial flight of El Al, Israel's national airline. His parting words to the newsmen and well-wishers who had gathered at the airport to see him off sounded the note of conciliation and optimism which he was to carry with him into the seclusion of Camp David. He was going to meet the President of the United States and the President of Egypt with "a maximum of good will." In an interview at the prime minister's office in Jerusalem, he had told Dean Fischer of *Time* magazine that a "very warm personal relationship" had developed between himself and Sadat during their meeting in Jerusalem the year before. Later, there had been a "metamorphosis" and "some bitter name-calling in Egypt," but he, Begin, had refrained from replying in kind "because I don't think name-calling solves any problems." When he would meet Sadat at Camp David, he, Begin, would say to him, "Mr. President, at Jersualem and Ismailia, you told me that you are my friend. Then there was a difficult period of relations between us. But I remember your statement, and I reciprocate it in my heart. Therefore, I suggest to you, 'Let us be friends.' "[21] Stepping before the microphones at New York's Kennedy airport that afternoon, he said "We want peace more than any other nation on earth . . . For the sake of peace, for our people and the people of Egypt, whom we wish well . . ."[22]

The Begins spent two nights in New York. This time they did not take a VIP suite at the Waldorf-Astoria or accept the hospitality of Mayor Koch but chose instead to stay at the Regency, an elegant but quiet hotel on Park Avenue and 61st Street.

Monday, September 4, was Labor Day, and the Begins spent it in relative quiet. In the late morning Begin, escorted by United States security men and trailed by a limousine carrying armed guards, took a stroll down Park Avenue from the Regency to the Waldorf-Astoria eleven blocks away. Due to the legal holiday the usual midday crowds of the avenue were absent, but here and there people — mostly residents of the neighborhood — gathered to cheer and applaud Begin as he passed. He stopped several times to shake outstretched hands, smiled, nodded and waved, apparently enjoying his morning constitutional . In front of the Waldorf, he hopped into the limousine that had been trailing him, and rode back to the Regency.

The next morning — Tuesday, September 5 — Begin boarded a U.S. Air Force DC-9 for the flight to Andrews Air Force Base, where he was met by Vice-President Mondale and Secretary of State Vance. Aliza was not with him; she had gone from New York to Toronto to attend a wedding and joined Begin at Camp David only later that week. At the Air Force base, Begin was escorted to an Air Force helicopter for the 35-minute ride to Camp David.

President Carter and his wife, Rosalynn, were waiting at the camp's helipad when Begin landed. They had similarly welcomed Sadat two hours earlier. Begin threw his arms around Carter, then kissed the First Lady's hands and cheek. After the brief welcoming speeches, he introduced every member of his entourage to the Carters, carefully explaining the duties of each individual. He singled out for special praise the legal advisor to his delegation, Aharon Barak. Until now, Begin informed the President, Barak had been attorney general of Israel, but now he was about to be promoted: he had been named a justice of Israel's supreme court. (Observers on the scene later contrasted Begin's style with that of Sadat who, after embracing the President and kissing Mrs. Carter, had walked off at once with the Carters, without so much as one look back at his staff, as if he had been totally unaware of their presence aboard his plane.)

The Carters escorted Begin to his cabin, Birch Cottage, just as, two hours earlier, they had installed Sadat at his quarters, Dogwood Cottage. Both cottages were approximately 50 yards away from Aspen Lodge, the large house reserved for the President's use. (Except for the barracks housing the U.S. Marine detachment which is permanently stationed at the camp, and the camp commandant's quarters, all the cottages at the camp are named for trees.) The Egyptian and Israeli aides were accommodated in six smaller cottages. At Begin's request, kosher food for the entire Israeli delegation had been brought into the camp by a Washington caterer. By no means all the Israelis who had come with Begin observed the Jewish dietary laws, but the prime minister considered it a demonstration of Jewish national identity that they should do so officially, while they were guests of the President of the United States at Camp David.

After Begin had settled down at Birch Cottage, Carter dropped in for a brief visit — as he had done earlier with Sadat — to explain the layout of the camp, and to invite Begin and his staff to make use of the camp's recreational and athletic facilities, including tennis courts, a one-hole golf course, a bowling alley and a heated swimming pool. (Begin preferred quiet walks along the camp's wooded nature trails. The one visit he paid to the tennis courts was on Carter's invitation to watch a doubles match played by Secretary of State Vance, U. S. Ambassador Samuel W. Lewis, National Security Advisor Zbigniew Brzezinski and Brzezinski's aide, Bill Quandt.)

Since no newspaper correspondents were allowed inside the camp, the communications media took up stations at a makeshift press center in the nearest town, Thurmont, Maryland, where they had to rely largely on Carter's press secretary Jody Powell for briefings. The reports that emanated from the camp during the 13 days of the summit conference were sparse. Only afterwards were newspapers and magazines in a position to reconstruct in part the activities of Begin, Sadat, Carter, and their aides between September 5, when they first disappeared into the seclusion of the camp, and September 17, when they emerged into the glare of publicity in the

White House to announce that, despite widespread rumors to the contrary, the conference had ended in an agreement between Israel and Egypt.[23]

On September 6, the first full day of the summit, Begin and Sadat joined Carter in a message calling on peoples of all faiths to pray that "peace and justice" might result from the deliberations that were about to begin at Camp David. It was a remarkable coincidence that, though so different from one another in background, personality, political outlook and social philosophy, these three leaders who jointly held the key to peace in one of the most crucial parts of the world should have in common a trait not usually ranked high in modern, sophisticated politics: the kind of personal piety which inspires them with a sincere belief in the modern-day relevance of religious traditions.

The first meeting between Begin and Sadat since Ismailia took place entirely by chance around noon on one of the camp's tree-shaded paths. According to one eyewitness, the two men shook hands cordially, with each complimenting the other on how well he looked. At that moment, Defense Minister Ezer Weizman pedaled by on one of the bicycles provided for Camp David's guests and received an enthusiastic embrace from Sadat. After a few minutes, the three men parted, promising to see each other at 3 o'clock that afternoon, when they were scheduled to have their first official meeting with President Carter.

The afternoon meeting took place on the outdoor patio of Aspen Lodge, where the Carters were staying. It was not a pleasant session. Sadat's initial working paper, which he read to Begin and Carter, sounded to Begin more like an ultimatum than a negotiating stance. It included all the Arab demands so well known from the past: Israel was to give up all the land she had occupied in the Six-Day War and to acknowledge that the Arabs of the West Bank and Gaza Strip had the right of political self-determination; that they were entitled to set up an independent state of their own, if they so chose. Begin saw visions of a new, intensely hostile Arab neighbor, ruled by the PLO and posing a mortal threat to Israel. Thoroughly upset, he said that if these demands were Sadat's last word, he, Begin, would have no other alternative but to leave the camp and take Israel's cause to the court of world public opinion. Carter asked Begin whether he could make a "grand gesture" equivalent to the one Sadat had made in visiting Jerusalem. Begin retorted that he and the people of Israel had already made such a gesture by giving a warm welcome to Sadat, who only five years earlier had "feigned routine autumn maneuvers and then deliberately attacked us at the precise moment that he knew we would all be in our synagogues." Sadat explained that the maneuvers prior to the Yom Kippur War had been a conventional piece of "strategic deception." This did not sit well with Begin. "Deception is deception," he said.

Begin, like Sadat (and Carter), had come to Camp David with working papers drafted by subordinates and describing his negotiating options. Produced by a committee under the chairmanship of General "Abrasha" Tamir, a close friend of Agriculture Minister Ariel Sharon, Begin's "Blue File" (so named because it was bound in a light blue folder) laid out a complete scenario: the objectives which Israel should seek to attain in the negotiations, the concessions she must be prepared, if necessary, to make to Egypt for this purpose, verbal gestures she might have to devise in order to placate the rest of the Arab world, and the limits beyond which Israel could not safely go in making concessions for the sake of peace.

Thursday, September 7, was devoted to meetings on a ministerial level involving Dayan, Weizman, Brzezinski, U.S. Secretary of Defense Harold Brown and Vice-President Mondale. Carter and Begin met privately for two hours, then, together, joined Sadat for more talks. Eyewitnesses noted that Begin treated Sadat with an exaggerated courtliness out of character with the informal setting of the summit meeting. Explaining that, as a prime minister, he ranked below Sadat, who was the president of his country, Begin meticulously observed such little formalities as insisting that Sadat precede him through doors. Except for official meetings, and social activities planned by Carter, Begin and Sadat were to spend almost no time together on an informal basis. As a matter of fact, it seems that most of the official negotiations between the two leaders were conducted with Carter acting as a messenger shuttling back and forth between them.

In the meantime, Aliza Begin had arrived from Toronto. (Sadat's wife had not come at all; she was in Paris with an ailing grandchild.) The Carters took both Begins on a tour of the camp grounds. Begin, who at first had kept to business suits, unbent and briefly changed to sports attire (a sweater instead of a jacket over his shirt.)

That Thursday evening, the Marine detachment that guarded the camp staged a tattoo, the traditional dress parade. During the colorful ceremony, which took about 45 minutes, Carter sat between Begin and Sadat. Trying to put both men at ease, the President exchanged whispers with them, once putting his arm around Sadat and once patting Begin on the back. Afterwards, the three leaders reviewed the Marines, then signed the Marines' guest book. In his entry Begin, somewhat inaccurately, referred to the U.S. Marines as "a great army."

Friday, September 8, was devoted largely to religious observances; the Moslems were keeping their day of rest, while the Jews were preparing for their Sabbath. At sundown Aliza Begin lit the Sabbath candles and, after the Friday evening services, presided over the traditional Friday evening dinner at Birch Cottage for the entire Israeli delegation and a few Egyptians who had accepted the Begins' invitation. The Marines from the camp acted as waiters, serving *gefilte fish*, chicken noodle soup, *tzimmes* (a sweetened mixture of carrots and prunes), noodle pudding and, for dessert, fruit and nuts. Between courses, everyone joined in the familiar Sabbath hymns and some modern Hebrew folk songs. Much to the delight of the Israelis, President and Mrs. Carter, along with Secretary Vance, dropped in. Given a place of honor between Begin and Aliza, the President of the United States put on an embroidered yarmulka and listened attentively as Begin explained each song to him. When Carter remarked that he had enjoyed *Fiddler on the Roof*, Ezer Weizman launched into a spirited rendition of "If I Were a Rich Man," one of the hit songs from the show.

Saturday, out of deference to the Jewish Sabbath, there were no formal meetings. In the evening, after the Sabbath had ended, Brzezinski invited Begin to play a game of chess. Begin accepted, but warned Brzezinski that he had not sat at a chess board in 38 years; the last time he had played had been in Vilna, and that game had been interrupted by the NKVD, who had come to arrest him.

On Sunday, September 10, the Carters, after attending early morning Baptist services at the camp, took the Begins, Sadat, Dayan and Weizman on a four-hour trip to the historic Civil War battlefield in Gettysburg, Pennsylvania, about half an hour's automobile ride away. The excursion had been made at the suggestion of Begin, who considers the study of American history one of his hobbies and is a fervent admirer of Abraham Lincoln.

Later in the day, Begin met with Carter and the U.S. delegation, and became involved in a discussion that lasted until 3 o'clock the next morning. In the process of drafting the framework to guide eventual peace negotiations, Carter asked Begin to sign a statement of principles which contained references to the "inadmissibility of the acquisition of territory by war." This phrase had been part of Resolution 242, which had been adopted by the United Nations in November, 1967, referring to Israeli troop withdrawals from Arab lands — with the word "all" deliberately omitted — in return for a genuine peace. Israel at the time had considered this resolution acceptable, because the "inadmissibility" clause had been linked to a provision urging the end of belligerency and asserting the right of all nations in the Middle East to secure and recognized borders. But, as Begin pointed out, if Israel were to endorse the thesis that territory conquered in a war had to be returned to its original holder, without the qualifying statements on peace and secure borders that had been operative parts of the UN resolution, she would place herself into an impossible position. She would then not only have to give up the entire West Bank territory, Gaza Strip, and the Old City of Jerusalem, but could be forced to abandon also the Golan Heights, from which, prior to the Six-Day War, Syrian guns had kept shelling Israeli kibbutzim. Begin argued that the "inadmissibility" clause was properly applicable only to territory conquered by an aggressor, not to land occupied by a victim of aggression in the course of a defensive war. If the clause were equally applicable to aggressor and victim, he said, it would constitute a license for aggression; an aggressor nation would see no reason for mending its ways if its intended victim were not permitted to keep strategic advantages in the form of territory occupied in its fight for survival.

Begin was not able to win over the Americans to his point that night, but two days later, Carter agreed to have the "inadmissibility" clause struck from the document. However, the following day — Wednesday, September 13 — the Egyptians balked at giving up the clause. Begin was furious. "Before I sign such a document," he told Carter, "may my right hand forget its cunning." Carter was impressed by the depth of Begin's emotion, and perhaps also by the Biblical language in which he expressed his feelings. (In his subsequent report to a public meeting of the Conference of Presidents of Major American Jewish Organizations in New York, Begin was to recall that Carter asked him for the original Hebrew text and the source of the quotation; he told the President that it was the fifth verse of Psalm 137: "If I forget thee, O Jerusalem, let my right hand forget its cunning"). In the end, Carter devised a compromise formula that made reference to the applicability of "Resolution 242 in all its parts" instead of stressing the "inadmissibility" clause out of its original context.

On Thursday, September 14, Sadat was ready to walk out of the conference because Israel had stated her wish to retain control of four airfields in the Sinai peninsula after the peninsula had been returned to Egyptian sovereignty. Carter persuaded the Israelis to drop that demand by promising American aid in building two new Israeli airstrips in the arid Negev region east of Sinai. (The airfields would be turned over to Egypt for civilian, not military use, and, as Begin was to tell the Knesset, Israel would not have to evacuate them until the new airfields to be built in the Negev had become operational).

On Friday, September 15, there was a meeting between Carter and Dayan. Believing that the business of the summit conference might be successfully completed by the weekend — it seemed likely that, no matter what befell, the meeting would end on Sunday, September 17 — Begin invited the Carters and Sadat to be his guests at a concert of the Israeli Philharmonic Orchestra in Washington on Saturday night. Carter accepted the invitation; no reply came from Sadat.

In the end, neither Begin nor Carter was able to attend the concert. There had been another snag in the negotiations, this one so serious that Begin told his son Benny in Colorado on the telephone after the Sabbath that the summit would probably end without an agreement. There had been heavy pressures, he said, but Israel had been able to withstand them, and would not be forced into an agreement detrimental to her interests. The cause of the difficulty was a "letter of disagreement" proposed by Sadat regarding the status of Jerusalem. In the draft of that document, East Jerusalem, which had been annexed by Jordan in the 1948 war but had been taken over by Israel in 1967, was described as "occupied territory." Begin threatened to walk out if such a document were adopted. On Sunday, September 17, the last day of the conference, he sent two of his key aides to Mondale and Vance in an effort to explain his views to them. The Americans, he said, had misunderstood the whole issue.

Fortunately, Begin was able to get the Americans to "understand." Earlier, Carter had suggested that he and Begin should have one more private meeting before the summit conference ended. Begin offered to call on Carter at Aspen Lodge, but on Sunday afternoon the President turned up at Birch Cottage with several photographs, autographed by himself and Sadat, for the Begin grandchildren. For a few minutes, the two men talked about their families. Begin felt that the right atmosphere had been created for a frank talk between them. Gently but candidly, Begin told Carter that the official designation of East Jerusalem as "occupied" territory could cause the summit conference to end in "complete failure." Certainly, after almost two weeks of intensive negotiations with both sides, and in view of the fact that he had staked his political reputation on the summit meeting, Carter was not eager to leave Camp David without positive results to report to the world. At any rate, he said to Begin, "If you feel that strongly about it, we shall couch the letter in terms more satisfactory to you."

Begin's message was taken to Sadat. What transpired then in Dogwood Cottage is not known, but Sadat decided not to insist on the offending statement. However, he made one more try for small favors. He requested Brzezinski to go to Begin and ask him whether he might not see his way clear to having an Arab flag hoisted over the shrines on the Temple Mount in Jerusalem. Begin told Brzezinski that, in view of the significance of the Temple Mount to the Jewish religion and the Jewish nation, this would be impossible. Brzezinski then suggested that, perhaps, in order to accommodate Sadat, an Arab flag might be permitted to fly over some other "institution" in Jerusalem. Before Begin was able to make a reply, Foreign Minister Dayan, his face dead serious, quipped, "Could it be over the Knesset?" The tension in the room at Birch Cottage dissolved in laughter. Begin promised that when peace came, there could be as many as 20 Arab flags on display all over Jerusalem — one on the embassy of every Arab nation that would recognize the State of Israel. That ended the conversation.

Afterwards, Begin paid a visit to Sadat at Dogwood Cottage, and Sadat returned the courtesy by calling on Begin at Birch Cottage.

All through the day, American radio and television stations had interspersed their regular programs with announcements that, in the evening, at 10:30, there would be a special report direct from the White House about the results of the Camp David summit conference.

At 10:30, the major television networks brought the East Room of the White House into the homes of millions of Americans. It was in this spacious hall, scene of elaborate state receptions and a host of sad and joyous events in the lives of Presidents and in the history of the United States, that the 13 days of secrecy at Camp David came to an end.

The cameras showed an audience of some 150 seated in rows of chairs, in a festive mood, as if awaiting the start of one of the many concerts presented in the East Room. Vice-President Mondale was there; so were the members of Carter's Cabinet and the top Presidential advisors, and leading members of the Senate and House of Representatives. Seated together in the front row were Rosalynn Carter and Aliza Begin.

The cameras slowly moved to the dais in front of the audience. There, behind a brown mahogany table with gilt trim, sat the three principal characters of the Camp David drama: Jimmy Carter in the center, flanked on the right by Anwar el-Sadat and on the left by Menahem Begin. Behind them, side by side, were the flags of Israel, Egypt and the United States.

The proceedings were opened by the President of the United States: "When we first arrived at Camp David," the President began, "the first thing upon which we agreed was to ask the people of the world to pray that our negotiations would be successful. Those prayers have been answered far beyond any expectations.

"We are privileged to witness tonight a significant achievement in the cause of peace, an achievement none thought possible a year ago, or even a month ago, an achievement that reflects the courage and wisdom of these two leaders."

As Carter went on to praise both Sadat and Begin for "determination, vision and flexibility," the cameras focused alternately on the President of Egypt and the Prime Minister of the State of Israel. Sadat, five years Begin's junior, seemed tense; he sat bolt upright, his face expressionless, his fists clenched. Begin, by contrast, seemed relaxed, all smiles and in a definitely happy mood.

Carter gave a brief description of two agreements which Sadat and Begin would sign that evening, witnessed by his own signature. The first, entitled "A Framework for Peace in the Middle East," contained the principles and "some specifics in the most substantive way" which would govern a "comprehensive peace settlement." The second, entitled "Framework for the Conclusion of a Peace Treaty between Egypt and Israel," in effect — though of course Carter could not say this in so many words — would make Egypt the first of the Arab nations to sign a peace treaty with the Jewish state. There also would be "accompanying letters," dealing with matters not explicitly resolved in the two main documents.

As Carter enumerated the main provisions of each document, it became clear that while some of the stipulations in the agreements represented Israeli concessions, Egypt had renounced her vision of total and unconditional Israeli military withdrawals. Israel had not been asked to endorse the establishment of a Palestinian

Arab state, nor did the agreements attempt to settle the delicate question of East Jerusalem. In fact, both "Frameworks" incorporated significant elements from the 26-point peace plan which Begin had put before both Carter and Sadat nine months earlier.

The "Framework for Peace in the Middle East" provided for a five-year transitional period for the West Bank and Gaza Strip regions. During this time span the Israeli military government would be withdrawn, to be replaced by an elected self-governing authority with full local autonomy. Jordan would be invited to help run police and border patrols. On the other hand, Israeli military forces would be permitted to remain in specified locations (as Begin had proposed) to prevent the two regions from becoming springboards for attacks on Israel. The question of the final political status of the West Bank and the Gaza Strip would not (as Begin had wanted) be held in abeyance indefinitely but would be decided in negotiations to take place at the end of the five-year transition period. (According to an agreement between Carter and Begin, settlements established by such groups as the "Gush Emunim" on the West Bank would remain for the time being, but Israelis were to establish no new settlements in the area during the negotiations; according to the original American interpretation, this meant during the five years of transition, while Israel was to say it meant only during the three months until the signing of the peace treaty with Egypt.)

The framework for an Egyptian-Israeli peace treaty called for negotiations leading to a full peace treaty between Israel and Egypt within three months of the signing of the "framework." Under the terms of this "framework," Israeli forces were to withdraw completely from the Sinai peninsula within three years. Between three months and nine months after the signing of the peace treaty Israel would make a partial, "interim" withdrawal, after which normal diplomatic, economic and cultural relations would be established between Israel and Egypt.

Carter announced one substantial difference still outstanding between Israel and Egypt: it concerned the future of the Jewish settlements which Israel — not splinter groups but the Israeli government itself — had established and promoted in the Sinai peninsula. Originally, Begin had envisioned the continued existence of these settlements even after Israeli military forces had been replaced by UN troops. At Camp David, Begin had stated that this issue should be resolved during the peace negotiations. Egypt, on the other hand, insisted that there could be no peace treaty without Israel's prior agreement to remove all Israeli settlements from Egyptian territory. When confronted with the Egyptian position, Begin said that he was not authorized to decide the fate of the settlements; he would have to refer the question to the Knesset after his return to Israel.

Carter was under no illusion that the peacemaking process would be quick and uncomplicated. He admitted that there still were "great difficulties" to be resolved, and that "many months of difficult negotiations" still lay ahead. Yet, he stressed that "substantial achievements" had been made at Camp David. He ended his remarks with the hope that the "foresight and wisdom" which had made the summit meeting a success would continue to guide Begin and Sadat "and the leaders of all nations as they continue the process toward peace."

Sadat was the next to speak. His statement, which he read from a prepared English text, was brief and formal. Praising Carter for his efforts, he stressed that which for him, Sadat, had been the most important accomplishment: that the United States had honored its commitment to be a "full partner in the peace process." The signing of the framework for the comprehensive peace settlement, he said, had a significance far beyond the event itself in that it signaled "the emergence of a new peace initiative with the American nation in the heart of the entire process." The continuation of Carter's active role in the peacemaking process was indispensable. "We need your help and the support of the American people. Let me seize this opportunity to thank each and every American for his genuine interest in the cause of peace in the Middle East."

Many who listened to Sadat that night were struck by the fact that he had addressed his remarks solely to "Dear President Carter." He said not one word about either Begin or the State of Israel. It was as if Sadat had been the only guest at the Camp David summit meeting and the only person to share the dais at the White House with the President of the United States.

The mood and style of Begin's speech were in every way the opposite of the tone used by Sadat that night. Begin spoke completely without notes; his words were informal, warm and laced with a playful sense of humor. He made frequent references to Sadat and the Egyptian people. He addressed his remarks not only to Carter but, significantly, also to "Mr. President of the Arab Republic of Egypt."

Like Sadat, he had high praise for Carter. The Camp David

Conference, he said, should be renamed the "Jimmy Carter Conference."

> The President took an initiative most imaginative in our time and brought President Sadat and myself and our colleagues and friends and advisors together under one roof. In itself, [this] was a great achievement.

He drew laughter and applause from his audience when he said he thought the President had worked harder at Camp David than the Children of Israel had done in Egypt building the pyramids.

"Yes, indeed, he worked day and night," Begin continued, "and so did we, day and night."

> We had some difficult moments; as usual, there are some crises in negotiations; as usual, somebody gives a hint that perhaps he would like to pack up and go home. It is all usual.

> But ultimately, ladies and gentlemen, the President of the United States won the day. And peace now celebrates victory for the nations of Egypt and Israel and for all mankind.

> Mr. President, we, the Israelis, thank you from the bottom of our hearts for all you have done for the sake of peace, for which we prayed and yearned more than 30 years . . .

And then he paid a warm tribute to "my friend, President Sadat":

> We met for the first time in our lives, last November, in Jerusalem. He came to us as a guest, a former enemy, and during our first meeting we became friends.

> In the Jewish teachings, there is a tradition that the greatest achievement of a human being is to turn his enemy into a friend, and this we do in reciprocity.

Since that time, Begin continued, they had had "some difficult days." But now this was all a thing of the past. Before leaving Camp David, he and Sadat had exchanged visits, shaken hands, and, "thank God, we again could have said to each other, 'You are my friend.' "

Begin, like Carter, did not allow himself to be carried away by undue optimism. Peace had not yet come. "We still have to go the road until my friend President Sadat and I sign the peace treaties." There still were "problems to solve," but "Camp David proved that any problem can be solved, if there is good will and understanding and some wisdom."

Sadat had thanked Carter's "able assistants" for their hospitality and dedication, but had said nothing about his own ministers and advisors who had been with him at Camp David. Begin, however, expressed his thanks not only to the "members of the American delegation," but also to his own team — to whom he referred as his "colleagues and friends" — because, as he put it "without them, that achievement wouldn't have been possible." He even thanked the Egyptian delegation, "who worked so hard together with us, headed by deputy prime minister Mr. [Hassan El] Tohami, for all they have done to achieve this moment."

At the close of his speech, Begin asked for permission to address the people of Israel, from the White House, in the Hebrew language. It was his way of impressing upon the world that the Jews were not merely a religion but also a nation, with a language and land of their own, both of which were very much alive and here to stay. Translated into English, this was Begin's message to his country:

> When you hear these words, it will be morning in Israel, an early hour, and the sun will shine in the land of our fathers and our sons.
>
> Will we be able to come to you within a few days and to sing with you, *Hevenu Shalom Alekhem?** I can tell you this: we have made every possible human effort up to now in order that the day may come when each of us can say, peace has come to our people and our land, not only in this generation but also for generations to come. With the help of God, together, we will achieve this goal, and we will be blessed with good days of upbuilding and brotherhood and understanding. May this be God's will.

After Begin had finished speaking, Secretary of State Vance stepped up to the dais and gave out copies of the "Framework" agreements to Sadat, Carter and Begin. All three men signed the documents. Afterwards, Begin rose from his seat and threw his arms around the President of the United States. For the first time,

---

*"We Have Brought Peace Unto You," a well-known Hebrew folk song.

Sadat smiled and applauded. Then Begin went over to Sadat and hugged him, too. Finally, as the audience applauded and the cameras flashed, Jimmy Carter, Anwar el-Sadat and Menahem Begin joined hands in a three-way handclasp.

In Jerusalem the next day, a correspondent of an American Jewish weekly walked through the streets and conducted random interviews with Israelis. How, he wanted to know, did Israelis feel about the news from Camp David and the prospects for peace at long last?

"It is a shock for me, something I just can't believe," one man said, and then added with fervor, "I hope it works. I hope so very much."[24]

Summer, 1977: Official portrait taken shortly after Begin assumed the premiership.
Courtesy Israel Government Press Office.

Epilogue

The day after the ceremony at the White House, Begin and Sadat attended a joint session of Congress at which Carter reported the results of the Camp David Conference. Seated in the gallery of the House of Representatives, on either side of Rosalynn Carter, they heard the President say, "This is the first time that an Arab and an Israeli leader have signed a comprehensive framework for peace. It contains the seeds of a time when the Middle East, with all its vast potential, may be a land of human richness and fulfillment, rather than of bitterness and conflict."

Four days later, on Friday, September 22, Menahem and Aliza Begin landed at Ben-Gurion airport. Smiling broadly, Begin descended from his plane to a red carpet, to be greeted by some 150 dignitaries.

"I bring you from Camp David an agreement with security and honor," he told the crowd of over 40,000 that had been waiting to receive him. "But can we say that we have brought peace unto you? No. Not yet. Very difficult days are still ahead of us. There are efforts we shall have to exert. But a sound and solid foundation has been laid down — a foundation for a peace agreement between us and our neighbors. Therefore, today I am the carrier of a message: the foundations of peace have been laid."

Then, he and Aliza entered their limousine for the drive home to Jerusalem. In front of the *Binyanei Ha-Umma*, Jerusalem's National Convention Hall, the city's mayor, Teddy Kollek, and his former deputy, Rabbi Menahem Porush, welcomed the Begins and offered them the traditional collation of bread and wine on a silver salver. But there was no time for more ceremony, because it was Friday afternoon and the Begins had to hurry home to unpack and to prepare for the Sabbath.

The weeks that followed were to be difficult ones for Begin; he had to obtain the approval of his Cabinet and of the Knesset for the course to which he was about to commit the country. Peace depended on whether the Knesset would be willing to have Israel part with the settlements in the Sinai peninsula, which over the years had become prosperous towns with enterprising populations and industries. If Israel gave them up, it would be the first time that she had ever voluntarily dismantled places where Israelis had established permanent outposts; even more distressing than this ideological wrench would be the fact that people who had invested their hearts, hands and minds into the upbuilding of the settlements would find themselves homeless and bereft of the fruits of their work. On the other hand, if Israel were to insist on keeping the settlements, Egypt would refuse to continue peace negotiations with her, the Camp David accords would be null and void, and the world would saddle Israel with the blame for allowing her "territorial expansionism" to vitiate the promise of peace in the Middle East.

In New York, before returning to Israel, Begin had told newspapermen and an audience of Jewish communal leaders that he would probably not attempt to influence the Knesset's decision one way or the other by participating in the debate.

On Sunday, September 24, two days after Begin's return to Israel, his Cabinet, by a vote of 11 to 2 — with three abstentions — accepted the peace framework documents formulated at Camp David.

The next day, Begin went before the Knesset to ask its approval. It was an agonizing time for him; he already knew that some of his closest friends in his own Herut party were adamantly opposed to the accords that had been signed at Camp David. He had seen demonstrators from the extreme right fringe of the Likud bloc wave black umbrellas at him, implying that, like Chamberlain at Munich four decades earlier, Begin had fallen into the enemy's trap and surrendered everything in the mistaken belief that he had obtained peace for his country.

In his report to the Knesset, he stressed that the agreements hammered out at Camp David did not hold the dangers and uncertainties of the interim, "step-by-step" accords Israel had been asked to accept in previous negotiations. Rather, they would lead directly to a complete and lasting peace. He spelled out the security arrangements Israel had received that would guard her against a sneak attack from the Sinai peninsula. Israel would give up the four airfields in the peninsula only after new ones, to be built in the Negev with American funds, would be ready for use. He also assured the legislators that there would be no PLO state, and that he had not agreed to negotiate with the PLO. (In New York, he had been asked what he would do if an individual elected from the West Bank or the Gaza Strip to the Arab self-governing council would turn out to be a member of the PLO. "We think it may happen," he had replied," But when we talk to them . . . we shall tell them simply: If you do not disturb the peace, represent the people properly and deal with their daily problems, we will talk. [But] If you represent the PLO and try to organize bombs, that we shall not tolerate.")[1]

Now, said Begin, the Knesset was faced with two alternatives: either to accept the loss of the Sinai settlements for the sake of peace, or "that the negotiations on a peace treaty will not even begin and all the things agreed on at Camp David will be completely done away with . . . These are the two possibilities. There is no third."

Originally, he had intended not to inject his own views into his report, but now he felt it was his duty to express his opinion candidly. "I declare that with a sorrowful and painful heart, but with a quiet conscience, I shall recommend opting for the possibility which we chose yesterday at the Cabinet session. Because that is the way that leads to peace. That is the supreme national interest — including that of my settler friends."

At one point his address was interrupted by the cries of Geula Cohen, the journalist and Stern Group veteran. Now one of Herut's representatives in the Knesset, she had taken an extreme stand. She was convinced that Begin's acceptance of the Camp David proposals was nothing short of craven surrender, if not treason. "Begin!" she shouted, "Stop cheating the nation!"

Begin paused for a moment, shook his head and muttered, "Terrible, terrible . . ." Clearly, he himself had agonized long and deeply over his decision. Once upon a time, he might have sided with Geula Cohen, but now Israel was faced with a new situation, demanding an appropriate response. At Camp David, Israel had not been presented with an ultimatum of unconditional surrender, which would have made her destruction only a matter of time. For the first time in her history, she had been offered a promise of genuine and lasting peace with her Arab neighbors, as a sovereign nation among other sovereign nations in the Middle East.

While other Knesset members surrounded Geula Cohen and escorted her out of the chamber, he continued:

Let each of you think his own thoughts, ask his conscience, and vote in accordance with his evaluation. . . . But I do request that all Knesset members — representatives of a great nation which has suffered much, fought much, sacrificed much — properly assess the moral significance of this turning point.

For 30 years we have longed for the moment when we could discuss directly the signing of a peace treaty; the complete normalization of relations; the cessation of the wars, the promise of life not only for our generation, but also for our children and our children's children.

This is the moment: A great moment. With God's help, may we very soon arrive at the great moment of signing the peace treaty.[2]

The formal debate in the Knesset began on September 27 and lasted 17 hours; it was one of the longest and most emotion-charged in the history of Israel's parliament.

The vote was taken in the early morning hours of Thursday, September 28. At 3:30 A.M., the results were announced from the rostrum by Speaker Itzhak Shamir, whose early political background had matched that of militant Geula Cohen; during the underground days he had been known as Itzhak Ysernitzky, a leader of the Stern Group.

Shamir declared that the Knesset, by a vote of 84 to 19 (another 17 members had abstained), had given its approval to the work for peace in which Menahem Begin had been engaged at Camp David.

Exhausted, but relieved and happy, Begin turned to his three principal colleagues in the Cabinet — Yigael Yadin, Moshe Dayan and Ezer Weizman — and embraced each one of them.

*   *
*

In New York, after the Camp David summit meeting, Begin told an audience that he hoped to achieve two goals for his country before he retired from politics: a permanent peace and the elimination of poverty, which he considers an insult to Israel's society.

He has said that he wants to retire from active political life at the age of 70. Now past his sixty-fifth birthday, he puts in a full working day. He rises at 5 or 5:30 each morning and listens to the news, a habit he acquired during the underground days when he tuned in on the daily news broadcasts of the BBC. Then he reads the newspapers, recites his morning prayers and has his breakfast. By 8 o'clock he is at his office reading reports, attending to official correspondence and holding conferences. At about 1 or 1:30 he goes home to his official residence and has dinner; like most Israelis, he takes his main meal at noon. After dinner he rests for two hours; this is a concession he has made to his heart condition. "It's true that I have to take a rest after dinner every day, and not a short one either," he said in an interview shortly after his return from Rumania. "In Rumania I did not have a chance to rest at noon and by evening I felt very tired. Then I said to myself and to my wife, 'I'll just have to watch myself and listen to my doctors.' And then I went off to rest. The reporters thought I was having a secret meeting with some delegates from Russia. They looked for me in all the mountains of Transylvania but they didn't find me. They might have looked in my bed, but that's the one place where they didn't look. The next day I felt stronger and not one bit tired."[3]

He stopped smoking long before his heart attacks, and drinks wine only on religious occasions. Instead of coffee, he takes Russian tea.

By 4 in the afternoon, he is back in his office, and remains there until 7. He spends his evenings quietly at home. Formerly, he was an avid moviegoer; nowadays, he watches TV until he is ready to go to bed.

He is widely read; during his school days he read the classics of Russian, French, German and English literature — mostly in Polish translation. He is as familiar with the writings of Tolstoy, Proust, Shakespeare, Goethe and Schiller as he is with the works of modern Hebrew authors. His favorite subject is history. He was particularly impressed with Jim Bishop's *The Last Year of FDR*, an account of Franklin D. Roosevelt's final illness. (As for his own health, he takes a philosphical attitude: "Everyone is in the hand of God. Any man can go to the next world at any moment," he says.[4]

He is deeply moved by music, but claims he does not really understand it. "I can't understand music," he says, "but I can feel it deeply. I can be profoundly moved at a concert, but I don't have much time to listen to concerts." He says that he does not seem to have a good singing voice. "Sometimes, when I would sing at home, the children would tell me, 'Stop it, *Abba*. You're no success at singing.' "[5]

But the pursuit which absorbs almost all his energies is his work. After his heart attack, he was relieved to learn from his doctors that he was, as he put it, "capable of doing every kind of work."

He is convinced that work is the best cure for ailments of both body and mind, and he is fond of quoting the song he and his friend sang when they were young: "Work is our life; it will save us from every ill."[6]

He has never owned a car or a home. His sister recalls that Begin gave away his first six months' salary as a Knesset member to help rehabilitate wounded veterans of his "fighting family." His salary as prime minister is less than $1500 per month.[7]

When interviewed shortly after becoming prime minister, he was firm about his intention to quit public life in 1983, when he reaches the age of 70. "It is true that, in general, a man of 70 is capable of remaining active in politics. We need only recall Gladstone, who headed his last government when he was 86."[8] But he would like to be free to engage in writing. There are, of course, his plans for a book about Garibaldi. But he wants to devote a number of years to a major work on Jewish history, entitled *The Generation of Destruction and Rebirth*. It will begin with World War I, continuing through the period between the two wars, the era of Vladimir Jabotinsky, the Holocaust, the period of the Jewish underground in Palestine, the rise of the State of Israel, and ending with a survey of his country's achievements as of the date his book is published.

"There are difficult days ahead of us, days of greatness . . ." he wrote recently. "We shall defend our populace and provide it with security. Only such a peace will exist for Israel, a peace with security. This is our belief, and in this spirit shall we act.

"But when all is said and done, when I scan the recent past and the more remote past, the present and the future, I wish to state: How fortunate am I that I am one of this generation which witnessed destruction and rebirth, a unique generation in the history of Israel, a generation which acquired everything it has through abysmal sacrifice and sublime heroism.

"How fortunate are we to be part of this generation."[9]

NOTES

CHAPTER 1

1. Nadav Safran, *Israel, The Embattled Ally,* Cambridge, Mass. and London, 1978, p. 197.

2. Begin's interview with Dov Goldstein, *Ma'ariv,* September 12, 1977.

3. William Safire, "The Authentic," *The New York Times,* August 4, 1977, p. A-19.

4. Interview with Dov Goldstein, *Ma'ariv,* September 12, 1977.

CHAPTER 2

1. Interview with Aharon Dolav, "White Nights and Stormy Days in the Life of Menahem Begin", *Ma'ariv,* June 10, 1977.

2. Ibid.

3. Ibid.

4. Abdullah's grandson is the present King Hussein of Jordan.

5. Aharon Dolav, "White Nights . . .", *Ma'ariv,* June 10, 1977.

CHAPTER 3

1. I.e., the Hebrew Bible and, by extension, Jewish religious law and custom.

2. Quoted in Joseph B. Schechtman, *Fighter and Prophet,* New York, 1961 (second of a two-volume biography of Jabotinsky), p. 289.

3. Jabotinsky used the term "colonization" not in the sense of occupying the land of an "inferior" race or people, but to denote settlement in previously unsettled and uncultivated areas.

4. Quoted in Joseph B. Schechtman, *Fighter and Prophet,* p. 293.

5. Walter Eytan, "Mr. Begin's First Hundred Days," *Hadassah Magazine,* August-September, 1977.

6. Aharon Dolav, "White Nights . . .", *Ma'ariv,* June 10, 1977.

7. Itzhak Gurion, *Triumph on the Gallows.* New York, 1950, page 176.

8. Vladimir Jabotinsky, *Evidence Submitted to the Palestine Royal Commission,* London, 1937, p. 13.

9. Ibid.

10. Aharon Dolav, "White Nights . . .", *Ma'ariv,* June 10, 1977.

CHAPTER 4

1. Quoted in Joseph B. Schechtman and Yehuda Benari, *History of the Revisionist Movement,* Vol. I, Tel Aviv, 1970, pp. 398-99.

2. *Toledot Betar Austria* (Hebrew and German), ed. Arje Koeppel, Tel Aviv, 5726 (1965-6), p. 40.

3. See Yehoshua Halevi, *Toledot Betar be-Tzechoslovakia* (Hebrew), Tel Aviv, 5621 (1960-1).

4. Chaim Weizmann, *Trial and Error,* Philadelphia, 1949, p. 397.

5. Menahem Begin, *The Revolt,* Jerusalem, 1951, p. 62.

6. For a report of the exchange between Jabotinsky and Begin at the 1938 Betar congress, see Aharon Dolav, "White Nights . . .", *Ma'ariv,* June 10. 1977 and Uri Avneri, "The Dam Breaks," *HaOlam HaZeh,* September 7, 1977.

7. Rafael Bashan, "Begin Talks About Begin," *Yediot Aharonot,* September 12, 1977.

8. Uri Avneri, "The Dam Breaks," *HaOlam HaZeh,* September 7, 1977.

9. I.e., Jewish Palestine. From Menahem Begin, *White Nights: The Story of a Prisoner in Russia,* London, 1957, p. 86.

10. Doris Katz, *The Lady Was A Terrorist,* New York, 1953, p. 40.

11. Interview with Shelly Gewirtz in *New York Daily News,* July 19, 1977.

12. Quoted from Menahem Begin, *White Nights,* p. 86.

CHAPTER 5

1. Uri Avneri, "The Dam Breaks," *HaOlam HaZeh,* September 7, 1977.

2. Quoted in William E. Farrell, "The New Face of Israel: Hawk on a Mission of Peace," *New York Times Magazine,* July 17, 1977.

3. Aharon Dolav, "White Nights . . .", *Ma'ariv,* June 10, 1977.

4. Menahem Begin, *White Nights,* p. 87.

5. Robert St. John, *Shalom Means Peace,* New York, 1949, p. 173.

6. Interview with Shelly Gewirtz in *New York Daily News,* July 19, 1977.

CHAPTER 6

1. Aharon Dolav, "White Nights . . .", *Ma'ariv,* June 10, 1977.

2. Uri Avneri, "The Dam Breaks," *HaOlam HaZeh,* September 7, 1977.

2a. J. Bowyer Bell, *Terror Out of Zion,* New York, 1977, p. 57.

3. Between 1939 and 1948 these men, along with other emissaries from Palestine and helped by refugees from Europe, were instrumental in the formation of at least half a dozen Jewish and pro-Jewish activist organizations in the United States, including the American Friends of a Jewish Palestine, the Committee for a Jewish Army, the Emergency Committee to Rescue the Jewish People of Europe and, most prominently, the Hebrew Committee of National Liberation and American League for a Free Palestine. Their supporters at various times included such well-known personalities as the author Ben Hecht and the Protestant author and clergyman, Pierre van Paassen.

4. David Niv, *Ma'arekhet HaIrgun Z'vai Leumi,* Vol. III, Tel Aviv, 1967, p. 274.

5. From article in *Herut,* organ of the Herut party (August 2, 1963), quoted in Niv, *Ma'arekhet HaIrgun Z'vai Leumi,* Vol. II, Tel Aviv, 1965, p. 275.

6. Menahem Begin, *The Revolt,* p. 41.

7. Jews were barred from the Wailing Wall (or the Western Wall, as it is known today) until Israeli forces expelled the Jordanians from the Old City of Jerusalem during the Six-Day War of 1967.

8. *The Revolt,* p. 89.

9. Niv, Vol. II, pp. 275-6.

10. Quoted in Niv, Vol. II, p. 276.

11. Eliahu Lankin, *Sipuro shel Mefaked "Altalena",* Tel Aviv, 5727 (1966-67), pp. 61-77

12. *The Revolt,* p. 44.

13. *The Revolt,* p. 78.

14. *The Revolt,* p. 85.

15. Lankin, *Sipuro shel Mefaked "Altalena",* pp. 66-71.

16. *The Revolt,* p. 73.

CHAPTER 7

1. Interview with Shelly Gewirtz in *New York Daily News*, July 19, 1977.

2. Tegart fortresses were heavy stone police towers built at strategic points. They were named for Sir Charles Tegart, who had undertaken their construction.

3. Menahem Begin, *The Revolt*, p. 113.

4. J. Bowyer Bell, *Terror Out of Zion*, 1977, p. 120.

5. Sir Harold MacMichael to the Secretary of State for Colonies, July 28, 1944 (Fo. 371/40126, 5052).

6. Eventually, in September, 1944, the British War Cabinet did approve the establishment of a Jewish Brigade which, under the command of a Canadian-born Jewish brigadier general, fought alongside the British Eighth Army in Italy. Shocked by its first contacts with the destitute, broken remnants of European Jewry, the Brigade men shared their own food rations, clothing and bedding with the survivors. As units of the Brigade entered Austria and Germany, they helped organize the concentration camp survivors and paved the way for their immigration to Palestine in the face of British restrictions. The British thereupon transferred the Brigade to Belgium and Holland, and decided to disband it as quickly as possible. But many members remained in Europe to assist in moving homeless Jews out of Europe and smuggling them into Palestine.

7. *The Revolt*, pp. 101-103.

8. Ibid. p. 142.

9. Born in Poland, Ysernitzky, who came to Palestine in 1935, Hebraized his last name to Shamir and in 1978 was speaker of the Knesset.

10. Thirty years later, in June, 1975, the Egyptian government released the bodies of Bet Zouri and Ben Hakim in return for the freeing of 20 Arab guerillas from Israeli prisons. Bet Zouri and Ben Hakim were reinterred in the national cemetery on Mount Herzl, and among the dignitaries attending the ceremony was Itzhak Rabin, a lifelong Labor Zionist, who was then the Prime Minister of Israel.

11. Unlike Irgun members, who were permitted to bear weapons only when they went to carry out an operation, Sternists were armed at all times.

12. J. Bowyer Bell, *Terror Out of Zion*, p. 134; Samuel Katz, *Days of Fire*, London, 1968, p. 85.

13. Eliahu Lankin, *Sipuro shel Mefaked "Altalena"* p. 85-86.

14. *The Revolt*, p. 152.

CHAPTER 8

1. Ephraim Dekel, *B'riha: Flight to the Homeland*, New York, 1972, p. 27.

2. Interview with *Ma'ariv* youth weekly, April 15, 1975, quoted in Aharon Dolav, "White Nights . . .", *Ma'ariv*, June 10, 1977.

3. Menahem Begin, *The Revolt*, p. 125.

4. Ibid. p. 178.

5. Jewish Agency, *Documents Relating to the Palestine Problem*, London, 1945, pp. 79-82.

6. Quoted in Jacob Rubin, *True/False About Israel*, New York, 1972, p. 53.

7. Quoted in Samuel Katz, *Days of Fire*, London, 1968, p. 71.

8. Quoted in *The Revolt*, p. 181.

9. Quoted in Michael Bar-Zohar, *Ben-Gurion, The Armed Prophet*, New York, 1967, p. 81.

10. *The Revolt*, p. 183.

11. J. Borisov (Joseph B. Schechtman), *Palestine Underground, The Story of the Jewish Resistance,* New York, 1947, p. 75.

12. *The Revolt,* p. 184.

13. Marie Syrkin, "Background to Attack," in *Hadassah Newsletter,* August-September, 1946.

14. Michael Bar-Zohar, *Ben-Gurion, The Armed Prophet,* pp. 84-85. The reference is to Vidkun Quisling, the Norwegian politician who betrayed his country to the Nazis and Marshal Philippe Pétain, leader of the French puppet government in Vichy.

15. Anny Latour, *The Resurrection of Israel,* New York and Cleveland, 1968, p. 303.

15a. "Israeli Who Was in Begin's Group Tells Why Hotel Was Bombed in '46," *New York Times,* September 17, 1977.

16. Quoted in *The Revolt,* p. 224.

17. Anny Latour, *The Resurrection of Israel,* pp. 306-07.

CHAPTER 9

1. Reprinted in *The Answer,* March 28, 1947, under the title "Irgun Commander Endorses Effort to Create Provisional Government Now."

2. Samuel Katz, *Days of Fire,* p. 143.

3. Col. Archer-Cust, former chief assistant to the Chief Secretary of the British mandatory government in Palestine, in a lecture before the Royal Empire Society, quoted in the *United Empire Journal,* November-December, 1949.

4. "Report of Conference Between Representatives of the United Nations Special Committee on Palestine and the Commander and Two Other Representatives of the Irgun Zvai Leumi." The copy of the report used by the authors was made available through the kindness of the Zionist Archives and Library, New York City.

5. Quoted in *The Revolt,* p. 335.

CHAPTER 10

1. Quoted in *The Revolt,* p. 337.

2. Haganah operated on the same basis as the Irgun, but its total membership was over 40,000. Of this total, 3,000 belonged to a special commando unit, the *P'lugot Mahatz* or "shock troops" known for short as Palmach, most of whom lived in kibbutzim. The extent to which Palestine's Jewish community was actively involved in the struggle, in Haganah, the Irgun or the Stern Group, can be judged from the fact that the total Jewish population of Palestine — men, women and children — in 1948 was no more than 700,000

3. *Terror Out of Zion,* p. 262. Another interesting sidelight: According to a report submitted in March, 1948 to the Palestine Committee of the Arab League by the command of the Arab forces operating in Palestine, the total number of Arab soldiers in Palestine during that period was 7,700. Of these, 5,200 were not inhabitants of Palestine but had come from neighboring Arab countries. According to conservative estimates, well over 100,000 Arab males between the ages of 18 and 36 were living in Palestine at the time.

4. Quoted in Dan Kurzman, *Genesis, 1948,* New York and Cleveland, 1970, p. 148.

5. "The former commander of the Irgun Zvai Leumi gives his personal account of Dir-Yassin. Why the Irgun fought the British," London *Times*, April 14, 1971.

6. Quoted in J. Bowyer Bell, *Terror Out of Zion*, p. 292.

7. Dan Kurzman, *Genesis, 1948*, p. 139.

8. Joseph Heckelman, *American Volunteers and Israel's War of Independence*, New York, 1974, p. 17.

9. Ibid., pp. 17-18.

10. *Al-Urdun*, April 9, 1953, quoted in Katz, *Days of Fire*, p. 217. The only factual inaccuracy in this statement was that the Irgun commander had been killed; actually, as already mentioned, Ben-Zion Cohen had only been wounded.

11. Israel Ministry of Foreign Affairs, March 16, 1969, "Background Notes on Current Themes." Preliminary notes in the same vein had been gathered by the Israeli embassy in Washington and released in July, 1957 "for internal use" in a pamphlet entitled "Arab Propaganda . . . And the Facts".

12. Quoted in *The Revolt*, p. 354.

13. J. Bowyer Bell, *Terror Out of Zion*, p. 303.

14. Quoted ibid. p. 311.

15. Quoted in *The Revolt*, p. 347.

16. Version printed in *The Answer*, May 28, 1948, pp. 4-5.

17. Ibid.

CHAPTER 11

1. J. Bowyer Bell, *Terror Out of Zion*, p. 326.

2. Jabotinsky had erroneously assumed that the Italian word *altalena* connoted "elevation" or a striving after higher things. Actually, it implies "see-sawing." Later, Jabotinsky said this did not alter the aptness of the pseudonym; at the time he had chosen it, he still had been at a "see-saw" stage in life, attempting to find his literary and intellectual bearings. Cf. Johanan Twersky, *Safrut 'Olam* (Dictionary of World Literature), Tel Aviv, n.d., vol. II, p. 280.

3. Actually, the correct translation for the title should be "Minister (Deputy Minister, or Ministry) of Security" because the literal meaning of *bitahon*, the Hebrew word describing this portfolio, does not mean "defense" but "security."

4. Samuel Katz, *Days of Fire*, p. 228.

5. Information from interview with Mr. Yitzhak Ben-Ami, New York, N.Y., June 2, 1978.

6. Samuel Katz, *Days of Fire*, pp. 228-29.

7. Cf. also Begin's broadcast following the *Altalena* incident, reprinted in *The Answer*, July 9, 1948.

8. J. Bowyer Bell, *Terror Out of Zion*, p. 320.

9. *The Revolt*, p. 155.

10. J. Bowyer Bell, *Terror Out of Zion*, p. 321.

11. Samuel Katz, *Days of Fire*, p. 238.

12. *The Revolt*, p. 168 and Samuel Katz, *Days of Fire*, p. 240.

13. Uri Avneri, "The Dam Breaks," in *HaOlam HaZeh*, September 7, 1977.

14. Samuel Katz, *Days of Fire*, p. 240.

15. Interview with Mr. Ben-Ami, June 2, 1978.

16. Dan Kurzman, *Genesis 1948*, p. 465.

17. *The Revolt*, p. 172.

18. Quoted in Samuel Katz, *Days of Fire*, p. 242.

19. Cf. Begin broadcast, reprinted in *The Answer*, July 9, 1948.

20. Ibid.

21. Samuel Katz, *Days of Fire*, p. 244.

22. Cf. Begin broadcast, reprinted in *The Answer*, July 9, 1948.

23. Samuel Katz, *Days of Fire*, p. 247.

24. Rabin was the future prime minister of Israel; Allon was to serve as foreign minister in his cabinet.

25. J. Bowyer Bell, *Terror Out of Zion*, p. 325.

26. See Fein's own account of the *Altalena* tragedy, quoted in Samuel Katz, *Days of Fire*, p. 246.

27. Cf. Begin broadcast, reprinted in *The Answer*, July 9, 1948.

28. Fein's account of the *Altalena* tragedy, quoted in Samuel Katz, *Days of Fire*, p. 246.

29. J. Bowyer Bell, *Terror Out of Zion*, p. 326.

30. Fein returned to the United States. He is married to a *sabra* of Yemenite origin, whom he met when he was stranded in Tel Aviv after the sinking of the *Altalena* and she was a nurse serving with the Irgun. Lankin was a member of Israel's first Knesset. He opened a law office in Jerusalem and later established a publishing firm in Tel Aviv. He is now married to Doris Katz, formerly the wife of Shmuel Katz. Yitzhak Ben-Ami is in business in the United States but still keeps in close touch with Irgun veterans.

31. *Palestine Post*, June 22, 1948. The daily's name was changed to *Jerusalem Post* on April 23, 1950.

32. Begin broadcast, reprinted in *The Answer*, July 9, 1948.

33. Ibid.

34. Ibid.

35. Samuel Katz, *Days of Fire*, p. 249.

36. Rabbi Fishman (Maimon) also held the portfolio of welfare in the provisional cabinet. After their return to the cabinet, Fishman was Minister of Religious Affairs and Shapira served variously as Minister of Social Welfare and Religious Affairs and as Minister of the Interior.

37. Monroe Fine in an interview with Myra Avrech, of Tel Aviv, in Avrech's article, "The Captain of the 'Altalena' Tells His Story," in *Jewish World* (monthly published by the United Zionist-Revisionist Organization of America), September, 1956, pp 14-16.

38. "Herut Bid Rejected in Unruly Session," *Jerusalem Post*, January 13, 1959.

39. Doris Katz, *The Lady Was a Terrorist*, pp. 153-54.

40. Samuel Katz, *Days of Fire*, p. .251.

41. Doris Katz, *The Lady Was a Terrorist*, pp. 177 ff.

42. Samuel Katz, *Days of Fire*, p. 252.

43. *The Revolt*, pp. 130-31.

44. Ibid. p. 66

45. *The Answer*, September 24, 1948.

46. *The Answer*, November 5, 1948, p. 7.

47. *Palcor News*, November 12, 1948.

48. Mapai received 46 seats; the Religious Front (a united front of parties based on religious Orthodoxy) 16; the Progressives (a middle-of-the-road party), 5; the Sephardim, 4 and the Arab Democrats 1.

CHAPTER 12

1. Asher Zidon, *Knesset; The Parliament of Israel*, tr. from the Hebrew by Aryeh Rubinstein and Gertrude Hirschler, New York, 1967, p. 17.

2. *The Revolt*, p. 316.

3. November 24, 1948.

4. *The Answer*, December 10, 1948. The account of Begin's first visit to the United States is taken largely from this issue and that of December 17, 1948.

5. J. Bowyer Bell, *Terror Out of Zion*, p. 343.

6. "Begin in Paris: Feted by French," *Jewish Chronicle*, December 31, 1948, p. 9.

7. "Knesset Debates Austerity Plan," *The Palestine Post*, May 4, 1949.

8. *Jewish Herald* (Johannesburg), May 23, 1952, p. 4.

9. This is the translation of the Hebrew title, *HaMered*.

10. Daily news report of the Jewish Telegraphic Agency, New York, January 8, 1952.

11. The text of Begin's speech from the balcony on Zion Square is reconstructed from reports in *The Jerusalem Post*, January 9, 1952 and the *Jewish Herald* (Johannesburg), January 11, 1952.

12. The quotations from Begin's speech on the Knesset floor are taken from *Divrei HaKnesset* (the records of Israel's parliament), session of January 7, 1952, Vol. 10, p. 903-08.

13. Quoted by S. Eliahu, in "Knesset Under Fire," *Jerusalem Post*, January 11, 1952, p. 4.

14. *Jerusalem Post*, May 7, 1952.

15. Reported by Uri Keisari in *HaAretz*, June 13, 1952, p. 3.

16. Daily news report of the Jewish Telegraphic Agency, New York, May 14, 1952.

17. *Jewish Herald* (Johannesburg), July 4, 1952.

18. Daily news report of the Jewish Telegraphic Agency, New York, May 16, 1952.

19. Daily news report of the Jewish Telegraphic Agency, New York, September 12, 1952.

20. Louis I. Rabinowitz in an article in *Herut* (in Hebrew), August 2, 1963, p. 7.

21. Translated from the Hebrew by Joseph Kuttner in *The Jewish World*, New York, pp. 5-8.

22. Quoted in Ernest Stock, *Israel on the Road to Sinai*, Ithaca, N.Y., 1967, p. 155. See *Divrei HaKnesset*, Vol. 16, p. 2558, August 30, 1954.

23. Quoted in *Jewish Herald* (Johannesburg), October 29, 1954, p. 1.

24. *Jewish Herald* (Johannesburg), November 26, 1954, p. 1.

25. *Jewish Herald* (Johannesburg), June 10, 1955.

26. Debate on October 18, 1955, quoted in *Jewish World* (monthly of the United Zionist-Revisionist Organization of America), November-December, 1955, p. 3.

27. Quoted in *Jewish World*, October, 1955, p. 14.

28. Netanel Lorch, "Sinai Campaign," essay in *Encyclopedia of Zionism and Israel* (2 vols.), New York, 1971, p. 1038.

29. Interview with Begin in *HaOlam HaZeh*, translated by Joseph Kuttner, in "Menahem Begin Answers Vital Questions: The Time Is Now," in *Jewish World*,

January-February, 1956, pp. 4-5.

30. Reproduced in *Jewish Herald* (Johannesburg), March 23, 1956, p. 3.

31. Interview with United Press News Agency, quoted in *Jewish Herald* (Johannesburg), September 5, 1956.

32. *Jewish Herald* (Johannesburg), September 14, 1956.

33. *Jewish World,* October, 1956.

34. *Divrei HaKnesset,* November 7, 1956, Vol. 21, pp. 201 ff.

CHAPTER 13

1. *Jewish Herald* (Johannesburg), January 4, 1957.

2. *Jewish Herald* (Johannesburg), February 15, 1957.

3. *Jewish Herald* (Johannesburg), March 15, 1957.

4. Ibid.

5. Daily news report of the Jewish Telegraphic Agency, New York, March 8, 1957.

6. *Jewish Herald* (Johannesburg), April 26, 1957.

7. Daily news report of the Jewish Telegraphic Agency, New York, May 3, 1957.

8. *Jewish Herald* (Johannesburg), May 17, 1957.

9. Daily news report of the Jewish Telegraphic Agency, New York, April 9, 1958.

10. *Divrei HaKnesset,* Vol. 24, 2243 ff.

11. *Jewish Herald* (Johannesburg), October 24, 1958.

12. Interview with Yohanan Ramati of *Jewish Observer and Middle East Review* (London Zionist weekly), September 26, 1958, pp. 11-13.

13. Knesset debate of February 19, 1962, quoted in *Jewish Herald* (Johannesburg), February 27, 1962.

14. Abba Eban, *Abba Eban: An Autobiography,* New York, 1977, p. 293.

15. See Dr. Rabinowitz's article in *Jewish Herald* (Johannesburg), September 15, 1965.

16. *Jewish Observer and Middle East Review,* (London), July 8, 1966, p. 7.

17. Menahem Begin, "Loyal Opposition, Positive Role in Israeli Politics," *Jewish Chronicle,* September 9, 1966, pp. 47 and 50.

18. *Jewish Herald* (Johannesburg), May 30, 1967.

19. Ibid.

20. Michael Bar-Zohar, *Embassies in Crisis,* tr. from the French by Monroe Stearns, New Jersey, 1970, p. 134.

21. Abba Eban, *Abba Eban: An Autobiograpy,* p. 387-88.

22. Michael Bar-Zohar, *Embassies in Crisis,* pp. 142-45.

23. For accounts of Begin's role in the decision to take the Old City of Jerusalem, see *Jewish Herald* (Johannesburg), November 7, 1967, p. 7, and article by Shelomo Nakdimon, reprinted in the same periodical on September 14, 1971, pp. 36 ff.

24. Television interview, broadcast over WNEW-TV, New York City, May 1, 1978.

25. The letter was dated July 10, 1967. See Abba Eban, *Abba Eban: An Autobiography,* p. 441-42.

26. David Niv, *Ma'arekhet HaIrgun Z'vai Leumi,* Vol. III, Tel Aviv, 1967, p. 280.

CHAPTER 14

1. Joel Marcus, political correspondent of *HaAretz,* quoted in *Jewish Herald* (Johannesburg), December 17, 1968.

2. Abba Eban: *Abba Eban: An Autobiography,* p. 593.

3. *Jewish Herald* (Johannesburg), August 1, 1967.

4. *Jewish Herald* (Johannesburg), December 19 and 27, 1967.

5. Israel T. Naamani, David Rudavsky and Abraham I. Katsh, eds. *Israel, Its Politics and Philosophy,* New York, 1974, pp. 316-30.

6. For the highlights of the discussions, see "Chiefs of the Pre-State Resistance Look Back," in *Jewish Herald* (Johannesburg), p. 19 ff.

7. *Jewish Herald* (Johannesburg), September 3, 1968.

8. *Jewish Herald* (Johannesburg), September 25, 1968.

9. *Jewish Herald* (Johannesburg), December 31, 1968.

10. *Jewish Herald* (Johannesburg), March 11, 1969.

11. "Begin Also Has a Plan," in *Jewish Observer and Middle East Review* (London), January 10, 1969.

12. *Jerusalem Post,* February 27, 1969.

13. Editorial in *Yediot Aharonot* (n.d.), quoted in *Jewish Herald* (Johannesburg), November 4, 1969.

14. Quoted in *Jewish Herald* (Johannesburg), November 4, 1969.

15. Quoted in *Jewish Herald* (Johannesburg), September 9, 1969.

16. Interview with Barry Gray, Station WMCA, New York, December 16, 1970, quoted in daily news report of the Jewish Telegraphic Agency, New York, December 17, 1970.

17. *Jewish Herald* (Johannesburg), August 4, 1970.

18. *Jewish Observer and Middle East Review* (London), August 7, 1970, p. 4.

19. *Jewish Herald* (Johannesburg), August 11, 1970.

CHAPTER 15

1. *Jewish Herald* (Johannesburg), August 18, 1970.

2. Address to the 20th convention of Bonds for Israel Organization at the Hilton Hotel, Jerusalem, quoted in *Jewish Herald* (Johannesburg), September 1, 1970.

3. *Jewish Herald* (Johannesburg), October 20, 1970.

4. Interview with Barry Gray, Station WMCA, New York, December 16, 1970, quoted in the daily news report of the Jewish Telegraphic Agency, New York, December 17, 1970.

5. Begin's article, "Encounters with Jewish Youth," in *Jewish Herald* (Johannesburg), February 2, 1971.

6. Cf. *Jewish Herald* (Johannesburg), February 23, 1971 and daily news report of the Jewish Telegraphic Agency, New York, February 26, 1971.

7. Excerpts from Begin-Rogers debate quoted in *Jewish Herald* (Johannesburg), May 11, 1971.

8. *Jewish Observer and Middle East Review* (London), January 7, 1972.

9. *Jewish Chronicle,* January 14, 1972.

10. Letter quoted in *Jewish Herald* (Johannesburg), February 15, 1972.

11. *Jewish Herald* (Johannesburg), September 12, 1972.

12. *Jewish Herald* (Johannesburg), November 28, 1972.

13. Ezer Weizman, *On Eagles' Wings,* London, 1976, p. 285.

14. Quoted in Begin's article, "More than P.M.'s Credibility is At Stake," in *Jewish Herald* (Johannesburg), May 15, 1973, p. 9.

15. *Jewish Herald* (Johannesburg), May 29, 1973.

16. *Jewish Herald* (Johannesburg), July 10, 1973.

17. Knesset debate of November 13, 1973, *Divrei HaKnesset,* 1973, No. 44, p. 4593 ff.

18. *Jewish Herald* (Johannesburg), November 27, 1973.

19. In an interview with Yohanan Ramati, *Jewish Observer and Middle East Review* (London), December 28, 1973.

20. Dated February 6, 1969; quoted in Aharon Dolav, "White Nights and Stormy Days in the Life of Menahem Begin," *Ma'ariv,* June 10, 1977.

21. Knesset debate of November 13, 1973, *Divrei HaKnesset,* 1973, No. 44, p. 4586.

22. See Begin's article, "We Can Look Forward With Confidence," *Jewish Herald* (Johannesburg), December 7, 1976, pp. 12-13.

23. *Jewish Herald* (Johannesburg), January 29, 1974.

24. *Jewish Herald* (Johannesburg), May 14, 1974.

25. Begin's article, "Nixon M.E. Peace Policy at Israel's Expense," *Jewish Herald* (Johannesburg), July 2, 1974, p. 7.

26. Begin's article, "No Need for Despair in Coming Year," *Jewish Herald* (Johannesburg), September 24, 1974, p. 5.

27. *Jewish Herald* (Johannesburg), December 31, 1974.

28. *Jewish Observer and Middle East Review* (London), January 17, 1975, p. 9.

29. The quotations are from the *Meet the Press* telecast of Sunday, April 6, 1975.

30. The quotations from the B'nai Jeshurun "dialogue" are taken from a transcript prepared by Congregation B'nai Jeshurun. The "dialogue," with Dr. William Berkowitz, rabbi of the congregation, as moderator, was held in the evening of November 15, 1976.

31. The report of this meeting, and the quotations, are based on Begin's article, "Will Carter's Team Honour His Election Pledges?" in *Jewish Herald* (Johannesburg), December 14, 1976, p. 7.

32. Yeshayahu Ben-Porat, Eitan Haber and Zeev Schiff, *Entebbe Rescue,* New York, 1976, p. 193.

CHAPTER 16

1. *Jewish Herald* (Johannesburg), January 18, 1977.

2. Interview with Milan J. Kubic, *Newsweek,* May 30, 1977, p. 37. Authors' italics.

3. Interview with Trude B. Feldman in Washington, *Balitmore Jewish Times* (Balitmore, Maryland), April 21, 1978.

4. "Ala," from Hebrew article in *Yediot Aharonot,* English translation in *Jewish Herald* (Johannesburg), September 6, 1977, p. 56.

5. In *Jerusalem Post,* May 24, 1977.

6. Interview with Rafael Bashan, "Begin Talks About Begin" (Hebrew), *Yediot Aharonot,* September 12, 1977.

7. *Jewish Herald* (Johannesburg), May 25, 1977.

8. Begin reported on that visit in his address to the Herut party convention in May, 1968.

9. The report on Begin's visit to the Wall and to Rabbi Kook is taken from *The New York Times,* June 14, 1977.

10. A detailed account of Begin's visit to the three rabbis is given in the *Algemeiner Journal,* a New York Yiddish-language weekly, issue of July 22, 1977.

11. *Newsweek* magazine, August 1, 1977.

12. Information from Prof. Tovia Preschel, New York City.

13. The *Time* interview was quoted in the *Jerusalem Post,* December 26, 1977.

CHAPTER 17

1. Recalled by Begin in his article, "Israel Will Not Submit to Threats," *Jewish Herald* (Johannesburg), February 21, 1978.

2. *Jerusalem Post,* November 13, 1977, (Quotation and Arab reaction).

3. *Time* magazine, November 28, 1977.

4. The translation of Sadat's address is from the *Jerusalem Post,* November 21, 1977.

5. The translation of Begin's address is from the *Jerusalem Post,* November 21, 1977.

6. Quoted in *Jewish Herald* (Johannesburg), December 6, 1977.

7. Columbia Broadcasting System telecast, *Face the Nation,* December 18, 1977. Quoted in *Jewish Week-American Examiner,* week of September 10. 1978, p. 2.

8. Ze'ev Schiff, "The Mood in Egypt," *Midstream,* May, 1978.

9. *Time,* September 11, 1978, p. 18.

10. Quoted in *Jewish Herald* (Johannesburg), December 28, 1977.

11. Begin's article, "Israel Will Not Submit to Threats, " *Jewish Herald* (Johannesburg), February 21, 1978, p. 7.

12. Ibid.

13. Address to the Conference of Presidents of Major American Jewish Organizations, New York City, March 23, 1978.

14. Quoted in *New York Times,* March 24, 1978, p. A-10.

15. *Jewish Herald* (Johannesburg), April 4, 1978.

16. *Jewish Herald* (Johannesburg), April 11, 1978, p. 3.

17. For quotations from Begin's Los Angeles speeches and the report of his visit to both cities see *The Jewish Week-American Examiner* (New York), week of May 14, 1978.

18. Ibid.

19. Marc Silver, "Is Begin an Obstacle to Peace?" *Baltimore Jewish Times,* July 28, 1978, pp. 10-11.

20. "An Exceptionally Hectic Week," *Baltimore Jewish Times,* July 28, 1978, pp. 11-16.

21. Interview with Dean Fischer, published in *Time* magazine, September 11, 1978, p. 15.

22. Daily news report of the Jewish Telegraphic Agency, New York, September 5, 1978.

23. Our account of day-to-day events at Camp David during the Begin-Carter-Sadat summit conference is based on reports in *Newsweek* magazine, October 2, 1978; Sidney Zion, "The Real Summit Story," *New York Magazine,* Oc-

tober 2, 1978, pp. 14-16; the daily news reports of the Jewish Telegraphic Agency, New York beginning with September 5, 1978; "Secrecy Shrouds Camp David Summit Meeting," *Baltimore Jewish Times,* September 15, 1978, pp. 10-14; Trude B. Feldman, "The View from Camp David," *Baltimore Jewish Times,* September 15, 1978, pp. 10-11, 14; *Algemeiner Journal* (Yiddish; New York), September 14, 1978.

24. Robert Wade, "Israel Reacts With Caution," *Baltimore Jewish Times,* September 22, 1978, pp. 51-52.

Epilogue

1. Interview with Foreign Editor Russel Watson and Correspondent Milan J. Kubic, *Newsweek* magazine, October 2, 1978, p. 33.

2. *Jerusalem Post,* September 26, 1978.

3. Raphael Bashan, "Begin Talks About Begin," (Hebrew) *Yediot Aharonot,* September 12, 1977.

4. Ibid.

5. Ibid.

6. Ibid.

7. Dial Torgerson, "World leader who has never owned a car or home . . .," *New York Post,* October 31, 1978.

8. Interview with Dov Goldstein, *Ma'ariv,* September 12, 1977.

9. *The Jewish Press* (New York), September 8, 1978.

Index

Brzezinski, Zbigniew, 279-80, 298, 333, 335, 336, 337
Bucharest, 47; Begin visits to, 15, 301-03
Buenos Aires, Begin visits to, 206
Bug (river), 17, 19, 106-07
Bunche, Ralph, 134, 135, 137, 189
Bund (Yiddishist socialist movement), 56
Burg, Joseph, 293

Cahan, Yaakov (poet), 135
Cairo, 11, 93, 96, 97, 141, 146, 225, 259, 292, 306, 307, 308, 309, 315, 318, 319, 328
Callaghan, James, 304, 316
Camp David, 15, 330-31, 332-39, 340, 341, 342, 343, 344, 345, 347, 348, 349, 350
Canada, 161; Begin visits to, 205, 206, 220, 231, 245, 260, 263, 277, 284
Canadian Jewish Congress, 205-06
Capitant, René, 195
Carey, Hugh (gov. of New York), 299, 326
Carter, Jimmy, 15, 30-31, 277, 279, 282, 294, 295, 297, 298, 299, 300, 301, 303, 316, 318, 320, 321, 322, 323, 324, 329, 330, 331, 332, 333, 334, 335, 336, 337, 338, 339, 340, 341, 342, 343, 344, 345, 347
Carter, Rosalynn, 15, 298, 332, 333, 336, 340, 347
Ceausescu, Nicolae, 303
Chicago, Ill., 160; Begin visits to, 221, 324, 325
Chief Rabbinate, Israeli, 91, 104, 309; Tel Aviv, 100
Chilewich affair, 92-93
Chomsky, Ben Zion, 205
Choral Synagogue (Bucharest), 302
Churchill, Winston S., 87, 95, 97, 111, 130, 134, 299, 331
Civitavecchia (Betar naval school), 43
Cleveland, Ohio, 138; Begin visit to, 221
Cohen, Ben-Zion (Irgun officer), 148
Cohen, Geula, 246, 247, 248, 252, 349

Cohen, Dov (Irgun fighter), 134
Committee for a Jewish Army, 228
Commons, House of, 97, 114, 115, 118, 130, 134, 135
Communism, 14, 18, 23, 45, 53, 194-95, 209, 217, 220, 221, 225, 248
Communists, 19, 38, 58, 214; in Israel, 87, 109, 187, 215, 217, 226, 270, 287
Conference of Presidents of Major American Jewish Organizations, 258, 296, 321-22, 326-26, 337
Conference on Jewish Material Claims against Germany, 206
Conference on Soviet Jewry (Brussels), first, 258-59, second, 277
Congregation B'nai Jeshurun (New York; Begin participates in "dialogue"), 277-78
Congress, U.S., 209, 277, 298, 323, 347
Council of Europe (Begin attends session), 277
Cronkite, Walter, 307
Cuba, Begin visit to, 196
Cunningham, Sir Alan, 116
Czechoslovakia, 45, 47, 211, 248, 273, Begin in, 40

Daiches, Paula, 56, 57
Davidson, Carter, 135
Dayan, Moshe, 65, 103-04, 215, 221, 231, 236, 237, 240, 241, 247, 250, 258, 272, 285, 290-91, 293, 303, 310, 311, 327, 329, 331, 335, 336, 338, 339, 350
De Gaulle, Gen. Charles, 195, 205, 214, 218, 227, 234
Deir Yassin (village), 12, 145-49, 150, 159, 260
Democratic Movement for Change (Israeli polit. party), 282, 286, 288, 293, 303-04
Detroit, Mich., Begin visit to, 285
Dinitz, Simcha, 295
Dock, Sgt. Peter (quoted), 261-62
Dreyfus affair, 32
Drohobycz (Poland), 45-46, 47, 50, 90

Jung, Rabbi Dr. Leo, 193

Waks, Israel, 137
Waldheim, Kurt, 299
Warhaftig, Zerach, 241
Warsaw, 17, 38, 39, 40, 43, 44, 47, 49, 50, 62, 66, 70, 193, 301, 247; University of, 39, 40
Washington, D.C., 234, 292, 303, 330, 331; Begin visit to, 15, 192, 193, 220, 260, 277, 295, 297-99, 316, 320-21, 322, 324, 338, 339-45
Wedgwood, Lord (Josiah Clement), 96
Weiss, Yaakov (Irgun fighter), 134-35
Weizman, Ezer, 252, 263-64, 284, 291, 293, 307, 315, 319, 323, 327, 331, 334, 335, 336, 350
Weizmann, Chaim, 25, 34, 41, 110, 112, 190, 198, 201, 228, 252, 264, 287, 291
West Bank area, 30, 140, 238, 239, 243, 246, 250, 263, 267, 268, 274, 275, 276, 283, 288, 289-90, 298, 300, 301, 310, 317, 319, 320, 322, 324, 329, 334, 337, 341, 349. *See also* Judea, Samaria
Western Wall, 241, 250, 292, 310. *See also* Wailing Wall
White Nights (Begin's account of his imprisonment in Russia), 55, 206
White Paper of 1939, 41, 63, 64, 72, 85, 87, 90, 105
Wiesel, Elie, 258
World Zionist Executive, 25, 33, 86, 87, 97, 112, 117, 123, 144, 159, 177, 206, 230

World Zionist Organization, 35, 112, 190

Yad Vashem memorial, 298, 310-11, 313
Yadin, Yigael, 149-50, 151, 172, 173, 187, 240, 282, 293, 303-04, 309-10, 311
Yadlin, Asher, 281
Yagur (kibbutz), 104
Yamit (town), 317
Yazur (village), 144
Yediot Aharonot (newspaper), 251
Yehudiyeh (village), 144
Yellin-Mor, Nathan, 247. *See also* Friedmann-Yellin, Nathan
Yemen, 139; Jews from, 76
Yeshiva University, 194, 325
"Yitzhak" (member of Irgun command), 99
"Yoel". *See* Eilberg, Yoel Bela
Yom Kippur War (1973), 267-70, 272, 281, 282, 288, 310, 335
Ysernitzky, Itzhak, 96, 124, 350. *See also* Shamir, Itzhak
Yunitchman, Shimshon, 56-57

Zionism, 21, 27, 34, 40, 53, 54, 58, 64, 67, 86, 87, 95, 96, 97, 229, 277; political, 17, 25, 28-29, 190, 311
Zionist General Council, 145, 151, 206
Zionist Organization of America, 192, 245, 257
Zondek, Dr. Hermann, 108, 132
Zurich, Begin visit to, 245